Indians in Minnesota

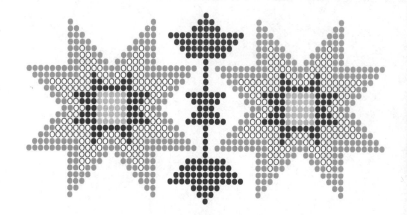

Indians

Judith Rosenblatt,
Editor

in Minnesota

Fourth Edition

Elizabeth Ebbott
for the
League of Women Voters
of Minnesota

UNIVERSITY OF MINNESOTA PRESS
MINNEAPOLIS

Publication assisted by grants to the League of
Women Voters of Minnesota Education Fund and to
the League of Women Voters Education Fund by
Grotto Foundation, The F.R. Bigelow Foundation,
and 3M.

Published by the University of Minnesota Press,
2037 University Avenue Southeast, Minneapolis, MN 55414.
Published simultaneously in Canada
by Fitzhenry & Whiteside Limited, Markham.
Printed in the United States of America.
Designed by Gwen M. Willems.

Library of Congress Cataloging in Publication Data
Ebbott, Elizabeth.
Indians in Minnesota.
Bibliography: p.
Includes index.
1. Indians of North America—Minnesota—Social
conditions. 2. Indians of North America—Government
relations. I. Rosenblatt, Judith. II. League of
Women Voters of Minnesota. III. Title.
E78.M7I53 1985   305.8'97'0776   84-28007
ISBN 0-8166-1354-0
ISBN 0-8166-1357-5 (pbk.)

Contents

Preface   vii

Introduction   3

CHAPTER 1 • Shifting Governmental Policies   7

CHAPTER 2 • The Tribes and the Land   18

CHAPTER 3 • Indian People   39

CHAPTER 4 • Tribal Governments and Federal Relations   53

CHAPTER 5 • State and Local Relations;
Hunting and Fishing Rights   65

CHAPTER 6 • Urban Indians   80

CHAPTER 7 • Economic Development   89

CHAPTER 8 • Employment   108

CHAPTER 9 • Education   122

CHAPTER 10 • Welfare   157

CHAPTER 11 • Housing   184

CHAPTER 12 • Health   199

CHAPTER 13 • Chemical Dependency   220

CHAPTER 14 • The Criminal Justice System   236

Conclusion   261

APPENDIXES   A. Federal Treaties and
Significant Legislation   265

B. Significant State Legislation   271.

C. Significant Court Decisions   275

D. Indian Media and Events in Minnesota   281

Acronyms   284

Notes   285

Selected Reading List   305

Index   311

MAPS

1. Treaties of land cessions and present reservations   21
2. Land ownership for a portion of
   Leech Lake Reservation (smallest unit is 20 acres)   26

TABLES

1. Minnesota Indian Reservations, 1983 Acreage   25
2. Indian Land Claims in Minnesota, November 1983   37
3. Change in Number of Minnesota Indians   40
4. Counties Where Minnesota Indians Live   41
5. Number of Indians Associated with Minnesota Reservations   42
6. Minnesota Urban Indian Population   43
7. Percentage of Increase in Urban Indian Population   43
8. Employment of Minnesota Indians
   in Industry and Government   109
9. Employment in Minnesota Private Industry   110
10. Indian Employment in Government in Minnesota   110
11. Minnesota Employment Figures for Indians and Whites   111
12. Indian Employment On and Near Reservations   112
13. Indicators of Problems in Indian Education   125
14. Indians in the Schools as Students and Personnel   133
15. Socioeconomic Characteristics of Minnesota Indians   159
16. Minnesota Children under 21 in Adoptive
    or Foster Homes in an Average Year   177
17. Children in Out-of-Home Placement in
    Hennepin County, December 1982   178
18. Indian Housing Compared with All Minnesota Housing   185
19. Indian Housing Needs on Reservations   185
20. New or Improved Housing on Minnesota Reservations   193
21. Infant Mortality Rate in Minnesota   202
22. Percentage of Deaths at Various Ages
    in Minnesota, 1975-76   204
23. Leading Causes of Death in Minnesota, 1979-81   205
24. Social Indicators Associated with
    Alcohol Abuse in Minnesota   224
25. Criminal Histories of Men in Halfway Houses, 1975   240
26. Arrest Rates of Minnesota Indian Adults, 1981   242
27. Crimes Leading to Incarceration   244
28. Arrests of Indian Juveniles, 1981   247
29. Detention of Indian Juveniles in Hennepin County, 1981   248

Preface

In 1962, the League of Women Voters of Minnesota published the first edition of *Indians in Minnesota*, bringing together for the first time information showing Minnesota Indians' needs and their relationship to government—tribal, federal, state, and local. Changes in the Indians' Minnesota since then have necessitated completely rewritten editions in 1971 and 1974 and this revised fourth edition, which reports conditions up to 1984.

The League hopes that its analysis of the issues will give the public a better understanding of Indian needs and a greater willingness to work with Indians towards solutions. Although this book focuses on the problems, the League does not intend to create or reinforce negative stereotypes that are both inaccurate and a great disservice to Indians.

This book deals only with issues that have direct impact on Minnesota's Indian population at this time. Other serious national Indian issues—water rights, control of reservation energy resources, and hunting, fishing, and land claims of Indians in other states—are of concern to Minnesota Indians and deserve the attention of the general public. They are not, however, within the scope of this book.

To help those who wish to do further research, sources of information are cited for each chapter in notes at the back of the book. When the information was obtained from the program or agency being described, it was not noted. A list of acronyms used in the endnotes and in the table footnotes faces the first page of the endnotes. Population figures are taken from the US census of 1980, unless otherwise specified. Most government figures are given in terms of fiscal year.

For quick reference, the appendixes list major treaties, important federal and state laws pertaining to Indians, and important court decisions, as well as general information about Indian community activities. A selected reading list is also included.

Twenty-six individuals, most of them members of the League of Women Voters from Bemidji, Cass Lake, Detroit Lakes, Duluth-Cloquet, Grand Rapids, Minneapolis, Moorhead, Morris, Red Wing, St. Cloud, St. Paul, Shakopee, and Winona, assisted in research. More than 400 interviews and 500 document sources were used.

Those contacted for information very graciously cooperated. Some agencies or authors made special computer runs of pertinent data or supplied unpublished studies and reports for the League's use. Experts in the various program areas provided generous help by critically reviewing the manuscript. Special thanks are extended to the photographers who granted the League permission to use their works.

The League gratefully acknowledges the grants to the League of Women Voters Education Fund provided by Grotto Foundation, The F. R. Bigelow Foundation, and 3M, and other grants to the League of Women Voters of Minnesota Education Fund that helped to fund the publication.

Indians in Minnesota

Introduction

When they were named by Europeans, "Indians" were not a group with uniform characteristics as the single name implies. They were many peoples spread over a vast continent, living according to the demands of various climates and food supplies. Political and economic styles, language, dress, and religion differed among the groups. Although many had common characteristics, their cultures were distinct.

Indians have made many contributions that endure into the twentieth century. Some were crop growers, cultivating the corn, potatoes, tobacco, peanuts, squash, tomatoes, pumpkins, and beans—unknown to Europeans—that were to become important plants not only for white settlers in America but for the world. Wild rice, maple syrup, blueberries, and cranberries, foods gathered and processed by Indians in Minnesota, still enhance the diets of people in the state. Such useful articles as canoes, snowshoes, moccasins, hammocks, smoking pipes, and dogsleds became widely adopted.

Indian herbs and drugs were valued by pioneers; belatedly, research is finding medical value in many of the treatments. Almost 200 drugs used by North American Indians are listed in two official drug compendiums.[1] With their holistic approach to physical and spiritual well-being, Indians were using dream analysis long before Freud.[2]

The political organization of the League of the Iroquois so impressed America's early statesmen that it became the model for the union of the colonies and the government of the United States as it was constituted in 1789. Senate and House conferees work out bills today in compromise sessions in a way that reflects the system of the Iroquois.[3]

Within this state, the legacy of the Indians is also reflected in place names that are Indian words, names of Indian leaders, or translations of names given by Indians. "Minnesota" is Dakota for "sky-tinted water"; "Mississippi" is an Algonquian word from the Ojibway for "great river." Twenty-seven of the state's counties have names of Indian origin, 15 from the Dakota and 12, Ojibway. "Manitou," meaning "spirit" in Ojibway, is widely used throughout Minnesota in place names. Several important Mdewakanton Dakota tribal leaders have given their names to cities, including Wabasha, Red Wing, and Shakopee.[4]

Indian Demographics

The state's Indian population (about 36,000, according to the 1980 census) lives primarily on 11 reservations (see map, p. 21) and in the major urban areas.[5] The following figures characterize Minnesota Indians in comparison with the state's general population. Although the data represent 1980–81 conditions, they paint a picture that is essentially accurate in 1984. (Note, however, that the accuracy of the census data has been questioned by many Indians; see chap. 3.)

- About one-half of the Indian population was under 20 years of age (median age, 20). One-third of the state's population was under 20; the median age was 29 (see chap. 10).
- Median income was 39% lower than the state average; 30% of all Indians lived below the poverty level (compared with 9% of the state population). Unemployment was four times the state percentage (see chap. 10).
- About 38% of Indian families were headed by women, compared with 10% in the state's general population (see chap. 10).
- As many as 50–60% did not finish high school. Of those over 24 years of age, 55% had completed high school, compared with 73% of the general population. Only 5% were college graduates; the state figure was 17% (see chap. 9).
- The average age at death for Indian men was nine years younger than that of white Minnesotan men. The gap in age at death between Indian women and white women was even greater. Indian women died an average 16 years younger. Minneapolis Indian infants died at a rate twice that of the general population (see chap. 12).
- Indians were 6.5 times more apt to live in overcrowded housing than the general population, 15% compared with 2.3% (see chap.

11). Unemployment, poverty, poor housing, and poor education contribute to other symptoms of social needs:

- One of every 10 Indian youths spent at least part of his or her childhood in a home or facility away from the immediate or extended family. Minnesota placed far more Indian children in foster homes than any other state (see Child Welfare, chap. 10).
- Indian adults were 4.4% of all Minnesotans arrested and made up 8% of the prison population, although they were 0.7% of the state population. At the state's juvenile correctional facilities, Indians were 12% of the residents (see chap. 14).
- Indian community workers estimated that the disease of alcoholism was a problem 6.5 times greater for the Indian population than the general population statewide (see chap. 13).

Indian Strengths

Indians and their communities embody great strengths and are an important asset to the state of Minnesota. They provide a culture and history that can be shared. They contribute the enthusiasm and dynamics of people who know what they want and need, and know that they will ultimately achieve it. They provide an economic asset through the programs they administer. The people's potential creativity and skills are being realized as more are assisted with education and training and allowed to be productive. The reservations are generating some of their own funding and are in turn providing the opportunity for greater investment and economic opportunity, not only for Indian communities but neighboring ones as well.

A League of Women Voters member who interviewed Indians at Fond du Lac Reservation commented on the experience: "There are over 150 employees [of the reservation] with excellent facilities. . . . They (the employees) are young, enthusiastic, dedicated to preserving Indian culture. In all the programs they are trying to retain and develop an individual sense of importance and worth, particularly in young people. Many funds are involved and the programs seem to be expanding. There is high morale and cooperation."[6]

Many positive things have occurred for Indians in the 10 years since the previous edition of this book was published. Most significant has been the increased recognition of tribal sovereignty and the concept of self-determination. Tribal governments are much stronger, and there is a deep resolve to protect and expand on their right to run their own affairs without the threat of federal termination of their status as Indians. Trained Indians are filling administrative positions, and Indians with skills are returning to the reservations as opportunities for employment expand.

Throughout the Indian communities, reservation and urban, capable leaders are putting together very complex financial packages and are operating programs that have great significance for their people. Skills have been developed to cope with funding and program changes while continuing essential services. Increased political understanding has helped Indians to be more effective in protecting their interests, protesting cuts, and demanding Indian shares in general programming.

The changes and challenges are accompanied by deep philosophical debate. Sam Deloria, an Indian recognized nationally for his work on tribe-state intergovernmental issues, has pointed out, "Indian tribes are engaged in some of the most delicate and complicated creative work that is being done in the world right now—trying to adapt social and political institutions to the needs of their own communities, questioning what to change and what to preserve."[7]

There are many natural splits within the various Indian communities. Although differences emerge during internal debates, there is no questioning of basic goals: the determination to remain Indian, to retain reservations, to protect and expand self-determination, to cooperate and assist each other when there are outside challenges, to attack the problems and try to help Indians in need.

In spite of the problems, individual and cultural strengths persist: "the beauty of Indian art, the accomplishments of Indian scholars, the love within Indian families, the dedication of Indian social service workers, the wisdom of Indian elders, the sacrifice of Indian spiritual leaders, and the gratitude of Indian people for being Indian."[8]

There is great optimism for the future. Ellen Olson, an artist who creates traditional Ojibway bead craft items at Grand Portage, commented, "I like the modern-day Indian. . . . They're better educated. They're more quick to appreciate their past. They're more curious about their language, about what their grandparents did. They have better insight into what their people are, who they are. They have accepted being Indian a lot better than my generation did. They have this natural pride that comes with understanding yourself."[9]

CHAPTER 1

Shifting
Governmental Policies

To understand how Indians view the world of the 1980s—their problems, their needs, their resentments, doubts, and fears—one needs some historical perspective. Briefly sketched in this chapter are governmental policies from the beginning of white settlement to the present. The effects of these policies on Minnesota Indians are discussed in subsequent chapters.

Treaties

Indian tribes, the dominant power on the continent as white settlement began, were treated as coequal sovereigns by the European immigrants. Treaties were the method of meeting the settlers' goals to keep peace and acquire land. The European concept of title to land, which could be acquired through purchase, became the basis of Indian-white relationships from the time of earliest English settlement.

Although they occupied defined territory, Indians had no concept of ownership and possession of land. "The country was made without lines of demarcation, and it is no man's business to divide it," stated Chief Joseph of the Nez Percé tribe. "Understand me fully with reference to my affection for the land. . . . The one who has a right to dispose of it is the one who created it. I claim a right to live on my land, and accord you the privilege to live on yours."[1]

Promises made by whites to Indians were usually lavish and not

7

kept. Perhaps the most quoted phrase was used by President Andrew Jackson in a letter to the Creek Indians dated 23 March 1829: "Beyond the great river Mississippi . . . your father has provided a country large enough for all of you, and he advises you to remove to it. There your white brothers will not trouble you; they will have no claim to the land, and you can live upon it, you and all your children, as long as the grass grows, or the water runs, in peace and plenty. It will be yours forever."[2]

The reality was quite different. Alexis de Tocqueville, who visited America in 1831, noted:

> The conduct of the Americans of the United States toward the aborigines is characterized . . . by a singular attachment to the formalities of law. . . . [They do not take] their hunting-grounds without a treaty of purchase; and if [the tribes cannot subsist] . . . they kindly take them by the hand and transport them to a grave far from the land of their fathers. . . . Americans of the United States have accomplished this . . . with singular felicity, tranquility, legally, philanthropically, without shedding blood, and without violating a single great principle of morality in the eyes of the world. It is impossible to destroy men with more respect for the laws of humanity.[3]

As demands for land by business interests and immigrants increased and the Indians became less of a threat, huge areas of land were "sold" by treaty to the United States and opened for settlement. In return, the usual pattern was an agreement to pay for the land, with the proceeds distributed over a period of years as medical care, education, rations, and payment of traders' bills. Indians were to confine themselves to a much diminished area, which would be reserved for them; and settlers were to keep out of the reservations. But as pressures again increased, the Indians were pushed into ever smaller, less viable areas.

Indian sovereignty was acknowledged in law. The Northwest Ordinance of 1787, which regulated settlement in the northern Midwest (including a major part of Minnesota) and predated the Constitution, declared:

> The utmost good faith shall always be observed towards the Indians; their lands and property shall never be taken from them without their consent, and in their property, rights, and liberty they never shall be invaded or disturbed, unless in just and lawful wars authorized by Congress; but laws founded in justice and humanity shall,

from time to time, be made, for preventing wrongs being done to them, and for preserving peace and friendship with them.[4]

Under the Constitution relations with Indian tribes were formalized. All treaties were to be considered supreme law of the land along with regular legislation (Article VI). Congress was granted the power to "regulate commerce with foreign nations, and among the several states, and with the Indian tribes" (Article I).

Administering Indian affairs was almost exclusively a federal responsibility (a few state reservations exist in eastern states). The Bureau of Indian Affairs (BIA) was created in the War Department in 1824 and transferred to the newly organized Department of the Interior in 1849. It has administered federal Indian affairs for 160 years. Federal law gives to the secretary of the interior the task of "management of all Indian affairs" (25 USC 2).

In 1871 the treaty-making process was replaced by congressional agreements. The tribes and agents of the government continued to negotiate as with treaties; however, approval was required by both houses of Congress. Legally, the agreements had the same status as treaties, and the change did not affect treaties previously signed and approved by the Senate.

Reservations

The traditional Indian way of life required a very low population density for an adequate food supply. Leaving the land "unused" was seen as wasteful and even sinful by whites, who wanted the rich, virgin land for timber, mining, and farms. Indians were seen as impediments, to be removed or destroyed. The traders, frequently selling liquor illegally, made profits by providing credit to Indians and then recovering the accounts from the federal annuities paid to the Indians under the treaties. It was in their interest to have more Indian land sold so that federal funds would continue to be available.

Confinement on reservations, with their greatly diminished land area, along with white settlement pressures and the destruction of the natural environment, greatly limited traditional Indian ways of food gathering. In addition, the rations provided by the treaties built a dependence on "handouts" that greatly modified living patterns. Supplying or withholding rations became a tool for controlling the population. By the 1890s, it was the practice to deny rations to Indian families who did not send their children away to school.[5]

The BIA had almost total control over the reservation population.

Use of this power, whether by dedicated, honest public servants or by those intent upon less noble purposes (and all kinds were represented), contributed to the destruction of tribal decision making and individual feelings of self-worth.

"Civilizing the Savages"

Well-meaning, "good" people who wanted to help became one of the major threats to the survival of Indian culture and identity. Missionaries were among the first white people to contact Indians. Representing the unquestioned view that Christianity and civilization were the same thing, they saw their role as converting the "savage" and changing "heathenish" practices and beliefs. They were not interested in seeing strengths in Indian beliefs. Christianity demanded total change, not only in matters of faith but in all aspects of life.

Bishop Henry Whipple, Episcopalian leader in Minnesota who was a great friend of Indians, urged in 1885 that the Ojibways should be made to agree to move to White Earth Reservation, freeing their other reservations for sale. The Indian annuities due from the existing reservations had expired or soon would. Unless they moved, the Indian people could not be "led to civilization."[6]

Allotments

Allotting land to individual Indian families was seen as the ideal tool for accomplishing the objectives of civilizing Indians, speeding assimilation, and opening the "surplus" reservation land to white settlement. The proceeds from selling the land could fund the cost of administering Indian programs.

The General Allotment Act (Dawes Act) passed in 1887 (25 USC 331) was intended, according to the commissioner of Indian affairs, "to break up reservations, destroy tribal relations, settle Indians upon their own homesteads, incorporate them into the national life, and deal with them not as nations or tribes or bands, but as individual citizens."[7] Although allotments had been made in Minnesota under earlier treaties, the Nelson Act of 1889 (25 Stat. 642) was the major legislation affecting the state (see Ojibway History, chap. 2).

Allotments, generally 160 acres, were assigned to individual families, but title to the land remained with the federal government. The land was held in trust and could not be taxed, sold, or transferred without BIA approval. Certain conditions were imposed before the land could be patented, that is, transferred to Indian ownership and out of trust status.

When the fee patents were issued by the federal government, the land could be taxed and individual Indians could dispose of it as they wished. (In some cases, although patents were issued, they were restricted so that the land continued under BIA jurisdiction, similar to trust lands.) The allotment process ended with passage of the Indian Reorganization Act (IRA) of 1934.

It was assumed that owning land would have the same value for Indian families as it did for immigrant settlers. Without any background or experience in European-style agriculture, Indians were expected to become farmers. Education was to be provided in agricultural skills, financed from the sale of the land.

The policy of allotment did not work; Indians did not become farmers. They were subjected to extreme pressures to sell, and the timber resources and land were rapidly acquired by others. The amount of reservation land subjected to allotment that is still held in trust by the federal government on behalf of Indians is only a small percentage of the original reservation acreage (see table 1, p. 25). Nationally, over 40 million acres were allotted to individual families; by 1976 only 10 million acres remained in trust.

Other Pressures to Assimilate

There were other strong pressures on Indians to become "civilized" and assimilate. The federal government established Indian police forces and courts to enforce white standards. For instance, the Court of Indian Offenses at Red Lake Reservation, established in 1884, was to enforce rules forbidding plural marriages, dances, destruction of property following death, intoxication, liquor traffic, interference of a medicine man with the "civilizing program," and an Indian's leaving the reservation without permission.

Schooling was the major vehicle of change. Children were sent to boarding schools, completely cut off from their culture, to be taught new ways. These schools remain a very close, bitter family memory for most Indians in the 1980s. Students were punished for speaking "Indian." The long hair and braids were cut, and things Indian were not allowed.

Citizenship

Citizenship, including the right to vote, was bestowed on Indians when they took title to (fee patented) their allotted land or met certain other requirements. For all other Indians, citizenship was granted in 1924 by an act of Congress. Until the late 1920s very little further attention was paid to Indians. It was commonly assumed that they would vanish. William Folwell, an eminent Minnesota historian, had no doubts in 1930: "The Chippewa Indians are a dying race."[8]

Indian Reorganization Act

In the 1920s, some citizens began to raise concerns about BIA mismanagement, exploitation, and corruption, and about the very impoverished situation in which Indians were forced to live. An extensive, objective study of reservation conditions published in 1928, *The Problem of Indian Administration*, became known by the name of the survey staff director, Lewis Meriam.[9] The Meriam report had a profound influence on legislation affecting Indians in the 1930s. Besides enumerating appalling physical conditions, the report cautioned that in trying to assimilate the Indians, the government should make haste slowly.

The Indian Reorganization Act of 1934 was a major change in federal policy. Regional hearings that solicited Indian opinion were held before passage of the act, marking a revival of bilateral relations in the formation of Indian policy.[10] The IRA ended land allotment, provided $2 million for the purchase of lands to be held in trust for the tribes, authorized the return to the tribes of original reservation lands still unsold since allotment, and allowed tribes to go into business with the help of a revolving credit fund. Tribes were allowed to decide by vote whether they wished to come under the act. Minnesota tribes all accepted.

The IRA acknowledged the tribes' right to self-government, thereby reversing the policy under the Allotment Act of splitting the individual away and destroying the tribe. The standardized form of governance developed by the BIA still provides the basis of most reservation governments in the 1980s. It is based on simplified federal government concepts, not on Indian styles of decision making. (See chap. 4 for a discussion of current governance of Minnesota tribes.)

The IRA reaffirmed the doctrine of limited tribal sovereignty, which had been all but ignored by the federal government. After so many years of dormancy, however, tribal government was slow to redevelop. Federally assisted services improved as New Deal programs reached the reservations.

Termination

By the 1950s, there was a very sharp reversal in Indian policy. Termination was seen as the final solution to the "Indian problem" and the way to get the government out of the "Indian business." The federal intent to shift responsibility was most clearly defined in House Concurrent Resolution 108 in 1953 (see appendix A). Although it spoke of "freeing" Indians from federal control and all the "disabilities and limitations specially applicable to Indians," the policy's goal was to abolish reservations, subjecting the land to taxation; to end federal programs and the special federal relationship; and to force the assimilation of Indian people.

Several tribes were terminated, including the Menominee of Wisconsin. The policy was very unsuccessful. The Menominee had great financial difficulties once they no longer had federal status as an Indian tribe. Land previously held by the tribe had to be sold to meet costs. An active lobbying effort was organized; in December 1973, federal recognition was restored (25 USC 903).

The goal of termination was also approached from other directions. For many years, tribes had sought redress for wrongs done and were pushing claims against the US government. Resolution of the claims, it was argued, would eliminate the need for Indians to affiliate with their tribes or reservations. Congress moved to speed up the process. The Indian Claims Commission was established in 1946 (25 USC 70).

A program to relocate reservation Indians to urban areas was also pushed, beginning in 1956. The BIA assisted in training, moving, and relocating Indians off the reservations, often intentionally far distant so that they would not return. Start-up services were provided, but support funds were limited. The result was the transfer of many Indians into urban areas and then their abandonment. The large migration of Indians into the Twin Cities of Minnesota began during this era (late 1950s).

Transferring legal jurisdiction to the states, another approach, was approved by Congress in 1953 as PL 280 (PL 83–280; 25 USC 1321). Five states, including Minnesota, that had been most responsive to the needs of their Indian citizens were given civil and criminal jurisdiction on the reservations, with some restrictions. Treaty rights and traditional hunting and fishing rights were protected. The state was not given jurisdiction over taxation or use of trust property.

The act passed without consultation with or approval of the tribes involved. Red Lake Reservation, at its request, was not included. In 1976, a major court case, *Bryan v. Itasca County*, established that the civil jurisdiction transferred to the states did not include taxing or regulatory powers.

PL 280 was amended by the Indian Civil Rights Act of 1968 to prohibit further transfer of jurisdiction to states unless the tribes agreed and to allow retrocession from state jurisdiction back to the federal government. At Bois Forte Reservation's request and with state agreement, jurisdiction in criminal matters was returned to the federal government for that reservation in 1975.

A New Direction: The 1960s and 1970s

Reclaiming Sovereignty

The 1960s saw Indians coming together in common purpose and speaking of their rights and needs that were being abused and neglected. In 1961, 400 Indians from 90 tribes assembled in Chicago and prepared a Declaration of Indian Purpose. Preserving and strengthening Indian sovereignty was the need. Looking back in 1981, Robert Treuer, a northern Minnesota writer, commented that "[Sovereignty] . . . had been whittled down, diminished, nibbled away by bureaucratic process, almost gummed to death, until a massive turnabout in the 1970s."[11]

Tribal governments, the embodiment of sovereignty, became the major vehicle for improved conditions on the reservations. Leaders became more successful in getting assistance programs for the reservations, influencing Congress, resisting federal domination, and using the courts to assert their rights.

There were other important outside influences. Antipoverty legislation passed in 1964 established a separate Indian Community Action Program (ICAP). For the first time, Indians were identifying their own needs and administering the assistance. The Indian communities came together, working with each other. Educated Indians returned to help. It was a route to services outside the bureaucratic BIA. Many of the leaders in Indian communities in the 1980s developed their skills and learned how to be administrators in ICAP.[12]

AIM

Indian activists formed the American Indian Movement (AIM) in Minneapolis in 1968. Since its beginning, it has publicized Indian issues, dramatizing and explaining Indian sovereignty and treaty rights to the general public.

In the 1970s, AIM members became very visible as militant activists challenging the system and bringing Indian needs into the headlines. Nationally, they sponsored the 1972 "Trail of Broken Treaties" to Washington, DC, with the occupation of the BIA, and the 1978 "Longest Walk to Washington." In Minneapolis, the Twin Cities Naval Air Station was occupied in 1971. In 1973, AIM took over the community of Wounded Knee, S. Dak. Protest of US abrogation of treaty rights continues in 1984 with the occupation at Yellow Thunder Camp in the Black Hills of South Dakota.

In Minnesota, AIM has concentrated on programs meeting needs of urban Indians. Building self-awareness and pride in being Indian is an important part of all programming.

The militancy of AIM has bothered many Indians, who see the violence and destructiveness of some of the activities that AIM has engaged in as excessive. AIM has been labeled an urban Indian protest movement; at times, there have been serious tensions between AIM and reservation leaders. Its objectives are not accepted by all Indians. But a great many Indians know and appreciate what AIM has done and what it has meant for all of them. "Possibly the only means of being heard was by being vocal and violent. . . . We're being taken seriously."[13]

Federal Policy Change

President Nixon in 1970 recommended an end to paternalism, a rejection of termination, and the adoption of goals of self-determination and self sufficiency. These policies were designed "to strengthen the Indian's sense of autonomy without threatening his sense of community . . . and to . . . make it clear that Indians can become independent of federal control without being cut off from federal concern and federal support."[14] Several important pieces of legislation followed.

One of the most important was the Indian Self-Determination and Education Act of 1975. It went a long way in committing Congress to a repudiation of termination. The act permits "an orderly transition from Federal domination of programs for and services to Indians to effective and meaningful participation by the Indian people in the planning, conduct and administration of those programs and services." Under the law, tribes can contract to run most of their own programs previously administered by the BIA and the Indian Health Service (IHS). Congress has provided for funding to build administrative capabilities. The act specified that it does not authorize the termination of any existing trust responsibility.

The American Indian Policy Review Commission was established by Congress in 1975 to look at Indian problems and barriers to effective programs. The commission, working through 11 task forces with majority Indian membership, examined many aspects of Indian life. The extensive hearings brought "more Indian participation than any other body developed by the federal government."[15] The reports were submitted in 1976.

The commission's final recommendation was that the "ultimate objective of federal Indian policy must be directed toward aiding the tribes in achievement of fully functioning governments, exercising primary governmental authority within the reservation . . . to do any and all of those things which all local governments within the United States are presently doing."[16]

During the early to middle 1970s, several major court decisions further defined Indian rights. Unextinguished treaty rights in hunting and fishing were reestablished throughout the country. Indians were affirmed in their right to have preference in employment in Indian programs. Tribal government jurisdiction was greatly strengthened when the Supreme Court ruled that the federal government cannot interfere when the tribe deals with its own members in such areas as membership, civil rights, and tribal voting rights.

The 1980s: Hopes and Fears

The 1980s have brought new challenges for Indian programming and fears that there might be another pendulum swing towards termination and abandonment. The memory of how fragile Indian rights are— how dependent on Congress, the administration, and the courts— dominates Indians' thinking as they evaluate any federal program.

Federal Policy

Federal policy toward Indians, as stated by President Reagan on 24 January 1983, was "to reaffirm dealing with Indian tribes on a government-to-government basis and to pursue the policy of self-government for Indian tribes without threatening termination. . . . [Tribes are to be assisted] in strengthening their governments by removing the federal impediments to tribal self-government and tribal resource development."[17]

These points are very important to Indian people, but Indians are skeptical about the value of self-government and freedom from federal domination in the light of major funding cuts and unfunded (though authorized) programs. "The solemn words of the laws you pass are only an offense to us when you take away the funds that will make them work."[18]

The Reagan administration proposed that all programs for Indians be transferred to the BIA and that nonreservation programs be terminated. If BIA definitions of "Indian" were used, many people now being served would no longer qualify; major education, health, and urban Indian center programs would no longer help Indians off the reservation. These proposals for consolidating Indian programs could mean a return to pre-1960s policies: only the BIA would be assisting Indians, and programs designed to serve all Americans would again be free to ignore unmet Indian needs.

Some court decisons since the late 1970s have put major limits on tribal jurisdiction over non-Indians on reservations. Liquor sales and sales tax decisions appear to expand state involvement on reservations. Tribal sovereignty continues to be reshaped by the courts.

Federal "Gyrations"

Always in the background of Indians' concern over federal poicy is that they are at the mercy of Congress. At any time, the unique relationship can be unilaterally altered—as was done with termination and PL 280. Exerting Indian rights can trigger local opposition and pressures for abrogating the treaty relationships and special status of Indian tribes. In this way, opponents of Indian rights would "make the problems go away" at the expense of Indians.

Speaking about changing federal policy, US District Court Judge Miles Lord commented in 1981:

> Justice for the American Indian is like a revolving door. It never leads anywhere very long and it eventually comes back to the same thing, assimilation. . . . The courts have flip-flopped on several decisions concerning Indian rights. How can a whole culture, a whole people, adjust to those kinds of gyrations? The "bottom line" is a governmental desire for assimilation of the tribes. But it's kind of hard to assimilate a sovereign nation. . . . Congress can be mighty fickle. What they didn't take away before, they can take away next. If you [Indians] can hold on to what you have, it will be by tooth and nail. Indians will need leaders who can deal with politicians.[19]

CHAPTER 2

The Tribes and the Land

History

Two major tribes—Dakota and Ojibway, speaking totally different languages—successively occupied the territory known as Minnesota. The Dakota preceded the Ojibway. It was not until after the earliest French explorers had visited the area that the Ojibway, equipped with firearms traded from the French, moved into Dakota territory from the Great Lakes, slowly pushing both southward and westward to the plains. In the middle 1800s, the Winnebago (or Hoshungras, as they prefer to be called) were moved from Wisconsin onto Minnesota reservations under treaty arrangements.

Sioux/Dakota

The Dakota ("friends" or "allies") were called Sioux by the whites, from the French corruption "Nadouessioux" of the Ojibway word "Nadowa," meaning "snake" or "enemy." Sioux was the title used in formal dealings with the federal government and has become the tribal name in governmental bodies. The people, however, prefer to use the name Dakota to refer to their identity and culture.

The Santee Sioux, represented by four major bands, were living in Minnesota at the time of treaties and white settlement. They were also known as the Eastern or Mississippi Sioux. Mdewakanton and Wahpekute were the Lower Sioux, located along the Mississippi River, in the

St. Paul area, and at the lower end of the Minnesota River. The Sisseton and Wahpeton bands were the Upper Sioux, living farther up the Minnesota River and around Lake Traverse on the present-day Minnesota–South Dakota border.

Chippewa/Ojibway

Chippewa was also a formal name used in treaties, and it remains in governmental designations. It was a corruption, however, of the Indian Ojibway, the term used by current members to refer to themselves. The name for these people in Ojibway is Anishinabe, meaning "original man" or "the people," a name many prefer.

The Ojibway are the largest tribe north of Mexico in North America. They have major populations in Michigan, Wisconsin, Minnesota, North Dakota, and southern Ontario, Canada. The Smithsonian Institution calculated the Ojibway population at 160,000 in 1970.[1]

The Ojibway are in the Algonquian linguistic family, which includes the Ottawa, Potawatomi, Fox, Cree, Menominee, and other tribes. Before the French arrived, the Algonquian groups extended from the Atlantic to the Rocky Mountains, from Hudson Bay to the Cumberland River.

In the area of Minnesota at the time of white contact, the Ojibway lived in small bands identified by their home location. The bands were made up of clans or families. Clan membership was inherited through the father, with each clan having a symbol or totem ("dodaim") such as the bear, loon, or moose. Clan identity still remains, and intermarriage within a clan seldom occurs.

For treaty purposes, the Ojibway were divided into five large, historic bands: the Superior in the northeast, the Mississippi south of the Superior band and in central Minnesota, the Pillager band in central Minnesota, the Red Lake band in the same location where the reservation is now located, and the Pembina to the west of the Red Lake band.

When the reservations were established, the bands were scattered. Today, Mississippi band member descendants may be enrolled members of Leech Lake, White Earth, or Mille Lacs reservation; a reservation such as White Earth has members from several historic bands. The smaller bands have also retained their identities.

Both Dakota and Ojibway adapted their economies to the resources and limitations of the Minnesota country. They hunted and fished; gathered wild rice, berries, and maple syrup; built houses of poles and skins or bark in semipermanent villages; traveled in summer by birchbark canoes along the countless waterways and in winter on snowshoes.

Early Contact with Whites

French traders and explorers were early to arrive in Minnesota, establishing a few forts and claiming the area for France. The British replaced them following the French and Indian War, and they enjoyed the loyalty of both Dakota and Ojibway during the Revolution—a loyalty that lasted to plague American agents through the War of 1812.

Captain Zebulon Pike, claiming the land for the United States in 1805, signed a treaty with the Dakota that ceded a nine-square-mile tract of land for a fort and trading post at the confluence of the Minnesota and Mississippi rivers. Some 60 gallons of liquor and $200 worth of gifts were used to encourage the sale. The treaty was never ratified by Congress, but ultimately the Indians were paid $2,000 for Fort Snelling.[2] The fort, which was intended as a base from which to maintain US sovereignty, control the fur trade, and stop intertribal warfare, became operational in 1820. (The accompanying map shows treaty areas and present-day reservations.)

Although the land remained Indian country (except for Fort Snelling), a white settlement huddled around the fort by 1830, and steamboats were coming up the Mississippi. Agent Taliaferro saw the need to speed the "civilization" of the Indians by turning their "excess" land into money, goods, and services. In 1837, major Ojibway and Dakota land cessions took place, and a wave of settlers and timber seekers moved in.

The 1847 treaties were made to establish new homelands for the Menominee and Winnebago, who were to be removed from their homes in Wisconsin and established as buffers between the Dakota and Ojibway. The Menominee successfully resisted being moved to Minnesota; the Winnebago came but did not like the land chosen for them, and they were settled instead in 1855 on land where the Blue Earth River joins the Minnesota River.

Treatment of the Dakota

After 1849, when Minnesota became a territory, the pressure on Indians to cede land increased. In 1851, two treaties with the Dakota took all their Minnesota and South Dakota land in exchange for two small reservations—adjacent strips along the Minnesota River, 150 miles long and 10 miles wide on each bank—and the promise of annuities, education, and farm equipment. The land rush was on. In 1858, these reservations were reduced by half, to just the southern bank.

1862 Uprising. Crowded together and starving, unable to hunt or maintain their way of life, lied to and cheated by the Indian agents and

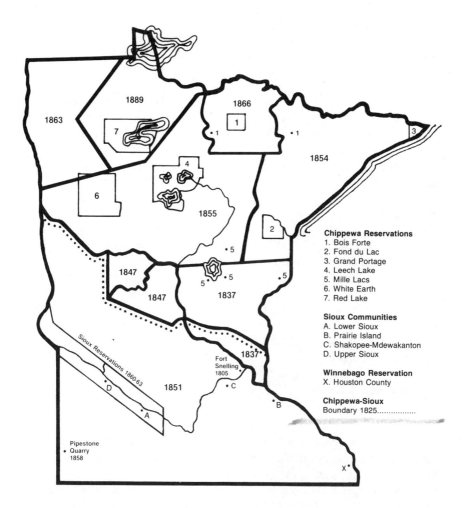

Map 1. Treaties of land cessions and present reservations

traders, the Dakota vented their anger over their suffering in the uprising of 1862. In a matter of a few weeks, about 1,400 people—as many Indians as whites—were dead. When the outbreak was quelled, 38 Dakota were simultaneously hanged at Mankato.

Congress retaliated in 1863 by abrogating its treaties with the Dakota, who were forced to leave Minnesota. They were first sent to a camp in Nebraska, where many died from lack of food; three years later they were settled in South Dakota. The response of the government was devastating to the Dakota people.

In 1861, the BIA roll showed over 6,000 Dakota living in Minnesota. After the uprising the Lower Sioux were sent out of the state. The Upper Sioux, who had not participated, fled in fear and eventually settled at Sisseton and Devil's Lake reservations in Dakota Territory. Some 2000 Winnebago were also shipped from their reservation on the Blue Earth River out of the state into what later became Nebraska.[3]

All annuities from the previous land sale were canceled and used instead to assist the white victims. The reservations were quickly claimed by white settlers. Although Congress had provided that "friendly" Dakota could take up land within the former Upper Sioux reservation, none did. White hostility was too great.

About 200 "friendly" Mdewakanton who had not participated wandered homeless in Minnesota for several years; other exiles drifted back to their home areas. In 1886 Congress authorized the purchase of land for these people, establishing the Shakopee-Mdewakanton Sioux, Prairie Island Indian, and Lower Sioux Indian communities (see appendix A). The Indians who had returned to the Upper Sioux Community area, mostly Sissetons, had land purchased for them in 1938 under the Indian Reorganization Act.

Treatment of the Ojibway

Treaties with the Ojibway living in the region that became Minnesota were first signed in 1825, in an effort to secure peace between them and the Dakota. A line was drawn diagonally across the state, with each group to remain in its own area. In 1837 a large area, including portions of Michigan, Wisconsin, and Minnesota north of the 1825 line extending to the Crow Wing River, was ceded by the Mississippi band. The Indians were not required to move.

Reservations Established. Treaties in which land was ceded and reservations established for the Ojibway in Minnesota began in 1854 with the Arrowhead region. In both the 1837 and 1854 treaties, hunting, fishing, and wild rice gathering rights were retained by the bands.

Under the 1854 treaty, present-day Grand Portage and Fond du Lac reservations were set aside. After minerals were discovered in northeastern Minnesota, previously set-aside Lake Vermilion Reservation and additional lands were ceded in 1866.

The 1855 treaty was for a major portion of north-central Minnesota; present-day Leech Lake and Mille Lacs reservations were established. Northwestern Minnesota was obtained through treaties in 1863 (amended in 1864) and agreements in 1889 (Nelson Act) and 1904. Red Lake Reservation remained, never having been ceded to the federal government.

Efforts to concentrate the Indians and release for settlement the reservations that had been established began in 1863. The 1867 treaty established White Earth reservation, where all Ojibway were expected to move.

The Nelson Act of 1889 provided for the allotment of Minnesota's reservations. Under the act, strong and skillful persuasion was used by the Rice Commission in an effort to get most of Minnesota's Ojibway bands to agree to move to the White Earth Reservation. Mille Lacs refused, although later some individuals did go. The act provided, however, that Indians could take up their individual allotments where they were on the various reservations, instead of moving to White Earth. Many individuals chose to remain, thus preserving their reservations.

Red Lake band had no interest in moving and was excluded from the Nelson Act. May-dway-gwa-no-nind, head chief of the Red Lake band at the time of negotiations, stated, "We think it is our duty to protect those that come after us. . . . We want the reservation we now select to last ourselves and our children forever."[4] Allotment was resisted and the reservation remains tribally held.

The Reservations

Reservations are the area of land originally set aside for Indians. Although there has been extensive transfer of land to non-Indian ownership, this has not removed the land from the reservation. The US Supreme Court has ruled that "the termination of federal responsibility and not the passing of legal land title within an area . . . determines whether a reservation exists in the eyes of the law" (*Seymour v. Superintendent*, 368 US351 [1962]). Unless Congress specifically acts to extinguish Indian rights, a reservation includes all the land "notwithstanding issuance of any patent" (18 USC 1151 [1948]). Reservations are the basis of tribal sovereignty, with the tribe holding the powers of government that have not been federally terminated.

Allotted land for which title has not been transferred to individual owners is held in trust. It derives from the original allotments made prior to the Indian Reorganization Act of 1934, which stopped the process. Most allottees took title to their land, and through the years it has been sold to non-Indians. The patented land still owned by Indians has no special status just because of Indian ownership.

Tribal Land

In addition to land allotted to Indian families, reservations contain tribal land. This is land held in trust by the BIA in the name of the tribe and controlled by the tribe's governing body. It may be used for community facilities, for economic development projects, leased to non-Indians for revenue production, or leased to members for their homes.

Tribal lands were increased through the Indian Reorganization Act of 1934. Land labeled as unneeded, which had been available for purchase but had not sold, was returned to the tribes. Some tribes, using their own resources, have made land purchases a high priority, rebuilding their land base. Land has been acquired for housing and economic development. The 1983 acreages of tribal, individually allotted, and government-purchased lands and their relationship to the original reservations are shown in table 1; land status in 1962 is given for comparison.

The amount of reservation land still in Indian trust status varies among the reservations. It is as low as 4% at Leech Lake. The accompanying map shows the typical checkerboard of land ownership, using a portion of Leech Lake as an example. No single tract of tribal land exceeds more than about two sections. The scattered pattern of ownership makes administration of the land difficult. Some reservations are finding that they do not have sufficiently large areas of solid ownership to embark on the kinds of economic development they would like to undertake.

Descriptions of the Reservations

Minnesota's reservations are discussed in three separate groups in this book. The largest consists of the six Ojibway reservations, Bois Forte, Fond du Lac, Grand Portage, Leech Lake, Mille Lacs, and White Earth, which have joined together to form the Minnesota Chippewa Tribe (MCT) for some governing functions. The Red Lake band is also Ojibway, but its reservation has a different history and government status that make it unique in Minnesota; it is therefore considered separately here. The four Sioux Communities of Dakota Indians have similar histories. They were established many years after the original Sioux reservations were abolished in 1863; they are independently run, however, by their own governments. Throughout the book, the reservations are dealt with as groups in the above sequence.

Table 1. Minnesota Indian Reservations, 1983 Acreage
(1962 Acreage in Parentheses)

| | Indian Trust Lands | | Govern- | | Original | Percent |
	Tribal	Allotted	mental	Total	Reservations[a]	Remaining[a]
		Chippewa Reservations				
Bois Forte	30,354	11,504	5	41,863	103,863	40%
	(25,976)	(14,301)	(5)	(41,282)		
Fond du Lac	4,784	17,034		21,818	97,800	22
	(3,932)	(17,702)		(22,634)		
Grand Portage	37,679	7,086	79	44,844	56,512	79
	(32,913)	(8,644)	(79)	(41,636)		
Leech Lake	15,448	12,075	4	27,527	677,099	4
	(12,320)	(11,402)	(4)	(23,726)		
Mille Lacs	3,781	68		3,849	Unresolved	
	(3,252)	(132)		(3,384)		
White Earth	54,125	1,953		56,078	709,467	8
	(25,382)	(2,070)	(28,610)	(56,062)		
Red Lake	564,426	102		564,528		
	(564,363)	(102)		(564,465)		
		Sioux Communities				
Lower Sioux	1,743			1,743		
	(1,743)			(1,743)		
Prairie Island	534			534		
	(534)			(534)		
Shakopee-Mdewakanton	258			258		
	(258)			(258)		
Upper Sioux	746			746		
	(746)			(746)		
		Winnebago Reservation				
Houston County[b]	296			296		
All lands	714,174	49,822	88	764,084		

Sources: For Chippewa reservations (except Red Lake), BIA, Minnesota Agency, Realty, *Annual Report* 30 Sept. 1983; for Red Lake Reservation, Sioux Communities, and Winnebago Reservation, BIA, Minneapolis Area Office, 1983.

[a]For those reservations where the original land was allotted.

[b]Administered by the BIA from its office in Ashland, Wis.

The following descriptions of Minnesota reservations are based on a variety of sources. Natural resources and forestry data are from BIA reports. Overall economic development plans (June 1980) and service unit health plans (IHS, July 1979) prepared for each reservation provided the general descriptions. The tribes and other governmental programs are major employers on each reservation; major tribal enterprises

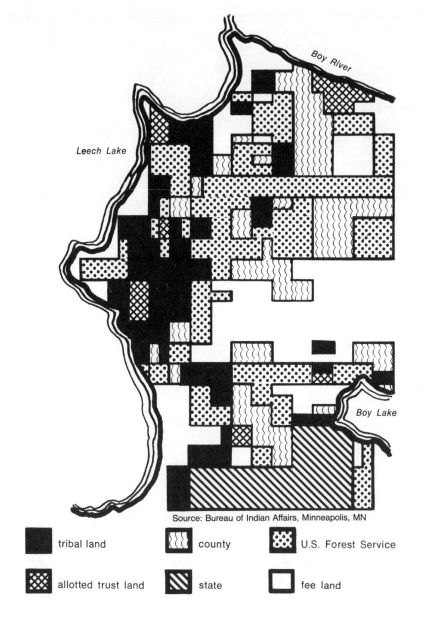

Leech Lake

Boy River

Boy Lake

Source: Bureau of Indian Affairs, Minneapolis, MN

- ■ tribal land
- ▨ county
- ▦ U.S. Forest Service
- ▧ allotted trust land
- ▨ state
- ☐ fee land

Map 2. Land ownership for a portion of Leech Lake Reservation
(smallest unit is 20 acres)

are listed in chapter 7. Refer to table 1 (p. 25) for reservation acreages and to table 5 (p. 42) for population size.

Bois Forte. The Bois Forte Indians of the Lake Superior band ceded their land in the La Pointe Treaty of 1854. By treaty in 1866, the current reservation at Nett Lake was established. Reservation land was added by executive order at Lake Vermilion in 1881 and at Deer Creek in 1883.

The reservation has beautiful pine forests, large lakes, and many streams. It is noted for its fine wild rice. Forest covers about 96% of the trust land; 90% is available as commercial forests, predominantly in black spruce, red pine, and aspen. When economic conditions are good, the timber industry provides some employment.

The Nett Lake portion of the reservation is located in St. Louis and Koochiching counties. The community center is at Nett Lake, which has the government center, a Head Start and day care facilities building, and an elementary school. Students attend high school in Orr, the nearest non-Indian community. Although both Nett Lake and Vermilion have outpatient clinic medical services, the nearest hospital is at Virginia, 65 miles away.

Vermilion, 65 miles to the east of Nett Lake and five miles north of State Highway 1, has a community center and facility for bingo constructed in 1984. Deer Creek is west of Nett Lake, in Itasca County.

Fond du Lac. The 1854 treaty with the Lake Superior and Mississippi bands established the Fond du Lac reservation. The land is in St. Louis and Carlton counties and has rolling hills along the St. Louis River. Much of the reservation is lowland, with about 20 lakes.

Wild rice and peat are produced locally. Only commercially poor, second-growth timber, used primarily for firewood, remains on the reservation.

Sawyer and Brookston are two communities within the reservation. The city of Cloquet abuts it on the east, with Duluth 25 miles to the northeast. US Highway 2 marks the north boundary of the reservation, and Interstate 35 the southeast corner. Tribal headquarters are at Cloquet, which has an administrative center and council chambers, an outpatient health clinic, vocational training facility, and a tribal school. Sawyer has a community center.

Four school districts split the reservation. Fond du Lac Ojibway School is a tribally run alternative school serving students on the reservation and from Duluth. Mash-Ka-Wisen, an Indian-run, residential, primary treatment facility for chemical dependency, is at Sawyer in facilities provided by the tribe.

Tribal operations include a construction company, the manufacture of furnaces, and a successful bingo operation. Off-reservation employment is provided in Duluth and by the wood products industry in Cloquet.

Grand Portage. The Grand Portage Reservation, created by the La Pointe Treaty of 1854, occupies the most northeasterly portion of Minnesota. The area is the historic site of early fur trade between Indians and voyageurs. The name comes from the nine-mile portage necessary to bypass the cascading waters of the Pigeon River, a 200-foot drop, to get inland to the lakes of northern Minnesota. The Grand Portage National Monument, with a reconstructed trading post, shares the community of Grand Portage with the tribe.

The area has much to attract tourists. The boat to Isle Royale National Park departs from Grand Portage. The reservation is bordered by the rugged, scenic shoreline of Lake Superior. The land is hilly and heavily forested with second-growth timber. Almost all of the land is commercial forest, with aspen, birch, and spruce-fir.

The city of Grand Portage, the community center and tribal headquarters, is located in Cook County on US Highway 61, 150 miles north of Duluth and near the Canadian border. An elementary school, the only log school in Minnesota, provides kindergarten through sixth-grade instruction. Junior and senior high are at Grand Marais, 35 miles away. The nearest hospital is also at Grand Marais, although a clinic serves the reservation in Grand Portage.

The Grand Portage Lodge and Conference Center, a 100-unit hotel on the shores of Lake Superior with a marina and campground, is a tribal business that employs all members who wish to work there. Additional employment is available in the lumber industry, commercial fishing on Lake Superior, and the National Park Service.

Leech Lake. The area that includes Leech Lake Reservation in north central Minnesota was the home of Ojibway bands located around the three major lakes of the region—Cass, Leech, and Winnibigoshish. The land was ceded by the Pillager and Lake Winnibigoshish bands in 1855, and the treaty of 1864 established the consolidated Leech Lake Reservation. The area was changed later by the treaty of 1867 and executive orders of 1873 and 1874. Well over half of the original reservation is owned by county, state, and federal governments. The National Chippewa Forest almost completely surrounds the reservation.

Drained by the headwaters of the Mississippi River, the area is generally swampy. It has low, rocky ridges and many lakes in addition to the three large ones. It is a prime sports fishing area of the state. Wild rice is a major crop. The land is 74% forested, mostly cutover timber usable for hardwood, fuelwood, waferboard (a wood chip product that replaces plywood in construction), softwood pulp, and sawtimber.

Located along US Highway 2, the reservation is 14 miles east of Bemidji and 53 miles west of Grand Rapids. Walker is on the southwest corner. Cass Lake, the largest community within the reservation, is the site of headquarters for Leech Lake Reservation, the MCT, the BIA Minnesota Agency Office, and a 23-bed IHS hospital and clinic. A community center and bingo facility is at the Leech Lake Veterans Memorial Complex. Other communities within the reservation, some of which have their own community centers and social programs, are Bena, Federal Dam, Ball Club, Onigum, Squaw Lake, Inger, Alwood, Spring Lake, Boy River, Mission, Pennington, and Sugar Point.

Parts of the reservation are in five counties — Cass, Itasca, Beltrami, Hubbard, and Crow Wing — and in seven school districts. The reservation has a tribal school, Chief Bug-O-Nay-Ge-Shig, which serves kindergarten through twelfth grades.

Employment is available in Bemidji as well as in several tribal enterprises. They include a restaurant, supermarket, and service station complex; a construction company; a logging company, lumber store, and firewood production and packaging facility; and waste disposal services.

Mille Lacs. The Mille Lacs reservation area was included in the 1837 treaty with the Mississippi band; the 1855 treaty established the reservation. Later treaties and acts of Congress were intended to make the Indians move. It was not until 1914 that major allotments were authorized. Additional land was added under the IRA in the 1930s.

The reservation is in four counties of central Minnesota, with the scattered sites divided into three separate areas for administrative purposes. The largest section is on the southwest shore of Mille Lacs Lake, around Vineland, where the tribe owns more than four miles of lakeshore frontage. Lake Lena area, 25 miles east of Hinckley near the Wisconsin border and St. Croix State Park, is the second portion. The third region contains settlements near Isle at the southeast end of Mille Lacs Lake; East Lake, five miles south of McGregor; Minnewawa, northeast of the East Lake area; and Sandy Lake, farther north, which had been an 1855 treaty reservation. Away from Mille Lacs Lake the land is mostly forest, used as firewood, with small scattered lakes.

The reservation portion at Vineland is on US Highway 169. The Minnesota Historical Society has an Indian museum nearby. The city nearest to this portion of the reservation is Brainerd, 45 miles away. The tribe's government center, school for grades seven through twelve (Nay

Ah Shing), and an outpatient health clinic are at or near Vineland. Community centers are located in the Lena and East Lake areas.

Employment is provided by several tribal enterprises, including an electronics manufacturing plant, construction company, and restaurant and marina. Jobs are also available in private tourist industries. Maple syrup is produced and sold by several members.

White Earth. The White Earth Reservation, established in 1867, was intended to become the home of all Ojibway in Minnesota. It was settled by members of four of the historic bands. In 1979 a court held that four townships on the northeast edge of the reservation had been ceded in 1889 and were no longer to be considered part of the original reservation.

White Earth is located in northwestern Minnesota in Mahnomen, Clearwater, and Becker counties. Indian communities within the reservation are White Earth, Pine Point/Ponsford, Naytahwaush, Rice Lake, Callaway, Elbow Lake, and Ebro. Ogema, Waubun, and Mahnomen are other cities within the reservation boundaries. The major cities outside the boundaries are Detroit Lakes, Park Rapids, and Bagley, with Bemidji 69 miles to the northeast. White Earth community is the location of the tribal school, Circle of Life. Pine Point has an Indian experimental school that is now tribally run. The reservation is divided among seven school districts.

The land is rolling, with several lakes and forests of aspen, northern hardwoods, and oak. Trees are harvested for sawtimber, sawbolts, hardwood pulpwood, firewood, and aspen for waferboard. The western portion of the reservation is used for farming, and the reservation also produces wild rice. Employment is provided by tribal programs and enterprises, including sawmill and construction, freeze-dried fishing bait, and clothing manufacturing companies; an IHS facility; businesses in nearby towns; and seasonal timber work.

Red Lake. In treaties and agreements in 1864, 1889, and 1904, the Red Lake band gave up land but never ceded the main reservation surrounding Lower Red Lake and a portion of Upper Red Lake. The current reservation is spoken of as the "diminished" or "aboriginal" land. It is 407,730 acres, of which 229,300 are water of the two lakes.

When land that had been ceded but not sold was returned after 1934, this restored land amounted to 156,696 acres. It included 70% of the Northwest Angle of Minnesota, as well as lands scattered between the reservation and the Canadian border. The total area controlled by the tribe, 564,426 acres, is about the size of Rhode Island. The land is located in nine different counties.

The reservation, called "closed," has never been subject to state law. Although Red Lake Indians are technically a Minnesota Chippewa tribe, the government of the reservation has remained separate from those of the other Chippewa tribes in the state.

The reservation is located in northwestern Minnesota. Bemidji, the closest city, is 35 miles to the south. The land is slightly rolling and heavily wooded, with 337,000 acres of commercial forestland under management. There are lakes, swamps, peat bogs, and prairies, with some land on the western side suitable for farming. The main areas with population are in Beltrami and Clearwater counties. Tribal enterprises include a construction company, sawmill, and fisheries.

The four reservation communities are Red Lake, Redby, Ponemah, and Little Rock. Tribal headquarters and the tribal court are located at Red Lake, as are the BIA Agency offices, the school, and an IHS hospital. The Humanities Building at Red Lake houses the Head Start program, a swimming pool, and other community facilities.

Ponemah, near the end of the peninsula separating Upper and Lower Red lakes, has a newly constructed elementary school, an alternative school (Bakaan Gwagak), Head Start, a health clinic, and other services. Redby is the location of the tribal sawmill and fisheries operations.

Sioux Communities. The Lower Sioux Indian Community at Morton, located along the banks of the Minnesota River, contains prime, flat agricultural land and about 250 acres of timber and brush in its 1,743 acres. Across the Minnesota River is the Birch Coulee battle site of the Uprising. Two Indians, Good Thunder and Charles Laurence, bought land at the location as early as 1834. The community was started in the late 1880s. The Lower Sioux is in Redwood County, two miles south of Morton and six miles east of Redwood Falls.

Lower Sioux Pottery manufactures handcrafted pottery. Tribal revenue is generated by leasing out a gravel pit and farm land. A major bingo facility, Jackpot Junction, five miles east of Redwood Falls, opened in 1984. There is a tribal office and a community building.·

The Prairie Island Indian Community is located on Prairie Island, which is formed as the Vermillion River joins the Mississippi. It is low-lying land, with about half of the community's property in the floodplain. Much of the land is leased to a tribal member for farming. The island is shared with Northern States Power Company's nuclear electric generating plant and the Army Corps of Engineers' US Lock and Dam No. 3.

The Mdewakantons of the Mississippi Dakota band had settled on the island as early as 1850; reservation land was purchased in the late 1880s. A community center and major facility for "big bingo" (large jackpot) began operation in 1984. Prairie Island Indian Community is considered part of the city of Red Wing, Goodhue County, having been annexed by the city.

The Shakopee-Mdewakanton Sioux Community, Prior Lake, consists of 258 acres that were part of the lands acquired by the federal government in the late 1880s for the Mdewakanton Dakotas. However, settlement on the land did not begin until the late 1950s. The land, 25 miles from downtown Minneapolis, is surrounded by the city of Prior Lake in Scott County. The community was incorporated into the city of Prior Lake in 1972.

The tribe has taken advantage of its location in the metropolitan area and its exemption from state liquor and cigarette taxes and gambling regulation to develop a very profitable big bingo operation—Little Six Bingo Palace (1982)—and limited cigarette and liquor sales. Unemployment has been virtually eliminated. Using proceeds from bingo, the tribe has built a day-care center, a health clinic, and a cultural center (the world's largest tepee, 85 feet tall). Tribal headquarters and the BIA Sioux Field Office are located in the community.

The Upper Sioux Community is located in Yellow Medicine County, three miles south of Granite Falls at the mouth of the Yellow Medicine River. It is settled by members of the Sisseton Dakota band on land purchased in 1938, under the IRA.

The reservation is along the Minnesota River, much of it in the floodplain. There are two community centers.

Land Issues

Original Treaty Claims

The Indian Claims Commission existed between 1946 and 1983 to deal with alleged wrongs done to Indians prior to 1946. The issues brought before the commission dealt primarily with inadequate payment to the tribes at the time of the treaties. Practically all treaties involving Minnesota Indians were reviewed and awards were granted. Once a claim was settled, no other claim concerning that treaty could be filed. Claims not handled by the commission were dealt with in the US Court of Claims, the regular system for suing the federal government.

The process of paying an Indian claim settlement is a lengthy one. Congress appropriates the money, and the BIA prepares a distribution plan after consulting with the Indians involved. Congress then has the right to disapprove of the plan. If it is approved, a roll is prepared of those eligible to participate.

Distribution plans usually set aside 20% of the funds for the tribe to use on common needs. The money paid out in claims is not subject to state or federal taxes, and it cannot be used to reduce welfare or payments from other government programs. Members of a band have or will receive only one payment from one treaty. The amounts awarded on Minnesota treaty claims have varied from $100 to $2,500 per person.

Heirship Problems

For land that has continued in trust (that is, where the owner[s] did not take title), it is not unusual for ownership portions to consist of a very small fraction. A 1983 example is an 80-acre tract with 94 heirs, most with less than 1% ownership. Splintered ownership makes it very difficult to get agreement to use the land for anything.

The Indian Land Consolidation Act, passed in 1983, is an attempt to deal in a small way with the problem. When an owner dies who held 2% or less interest in an allotted piece of property that earned less than $100 in the previous year for the owner, the property will pass into tribal ownership.

Special Problems

Mille Lacs Reservation. Most of the Ojibway reservations are defined today as the areas originally set aside. The extent of the Mille Lacs Reservation is in dispute. Originally (1855), portions of four townships (61,000 acres) were designated, with additional land at Sandy and Rice lakes.

Today's reservation, according to the BIA, is only the land held in trust by the federal government. The Mille Lacs band contends that the original reservations remain, with about 3% of the land now in trust status. The issues revolve around interpretation of the treaties and laws dealing with the Mille Lacs band and Indian understanding of them: the 1864 treaty, the Nelson Act, and 1902 legislation (see appendix A). The extent of the reservation is an important current issue because band sovereignty, which carries with it several important powers and rights, extends throughout reservations, not just on trust-held land.

Indians at Mille Lacs have had an especially difficult history of dealing with white people. While the Indians were not able to get allotments, lumbering interests took the timber; later, immigrant farmers purchased the land and were given legal titles.

As the secretary of the interior acknowledged in 1890, "The rights of the Indians upon this reservation have been a vexed question, full of difficulties and embarrassments. Their principal fault seems to be in possessing lands that the white man wants."[5]

To force the removal of the Mille Lacs Indians, whites burned and destroyed their homes. In May 1901, the sheriff of Mille Lacs County destroyed the homes of about 100 Indians because whites had claimed title to the land.[6] Reservation residents still living witnessed their homes being destroyed.

The Taking of White Earth Reservation. Special legislation for White Earth Reservation, the Clapp Rider of 1906, greatly reduced the restrictions on transfer of Indian land so that timber interests and farmers would not have to wait the 25 years required under general allotment laws. The Clapp Rider provided that all adult "mixed bloods" could take title to their allotments and sell them if they wished. Adult "full bloods" were also allowed to sell their land when the secretary of the interior believed that they were competent to handle their own affairs. The legislation was interpreted as immediately passing title to the adult mixed bloods.

The details of how the land changed ownership in the early 1900s are again important in the 1980s because the Minnesota Supreme Court ruled in State v. Zay Zah (1977) that the trust status of the Indian land should not have ended unless the Indian had consented to taking title and the land should not have been subject to taxes.

The Clapp Rider triggered the rapid transference of land. By 1909, fully 90% of the allotments to full bloods had been sold or mortgaged; 80% of the whole acreage of the reservation had passed into private hands.[7] Fraud and improper dealings were extensive, as subsequent investigations (1911–20) were to show.[8]

In a 1978 interview, an 85-year-old White Earth Ojibway recalled her mother's experiences:

> My mother told me how she put down her thumbprint
> on a piece of paper. She couldn't write. She couldn't
> speak English. My mother lost her land that way. She
> didn't know she was losing her allotment. . . . She
> was full blood. She wasn't supposed to be able to sell
> her land, according to the law. . . . The Indians went
> through their land money in a hurry. It took maybe a
> year. They bought horses and buggies and clothes. Then

it was all gone and they had to live the way they did before.[9]

Since full bloods could not sell their land immediately, blood designation was important. A roll taken in 1910 (the Hinton Roll) showed 927 full bloods. In 1913 Congress authorized that another roll be taken. Lawsuits and court action depended on who was a full blood. An anthropologist from the US National Museum, Ales Hrdlicka—an "expert" on identifying full blooded Indians—came to White Earth to prepare the roll.

He used "scientific" standards: shape of head; color of eyes; color of skin and its reaction to pressure; color, thickness, and character of hair; structure of teeth. His report was filed as the 1920 Blood Roll and accepted by the federal court in 1920. He had found only 126 full bloods. The federal government is now bound by this roll because it was accepted at that time, even though there are known obvious errors, such as brothers and sisters (children of the same parents) reported as one full blood, one mixed blood.

White Earth Probate Problems. Because of the Clapp Rider and the assumption that there was no longer a trust relationship, the BIA stopped probating estates at White Earth in 1915. There is now a tremendous backlog of estates that need to be processed, covering several generations. Research has found that for 950 allotments the original allottees are recorded as still living, while the best estimate is that all but about 30 are dead. In all of these cases, records are either very sketchy or nonexistent. Identifying the heirs to complete the probate and clarify land titles is exceedingly laborious and may be impossible in some cases.[10]

Trespass Claims

A deadline was imposed on the federal government's right to act in cases of trespass. This includes violation of an individual's property, such as taking rights of way for roads or public utilities without payment; abandoning rights of way but not returning the land to the owner; taking timber, harvesting wild rice, damming streams or flooding property and destroying the natural resources, all without compensation to the rightful owner; and gaining economic benefit from land improperly taken.

The legislation, called "2415" (28 USC 2415), required that the federal government file suit for money damages in cases of trespass on trust or restricted fee Indian land that took place before 1966, or the claim would be forever invalid. As of 1984, all possible trespass cases have been identified and are being processed by the BIA and the US Department of Justice.

If the federal government decides not to pursue a case, the tribe (and presumably, through the tribe, the individuals) involved will be notified and may still bring suit on their own within a year of the notification. If the BIA proposes legislation in lieu of litigation, three years remain for individual action before the claim dies. There is no time limit on when the BIA must make a decision and go to court, drop the case, or seek congressional action.

The legislation applied specifically to trespass cases, but because improper land title transfers might also involve subsequent trespass damages, all types of cases have been identified. (In cases establishing title or right of possession, there is no statute of limitation barring the US government from recovering for tribes or individual Indians; court cases can be brought at any time.)

Problems in Minnesota. The MCT, under contract with the BIA, investigated cases on the six MCT reservations beginning with the 12,178 original allotments; additional research was done on the other reservations. Several types of problems were identified.

Indian land was improperly subjected to taxes and then forfeited for nonpayment. This was a major problem on White Earth Reservation, where the Clapp Rider was interpreted incorrectly, but it also occurred on other reservations. County courts probated Indian estates, including allotted land that should have remained in trust, and authorized the sale of the land. Old Age Assistance (welfare) liens were placed against trust property. When estate income was realized or the land was sold, the lien was repaid to the county.

Fractionalized heirship sales were one of the biggest problems on the Leech Lake Reservation. The BIA had allowed the sale of trust allotted property without getting the consent of all heirs. These sales, called "partial consents" or "secretarial transfers" (carried out by the secretary of the interior), were authorized by many of the heirs but not all. The solicitor of the Department of the Interior directed that such sales should cease in 1956. Many unsettled claims remain from those sales. The legality of the transfer of titles without full consent of all heirs has not been decided.

Extent of the Cases. The mishandling of land that had been allotted to individual Indians and was supposed to be protected by the trust relationship with the BIA is now known to be a problem on almost all Minnesota reservations. Those who now hold the land or trespassed on it and might be responsible for damages include state and county governments, the US Forest Service, Indian tribes, private individuals, and companies. Problems are especially extensive on White Earth Reservation, where irregularities occurred in about one-fourth of the sales of trust land.

Of the possible claims identified in Minnesota, 2,328 were known to present problems as of November 1983. Although the various categories of claims will be reconsidered, and the reason must be identified for all claims rejected, the federal government concluded that litigation will probably be necessary in 301 cases (see table 2) involving primarily Old Age Assistance and tax forfeiture.

Table 2. Indian Land Claims in Minnesota, November 1983

Reservation	Cases Slated for Litigation[a]	Unresolved Cases
Bois Forte	23	90
Fond du Lac	33	72
Grand Portage	18	50
Leech Lake	72	705
Mille Lacs	14	92
White Earth	141	971
Red Lake	0	45
Total	301	2,025

Source: Federal Register, November 1983.
[a]Litigation considered by the BIA; however, no action had been taken.

The bulk of the cases, 2,025, are considered unresolved. These include secretarial transfers for which the legal position is not clear; title cases on White Earth Reservation, in which a legislative solution is seen as a better choice; and instances of trespass, such as establishment of rights of way, where the result was considered beneficial to the property. Of the Sioux Communities, only the Upper Sioux has one case for possible litigation.

Dealing with the Problems. The claims have raised a multitude of problems that will be with Indian claimants, tribes, owners of reservation land, governments, courts, and legislators for a long time to come. It will be very difficult to balance the interests of those who had property and rights taken illegally and the present owners who, in good faith, bought land on which they thought title was free and clear of any disputes. Although issues remain unresolved, the possibility of suits has clouded land titles and affected property values.

By not fulfilling its trust responsibilities, the federal government allowed the damages to occur. Now federal agencies must act on the claims: the BIA is processing the cases, and the Department of Justice is deciding which cases to litigate and which to drop. Strong interests, including other agencies of government, currently hold the property that was wrongfully taken. Some Indians fear that decisions will be made on a political basis rather than with full justice for those who have been harmed.

Any solution—legislative or court determined—will entail the monumental job of establishing the nature and extent of the damage, deciding on a suitable settlement, and identifying and locating the heirs. Even with help from the tribes (and the trespass law uses the tribes as the vehicle for communicating with individuals), it may be impossible to find the heirs: they may not be Indian; they may not be tribal members; they may have lived away from the tribe for several generations.

Tribes are speaking on behalf of individual claimants and are recommending that property transfers or other settlements be made with the tribes, especially as it may be impossible to find the heirs. The tribes, however, may also have been beneficiaries of the illegal taking of land. In these situations, the individual's claim would be against the tribe.

Legislation is seen by many as the answer to the problems. A federal proposal for the White Earth Reservation cases would validate all past sales and provide compensation to the Indian heirs. Minnesota passed legislation in 1984 authorizing the transfer of 10,000 acres of state-held land to be held in trust for the tribe. The land transfer would occur only as part of an agreement between the tribe and the federal government settling the land claims.

The specific amounts of money and land proposed were considered inadequate by tribal officials. Individuals would receive payment based on the value of the land when the wrong occurred, with no provision for compensation for the loss of the use of the land and its resources. Estimated costs of administering the claims were well in excess of the proposed compensation. The amount of land offered for transfer was approximately one-tenth of the acres subject to claims. Congress did not pass the proposed federal law in 1984. The state offer of land becomes void if there is no federal legislation by 31 December 1985.

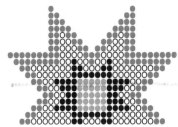

CHAPTER 3
Indian People

Who Is Indian?

The definition of "Indian" depends on who is doing the defining. Within Indian communities, urban and reservation, people are known as Indian because they wish to belong and the communities consider them Indian; the US census counted those who identified themselves as Indian. Other Indian counts are also undefined. The annual sight count taken in all of the state's public schools includes those students the teachers consider to be "American Indian." The designation in state birth and death records, kept by race, depends on the information supplied by whoever fills out the form.

Tribal Membership

Tribal membership is formal recognition of being Indian; in terms of tribal sovereignty, it is argued that only the tribes should have the power to state who is Indian. The Minnesota Chippewa Tribe requires that a member be at least one-fourth MCT Indian blood. Application for enrollment is to be filed within one year after a child's birth. American citizenship is required. The governing body of each reservation determines the enrollment, and an appeal process is provided.

The Red Lake band and the Sioux Communities have similar requirements. At Red Lake, membership applications must be filed within 180 days after a child's birth. The Shakopee-Mdewakanton Sioux,

Prairie Island, and Lower Sioux Indian communities link their membership to being one-fourth or more Mdewakanton and able to trace ancestry to Minnesota residence on 20 May 1886. Many of the Upper Sioux Community are enrolled through other reservations; requirements for membership in the community are Dakota Indian blood and residency.

Qualification for Government Programs

Qualification as an Indian for Indian-designated programs may be based on different definitions; most programs have their own specific criteria. The National Tribal Chairmen's Association examined the criteria of federal agencies in 1980 and found 47 definitions of "Indian."[1] They vary from that of the BIA—one-fourth Indian ancestry of an individual living on or near a reservation—to that of the Indian Education Act—an individual living anywhere in the country who has one grandparent a tribal member. Minnesota laws, while consistent in defining Indians as having one-fourth or more Indian blood, differ on whether the person needs to be tribally enrolled.

The Numbers

In 1980 the US census reported 35,016 Indians in Minnesota, 0.9% of the state's population. Minnesota had 2.6% of the US Indian population, twelfth largest in the country. Table 3 shows the changes in the state's Indian population in the years since 1860. In 1980, Indians lived

Table 3. Change in Number of Minnesota Indians

Year	Number of Indians	Percentage Increase over Previous Decade	Percentage of the Population
1860	2,369	—	1.4
1900	9,182	—	0.5
1920	8,761	Decline	0.4
1930	11,077	26	0.4
1940	12,528	13	0.4
1950	12,533	0	0.4
1960	15,496	24	0.5
1970	23,128	49	0.6
1980	35,016	51	0.9

Source: US Census.

primarily in the seven-county Metropolitan Area (45%) or in nine northern counties (41%); see table 4. The reservation population (28%) and

Table 4. Counties Where Minnesota Indians Live

More than 1,000 Indians		2.5% or More Indian	
County	Number of Indians	County	Percent Indian
Hennepin	10,479	Mahnomen	18.1
Beltrami	3,917	Beltrami	12.6
Ramsey	2,993	Cass	9.0
St. Louis	2,815	Clearwater	6.8
Becker	1,720	Becker	5.9
Anoka	1,112	Carlton	2.7
Itasca	1,087	Mille Lacs	2.7
Mahnomen	1,003	Itasca	2.5

Source: US Census, 1980

the Minneapolis population (26%) were almost the same. Indians were the second largest minority population in the state, after Blacks with 53,344.

On the Reservations

The 1980 census, Bureau of Indian Affairs, Indian Health Service, and tribal enrollment counts of Indians associated with the state's reservations are shown in table 5. Some of the difference in counts can be traced to the definitions used. The census reservation totals include only Indians on census tracts with land held in trust; the BIA includes the whole reservation and certain off-reservation areas; the IHS counts all Indians living in counties that contain reservations, as well as abutting counties. Duluth Indians, for instance, are included in the IHS count for Fond du Lac Reservation, while they are not in the BIA figure.

Enrolled members of the tribes far exceed those living on the reservations. These individuals may live anywhere. They may or may not continue to identify in an active way with an Indian community and their reservation.

Urban Indians

In 1928 the Meriam report estimated that 800 Indians lived in Minnesota's three major cities, about 5% of the state's Indian population.[2] In 1980 the total for the three cities was 12,815, 37% of the Indians in the state (see table 6). In Duluth, Indians were the largest minority population, whereas Minneapolis had more Blacks than Indians. In St. Paul, Indians were the fourth largest minority group (after Blacks, Asians, and Spanish-speaking).

Table 5. Number of Indians Associated with Minnesota Reservations

Reservation	1980 Census[a]	Bureau of Indian Affairs, 1980[b]			Indian Health Service, 1980[c]	Enrolled Members, 1982[d]
		On	Near	Total		
Bois Forte	502	680	250	930	1,449	1,921
Fond du Lac	514[e]	882	430	1,312	2,541[f]	2,825
Grand Portage	187	301	80	381	278	788
Leech Lake	2,759	3,026	1,500	4,526	4,124	5,841
Mille Lacs	293	710	203	913	912	2,075
White Earth	2,554	3,367	217	3,584	3,547	19,836
Total MCT[g]	6,809	8,966	2,680	11,646	12,851	33,286
Red Lake	2,823	4,069	330	4,399	3,297	7,200
Lower Sioux	65	163	39	202	192	
Prairie Island	80	59	59	118	222	
Shakopee-Mdewakanton	77	116	0	116	194	
Upper Sioux	51	62	62	124	121	
Total Sioux Communities	273	400	160	560	729	
Total Minnesota	9,905	13,435	3,170	16,605	16,877	

[a]Only Indians on census tracts with land held in trust.
[b]Indians on whole reservation and certain nearby areas.
[c]Indians in reservation counties and abutting ones.
[d]Enrolled tribal members living anywhere.
[e]A special census counted 959 in 1983.
[f]Includes Duluth.
[g]Minnesota Chippewa Tribe.

Of all major US cities, Minneapolis had the third highest percentage of Indian population (2.4%, after Tulsa and Oklahoma City); it had the largest concentration of Indians in the state. Only Red Lake, Leech Lake, and White Earth reservations exceeded the populations of either St. Paul or Duluth.

Within Minneapolis, the Phillips neighborhood has by far the largest concentration of Indian population. It is sometimes called "the largest reservation in the state." In an area one and one-half miles square, 3,026 Indians were living in 1980.

Migration to the Twin Cities took a big jump between 1960 and 1970. During the 1970s the urban increase slowed, although generally still exceeding the state growth of 49% in 1960–70 and 51% in 1970–80. Duluth and the metropolitan suburbs had the most rapid increase (see table 7).

Problems with the Census Count

Until 1950, the enumerator identified who was Indian. Starting with the 1960 census, when questionnaires were handled by mail and

Table 6. Minnesota Urban Indian Population

Urban Area	1928	1960	1970	1980
Minneapolis	300 (2%)[a]	2,077 (13%)	5,829 (25%)	8,933 (26%)
St. Paul	300 (2)	524 (3)	1,906 (8)	2,538 (7)
Suburbs		710 (5)	2,223 (10)	4,194 (12)
Total, Seven-County Metro Area		3,311 (21)	9,958 (43)	15,665 (45)
Duluth	150–200 (1)	402 (3)	615 (3)	1,344 (4)
Total, Minneapolis, St. Paul, Duluth	800 (5)	3,003 (19)	8,350 (36)	12,815 (37)

Sources: Lewis Meriam, *The Problems of Indian Administration* (Baltimore: Johns Hopkins Press, 1928), 197, 727; US Census.
[a]Percentage of state's Indian population given in parentheses.

people were free to identify themselves as they chose, the Indian population showed a major increase. Identifying Indians and getting their cooperation have been continuing problems for the census.

When the 1970 census count of Minnesota Indians was compared with that for 1960, it was realized that in its annual projections the state had been undercounting the Indian population by 20%. Throughout the 1970s, an adjustment factor was used for the yearly figures.[3]

The Indian communities are certain that the 1980 census did not count all Indians in the state, although state officials who deal with population believe that it was accurate. The count by reservations had only 36 Indians on Mille Lacs Reservation, an obvious undercount. The US census subsequently acknowledged the undercount and in November 1983 raised the figure to 293.[4] Fond du Lac Reservation had a special census taken in November 1983 that showed 959 Indians; only 514 were reported in 1980.

Leaders at the urban centers gave the following estimates for 1980, based on the numbers of Indians they served: Indian Health Board, 17,000 in Minneapolis; St. Paul American Indian Center, 6,000 in St.

Table 7. Percentage of Increase in Urban Indian Population

Urban Area	1960 to 1970	1970 to 1980
Minneapolis	181%	53%
St. Paul	264	33
Suburbs	213	89
Total, Seven-County Metro Area	201	57
Duluth	53	119
Total, Minneapolis, St. Paul, Duluth	178	53

Source: US Census.

Paul; American Indian Fellowship Association, 2,600 in Duluth.[5] The director of the Indian Affairs Council estimated the state's Indian population at 45,000 in 1982.

Many reasons are mentioned by Indians for the undercount. Administratively, some of the reservations were split between two census district offices, causing confusion about who was responsible. The enumerators chosen did not always relate well to the people. Indians have a dislike and perhaps fear of what seems like white authority coming to their doors, checking on them and interfering with their lives. The census is viewed as "for whites and by whites and Indians are out of it from the beginning."[6] Indians do not want to be studied and made to fill out forms that they think have no relevance to them. In some instances, people may have chosen not to identify themselves or their adopted Indian children as Indian.

A serious result of an undercount is the effect it has on programs for which funding is based on population. Revenue sharing was distributed annually during the 1970s based on BIA figures by reservation. The 1980 census figures were so low in comparison that sharp cuts in funding were made, and these figures will be the basis of funding for many programs in the next decade. This meant, for instance, significantly less employment assistance for the northern reservations and higher funding for the urban Indian programs in 1983. The census also, in effect, abolished two of the state's reservations for funding purposes. Prairie Island and Shakopee-Mdewakanton communities are totally encircled by cities. They were included in the city populations and were not given status as reservations.

Although there are good reasons to doubt the accuracy of the census count, it is the official US measurement and no other more accurate information is available. Throughout this book, therefore, 1980 census data have been used.

Indian Culture

Values

Indians have resisted tremendous pressures to destroy their culture, which gives them a distinctly nonwhite view of the world and ways of relating to others. "The world views of Indians and whites differ and it is foolish to try to make them the same. Maybe when society learns that lesson, there will be understanding."[7]

The traits that are called Indian were developed to meet the group's needs and to ensure survival. Sharing, and stressing the group over the individual, were necessary to maintain the group's existence. Respect was one of the highest ideals: for nature, which was home and provided sustenance; for elders, who embodied the tribe's wisdom; and for individuals who had skills in healing, war, or leadership, when those particular abilities were needed by the group. Other traits and values are commonly cited by today's Indians:

- Living in balance with nature is desirable, and respect for the earth is basic. If people accept this world as it is and live as they should with it, there will be no sickness or lack of food. The non-Indian world stresses control and mastery of the physical world, attitudes that Indians view as disrespectful.
- Little importance is placed on material possessions, which are shared and given generously to those in need.
- Although Indians compete fiercely in sports and games with other Indians and wage aggressive political contests, there is a general tendency not to compete to get ahead at the price of another's failure.
- Indians respect the elderly for their wisdom. Age is not concealed.
- Indians develop great skill in learning and absorbing information through indirection and innuendo. "You white people live in the world of words, printed and spoken. We Indians live in a quieter world, fewer words and facts, but more understanding."[8] Indians are brought up to be silent; however, they are trained to pick up emotions and meanings from the tiniest nonverbal clues.
- Respect for others is also manifest in the decision-making process, where the Indian way is to wait. It is a greater virtue to wait one's turn than to jump in. All will be asked to speak. Action is taken by the group when there is agreement by all involved, and there is resentment of decisions made without giving everyone a chance to have a say.
- Children are taught through example and the use of external consequences, rather than through admonition and punishment. Storytelling is used to convey values.
- The extended family and the group are greater than the individual. Indians have extensive family responsibilities. Many relatives are available for help and support whenever members of the network are temporarily incapacitated and unable to provide for themselves. The family interdependence system works much like a form of social insurance. Grandparents and older namesakes (somewhat like godparents) become superegos within families, with a responsibility to transmit a world view derived from the wisdom of years.[9]

For Indians who administer programs, government requirements often pose a cultural adjustment problem. The administrator of the Minneapolis American Indian Center commented, "As Indians, we didn't care who came in, or what they wanted. We just tried to give help to the people who needed it . . . and never bothered to count them or find out who was who, because that would be kind of impolite and would imply something about authority and status that is distasteful to Indians."[10] The program was computerized, however, to aid record keeping. "You cannot know how grotesque it is, how demeaning that is to us, to put an Indian's life on a punch card so that it can be run into a computer. It's just wrong. In this job, I do things that I know are wrong because I can feel that they're wrong, but we have to do them if we are going to survive."

Non-Indian Attitudes

Critically important to the Indian's self-concept is the non-Indian view of Indians. Since the beginning of contact between the two races, misconceptions have accumulated and little has been done to dispel the myths. Stereotypes are still being mass-produced through television, movies, advertising, and newspapers; beyond these images, Indians are ignored. A Boston study of 38 hours of children's television during January 1981 found that American Indians were represented solely by "Tonto."[11] Indians are not presented with reality in history books. Equally ignored are the accomplishments of modern-day Indians.

Personal discrimination has been felt by most Indians. For some the experience was very direct, "I can remember once when my sister missed the [school] bus. We didn't have a car then and rather than the school bringing her home, they put her in the jailhouse overnight. My mother was furious, but couldn't do anything . . . no money, no car. I remember that incident. I cried."[12]

When discrimination against Indians has become blatant, court action has been used to stop it. In recent cases of racial abuse against Indians, the Minnesota Supreme Court ruled against the abusers—a building inspector who made a racist remark about Indians (Thompson v. City of Minneapolis, 1980) and the police chief of Bagley, who demeaned an Indian police officer in a racially discriminatory way (Lamb v. Village of Bagley, 1981).

Effects of Negative Treatment

Indians are the only race in the United States that has experienced the deliberate, official governmental effort over decades to wipe out its way of life, language, and culture. They were conquered; colonized; and subjected to social engineering, culture shock, relocation, and forced negative education. Indians retain very little trust of the white system. As they face the questions of who they are and what the system has done to them, they react in a variety of ways.

For some the response is violence. Anger may be turned inward, resulting in self-destructive acts, suicide, interfamily problems, poor achievement in school, or chemical dependency. Others feel that because of past wrongs the government owes them a living. Some develop a distrust of non-Indians in any relationship and a heightened sensitivity to disrespect or conflict from whites.

Many Indians have to endure the destructiveness of poverty, in which a person's main concern is survival on the most minimal level. The need to rely on welfare assistance can foster dependency and discourage initiative. Being continually directed by others helps to destroy a person's image of self worth.

Vitality of Indian Culture

Although the problems are extensive and the causes go deeply into past history, which cannot be changed, there is tremendous determination and universal agreement among Indians that as a race and culture they will survive.

Different Indians express the challenge in different terms:

- "We must adjust and adapt to change and within our means control it. In many respects we are the final generation of an old tradition and the first generation of a new one" (chairman of the Mille Lacs band, 1980).[13]
- "White culture can very well ignore the Indians. It could annihilate us without noticing it, but there's no way we Indians can ignore white culture because it's too big, it's all around us, and it isn't going to go away. To save ourselves we have to be able to at least work with it, to try to understand what white culture is doing" (director of the Minneapolis American Indian Center, 1979).[14]
- "Twentieth-century Indian people are as distinct and self-determined as they were before contact with European nations. The blending of traditional values and contemporary life styles is a creative act of survival, not a compromise" (White Earth Reservation photographer-artist, 1982).[15]

Indians have strong feelings about other Indians' ways of meeting the non-Indian world. A hundred years ago, some Indians were willing to go along with the white man's ways and some were unwilling: "farmer Indians" versus "blanket Indians." Today, Indians may use such labels as "apple" (red on the outside, white within), "Uncle Tomahawk," "conservative," "traditional," or "militant" to describe each other. Whatever the terms, they are used to connote the different ways Indians are combining their pride in being Indian with their place in the dominant culture.

A study done in 1967 compared Ojibway families who had married Ojibway, retained the traditional beliefs, and spoke only Ojibway with those who had married white people, converted to Christianity, and spoke only English. The assumption was that the latter group would show acculturation and would not retain Ojibway personality characteristics. Contrary to expectations, the study found that core personality patterns remained constant across all levels of supposed acculturation.[16]

Building understanding of Indian culture is a strong priority of Indian communities. Classes and other learning opportunities in language, stories, and crafts are widely used by the various Indian groups. The importance of this, especially to the urban Indian peoples not involved in the reservation experience, has been noted by Indian educators. With the learning come positive attitudes toward Indian values, tradition, and spirituality.

An Indian middle class is building, and it is devoting its energies to the Indian communities. Indians whose parents had passed as whites and who were brought up as whites have returned to the Indian community to find their Indianness and offer their skills to their people. "There is a time to stop mourning our loss, and go on with our present. We must continue to set up our own support systems. We know, and have always known, what is the best for ourselves."[17]

Pow wows. Pow wows are an important part of Indian culture. The word comes from the Algonquian "pauau," meaning a gathering of people to celebrate an important event.[18] Most tribes and Indian communities have pow wows, many of them yearly (see appendix D). They have become pan-Indian, intertribal in attendance and in the dances and songs.

The traditional dress, composed of many spiritual and symbolic items and decorations, is highly respected, with eagle feathers especially revered. Pow wows may include singing and dancing contests, "giveaways," ceremonials, games, general intertribal dancing, feasts, other cultural activities, and a great deal of socializing and fun.

Pow wows are traditional spiritual gatherings to honor the drums, the songs and dances, and to learn from the elders about traditional ways. The drums and dance are expressions of prayer and thought, and drums are respected as spiritual beings. "Intensity of the dance is meant to restore conditions of harmony within oneself and for the ultimate good of the tribe. There are many different dances in a pow wow— Snake, War, Spear and Shield, Eagle, Hoop; however all are prayers to the life forces."[19]

A pow wow is "something more than a celebration. . . . [It] is a traditional way to commemorate an individual's pride in being Indian, renewing old friendships with other Indian people and an unsaid prayer that the American Indian way of life will continue. Even more so, a pow wow signifies the heartbeat of 'Indian Country,' like the steady rhythm of the Indian songs and drumming is meant to signify the human heartbeat."[20]

Art and Media

Indian expression through visual art is an outgrowth of the making of traditional ceremonial and ritualistic objects. Although these may have been prescribed by the culture, technical skill was noted and appreciated. Great skills were also developed in the decorative arts and manufacture of household utensils, clothing, ceremonial dress, jewelry, and other objects.

Minnesota has many good practitioners of the various arts using a variety of mediums, including painting, sculpture, graphics, and photography. Fine crafting and artistic skill are continued in the traditional areas of beadwork, clothing decoration, and basketry. A competition for Upper Great Lakes Indian artists, the Ojibwe Art Expo, is held annually at Bemidji State University; the works are then exhibited at Augsburg College in Minneapolis.

Indian newspapers serve Leech Lake and White Earth reservations, and the MCT also publishes a monthly paper, *Ourselves*. The *Circle* is the newspaper of the Minneapolis American Indian Center. Weekly television programming is produced in the Twin Cities and Duluth; and public television in Bemidji, KAWE (Ojibway for "top priority") has active Indian participation and a weekly program, "Ojibwe Issues," begun in 1984 (see appendix D).

Minneapolis is the home of Migizi ("eagle" in Ojibway) Communications, the nonprofit organization that produces "First Person Radio," the only nationally aired American Indian news program. It is a half-hour magazine format distributed by the National Public Radio satellite system. The board of directors and radio production staff are all Indian. In 1984, 48 stations in 18 states subscribed to it, including 8 stations in

Minnesota. Migizi also trains Indians in radio and other communications skills with a program for high school students, Achievement through Communications.

Spiritual Beliefs

Before white interference, Indians had a rich spiritual life. It included the gift of the spirits through the wisdom of visions and dreams; respect for elders and their wisdom; and understanding and respect for the natural world—the directions, the seasons, and all living things.

For the Ojibway, Midewiwin (Grand Medicine Society) was the method of preserving spiritual knowledge. "The principal idea of the Midewiwin is that life is prolonged by right living and the use of herbs which were intended for this purpose by the Mide manido (Grand Medicine spirit)."[21] Midewiwin taught that one must adhere to moral standards and that evil inevitably reacts on the offender. Lying, stealing, and the use of liquor were strictly forbidden.

Indian Spirituality Today. "Indians are among the most spiritual people in the world. The culture doesn't break into compartments like white culture with its 'sacred' and 'profane.' Indians have a holistic view where all life is sacred."[22]

Many Indians consider themselves "traditionalist," believers in and practitioners of the traditional culture. There has been increased interest in learning about traditional ways. Elders are sought out and listened to at alternative schools, community events, and ceremonies. There is a resurgence of vision quests, healing ceremonies, naming ceremonies, and rites of passage. Pipe ceremonies, sweat lodges, pow wows, drums, and dancing contribute spiritual strength.

For many Indians, traditional beliefs require that they have no structured organization, no physical place to go, which is an antithesis of organized Christian practice. Other traditionalists can be very comfortable also participating in Christian churches.

The Native American Church is a structured denomination incorporating traditional beliefs. Peyote is used as a sacramental element in its religious ceremonies and is specifically allowed under federal drug laws. There are Native American Church congregations in Minnesota, with the largest one in St. Paul.

Indian religious activity has several protections in federal law. The right to participate in traditional ceremonial rites, the protection of religious sites, and the use and possession of sacred objects have been guaranteed to Indians under the American Indian Religious Freedom Act (PL 95-341, 1978). On reservations, the US constitutional guarantee of separation of church and state does not apply. Tribes may establish religions; however, an individual's free exercise of religion cannot be prohibited.

Denominational Activity. Emissaries of the Christian religions were among the first to come among the Indians in Minnesota. They played an active role, supported by the federal government, in trying to eliminate "pagan" beliefs and to educate Indians into accepting Christianity and "civilization." Because the churches played a large role in the forceable destruction of Indian culture, some Indians still feel hostility and anger at church organizations.

About half of all Indians nationwide have had Christian church training; presumably, the figure is similar in Minnesota. The Protestant Episcopal and Roman Catholic churches have historically had the strongest programs on the reservations. Both denominations operated Indian boarding schools. For over 125 years, the Episcopalians have trained Indians in Minnesota to be priests. The oldest surviving Indian Christian congregation is St. Columba's at White Earth, begun in 1852 and moved to the reservation when it was settled in 1869. The Catholics continue to operate St. Mary's Mission School, a day school on Red Lake Reservation.

Various denominations have congregations and active programs for Indians on the reservations and in the urban areas; several are served by Indian ministers or priests. These churches are increasingly enriching their services and liturgy by incorporating traditional Indian symbols, music, drum, and pipe ceremonies in a way to honor them as sacred.

The Native American Theological Association helps Indians attend seminary schools and assists the seminaries in becoming more aware and concerned about Indians. It works through several institutions, including United Theological and Luther-Northwestern seminaries in the Twin Cities.

Good Works. As denominations, through umbrella groups, as congregations and individual members, churches are very active in funding and assisting social and welfare programs, including emergency food and care services that are important in the Indian communities (see chap. 6). The Minnesota, Minneapolis, and St. Paul councils of churches all have Indian programs; the Minnesota council funds a worker in Duluth.

Church denominations provide assistance for other Indian programs. The Lutherans have given support to the AIM organization, and Methodists hold the contract for deed of the Heart of the Earth Survival

School in Minneapolis. Both denominations and the Presbyterians have helped fund the Indian radio news program, Migizi, and the Episcopal church is assisting an economic development program on White Earth Reservation. Several denominations have education programs to inform their members and the public about Indian needs. Through the Mennonite church, volunteers serve Indian programs in the Twin Cities.

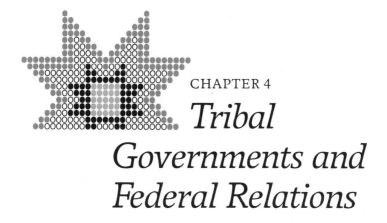

CHAPTER 4

Tribal Governments and Federal Relations

Tribal Governments

Traditionally, Ojibway leaders were accepted by the tribe for some immediate purpose and were followed only so long as they fulfilled it. No permanent commitment was made to a leader or to a highly centralized authority system. Because traders and government officials preferred to deal with as few people as possible, however, a "leadership" was designated for transactions with outsiders. Emergence of a permanent leadership, some believe, was the creation of white economic control and influence, not necessarily the result of developments within the tribal culture itself.

Ojibway from the various reservations who were being pressured to move to White Earth began an informal coalition, the General Council of the Chippewa Indians of Minnesota, in 1913.[1] All seven Chippewa reservations were members; Red Lake band withdrew in 1927.

A written constitution formed the General Council of the Red Lake band in 1918. It was based on a traditional system; hereditary chiefs and their appointees formed a 42-member deliberative body. Present-day constitutions for Minnesota's other reservations came into being after the passage of the Indian Reorganization Act in 1934. In 1959 Red Lake band changed to a government based on majority vote and elected representatives, similar to those formed by the other reservations under the IRA.

Under their constitutions and bylaws, the tribes exert powers very similar to those of other local governments. They represent the people's sovereignty in entering into contracts, hiring counsel, negotiating and lobbying with other levels of government, and passing and enforcing laws. They set membership criteria and pass on all tribal enrollment. They hire staff and administer programs.

To comply with legal requirements, the tribes establish housing authorities, development corporations, construction companies, and other enterprises. They hold elections, establish courts and advisory groups, grant income-producing leases, and grant housing and other leases to members. They have sovereign immunity and can be sued only if the action is first approved by Congress.

Unlike other governments, Indian tribal governments must seek BIA approval before they may take some actions; the degree of federal involvement varies with the wording of the specific tribal constitution. Constitutional amendments must be approved by the BIA as well as by the tribal governing body (a two-thirds vote in the case of the MCT) and a majority of those voting in an election, provided that at least 30% of eligible voters have voted.

Voting in elections is limited to enrolled members who are 18 or older. Absentee voting is allowed on all reservations except three of the Sioux Communities (Prairie Island does allow it). Elections are often hotly contested, and there may be a large absentee vote. In the race for secretary-treasurer of the White Earth Reservation in 1982, the winning candidate got 203 of his 378-vote total from absentee voters.

Organization of Government

Minnesota Chippewa Tribe. The MCT Constitution was first adopted in 1936 and amended in 1963 and 1972 into its present structure. It is the constitution for the Bois Forte, Fond du Lac, Grand Portage, Leech Lake, and White Earth reservations and for the Nonremovable Mille Lacs band. It is also the constitution for the MCT itself, the umbrella organization of the six reservations.

Each of the six reservations elects at large a chairman and secretary-treasurer and one to three representatives by district, all for four-year terms. These officials form the Reservation Business Committee (RBC), the governing body of each reservation.

The MCT also has powers as a tribe. (Throughout this book, "tribe" refers to the RBC of a reservation unless MCT is specifically mentioned.) Its governing body is the Tribal Executive Committee (TEC), which is

composed of the chairman and secretary-treasurer of each reservation—
12 members in all. A president, vice-president, secretary, and treasurer
are selected from the TEC members for two-year terms. The appointed
Urban Advisory Committee is made up of one RBC-chosen representative for each reservation. Some reservations also elect local Indian councils, which are active at the community level but not a formal body under the tribal constitution.

The MCT headquarters is located at Cass Lake; additional offices
in Duluth and Minneapolis serve members and administer programs
that extend off the reservations.

In the early 1980s, the MCT was operating many programs and had
a staff of 250; by 1982 the staff had been cut to about 100. Program funding had been cut or eliminated, and individual reservations in several
instances were choosing to administer programs themselves. In view of
these changes, the MCT and the RBCs have been reviewing their practices to determine the level of government that can best provide particular services.

In 1981, Mille Lacs Reservation began reorganizing its government
into three separate branches that became fully functional in 1984. The
tribal chairman heads the executive branch; the Legislative Assembly
includes the secretary-treasurer as speaker, with three remaining members elected by district; and the seven-person Court of Central Jurisdiction enforces laws and resolves disputes. The court uses unwritten cultural tradition as well as tribal ordinances in making its decisions.
Among the appointed positions are an advisory council of elders and a
spiritual adviser.

The reservation is still formally a part of the MCT structure. Mille
Lacs leaders explain, however, that the new form of governance is based
on the inherent sovereignty that rests with the band, on a provision in
the MCT constitution that RBCs may define the duties of officers and
committtees, and on an opinion by the Department of the Interior solicitor that a tribe in a PL 280 state retains "sovereign power to enact its own
law and order code, establish a tribal court, and authorize tribal police
to enforce tribal law."[2]

Red Lake. Red Lake Reservation's revised constitution and bylaws
were adopted in 1959 and amended in 1974 and 1979. The tribal council
is composed of a chairman, secretary, and treasurer (all elected at large)
and eight council members (two elected from each of four districts).
Descendants of the seven hereditary chiefs continue to serve as an advisory council.

Sioux Communities. Of the Sioux Communities, Prairie Island and Lower Sioux Indian communities have similar, standard IRA constitutions ratified in 1937 that provide for tribal councils composed of a chairman and four council members elected for two-year terms.

Shakopee-Mdewakanton Sioux Community was affiliated with the Lower Sioux for governmental purposes until 1969, when it formed its own government. Membership began with those on the rolls at that time and their descendants. The governing body for the community is the general council, which is composed of all qualified voters, who must be residents. The Shakopee-Mdewakanton General Council has the authority to delegate the administration of the community to the business council, composed of the chairman, vice-chairman, and secretary-treasurer chosen by the general council.

The Upper Sioux Community does not have a constitution and is not considered a tribe for enrollment purposes because residents are enrolled at other reservations (primarily Sisseton or Flandreau in South Dakota). Community affairs are run by a board of five trustees, who are elected at large for four-year terms, under provisions for governance adopted in 1962.

In the past (1971–84) the Sioux Communities had an umbrella organization, which changed its name and membership over the years. The organization was disbanded in 1984 because the communities decided that their different needs could be served better if they handled their affairs individually. All four communities participate in the Minnesota Dakota Indian Housing Authority, which administers state and federal housing programs for the total group.

National Groups

Representing Indian interests at the national level are several groups that have had leadership from Indians in Minnesota. The National Congress of American Indians, the oldest (founded in 1944), includes a broad spectrum of Indian views and interests. Lee Cook of Minneapolis has served as national president.

The National Tribal Chairmen's Association, begun in 1971, is composed of leaders of the federally recognized tribes. Roger Jourdain of Red Lake was active in establishing the group and has served it for many years in leadership positions. The Council of Energy Resource Tribes represents 29 tribes with energy resources of gas, oil, and coal; Minnesota tribes are not involved.

Minneapolis was one of the major cities to shape the American

Indian Movement and provide it with national leadership. In 1983, Clyde Bellecourt of Minneapolis was a national director. The International Indian Treaty Council (IITC), composed of Indian nations throughout the Americas, grew out of AIM leadership. The IITC has been granted nongovernmental organization (NGO) status at the United Nations. Minnesota AIM officials, as part of IITC, participated in the UN conferences on indigenous peoples held at Geneva in 1977 and 1981.

Other groups are active in special areas of Indian concern. The American Indian Law Center and the Native American Rights Fund are legal organizations working for Indian rights through the courts. The National Indian Education Association got its start in Minnesota and has its national office in the Twin Cities.

Tribal Sovereign Rights

Basis in Treaties

The importance of treaties was stressed by Felix Cohen, the noted authority on Indian legal matters, in 1942: "One who attempts to survey the legal problems raised by Indian treaties must at the outset dispose of the objection that such treaties are somehow of inferior validity or are of purely antiquarian interest. . . . Such an assumption is unfounded. . . . The reciprocal obligations assumed by the Federal Government and by Indian tribes during a period of almost a hundred years constitute a chief source of present-day Indian law."[3]

Although Indians granted rights to the federal government through treaties, they retained all rights not granted. As an attorney who deals with Indian issues has said, "The honored role of treaties is put down in the Constitution itself. . . . Treaties are part of the supreme law of the land. It is because of this that treaties are such a strong weapon today . . . a weapon that can be used to force the United States to honor obligations it has made."[4]

As instruments of law, however, treaties are not that secure. The US Commission on Civil Rights noted that "no international forum or court has yet been able to enforce treaties or hold the United States accountable for the violations of any of its pledges to Indians."[5] US courts have allowed treaties to be violated, ruling that they are only equal to regular laws and that the latest approved is considered to be the closest to congressional intent. The only advantage courts accord to treaties is to require that congressional intention to override the terms of a treaty be clear.

Congressionally Imposed Limitations

The Constitution grants Congress the power to regulate commerce with Indian tribes, a provision that has been broadly construed to give Congress authority in many areas beyond just regulating commerce. Indians on their reservations do not come under any of the other protections or clauses of the Constitution except as Congress uses its power under the commerce clause. This "plenary power" gives Congress extraordinary control over Indian tribes. "It can, without regard to most Constitutional safeguards, do whatever it wants in Indian affairs."[6] Congress is the "bottom line" on Indian issues.

Questions are being raised about whether it is proper for Congress to have extraordinary power over Indian tribes. At the time the principle of plenary power was applied (*US v. Kagama*, 1886), Indians were in a very dependent role. But "incompetents, needing a guardian" or "wards" is not now a valid characterization of Indians in their relationship to the federal government. Rather, the relationship is based on the trust obligation.

As pointed out by a tribal attorney, the plenary power of Congress holds over Indian tribes the constant threat that everything can be taken away. In political terms, this becomes the unstated or overt threat that Indians must agree to proposals or Congress will act to make things worse. The attorney maintained that the concept of plenary power is inconsistent with respect for human rights and with other fundamental American principles of democratic self-government.[7]

Because Indians are weak politically and are at the mercy of governments that they are unable to influence alone, their survival becomes the necessary concern of all Americans. The US Commission on Civil Rights commented that "Indian tribes have had to rely upon the constitutional-legal system and the moral conscience of society for their survival."[8]

Powers Remaining

The concept of tribal sovereignty as identified by Felix Cohen is considered the standard. There are three fundamental principles:

(1) An Indian tribe possesses . . . all the powers of any sovereign state.
(2) Conquest renders the tribe subject to the legislative power of the United States . . . terminates the external powers of sovereignty . . . e.g. its power to enter into treaties with foreign nations, but does not by itself affect

the internal sovereignty of the tribe, i.e., its powers of
local self-government.

(3) These powers are subject to qualification by treaties
and by express legislation of Congress, but . . . [unless]
expressly qualified, full powers of internal sovereignty are
vested in the Indian tribes and in their duly constituted
organs of government.[9]

Cohen also noted that the right to self-government has been "consistently protected by the courts, frequently recognized and intermittently ignored by treaty-makers and legislators, and very widely disregarded by administrative officials."[10]

On reservations, individual rights are defined by tribal constitutions and the Indian Civil Rights Act of 1968. Tribal sovereignty is acknowledged and, in general terms, "most of the constitutional protections of individual rights do not apply to the operations of tribal governments. Neither Indians nor non-Indians on the reservation have the same rights with respect to tribal governments that they both have with respect to federal, state, and local governments."[11]

Some Bill of Rights protections have been extended: freedom of speech and religion are specified, although tribes may have established religions. Jury trials are provided for in criminal cases if there could be a jail sentence, but free counsel is not mandated. If violations of rights are alleged, tribal courts deal with them, with the exception of petitions of habeas corpus in criminal cases (which may be taken to federal courts).

The Role of the BIA

The BIA has the power to limit tribal sovereignty and decision making on the basis of laws and tribal constitutions. This stems from several sources. Laws define the agency's purposes as (1) preserving inherent rights of tribal self-government and providing resources and help in strengthening tribal capacity to govern; (2) pursuing and protecting sovereignty rights; and (3) fulfilling the trust obligation, for which it is held liable.

Fulfillment of the trust obligation by the BIA implies some control over tribal governments. The Indian Self-Determination Act, however, gave the tribes the right to contract to run their own programs, subject to BIA approval reached through negotiation. The extent of residual control and its administration by the BIA have been difficult issues to resolve in some cases. There is greatest agreement that the BIA is responsible for land and natural resources like timber. The MCT and the BIA have been unable to reach agreement on the MCT proposal that it assume the operating function of the BIA Minnesota Agency Office, including handling the tribe's timber resources. Red Lake Reservation has shown less interest in taking charge of its programs, perhaps having a greater fear of termination and cutoff of federal funds (see the discussion of the BIA embargo on funds, below).

Tribal constitutions, which are based on BIA models, specify the federal approval of several functions. The MCT Constitution, for instance, mandates approval of proposed constitutional amendments, attorney contracts, transfer of funds from the federal government to the tribe, and ordinances to license or impose fees on nonmembers.

The BIA acknowledges that the 1934 standard tribal constitution requires more BIA approval than is now necessary because tribes are more capable and need less supervision.[12] Changing a constitution is a laborious process, requiring not only tribal council and voter approval but also approval of BIA offices at the local, area, and national levels and the US solicitor's office, Department of the Interior.

Differences have arisen between the MCT and the BIA on questions of constitutional powers. Tribal leaders believe that the MCT is already empowered by the document to "exercise all powers granted and provided Indians." If they wish to take actions exercising aboriginal sovereignty and allowed by federal law, they claim that they do not need to seek BIA permission first.

The BIA sees the constitution as a narrow document, the limited delegation of the sovereign power from the tribal member to the MCT leadership. Lacking specific authorization in the constitution, the leadership must seek an amendment before it can act.

The BIA is also authorized by statute to review and approve all tribal contracts and ordinances. Although this broad authorization has never been followed, federal law allows a great deal of supervision.

Approval of ordinances that would apply to non-Indians as well as tribal members on the reservations has been a politically sensitive issue with the BIA. Although jurisdictional questions have not been resolved, a 1982 letter from the secretary of the interior circulated within the department recommended that approval should not be granted unless more than 50% of the reservation was under Indian control. Although not formal policy, the letter indicates that tribes that have only small portions of their reservations remaining in federal trust might have difficulty getting approval for regulations that apply throughout the reservation.

Intervention at Red Lake. In 1979, violence erupted on the reservation when the Red Lake Tribal Council, upset with the actions of an elected official, removed that person from office. Tribal members critical of the tribal government, seeing no opportunity to have their complaints dealt with by an impartial authority, resorted to violence at great cost to the reservation.

In an attempt to modify the tribal council's actions, the BIA stopped all federal program funding and threatened to withdraw federal recognition of the Red Lake band. Despite an embargo on funds that lasted nearly a year, the tribal council did not change its position.

According to a solicitor in the Department of Interior, the BIA's actions were authorized because the agency was a party to the approval of the tribal constitution. As such, it had a role in seeing that the tribe did not "stray too far from the path of democracy" in running the reservation. In his view, because tribes are outside of the US Constitution and there is no basis in law for judicial review of tribal actions, "the secretary of interior has the authority to suspend support of that government" if the BIA considers that a tribal constitution has been violated.[13]

The Red Lake government saw the BIA action as improperly infringing on tribal sovereignty. Roger Jourdain, Red Lake tribal chairman, commented on the federal government's action: "We were determined that the BIA would not break us up. That was the tactic. . . . I could not give up. It was the principle. The BIA tried just about everything."[14]

Control through Funding Powers. Reliance on government funding is a major restriction on tribal sovereignty, and funding agencies come to dominate policy decisions. "Over 90% of all money coming on the reservation is federal. That's slavery, colonialism. The federal government can dominate a reservation," said an Indian active in government programs for many years.[15] "[Government] . . . can't possibly bestow self-determination upon Indian people at the same time it orchestrates their future."[16]

Because tribes depend heavily on BIA funding, they support adequate appropriations and strong, energetic programs. Rather than earmarking funds for specific programs, however, they ask that tribes be given the administrative power to decide priorities and focus programs on their greatest local needs.

Indian View of the BIA. Many Indians have a special love-hate feeling about the BIA. It is the protector of the reservations and the

tribes and a major source of funding for needed programs, but it is accused of "inept bungling" and being a law unto itself.

BIA dominance over tribal government is an unresolved issue. The
American Indian Policy Review Commission noted that "tribal governments are simply not true governments if the Secretary of Interior and
his agents [BIA] continue to possess and exercise authority to veto virtually all forms of tribal government action."[17] In a statement on 24
January 1983, President Reagan blamed excessive regulation and bureaucracy for having "stifled local decision-making . . . [and] pro-
moted dependency rather than self-sufficiency."[18]

Programs for Indians

Through the BIA

The BIA funds and is involved in many programs that are discussed in later chapters of this book. Some are specifically authorized
and defined by Congress, but the BIA's basic authority comes from the
Snyder Act of 1921 (25 USC 13), which authorizes it to provide programs
for general support and civilization. Program specifics are set by regulations prepared by the BIA.

Unlike the programs of most federal agencies, BIA programs do
not go through an authorization process. Rather (as stated in the Snyder
Act), the BIA spends "such moneys as Congress may from time to time
appropriate." The US Supreme Court and further legislation have mandated Indian preference in hiring and promotion within these programs
as well as contracting and purchasing.

BIA programs are generally restricted to persons who are one-
fourth degree Indian or more, are members of federally recognized
tribes (this excludes terminated tribes), and live on or "near" a reservation. BIA rules define "near" Indians as those living on land that is con-
tiguous, where administration is feasible; living where there are other
Indians; socially and economically affiliated with the tribe; or designated
by the tribe as qualified, and so listed in the Federal Register. With very
limited exceptions, BIA programs are not available to Indians in urban
areas. Further, services are to be provided only if no other assistance is
available: regular programs that are available to all citizens are intended
to be used first.

Agency offices that administer the programs are located on the
reservations. The Red Lake Reservation Agency Office is at Red Lake,
the Minnesota Agency serving the six MCT reservations is at Cass Lake,
and the Sioux Field Office is at the Shakopee-Mdewakanton Commun-

ity. The BIA Area Office, serving reservations in Minnesota, Wisconsin, Michigan, and Iowa, is located in Minneapolis. Tribal leaders have advocated abolishing the area office level to move decision making closer to the tribes at the agency level.

Other Programs

Since 1955, when health services were transferred from the BIA to the Public Health Service in the Department of Health, Education and Welfare, there has been an expansion in Indian-targeted programs outside the BIA. When the American Indian Policy Review Commission on Tribal Government analyzed federal programs for its 1976 report, it found that Indian tribal governments had direct access to only 65% of some 600 programs.[19] Barriers still exist to Indian participation in programs intended to serve the general population, but several important programs now have Indian set-asides, Indian desks, or specific provisions mandating Indian participation; some of these are detailed in later chapters.

Although this book focuses on rights and services that are uniquely intended for Indians, Indians are US citizens who are fully entitled to all privileges and responsibilities of citizenship; programs cannot be denied on the basis of race. When programs are designed to help low-income, disadvantaged, unemployed, or other citizens with special needs, or when they are funded based on the numbers of those with special needs, Indians are included in the distribution formulas. They often add numbers well in excess of their percentage in the population.

Are Indians being served by governments as their citizenship status and special needs entitle them to be? The researchers for this book tried to verify Indian use of the specific programs that are discussed. With very few exceptions, Indians are not receiving the help that their documented needs warrant.

Poor utilization is linked to agency insensitivity to cultural differences or lack of understanding of Indians, as well as to Indian hesitancy in approaching white systems. When a program is run by Indians or oriented to their culture, it is far more succesful; the heavy use of these programs shows their value. A Hennepin County commissioner has acknowledged that "the most effective programs for Indians are those that are planned and operated by Indians."[20]

Most non-Indian professionals who have Indians as clients or patients admit that they do not do a good job communicating with them. What this barrier means to the Indian is recognized by some agencies. As funding cuts in 1984 threatened the program of the Indian Health

Board, which provides clinic services to low-income Minneapolis Indians, the chief of family practice at Hennepin County Medical Center commented that if the program were ended it "would effectively reduce the services that Indian people take advantage of. They would deny themselves needed services because of their discomfort in approaching other resources."[21]

Indians are raising concerns about the fragmentation of services and the way current systems of program delivery isolate the person or problem being addressed. This kind of treatment is seen in child and family welfare services, in family abuse and battered women programs, and in mental illness and chemical dependency treatment. Because the problems being treated are not isolated, a holistic approach is urged that would involve the whole family and use the strengths of the family and the Indian community.

Government Funding Practices

Government programs can be subject to rapid changes in policy, funding levels, and target groups to be served; no long-term commitment is guaranteed. Such changes can have devastating effects on those abandoned or overlooked by policymakers. Indians depend on government programs for economic survival, and these changes can have great impact on their lives.

Through the grant system, government, not those in need, defines the needs to be addressed. Other problems: Most grants are for a limited time, and when they end other levels of government do not usually continue funding the programs that have proved valuable. Grant distribution on a per capita basis means that reservations with small populations get so little funding that effective programs are impossible. Competition for grants puts a great burden on less organized agencies with small staffs, perhaps the ones in greatest need of funding help.

The block grant system of funding from federal to state and from state to local government is opposed by most Indian tribes because their share of the funding must come from state or county governments, which have been less responsive to Indians than has the federal government. Block grants have also usually meant that less total funding is provided.

CHAPTER 5

State and Local Relations; Hunting and Fishing Rights

Tribal Relations with the State

The role that state governments have been willing to play in the solution of Indian problems has evolved slowly. Because Indian reservations were located by federal decision within only some state boundaries, those states have complained about being expected to provide aid to Indians when other states are free of such responsibility. The 1928 Meriam report noted that several states with fairly large Indian populations still tended to regard services for the Indians as purely a federal function. In many of those states, this attitude still dominates.

But the report found a few states, including Minnesota, where "governments have evidenced a growing sense of responsibility for Indian affairs."

> Their state departments concerned with education, health, and public welfare appreciate that it is a matter of grave concern to the state to have in its midst groups of people living below reasonable hygienic and social standards. To them the question of whether the responsibility rests on the state or on the national government is very properly being relegated to a minor place and the real question is being faced as to whether these inhabitants of the state are being fitted to be assets rather than liabilities.[1]

Minnesota began assuming some responsibility for its Indian residents in the 1920s, when public health nurses were assigned to work with Indians. State public education was provided, with federal assistance, when the BIA closed its schools. In 1936, the state contracted to take over the provision of public education under the Johnson-O'Malley Act.

When federal policy in the 1950s encouraged termination of federal responsibility toward Indians, the state became active in trying to keep the federal government involved in the funding of Indian programs. The unilateral federal decision in 1953 to turn over to Minnesota civil and criminal jurisdiction for all reservations except Red Lake (PL 280) was made with no provision to assist in funding the increased law enforcement costs that were transferred to county governments.

Gradually, the state began to respond to the need for more Indian services. A higher education scholarship program was begun in 1955; by the 1970s, there were several Indian-targeted programs.

Indian Affairs Council

The Minnesota Indian Affairs Commission in 1963 became the first legislated state body to focus on Indians, develop information about Indian problems, assist in coordinating governmental and private programs for Indians, and make legislative recommendations (Mn. Stat. 3.922). In 1976, the name was changed to the Minnesota Indian Affairs Intertribal Board. The current name, Indian Affairs Council (IAC), was approved in 1983. Voting members include one representative from each of the state's 11 reservations, selected by that reservation's governing body. Two representatives are also elected for four-year terms by Indians living in Minnesota but enrolled in federally recognized tribes located outside the state.

Nonvoting members include three state senators, three house members, and representatives of the governor and of the commissioners of nine state agencies. The council appoints an urban Indian advisory council, composed of five members with at least one each from Minneapolis, St. Paul, and Duluth. The IAC has offices in Bemidji and St. Paul.

By law, the Indian Affairs Council is mandated to "clarify for the legislature and state agencies the nature of tribal governments and the relationship of tribal governments to the Indian people of Minnesota" (Mn. Stat. 3.922, subd. 6, 1). It has power to make legislative recommendations, to administer programs, to help establish Indian advisory councils to state agencies, and to act as an intermediary in Indian-state government questions, problems, or conflicts. The council has been effective in seeking state laws in areas of Indian concern.

The State/Indian Relations Team, a task force within state government, proposed in 1984 that additional state agencies as well as the BIA and IHS be added as ex officio members. It recommended that other agencies of state government make greater use of the IAC as a primary resource and coordinating agency between state programs and the tribes and that professional staffing be increased in human services and economic development areas.[2]

State Laws and Programs for Indians

Indians are recognized in several areas of state law that are designed to meet various needs (see appendix B). In some cases, the laws were needed to allow the state to receive federal Indian program funds; by the 1980s, however, most of these programs were channeled directly to the tribes. Laws were also needed to make some statewide programs available to reservation Indians, such as the state's housing program for low-income people. Other laws channel funding to agencies identified as Indian to ensure that Indians are served.

In addition, Minnesota has made innovative efforts to provide services to Indians in areas where needs have not been met. The state funds a large postsecondary scholarship program, and it provides special help to several school districts so that they can incorporate Indian culture and curriculum into their programs (Chapter 312). Programs staffed by Indians and with an Indian orientation are funded to deal with chemical dependency problems.

The laws usually specify that the programs apply to all Indians, regardless of residency. For instance, the revolving business loan program for Indians requires a reasonable balance between recipients living on and off reservations. When they first began, Chapter 312 programs were required to serve at least three urban and three reservation schools.

Special legislation has made the state a leader in protecting Indian burials and prohibiting their molestation. Funding was provided in 1984 to purchase 20 acres of a proposed Red Wing industrial park near Prairie Island Indian Community that contain burial mounds 500 to 1,000 years old. The law also prescribes how to deal with accidentally disturbed remains.

The 1983 legislature authorized the redesign of the state seal, with active participation of the IAC, to show the Indian more prominently. Instead of appearing to be fleeing, he is now turned, looking at the farmer.

The state is increasingly using Indians on major policy boards and commissions. During 1982–83, gubernatorial appointments of Indians to state boards and commissions totaled 23 of 351, or 6.6%.

Jurisdictional Powers

"State and municipal governments are constitutionally required to extend both services and the franchise to reservation Indian people despite the fact that they lack jurisdiction over them."[3] The state does not have the power to take away tribal sovereignty rights, which are determined by the relationship between the tribe and the federal government. PL 280 transferred criminal and some civil jurisdiction over Indians on reservations to the state; Red Lake Reservation was not included. Indian governments on reservations retained taxing, licensing, zoning, and other regulatory powers.

The state cannot tax Indians on any income earned while living and working anywhere within the reservation, whether or not trust land is involved. If, however, the Indian lives off the reservation or the income is earned off the reservation, it is subject to state taxes. Indians pay federal income taxes regardless of the source of income. (See chap. 7 for further discussion of taxation issues.)

Questions of regulatory and zoning power have not been fully resolved. State regulation probably does not extend to Indians or Indian-held land on reservations, where the tribes have authority. State or county regulation probably does apply to non-Indians and non-Indian land on reservations. Cooperation is vital, however, if the interests of both groups are to be served. The MCT has zoning ordinances governing Indians on the reservations. A more comprehensive code was prepared to cover all reservation lands—including those held by non-Indians. Because of jurisdictional questions, the latter ordinances have not been implemented.

State legislation establishing a land use planning board for the upper Mississippi River included the provision that the counties involved cooperate with the Leech Lake Reservation. The question of zoning power was skirted by stating that the law should not be construed to "alter or expand the zoning jurisdiction of the counties within the exterior boundaries of the Leech Lake Reservation" (Mn. Stat. 114 B.03, subd. 4). The "cooperative management and jurisdictional agreement" with the Indians envisioned in the legislation has not been implemented.

Red Lake Reservation is totally separate from state jurisdiction except where specific agreements have been made. The band issues its own car licenses and is exempt from Minnesota's auto registration and licensing laws; the state grants reciprocity as it does with other states or territories. Through state legislation and by agreement in 1983, tribal court commitments for treatment in state institutions are recognized under state law.

State Indian Policy

In some areas of state-tribal relations, cooperation and agreements have come only after extensive court processes; in other areas, the issues remain unresolved. The settlement of disputes over hunting and fishing rights has been especially slow because non-Indian pressures against accommodation have been strong.

The state has no overall policy to guide its responses to questions involving Indian issues. Decisions that actually set policy are made within various agencies of government as programs are funded, rules are written, existing programs are modified to reach Indians better, or Indian actions are challenged and tested in the courts. Although the IAC is brought in when state-tribal conflicts arise, it is not consulted in policy decisions.

The State/Indian Relations Team proposed a series of steps to improve this situation. Beginning with a governor's proclamation that the state recognizes the authority of Indian governments, a general policy of intergovernmental cooperation and coordination would be implemented. All state agencies would designate an Indian liaison person, increase employee understanding and knowledge of the state's Indian population, and use Indians in policy, planning, rule-making, and program administration. The team recommended that the state goal should be the elimination of disparities between Indians and non-Indian citizens in education, employment, economic development, income, health, housing, and criminal justice, with each state agency developing legislation and budgetary proposals to meet the specifics of this goal.[4]

Jurisdictional Ambiguities

Answers for the many unresolved jurisdictional questions are often sought in further federal legislation or in the courts. Minnesota's justification for its willingness to go to court, especially in the areas of taxation and hunting and fishing rights, is the ambiguity of the laws; jurisdictional issues are complex, and the decisions far reaching.[5] For this reason, the tribes are also interested in having the courts resolve some of the conflicts.

Litigation, however, "tends to polarize the opponents rather than encourage government-to-government relations and is often followed by another lawsuit. . . . Policy decisions in this atmosphere are often influenced more by litigation strategy than by the needs and resources of the governments involved."[6] The court process causes great delay and is a drain on very limited resources. Some Indians see this process as the state "trying to take the rights away in any way possible."[7]

Tribes may be reluctant to develop a close relationship with state government, fearing that such cooperation might end up with Congress punishing them by limiting tribal powers and expanding state powers on reservations.[8] For example, the state Indian housing program requires the tribe to agree to be sued and be liable for ultimate repayment of the mortgages. As the Mille Lacs band tribal chairman has stated, "Our rights can never be bought, sold, nor transferred."[9] The band's policy is that members should not serve on state agencies. Seeing its relationship with the state as one of mutual sovereignty, it maintains that participation would be an act consenting to the jurisdiction of the state.

The jurisdictional ambiguities do not necessarily have to be resolved so that one or the other government has exclusive power. Cooperative arrangements can be worked out "without sacrificing the legislative interests of either government or the cultural diversity which the present situation allows."[10]

In general Minnesota has been and remains a leader in recognizing its responsibility in working with the Indian communities and assisting with the problems facing Indians. This effort has been noted and is appreciated by the Indian leaders. "Other state governments with significant Indian populations have marveled at the ease with which Minnesota state officials are able to sit down and meet with tribal officials on topics involving mutual concerns."[11] According to the president of the MCT, "Minnesota Indians are fortunate indeed to have their needs understood and enjoy the confidence of the legislators in promoting Indian self-sufficiency."[12]

Hunting and Fishing Rights

Judge Edward Devitt noted, "It is difficult to conceive of a subject matter in which Indian tribes would have a stronger traditional interest than in hunting, fishing and food gathering" (*White Earth Band v. Alexander*, 518 F. Supp. 536 [D. Mn., 1981]).

Hunting, fishing, trapping, and the harvesting of wild rice were the sources of food and survival for early Minnesota Indians; they are still important sources of food. The power to regulate and control these activities of Indians, and of other people on reservations, has been disputed in many court cases. It is a primary cause of tension and ill feeling between Indians and the white communities in Indian areas. Starting with the 1971 US district court decision in a case brought from Leech Lake Reservation (*Leech Lake Band v. Herbst*), there has been a dramatic alteration of control responsibilities for hunting and fishing on reservations in northern Minnesota. (See appendix C for summaries of the court decisions.)

Growing out of the Leech Lake court decision, the state and the tribe entered into an agreement that was incorporated into state law as statute 97.431. The tribe agreed to give up its right to commercial hunting and taking of game fish on the reservation and to have a conservation code acceptable to the Department of Natural Resources (DNR), with tribal enforcement officers and a court. In return, the state agreed to acknowledge the Indians' hunting and fishing rights and to pay a portion of state-collected hunting and fishing license fees to the tribe. Following a 1980 amendment of the law, the state now pays 5% of all money collected for hunting and fishing licenses throughout the state — over $1 million in 1983.

Current Regulation

Indians, as original owners who never gave up their rights, continue to have the right to hunt and fish throughout their reservations without state interference. The right belongs exclusively to the tribe. This means that the tribe determines who may use the resources, the number and kind of fish and game that can be taken, the method of catching, and the seasons.

Indians can also require non-Indians on Indian-held land to abide by tribal regulations (18 USC 1165). If non-Indians violate these laws, they can be arrested by federally licensed police and turned over to the US magistrate's office for fining and confiscation of their equipment. The state, however, continues to regulate hunting and fishing by non-Indians anywhere within reservations.

All of the state's Chippewa reservations require licensing, and have conservation codes, conservation officers (game wardens) to enforce the codes, and conservation courts to deal with violations; the BIA provides funding. Seventeen Indian conservation officers now work in Minnesota. Leech Lake Reservation, which has the largest operation, has nine officers and a full conservation court system: a judge, clerk, prosecutors, and defense attorneys. The major funding is from the BIA, with $50,000 (1982) from the DNR and other funding from the tribe's share of license fees.

On both Leech Lake and Fond du Lac reservations, state and tribal conservation officers are cross-deputized. The Indian officers are empowered to arrest non-Indians who violate state law, and state officers may arrest Indians who violate the tribal ordinances. Indians are dealt with in tribal court; non-Indians, in state court.

The tribal conservation codes are quite similar to state law. Seasons and limits are established, and the taking of fish with gill nets—the traditional harvest method—is allowed with various restrictions. On Leech Lake Reservation, sports fish may be taken for personal sustenance, and the commercial taking of rough fish (primarily whitefish and some tullibees) is allowed.

Mille Lacs Reservation allows gill netting only in special cases for subsistence needs, and a special limited license is required. If necessary, the tribal code is enforced by confiscating nets and boats and imposing fines.

Problems

Jurisdiction. The White Earth Reservation decision (*White Earth v. Alexander*) allows separate tribal and state jurisdictions to operate simultaneously when people who are not members of the tribe hunt, fish, or harvest wild rice on Indian land. Judge Devitt noted that the dual regulatory systems "will always be in conflict to some extent" (518 F. Supp. 537). People might avoid Indian lands and not purchase tribal licenses, or enforcement by the state of its laws on Indian land could disrupt the reservation's conservation efforts; however, the judge did not believe that either situation would be a hardship.

Local Opposition. Hostility from non-Indians who believe that the state should have total control of these natural resources has been a continuing problem. Resort owners and county governments in the Leech Lake Reservation area challenged the 1971 decision in court over a six-year period. The unsettled nature of rights is a fertile field for extremists and those willing to take advantage of the uncertainties.

Non-Indians interested in fishing often express concern over the fishing done by Indians, especially the taking of fish in nets. Leech Lake Reservation encompasses some of the best walleye fishing lakes in Minnesota, and these fish are a source of livelihood to many white resort owners on the reservation. They are important to the state for tourist dollars, and they are important to the Indians not only as food but as the symbol of aboriginal rights that still remain with the tribe.

To evaluate the impact of Indian netting, the DNR did a survey of fishing on Leech Lake in 1978. It found that the vast majority of Indians were in compliance with the band's regulations. By commercially harvesting the lake's rough fish, the Indians were benefiting the lake. Netting is the way to catch these fish, and if the Indians did not remove them they would have to be removed at DNR expense—as is done in other lakes. Game fish taken by the Indians were only about 1% of the total poundage harvested by non-Indians. The conclusion was that there had been no ill effects on the fish population of the lake.[13]

Unresolved Treaty Issues. In the Arrowhead region of the state, hunting and fishing rights were reserved by the Indians in the 1854 treaty and have not been subsequently revoked. The state is unwilling to acknowledge the existence of these rights, which would be of value to Bois Forte, Grand Portage, and Fond du Lac reservations.

At Grand Portage, a few tribe members commercially fish in Lake Superior; it is regarded as a possible resource for development by the tribe. The state, however, does not acknowledge this fishing to be an Indian right. The DNR has allegedly harassed buyers of Indian fish "with the notion that Indian marketed fish are illegal fish because they have not a State of Minnesota tag on them."[14] Concern for fishing on Lake Superior and Indian rights led to the formation of the Great Lakes Indian Fisheries Commission, a consortium of six Indian tribes around the lake; Grand Portage and Fond du Lac reservations are members. The commission helps the tribes with management of fishing operations, maintenance of lake quality, and preservation of tribal rights to fish. Funding has been provided by Congress.

At Mille Lacs Reservation, treaty rights are also unresolved. The band considers itself a "boundaryless reservation," with hunting and fishing rights stemming from the 1837 treaty. The US Circuit Court for Wisconsin has ruled (*Lac Courte Oreilles Band v. Voight*) that the treaty is still valid and that hunting and fishing rights were not taken away by later action. The state of Wisconsin has granted these rights to Minnesota's Mille Lacs band in the treaty area of that state. Minnesota and the band have not resolved the question of whether or how the decision applies in Minnesota.

With tribal rights to control Indian hunting and fishing on White Earth Reservation determined by the courts, and with similar rights strongly asserted by the Mille Lacs band, the Minnesota legislature has directed the DNR to negotiate financial agreements with the two groups. A payment of 2.5% of state-collected money from licenses and fees for hunting and fishing was authorized by the legislature for the White Earth Reservation, which would have meant an estimated half-million dollars in 1983. In neither case has an agreement been reached.

The reason for not acting, according to both Indians and the state, is the strong hostility from whites: for political reasons, the state believes that it cannot enter into such an agreement. The DNR commissioner stated, "I wish I had enough nerve to go ahead, but there is no reason because the public is so against it."[15]

Hunting seasons for migratory birds are federally controlled. The law and its relation to tribal hunting rights have not been tested in the courts. In 1984, Leech Lake, Mille Lacs, and White Earth reservations were considering setting their own migratory bird hunting seasons.

Protection of Natural Resources

Indians are very concerned about the quality of the lakes and maintaining the fish supply. To acquire a data base about lake quality on the reservations and to monitor what is happening, the MCT has had a BIA contract to test the waters. Base work has been done on 30 lakes and 10 to 12 streams. It is the tribe's goal to follow at least two lakes per reservation. They have built a well-equipped laboratory at Cass Lake to handle the work. In 1984, the US Geological Survey and White Earth Reservation were cooperating on a study of the water resources on that reservation.

White Earth Reservation has a strong program staffed by a fish biologist and an environmental specialist, along with support staff. Leech Lake, Mille Lacs, and Red Lake also have active programs. White Earth and Red Lake operate fish hatcheries and stock the lakes with walleyes. At Red Lake, the program primarily serves to maintain the fisheries business; White Earth is stocking lakes for game fishing to benefit Indians and non-Indians alike. The federal government stocks fish on Grand Portage Reservation.

Great concern has been expressed by both Indians and whites about the future of Mille Lacs Lake because the size and number of game fish are seen as declining. The Mille Lacs band asked the MCT to do a detailed, three-year study of the lake, which found that it faced problems from increased nutrients (human waste and agricultural fertilizers) and other forms of pollution (atmospheric chemicals, roadside salt, and nonpoint source pollution).

The enrichment of the water was beginning to disrupt the normal food chain; in some layers of water, the oxygen supply was too low to support game fish. The increased nutrients were also harming the wild rice crop.[16] The DNR is continuing to study the lake, evaluating fish size and catch numbers.

Community Cooperation. In 1982, with tensions in the white community increasing over net fishing and the Indians upset because their gill nets (which cost $200 apiece) were being taken or damaged by motorboats, the Greater Leech Lake Reservation Advisory Alliance was formed. The tribe and some 14 local and state groups make up the membership. It provides a forum for mutual understanding and for preventing polarization on fishing issues by allowing those concerned to talk over problems. The group is interested not only in fishing but in water, land, and air quality issues.

The alliance has helped to improve communication among people who for well over 10 years have been seeing each other as having opposing vital interests. From a member of the white community: "Every one of those meetings have been absolutely excellent. There has been no finger pointing." From an Indian official: "It's been just great. Members are talking like grown-ups and not talking about shooting Indians."[17]

Leech Lake Reservation officials have also taken an active role in seeking solutions to the sewage problems of the city of Bemidji. When the city sought to dump the pollutants directly into the Mississippi River (which then flows through the reservation), the tribe joined with others in lobbying to block the city. It later joined Bemidji in requesting help from the Minnesota Pollution Control Agency in funding a wastewater treatment facility. White Earth Reservation is conducting air quality studies under a grant from the US Environmental Protection Agency.

Tribal Relations with Local Governments

Indian Exclusion from Programs

Indian tribes continue to have their most difficult relations with local governments, which often do not include Indians in programming and do not extend programs into Indian communities when a service is to be provided to all citizens. In 1980, the Upper Sioux Community Comprehensive Plan noted:

> There are several agencies which Indian communities tra-
> ditionally have not used because the agency programs
> were not specifically designated to serve Indian clientele.
> The target group may have been low income families but
> the agency in turn may have assumed that the target
> group excluded Indian reservations because they are under
> federal jurisdiction and were probably eligible for similar
> federal programs.[18]

Poor communication often exists between reservations and the many groups responsible for services. These include county commissions and agencies, community action poverty programs, highway programs, police or sheriff and fire departments, and regional development commissions.

Some officials also believe that asking local government (or state government) to assume costs that should be federal is unjustified. The fact that reservation Indians do not pay property taxes and are exempt from some state taxes is seen by some as unfair. In his dissenting opinion in *Minnesota v. Zay Zah*, Minnesota Supreme Court Justice Yetka summed up these attitudes:

> While property tax exemption is viewed by the Indians as a right deriving from special historical status and a means of strengthening cultural identity, it is viewed by whites as a privilege and a lack of fundamental fairness. . . . If Federal policy contemplates strengthening tribal governments with reliance on state and local governments to provide services that would otherwise be unavailable, then the Federal government must accept the financial responsibility for providing services (259 NW2d 550 [MSC, 1977]).

Community services block grant programs and community action agencies that administer them are required to have one-third representation of the poor deciding the programs. The major block grants, state and federally funded, that provide community social services and community health programs are required to involve needy groups in drawing up plans to assure that needs are dealt with. Interviews conducted for this book and study of some filed plans, however, showed that Indians are rarely included in programming or decision making—even though they have major needs (child welfare, adolescent pregnancies, chemical dependency) that should be included and may even form a significant proportion of the population to be served.

In several instances, Congress has recognized this problem in delivery of services by providing that the federal department handling the program "determine whether low-income Indian tribe members are receiving equivalent benefits to others in the state and whether the tribe would be better served by a direct grant to the tribe."[19]

Attitudes of Local Officials

Local prejudices often become a real barrier to providing services. A Leech Lake RBC official has commented, "There has been so much mistrust for so long. It is hard to get across to the county commissioners that they represent Indians, too."[20]

The city council of Prior Lake annexed the Shakopee-Mdewakanton commmunity in 1972 without Indian consent, then refused to provide police services or handle misdemeanor cases for the community. In 1983, the city argued that since the annexation was done without Indian consent, it was invalid and that the community should not be a part of the city. Prior Lake drew new voting lines excluding the Indians.

According to the city manager, the intent was to keep the Indians from voting in city elections. "There is . . . the possibility that someone [from the reservation] could get elected to [a city] office. Then you would have a situation where they would be voting to spend the city's money, but they wouldn't have any direct involvement in where that money comes from. A decision to raise taxes wouldn't affect them."[21]

The tribe took the issue to federal court, where the judge ruled that the community was a part of Prior Lake. The city was ordered to allow the Indians to vote, to provide the community with fire and emergency services at no extra fee, and to pay the expenses of the lawsuit. The city filed an appeal in 1984.

In some places, relations with local governments are good. Leech Lake representatives meet on a regular basis with county commissioners; counties are providing some direct services to the reservation, and there is agreement that understanding is improving.

Laws on Discrimination

It is against the law in the United States to discriminate in employment, public education, housing, public accommodations and facilities, and voting. Discrimination is forbidden by employers of 15 or more persons, labor organizations, governments, recipients of federal funds, and government contractors. (Specific provisions protect Indians and Indian contractors working on reservations.) Discrimination is prohibited on the basis of race, sex, or several other categories. These protections and remedies are contained in the Civil Rights Act of 1964, its subsequent amendments, and in executive orders.

The Minnesota law has similar provisions (Mn. Stat. 363). It specifies that Indian citizens are to be assisted "to assume all rights, privileges, and duties of citizenship." Minneapolis and St. Paul also have civil rights ordinances. A person who believes there has been discrimination can file a complaint; depending upon the nature of the problem, federal, state, or local agencies may be used.

A large backlog of cases filed with Minnesota's Department of

Human Rights (DHR) has meant that resolving a claim may take several years. In 1984, efforts were being made to improve administration and reduce the backlog. Indians file very few complaints with the DHR; in 1982, 30 Indian complaints were filed—1.8% of the total.

In its 1982 annual report, the Minnesota Indian Affairs Intertribal Board commented that although Indians are reluctant to file complaints with the DHR, the St. Paul and Bemidji offices of the board "regularly are contacted by Indian people who believe they are victims of discrimination. We refer those people to the Human Rights Department and appropriate federal agencies, but more often than not the matters are not pursued by the complainants."[22]

The US Commission on Civil Rights is an independent agency with statutory mandate to make findings and recommendations to the president and Congress concerning discrimination or denials of equal protection of the laws. Several studies have dealt with Indian issues. Minnesota's state advisory committee to the US commission has Indian membership (including an Indian woman chairperson in 1982) and has published studies on Indians in Minneapolis and St. Paul.

The commission has noted that for Indians, civil rights goals are the opposite of those of other minorities.[23] Other groups have sought integration and the ending of separate government institutions, with the goal of making the existing system involve them and work for them. Indian tribes, on the other hand, have always been separate political entities interested in maintaining their own institutions and beliefs. Their goal has been to prevent the dismantling of their own systems. Unlike other minorities, Indian tribes on reservations do not desire desegregation if it means the end of the separate political rights and sovereignty that tribes have fought so hard to maintain.[24] Indians also do not favor desegregation as it applies to schools because it breaks up the Indian community, isolating the children and diffusing the impact of special Indian education program funds.

Indian Preference

Several legal exceptions allow Indians to be unaffected by some nondiscrimination laws. These provide Indian preference primarily in employment, contracting, and purchasing for Indian programs. The US Supreme Court upheld this preference as "reasonable and rationally designed to further Indian self-government" (*Morton v. Mancari*).

In programs operated by the Department of Housing and Urban Development, Indian housing authorities are allowed to serve only tribal Indians because of the special obligation of the federal government to Indians. A federal rent subsidy program was ruled to be a proper extension of the Indian trust relationship and nondiscriminatory if it was used in an urban Indian housing program just for Indians (*St. Paul Intertribal Housing Board v. Reynolds*).

The Minnesota American Indian Language and Culture Education Act (Chapter 312) declared that "programs and activities . . . shall be deemed to be positive action programs to combat discrimination" and not in violation of antidiscrimination legislation (Mn. Stat. 126.55).

Voting Rights Act

The Federal Voting Rights Act, as amended by PL 94–73 in 1975, requires that bilingual federal elections be conducted where more than 5% of the citizenry are of a single non-English language group and where there is higher than national average illiteracy (as determined by those who failed to finish the fifth grade, according to the US census). When the language is unwritten, interpreters are to be provided.

In Minnesota, two counties come under this provision, Beltrami and Cass. County auditors are responsible for administering the law, which is intended to ensure that assistance be provided in the other language to help with registering and voting. In Minnesota, election officials believe that unfamiliarity with English is not a problem; the service of Indians as election judges is thought to satisfy the law.[25] Under Minnesota law, anyone who needs an interpreter may bring one to the polls.

CHAPTER 6

Urban Indians

The Urban Population

In 1928, the Meriam report spoke of the Twin Cities urban Indian population as being middle class and fiercely determined to remain Indian:

> One gets the impression in St. Paul and Minneapolis that most of the persons claiming to be Indians have but a slight degree of Indian blood. From "lists of Indians" furnished by the several reservations, many were reached whose personal appearance indicated French or Scandinavian blood rather than Indian. In a number of cases a claim of only one-sixteenth, one-thirty-second, or one-sixty-fourth Indian blood was made, yet great insistence was put upon the right to be designated "Indian." Some of the so-called Indians were found to be persons generally believed to be white, who were living in the type of home that fairly prosperous young professional or business folk generally enjoy.[1]

In the 1980s, similar people are living in the urban areas. They may or may not associate with the Indian communities, and they have little need for government assistance. The Twin Cities suburban population provides the census statistics to characterize this group: it is the fastest growing segment of the urban Indian population, with better education, more stable families, less unemployment, and more affluence than the state's average Indian.

In this book, however, "urban Indians" refers to the large group living in the major cities who have problems that need the attention of government agencies. As statistics show (see chap. 10) and as the urban Indian community knows, there are severe problems, and being Indian frequently adds a unique dimension to difficulties that are shared with others who are poor or minorities. Life in the cities brings isolation, disorientation, bureaucratic complexities, and great disillusionment. Indian-oriented programs often do not exist, and Indians have difficulty in relating to white-run services.

Ties to the Reservations

Many Indians who came to the cities in the 1950s and 1960s stayed, had children, and now are into the third generation of urban population. Interviews with 587 Minneapolis Indian residents in 1978 found that 15% of the respondents had lived in Minneapolis all their lives, and 80%, for more than five years. The population was much more stable than the usual stereotype of constant migration back and forth from the reservation, but reservation ties were strong; 94% were enrolled tribal members.[2]

Nonetheless, migration remains a characteristic of the life of urban Indians. The Indian Health Board, serving the low-income population in the Phillips neighborhood of Minneapolis, has an average of 20% new patients each year, and even higher during times of recession.[3]

Many factors are involved in an individual's decision to migrate from the reservation or to return. A study done on the St. Croix Chippewa Reservation in Wisconsin identified both advantages and disadvantages of living on reservations.[4] Among the advantages are the "majority status" of Indians and the opportunity to serve in decision-making positions. The extended family provides security, and poverty is not an isolating condition—it is shared. Some natural resources are available, including wood, game, fish, and wild rice. There are no property taxes, housing assistance may be available, and health care services are provided. Finally, individual freedom is respected.

Disadvantages include severe unemployment and economic depression on most reservations. With the close-knit community, individuals may lack privacy; family and friendship ties can lead to factionalism and nepotism. The federal government, through the BIA, continues to exert a great deal of paternalistic control. Especially for youth, the reservations lack excitement and activity.

Those who leave tend to be younger, single, more highly educated, and more prosperous. Although those who return to the reservations are probably coming from a marginal life in the city, they most frequently give housing, not employment, as their reason for returning.

Strains on the Culture

Transition to urban life puts strains on traditional Indian culture. Those who come to the cities encounter a physical environment, social organization, interpersonal behavior, attitudes, values, and sometimes even language that are foreign to what they have known. The traditional source of support—the extended kin group—may be undermined or totally lacking. The sense of community, with family and elders to pass traditional ways on to children, is often disrupted; people may live in isolation from each other.

An Indian educator has noted, however, that "there is nothing inherently wrong with the city. We marvel at a beaver building a dam and call it a glorious work of nature. I think, too, the human-built city is a glorious work of nature, if we learn to live well with it."[5]

The city experience has caused Indians to be concerned about their culture. For many urban Indians, especially the young people, ties to the reservations have been weakened. The director of Indian education for the Minneapolis Public Schools estimates that 85% of Indian children born in the cities have no experience with the reservation.[6]

The interest in learning about Indian ways is strong in urban communities. Not only is it seen as essential for preserving the culture, but also as the way to solve the many problems that Indians face. An urban Indian leader explained this growing interest in Indian culture. Tribal leaders, who are secure in their Indian heritage, view reservations in very realistic terms of "logging, computers, and administering programs." It is the urban Indians who are finding the need to identify and assert their culture. They have become neotraditionalists with a "strong emotional, philosophical 'hook' to the land, to 'feathers and blankets,' to 'old ways and mother earth.' "[7]

There are sometimes clashes of interest between urban and reservation Indians, with strong differences of opinion over the funding of programs and their administration. But urban Indians have a universal, underlying commitment to the reservation because only through it and tribal enrollment is one an Indian.

Programs for Urban Indians

Rationale for Providing Services

A task force of the American Indian Policy Review Commission argued that special programs should be provided to assist urban Indians because they have needs that are not being met by existing programs.[8] As Indians, they retain unique rights, based on the federal trust relationship growing from the treaties, that should apply to the individual as well as the tribe. If the tribe is sovereign, then the individuals who make up the tribe are equally sovereign. By providing services based on residency to a part of this group only, the government is in effect coercing people into adopting a particular place to live. Returning to the reservation may be seen as the only way of getting the services to which Indians are entitled but which urban Indians are denied.

It was further argued that federal policies were primary causes of urban migration. If the federal government had fulfilled its trust responsibilities by helping to develop more viable reservation economies, the urban migration would have been unnecessary. The commission also noted that the law authorizing most of the BIA programs, the Snyder Act, directs that programs be provided "throughout the United States."

BIA policy, linked to the trust responsibility, is to provide programs primarily on reservations, but funds are very limited now, and many reservation needs are unmet. Trying to serve the urban population, too, is seen as impractical. Any change in current policy would also be strongly resisted by reservation leaders, who point out that urban Indians have chosen to reside in another governmental jurisdiction where they can participate in and are counted for urban-provided services. The tribes do not benefit because their urban members are not counted for the distribution of population-based services on the reservations.

Tribes extend a few of the programs they administer into the cities, including the federal higher education scholarship program, the Indian Child Welfare Act, and economic development assistance. Fond du Lac Reservation is operating an IHS clinic in Duluth as a reservation program. A limited number of federal programs specifically for Indians serve the urban communities in education, health services, and funding for Indian centers; these have been threatened by the 1983 administration proposal that only the BIA administer Indian-oriented programs. Some Minnesota state programs that are designed to reach all citizens are targeted to serve urban Indians.

Representatives of the urban Indian communities serve on a few governmental bodies. Under state law the Indian Affairs Council appoints a five-member urban advisory council that includes at least one representative each from Minneapolis, St. Paul, and Duluth. The MCT (which has offices in Minneapolis and Duluth) also has an urban advisory group for which each reservation selects one member living in an urban area.

Since the mid-1970s, the Indian community in Minneapolis has had an advocate in city government to improve understanding and seek better services from the city. In 1983 a new position of Indian liaison was created in the Minneapolis Center for Citizen Participation, with federal funding from a community development block grant.

Minneapolis Programs

Indian leaders in Minneapolis have done a great deal to coordinate their activities by organizing task forces or more formal groups when support is needed or problems require attention. A nonpartisan American Indian Political Caucus has been active in voter registration and education. In 1982, after considerable controversy, Indians assumed leadership roles in two important programs that serve minorities in Minneapolis—the Community Action Agency (the city's poverty program) and the Civil Rights Commission. Indians have recently served on the Planning, Charter, and Arts commissions.

The Minneapolis Indian community can take pride in the leadership that has given them many innovative programs, which are described in detail below and in later chapters:

- The Minneapolis American Indian Center, offering many programs in the heart of the Indian area in a building designed to reflect Indian culture and constructed under the direction of an Indian.
- Indian alternative schooling, stressing culturally based education; Indian programming in the public schools.
- The first federally funded urban Indian health clinic in the nation.
- A halfway house for parolees that is based on traditional spirituality.
- The first urban Indian shopping center, helping to revitalize Franklin Avenue.
- A low-income housing community run by Indians.

To the Indian community, the *Minneapolis American Indian Center* (MAIC), located at 1530 East Franklin Avenue is "the center." It opened in 1974 and is run by a board elected by Indian residents of Minneapolis or its suburbs.

As of October 1982, 14 programs were operating at the center, with funding supplied by federal, state, city, and county programs; private foundations; and the United Way. The center provides a community gathering place for pow wows, feasts, and festivals. Recreation facilities and youth programs are provided. Teaching about Indian art and culture is emphasized, Indian art exhibits and performances are offered, and a monthly newspaper—the *Circle*—is published.

Congregate dining serves two meals daily to about 100 senior citizens. Many social service programs are offered: chemical dependency, adult basic education, employment assistance, a branch office of the Hennepin County Welfare Department, an Indian housing advocate, a senior citizen advocate, and a youth program offering alternatives to incarceration. A sewing project that makes tote bags was begun in 1982, and handicraft items are sold at the Woodland Indian Craft Shop.

One of the oldest Indian organizations, *Upper Midwest American Indian Center* at 113 West Broadway on the northeast side, was founded in 1961. United Way has provided funding since 1970. Upper Midwest operates out of a storefront, administering a youth leadership program, energy assistance funds, BIA-funded Indian Child Welfare Act services, and assistance for sexual assault victims.

The *Division of Indian Work* (DIW) at 3045 Park Avenue South, which began in 1952, is a division of the Greater Minneapolis Council of Churches. Support is also provided by individual denominations, churches, individuals, and the United Way. The DIW provides a community center that is used by two Indian-oriented church congregations— All Saints Episcopal and All Nations Indian churches. Emergency assistance for urban Indians, especially new arrivals, has been a major service provided by DIW since its beginning. Services include a food-shelf program, help with clothing and transportation, and limited housing assistance. In 1983, the Emergency Assistance Program provided 48,000 services.

The DIW offers several other human service programs: youth leadership, including a scouting program; work with young parents to enhance parenting and housekeeping skills; help to those experiencing domestic violence; and chemical dependency programs. Culture classes are offered, and a monthly newsletter—*Vision on the Wind*—is published.

Other sources of emergency help for the Indian community include the Indian Neighborhood Club, 736 East Franklin; the Loaves and

Fishes program, Holy Rosary Church; and three Catholic Charities Branch drop-in centers.

Na-way-ee, at 24th and Bloomington, has an alternative school—Center School—for grades 9 through 12. It also administers a state-funded youth chemical dependency program and the Red Star program for women, providing social services and cultural programs. It receives United Way money.

Many other agencies provide services of more limited scope to the Minneapolis Indian community. These efforts are either run by Indians or, because of location and Indian staff, are oriented toward them.

St. Paul Services

Although the St. Paul Indian community leaders are aware of many unmet needs, Indians lack the numbers in that city to attract substantial programming. One goal is a multipurpose Indian center similar to the one in Minneapolis; however, St. Paul distributes funding for such community projects on a neighborhood basis and Indians lack a population concentration large enough in any one neighborhood to influence decisions. The government of St. Paul has no formal liaison with the Indian community.

The *St. Paul American Indian Center*, located at 506 Kenny Road (near Payne Avenue and Seventh Street), provides some programs. Its basic support comes from the Administration for Native Americans (federal) and the United Way, with additional foundation assistance. The center sponsors social events and a newsletter, *Smoke Signals*. Services provided include employment assistance, counseling, emergency food help, legal aid, and BIA-funded Indian Child Welfare Act assistance. A state-licensed private child placement agency, the American Indian Family and Children Service, was established by the center in 1984. A gardening, food utilization, and nutrition program is operated in cooperation with Ramsey County Extension Service.

AIM, at 643 Virginia Street, is a community center incorporating the Red School House (the survival school begun by AIM), day care, adult education, the St. Paul Indian Health Board, and legal advocacy services. It provides counseling, help with employment and housing, and emergency help (including a foodshelf).

The *Department of Indian Work*, St. Paul Council of Churches, at 1671 Summit Avenue, offers social services and emergency help. St. Paul's government agencies pay relatively little attention to the special needs of Indians. An exception is the Juel Fairbanks Aftercare Residence for chemical dependency treatment, an outstanding Indian-oriented program.

Duluth Services

Indians in Duluth are physically, and in terms of outlook, closer to the reservations than are the Twin Cities Indian communities. For instance, the American Indian Movement has not been active in the city. The Duluth Indian community also indicates greater tensions with city government than do Indians in Minneapolis and St. Paul. Lack of Indian employment by the city, failure to incorporate Indians into city programs, and discrimination are identified as problems.[9]

The *American Indian Fellowship Association*, at 8 East Second Street, is the city's Indian center. Begun in 1966, its services include a breakfast and hot lunch program, Indian Child Welfare Act services (BIA funds), the urban Indian health program (state-funded), and an employment assistance program.

The MCT office in Duluth houses a program to provide economic development assistance and the state Indian housing program. Fond du Lac Reservation operates an Indian Health Service satellite health clinic. Other Indian-oriented programs include two chemical dependency halfway houses, a group home for Indian males aged 16 to 18, Indian Legal Services, and the state-funded adult Indian education program. The strong Indian programs at the University of Minnesota, Duluth, contribute to Indian leadership in the community.

Services in Other Cities

Although some smaller Minnesota cities have significant numbers of Indians, the Indian Fellowship Center at South International Falls is the only other organized center that has come to the attention of the League of Women Voters. It administers state-funded chemical dependency programs.

Nongovernmental Sources of Aid

Foundations, charities, corporations, and other nongovernmental bodies have been very important to Minnesota Indians on the reservations and in urban areas. They have provided money to pay start-up costs and in some cases to cover ongoing operations for most of the major Indian programs in the Twin Cities and several important projects on the reservations.

Some examples of the types of foundation, corporate, and private assistance are the following:

- The Minneapolis-St. Paul Family Housing Program, combining McKnight Foundation money with city and federal funds, which assists low-income people (including Indians) by making reduced-interest mortgages available.

- Blandin Foundation funding of a $250,000, three-year expansion of the Service to Indian People program to encourage and assist Indian students throughout the Arrowhead Community College system.
- Companies aiding Indians through their business practices: an insurance firm making a loan for a portion of the Franklin Circle shopping center funding; other companies using the American Indian Bank, Washington, DC, as a regular bank depository or working through the Minnesota Minority Purchasing Council to use minority firms to supply needed items.
- Dayton-Hudson Foundation, in addition to providing funding, also actively assisting in management training to handle the business needs of Migizi, the *Circle*, and the Multi-Service Center on the Bois Forte Reservation.
- Honeywell Corporation, which provides funding to encourage employees to take part in community affairs, funding the employee Indian Concerns Committee in its support of the Ojibwe Art Expo; and helping small neighborhood businesses like Phillips Bindery with seed money, purchase of services, staff assistance, and marketing.
- Episcopal Diocese of Minnesota, arranging funding help and personal involvement of skilled business leaders for Indian Enterprise, an economic development project on White Earth Reservation.
- A corporation president donating a resort to Leech Lake RBC to use as Leech Lake Youth Lodge.
- Individuals donating time and services: medical people in health clinics, attorneys providing legal services, loaned and retired executives helping with management problems, volunteers at emergency foodshelves, the service programs funded by churches.

United Way is an organized system of collecting charitable contributions from great numbers of individuals and corporations and distributing them to programs that serve the needy within the community. Despite efforts to do a better job funding priority needs, most of the money continues to go to long-established programs that lack an Indian outreach and do little to help in the Indian communities. In 1983, United Way of the Minneapolis Area allocated 2.5% of its funds to six Indian-oriented programs.

CHAPTER 7

Economic Development

Tribal governments today have a great deal more power and autonomy than they did ten or twenty years ago. Most reservations are now more viable economically than they were in the recent past. Much of the improvement, however, has been generated by transfer payments via federal and private grants. Grants are only a means to an end, the end in this case being to develop the reservation economies so that the residents can receive their full and rightful share of the prosperity of this nation.[1]

Progress

In contrast with just a few years ago, there has been a great increase in the vitality of reservation economies. The MCT and the individual reservations have taken over management of many of their own programs, and several tribal enterprises are operating successfully on the reservations. Strong resources remain: timber, water, the land, and—most valuable—the people.

Leech Lake Reservation has probably done the most to begin its own tribal enterprises. The tribe employed 348 in the spring of 1982, increased from only 75 just two years before; these were not necessarily new jobs, but they were in programs newly administered by the tribe's

RBC. In 1982, there was a payroll of some $4 million. The tribe was operating 12 businesses, which provided the funds to invest in new projects.

Value of Development to the Region

Healthy, growing economies on the reservations provide great benefit to surrounding areas. Two studies by the Ninth District Federal Reserve Bank of reservations in the Dakotas in the 1970s documented the importance of reservation dollars and jobs. The income received by Indians on one reservation was respent almost four (3.88) times before it left the area. For every 10 basic jobs provided on the other reservation, eight additional jobs were generated in support activities.[2]

A banker in Cass Lake has acknowledged that the growth in financial activity by the Leech Lake Reservation and other Indian programs has been important to the white community. "The impact on the local economy . . . is noticeable in the increase of spendable income in town. Reservation monies are providing a lot more people with salaries and wages. The standard of living has noticeably increased. . . . From a downtown with a lot of boarded up buildings, where many businesses were just existing, Cass Lake has converted to prosperity unknown before development of the Leech Lake Reservation."[3]

In 1978 the combined value of Indian activity in the area of Bemidji was estimated at $55 million, including programs of the MCT, the Red Lake band, Indian Health Service, and BIA.[4]

The economic importance of Indians to the communities in northern Minnesota is usually not acknowledged; this is seen by Indians as an example of local discrimination. Although Indian economic improvement leads to more business for nearby white communities, Indians believe that "when a white business prospers, there is little or no effect on the Indian community for there is no employment opportunity available to Indian people, and no purchasing done through Indian firms."[5]

Problems

Economic development is a very difficult process. A *Wall Street Journal* article noted, "The creeping, inching, painful nature of the Indians' progress . . . reminds us that development is a tedious job that remains to be done."[6]

Northern Minnesota

There are several drawbacks to major economic development in northern Minnesota, for Indians and non-Indians alike. Commercial resources are limited, and the industries that are important in the area—such as timber and tourism—are often in depressed circumstances. The distance from major population centers increases transportation costs, and energy costs are high.

Problems also arise from limitations in the infrastructure, including lack of good roads and inadequate sanitation facilities, emergency services, and electric power. Limited fire protection adds to insurance costs, and local investment capital may not be available. Some of Minnesota's reservations lack enough land, or have land that is too fragmented, to permit development.

Labor Force

The availability of a labor force is one of the major strengths of the reservations, but most of the people have low-level job skills and little formal education. One solution may be small-scale industries that can use the low-skill employee, although successful operations on this scale do not begin to provide enough jobs.

Inexperienced management, poor marketing, and unrealistic planning often contribute to Indian business failures. In their economic plans, Minnesota's reservations almost without exception have identified the need for trained managers. Indians have not traditionally chosen to learn business skills; they have had few role models or experiences with the business world.

Conflict with Indian Culture

The commitment to creating jobs is also tempered by tribal concern to retain control and to avoid development that might be destructive to the tribes or to Indian culture. Mille Lacs band expressed determination that the benefits of economic development not come with a loosening of traditional cultural beliefs, a breakdown of sociocultural structure that would pit Indian against Indian. Tribally owned and generated businesses should have the sole purpose of producing social profits that benefit tribal unity, individual and community pride, and the attainment of reservation self-sufficiency.[7]

Tribal decision-making processes and goals may be in conflict with good business management. Some difficulties were identified in the *Wall Street Journal* article: the process of collective agreement—"unremitting democracy"—is slow and cumbersome and may result in or bring erratic results; there is an overwhelming bias toward political rather than economic decisions; some Indian groups may not want to be in the business at all; and a community priority of employment at the expense of profit can cause businesses to fail.[8]

These difficulties may be encountered in the development of tribal enterprises as well as privately funded ones. Indians trained as business managers may find they lack the freedom to manage and make tough business decisions. By having independent corporations run the businesses, reservations are attempting to insulate the money-making function from community politics.

Outside Investment

The reservations have many strengths to offer outside investors. They have land, resources, and a large labor pool with an increasing number of individuals well trained through government programs. Operating from Indian areas can also provide tax breaks, flexible financing, and other financial incentives. Despite these advantages, attempts by non-Indian entrepreneurs to operate businesses on Minnesota reservations have not generally been successful.

The status of the land and tribal sovereignty cause unique problems for business investment. The land cannot be collateral for a loan, nor can it be sold, which poses problems in getting commercial loans. As sovereign bodies, the tribes are immune from lawsuits except when they waive immunity.

Reservations have on occasion attracted businesses interested in getting something for nothing. Businesses that invested primarily to benefit from the various government programs of financial incentives available for locating on reservations were rarely willing to provide the necessary management and financial resources to make the operation successful.

Developments that do succeed require a "prodigious amount of persistence."[9] A study of a successful operation on a Nebraska reservation pointed out that "Indians come from a culture that is foreign to the typical business executive. Our ways are not their ways, but each can accommodate the other. . . . Business people considering a deal with Indians must develop and demonstrate a commitment that transcends mere dollars and cents."[10]

Development Administered by the Tribe

As governing bodies, tribes have powers similar to other governments to raise and receive money. They get federal revenue sharing based on population (31 USC 1227 [b 4]). They do not have to pay federal excise tax on purchases, and they can sell tax-exempt bonds for public improvements. Community Development Block Grants, with separate funding for Indian tribes (PL 86–372, Sec. 107 [a 3]), are available for reservation projects; money is granted on a competitive basis. Major amounts of development capital funds are spent by the BIA and IHS in building reservation infrastructure: roads, schools, hospitals, clinics, housing for hospital personnel, sanitation and water systems, and forestry services.

An increasing array of tribally run government programs have been brought to the reservations. Tribal control of programs was greatly expanded by the Indian Self-Determination Act of 1975, which gave tribes the right to contract for BIA and IHS programs and to administer them directly. Some funding was also provided for technical assistance to strengthen the tribes' administrative skills.

Taxation

Indians on reservations are not subject to state taxes. State tribes and the Minnesota commissioner of revenue made an agreement in 1977 that sales taxes collected on the reservations would be returned on a per capita basis to each reservation's governing body (Mn. Stat. 270.60). Red Lake does not participate in the sales/motor vehicle tax refund because those taxes are not collected on the reservation. Tax refunds have provided large amounts of money to the tribal governments. In 1981, $451,000 in tobacco tax, $302,000 in alcohol tax, and $59,000 in petroleum tax were refunded.

In January 1982, the Shakopee-Mdewakanton Sioux Community terminated its cigarette excise tax agreement with the state. Without the state tax, the cigarettes can be sold a good deal cheaper. By ordinance, sales to non-Indians are limited to two cartons.

Fearing a major loss of tax revenue if there were widespread sales to non-Indians, the state passed a law in 1982 (Mn Stat. 297.041) to deny wholesalers the right to do business in the state if the tribes did not collect and pay the tax to the state for cigarettes sold to nonmembers. The commissioner of revenue can also seize any cigarettes destined for delivery to the tribe. The effect of the law has been to shift tribal purchases from Minnesota dealers to out-of-state wholesalers.

The US Supreme Court has ruled that Indian retailers can be required to collect and remit state taxes collected from non-Indian buyers on reservations (*Washington v. Colville*, 1980). In the view of a Department of the Interior official, this does not apply to the Minnesota situation, where the tax is an excise tax on the retailer, not the buyer. Under the circumstances, the state lacks jurisdiction to collect from the tribe.[11]

Liquor Licenses

In 1981 the MCT began issuing liquor licenses to Indians for alcohol sales on the reservations. The tribe had established an ordinance regulating liquor licensing as early as 1954, but the state blocked it by threatening wholesalers with loss of their licenses if they sold to Indian establishments. Federal law governs liquor sales on reservations (18 USC 1154 [c]), giving Indian tribes control over liquor except in "non-Indian communities within the reservation."

A case to test whether the MCT could issue a liquor license was resolved in favor of the tribe in Cass County District Court in 1981. The state attorney general then issued an opinion that the state would honor tribal liquor licenses.

The power to license liquor sales is important to tribes not only as a source of economic benefit but as a means to regulate sales to protect the interests of their people. As of 1982, the MCT had issued a dozen licenses.

In July 1983, the US Supreme Court ruled that, in addition to the tribe, the state of California also has the power to license liquor sales on a California Indian reservation (*Rice v. Rehner*). It is not clear what this decision will mean for Minnesota.

Gambling

If state law allows gambling, such as bingo, the activity on reservations cannot be regulated by the state. This tribal power, confirmed by court decisions, has led to the establishment on several Minnesota reservations of professional bingo operations that produce major revenue for tribal purposes.

The first of these operations was the Little Six Bingo Palace at Prior Lake. It provides bingo seven nights a week with large jackpots. The $950,000 facility seats 1,300 people; free shuttle bus service brings customers from the Twin Cities. The operation is managed by New England-Pan American Entertainment Company under contract with the Shakopee-Mdewakanton Sioux Community, with the profits divided 55% to the Indians and 45% to the management company. About 130 people are employed.

Little Six opened in October 1982. By June 1983 it had generated enough profit to pay off the mortgage and pave reservation roads and driveways. In 1984, it was the largest employer in Prior Lake and was expected to earn $12 million. Profits fund a reservation health clinic, a day-care center, and a culture center. Some of the funds are used for per family payments, the first time in Minnesota that income generated by a tribe has been distributed to tribal members. Reservation unemployment has been virtually eliminated.

By 1984, facilities to accommodate large bingo programs had been built or were under construction at Lake Vermilion, Bois Forte, Fond du Lac, Leech Lake, Prairie Island, and Lower Sioux reservations. The Prairie Island facility is similar to the one at Prior Lake, seating 1,400 and employing about 200 people. The Lower Sioux facility, Jackpot Junction, 5 miles east of Redwood Falls, is a half-million-dollar building seating 600 and employing about 50 people. Profits of all the reservation bingo operations are earmarked for such uses as preschool programs, construction projects, or support of community activities, depending on the tribe's priorities.

State and federal governments are being pressured to change the laws so that Indian reservations no longer have the advantage of being unregulated by state laws. Indians, who have traditionally been avid participants in games of chance, see those efforts as another instance of the white man's taking from Indians any resource that might give them the chance to have a viable economy that they themselves control.

A 1983 proposal of the Bois Forte band to build a complex for bingo and pari-mutuel betting on horse races at Gilbert, in cooperation with that city, was subjected to strong state political pressures. The proposal was dropped. Fond du Lac Reservation and the city of Duluth agreed in 1984 to transfer property in the city to the tribe for a bingo facility. To establish the land as Indian, the BIA must approve. By fall 1984, opposition to the plan had been voiced by some state legislators and a decision had not been made.

Government Programs for Economic Development

Reservation development projects may require the tribe to bring together several federal agencies; perhaps state, county, and local interests; private businesses; and foundations with varying requirements, funding cycles, and bureaucratic "white" tape. To add to the problem, the major financial help—the Economic Development Administration (EDA)—was ended in 1982. That program, providing grants and loans, invested more than $12.5 million in projects on the state's reservations. Practically all development projects until 1982 included EDA money. EDA-funded planners enabled each reservation to prepare and maintain an overall economic development plan, which started the process of realistic, comprehensive, long-term thinking about reservation development.

The BIA administers the Indian Financing Act, with the goal of helping Indians to develop and utilize their resources so that "they will enjoy a standard of living from their own productive efforts comparable to that enjoyed by non-Indians in neighboring communities" (25 USC 1451). The act provides for a revolving loan fund, federal guarantees for up to 90% of loans (with interest subsidy available), grants of up to $50,000, and technical assistance. The program is "of last resort," usable only if financing from other sources is unavailable on reasonable terms and conditions. Projects must be profit oriented and at least 51% owned by Indians.

BIA policy in 1982 was to provide no more than 30% of the grant, with the tribe committing additional funds up to 50–60% of the project. The remaining share was to come from private sources, although for projects on trust land this was not feasible. The MCT has contracted with the BIA for one person to assist the tribes in using the act, working with the reservations on building loan packages.

The Farmers Home Administration in the US Department of Agriculture has a program for industrial development, business loans, and community facilities loans that is available for Indians (7 USC 1989). It has not been widely used in Minnesota. Tribes can also use Small Business Administration programs and other government programs.

Tribal Businesses and Economic Resources

A corporation is usually formed by the tribe to administer its reservation business interests. Examples are the Grand Portage Local Development Corporation, founded in 1971, and the White Earth Community Development Corporation, begun in 1980. The latter group has had the help of Indian Enterprise, a support program of volunteer professional assistance, and funding from the Episcopal Diocese of Minnesota.

The following discussion identifies tribal businesses on the state's reservations. They include manufacturing and processing, construction, tourism, service operations, and businesses using the natural resources. Over the years several enterprises have failed, and others are operating at a loss and are in arrears in repaying government loans. Several make profits that are then used by the tribes for further economic development.

Manufacturing and Processing. Manufacturing companies include Fond du Lac Manufacturing, which makes wood-oil and wood-gas furnaces; they are marketed nationwide by Wilson-Yukon Industries. The company has been operating since 1977, employing from 15 to 28 seasonal workers. In 1982, the tribe undertook a gasification furnace research project to study the feasibility of converting wood chips to gas.

Mille Lacs Reservation Business Enterprise was begun in 1968. The company, which employs about 30 people, does a variety of contract electronics work.

Leech Lake Firewood Company cuts, splits, seasons, packages, and markets wood for home heating, retail and wholesale. Eight employees run the operation, with additional people involved as loggers and haulers. Indian Wood, Incorporated, is a White Earth Reservation operation that processes and ships fireplace wood.

The White Earth Reservation has Ojibway Bait Company, which freeze-dries minnows, leeches, shiners, suckers, crayfish, and worms and sells them as fishing bait. The product, Jib-Way Bait, is far easier to handle than fresh bait. When restored by soaking in water, the lifelike bait is reportedly very successful in catching fish.

White Earth Garment Manufacturing Company, begun in 1982, contracts with several companies to make items ranging from uniforms for professional sports teams to baby pajamas. The reservation has also organized the manufacture of quality handicraft items to be marketed through an established mail-order catalog operation.

Lower Sioux Pottery is the only manufacturing company in the Sioux communities. Located at Morton, it manufactures handcrafted pottery from local clays and glazes. Either traditional Dakota designs or individual artists' creations are used to decorate the pieces. Six people are employed.

Construction. Most of the reservations have construction companies. The MCT Construction Company was chartered by the state in 1972. It has qualified as an 8A (minority) business and has worked on several federal government contracts, as well as projects for the MCT.

The Fond du Lac Equipment and Construction Company, the Leech Lake Construction Company, the Ojibwa Construction Company (White Earth), and Red Lake Builders do construction work on the reservations. Mille Lacs Reservation Construction Company was a local concern that the tribe purchased. The previous owner was hired to operate it and provide on-the-job training for tribe members. Growing out of the construction work, building and supply companies were begun by the MCT and the Leech Lake and White Earth reservations.

Resorts and Tourist Industry. Recreational facilities are operated by tribes on Grand Portage and Mille Lacs reservations. The 100-room Grand Portage Lodge and Conference Center was built in 1973 at a cost of $3 million. Conference facilities to accommodate 300 people were added later, along with staff housing. The lodge is located on the north shore of Lake Superior near the reconstructed Grand Portage Fort and Trading Post and the ferry for Isle Royale National Park. The restaurant, swimming pool, and conference facilities are available year-round. Among the 100-person staff are about 45 Indians and an Indian manager. The tribe also operates a tourist information center and a small marina.

Mille Lacs Reservation has the Marina and Tourism Complex at Vineland, built in 1975 and consisting of 11 cottages, a marina, a restaurant, and an auto service center. The Drift Inn, located three miles south of the reservation, was purchased in 1980 and is operated by the tribe. The Shakopee-Mdewakanton Sioux Community in 1984 opened the Tado Teepee restaurant and gift shops selling Indian handicrafts in the culture center.

Service Operations. A current focus of reservation development strategy is the "recapture" of spending on the reservation; that is, reusing Indian dollars in Indian establishments. As one tribe noted in its community development plan, "Historically the reservation economy has lacked a circulatory system. Indian funds quickly made their way to off-reservation retail establishments and financial institutions."[12]

The Federal Reserve Bank report cautioned, however, that Indian-built service operations may prove to be a source of frustration because the small population of a reservation "lack[s] the critical mass necessary to the development of a diversified and viable local economy." Competition is another hazard.

> Relationships with neighboring communities are usually
> strained by racial, cultural, and value differences; thus
> many Indian people would prefer to develop their econ-
> omy independently rather than in cooperation with the
> surrounding non-Indian communities. Many times this
> becomes a source of further frustration as Indian people
> find it difficult to compete with well-established and better-
> capitalized non-Indian enterprises.[13]

In Minnesota, tribally run laundromats and a bowling alley have closed, being unable to earn sufficient income.

Leech Lake Reservation successfully operates a restaurant, service station, and grocery store—Che-Wa-Ka-E-Gon (big house)—at Cass Lake on Highway 2, a major east-west road across northern Minnesota.

A $1 million expansion was added in 1981. The tribe also provides sanitation services for the reservation area.

Bois Forte Reservation opened the Multi-Service Center—a grocery store and service station—in 1982. Before these became available on the reservation, it was a 70-mile round trip to a supermarket, and 36 miles for a loaf of bread.

Fishing. Red Lake Reservation has a commercial fisheries operation, Red Lake Fisheries Association, which was started in 1929 when the fishermen and the reservation tribal council organized the World War I fishing operation into a cooperative. The enterprise was set up under state and federal law. (Mn. Stat. 102.30 allows fish taken on Upper and Lower Red lakes to be transported for sale.) About 300 members form the association, with about a third to a half active at any one time. They are paid for their catch, and the tribe is paid a royalty for the fish taken. The profits are divided among association members. For the fishermen, work is part time, to provide supplemental income.

In 1975, a new building was constructed and equipped with machines that scale, dress, fillet, and flash-freeze the fish. The fish are sold fresh or are frozen and shipped throughout the Midwest; smoked fish are also prepared. Processing the catch employs about 25 people. The operation takes in about $1 million a year.

To protect fishing in Red Lake, a yearly harvest limit of 650,000 pounds is imposed on the walleye catch. The other fish that come in with the walleyes are also processed and sold. About 100,000 pounds of perch and 50,000 pounds of northerns and whitefish are handled annually, and the fisheries association also buys whitefish taken at Leech Lake. It operates a fish hatchery to keep the Red Lakes stocked.

The Leech Lake tribe's agreement to restrict Indian hunting and fishing and in return to receive a portion of state-collected license fees provides them with over $1 million annually (1983). A few individuals sell fish from Lake Superior at Grand Portage Reservation.

Timber. For most of the reservations, timber is the greatest natural resource.[14] The forests are managed by the BIA, with tribal governing bodies setting policy and approving sales. The BIA provides at least one forester on each northern reservation.

Timber resources are managed on a perpetual harvest basis, with species and total allowable cut limits. Replanting is done on about 10% of the harvested areas. Red Lake Reservation replants from 300 to 700 acres annually with seedlings from its own nursery, which employs up to 12 people.

Sales of timber and the products made from it were very depressed in the early 1980s. The Red Lake band averaged sales of 17,400 thousand board feet (MBF) of timber between 1965 and 1981; in 1981 the cut was 12,000 MBF worth $263,000. Over the same 17-year period, the MCT reservations averaged 8,500 MBF; just under 6,000 MBF were sold in 1981, one-half from Grand Portage and a third from White Earth reservations, for a total income of $90,000.

Indian timber and forest products are used by pulp and paper mills in the region and for the manufacture of a new product—wood chip waferboard, a substitute for plywood. Aspen, a tree largely overlooked in the past, can be used for it.

Reservation sawmills use tribal timber to manufacture lumber and other wood products. Red Lake Mills, which was authorized by federal legislation in 1916 (39 Stat. 137), is operated by the BIA. In addition to the sawmill, the facility includes a drying kiln and equipment for cedar post production. Depending upon the market, between 30 and 60 people are employed.

Profits from the mill, put into a trust account to benefit the tribe, have enabled it to repay the government loan that was used to improve the facility; it is the only tribe that has made such a repayment. In recent years, there has been an operating loss, and the federal government has taken money from the trust account to cover the deficits. By fall 1983, the issue was in federal court, with an audit ordered. The financial stewardship by the BIA of the tribe's resources, the legal status of the mill, and the role of the tribe in its operation are all issues to be resolved.

Ojibwa Forest Products on the White Earth Reservation saws lumber and railroad ties and manufactures storage sheds, wood packaging materials, and shipping pallets. Bois Forte has a sawmill that had a major expansion of equipment in 1980, but during the recession of the early 1980s, the mill went bankrupt and closed down. Leech Lake Logging Enterprises is a logging operation that employs eight people; Grand Portage Forest Products Enterprises is a timber-hauling operation.

White Earth Reservation Ranch, site of a former Job Corps facility, has been used for a variety of economic development programs through the years, none of which has been successful. In the late 1970s, the tribe ran the 10,000-acre ranch as a cattle-raising enterprise, but it was not economically viable. A pilot project (funded by the US Department of Energy) to make alcohol from cattails was tried, whereupon it was discovered that cattails have an enzyme that resists the conversion. In 1983, the farmland was leased.

Peat and Other Power Development

A comprehensive report prepared by the Minnesota DNR in 1981 indicated that peat having commercial potential is on or near several reservations.[15] Development would have many ramifications, positive and negative: although the jobs and economic stimulation would be welcome, peat processing and conversion on a major scale could damage the environment.

A 1978 study at Red Lake assessed the impact that peat development would have on the reservation and concluded that a peat gasification plant would provide little benefit. Employment would require skill levels and work experience exceeding that of many Red Lake members, and the indirect effects would primarily benefit the off-reservation retail service centers. Moreover, the potential for damage was thought to be great, with resources of fish, timber, wild rice, and wildlife likely to be affected to some degree. Reservation residents believed that they were using the peat resources in the best possible manner—as habitat for wildlife, as land for forestry and wild rice production, and as a water source for the Red lakes. They also thought the potential value to them of peat development did not justify risking resources so much a part of their tribal heritage.[16]

By federal law, Indian reservations are allowed to apply for and be certified as class I air quality areas, or the same as wilderness areas, where air quality deterioration is not allowed. Although Minnesota's Indian reservations are now in the class II group, with less stringent standards, they can at any time petition to be reclassified as class I. Because a change in status is time-consuming and no threats to air quality have yet been proposed, the reservations have not sought the change; but the issue may become significant if major peat development and gasification plants are proposed for reservation areas.

Citizens concerned about nuclear power plant safety sometimes raise questions about the environment at Prairie Island, which the Indian Community shares with a nuclear-powered electric generating plant. Although questions of possible contamination have been brought up at tribal council meetings, the Indian community has had no discernible health problems from the power plant and is not concerned about its presence.[17]

Wild Rice

In the view of Minnesota's Ojibways, wild rice is much more than a product to be used for economic benefit. "There's a feeling you get out there that's hard to get other places. You're close to Mother Nature, seeing things grow and harvesting the results of the water and sun and winds. . . . We sort of touch our roots when we're among the rice plants."[18]

Wild rice or "manomin," (Ojibway for "good berry") has been the staple food of Minnesota's Indians for centuries. Considered a sacred gift, wild rice is associated with happy reunions and festivals at harvest time. It is an important part of the Indian diet, served at every celebration, and an integral part of Indian culture.

Wild rice is a tall, oatlike, aquatic annual grass (*Zizania aquatica*) that grows in the rich, silted shallows of lakes, rivers, and ponds. In harvesting methods developed by the Indians, two people use a canoe propelled by a forked pole. The rice stems are bent over the canoe with one stick while the matured grains are tapped into the canoe with a second one. Because the grains ripen on a staggered basis, the rice beds are harvested several times during a period that lasts two to three weeks. This process harvests perhaps 15% of the natural grain and ensures seeding for a crop the next year.

Traditional Indian processing includes parching the harvested rice to remove excess moisture. It is then put into a pit lined with a hide or canvas and "jigged," danced on until the husks separate from the grains. The hulls are then winnowed away, leaving the grain.

By Minnesota law (Mn. Stat. 84.09), harvesting of all natural wild rice must be done in the Indian nonmechanical way, and only Indians or people residing on the reservations can harvest the reservation wild rice. About one-third to one-half of the state's water acres producing natural wild rice are on Indian reservations.[19] Harvesting is regulated by the tribes on the reservations and by the state elsewhere. Alternate days and specific, limited hours are set, with a license fee imposed. The White Earth Conservation Department, concerned about declining natural stands on the reservation, began a reseeding program in 1983; over 700 acres were replanted in 1984.

Nonshattering varieties of wild rice, developed by the University of Minnesota, have made a major impact on production. Paddies can produce up to 1,000 pounds per acre, while a natural lake that produces well yields about 50 pounds. Between 1978 and 81, around 4.5 million pounds were produced annually in Minnesota paddies.

Lake rice production has wide fluctuations. In 1980, production was 4 million pounds; two years earlier, however, it was less than 500,000 pounds. On the average, for the 10 years 1972–81, lake rice harvest was about 1.4 million pounds, 37% of the state's total wild rice production. About 40% of the lake wild rice comes from reservations.[20]

The paddy-grown wild rice has caused great concern to Indians in Minnesota. It is seen as an inferior product that has reduced the commercial value of natural wild rice production. In a study done on Indian potential in the wild rice industry, the quality differences were analyzed. Quality was equated with the number of long grains harvested. The natural lake wild rice had a greater percentage of long grains, but (the study pointed out) the market does not pay a premium on this basis.[21]

In 1981, the Minnesota legislature passed legislation sought by Indians (Mn. Stat. 30.49) that requires all cultivated wild rice to be labeled conspicuously as "paddy grown" when offered for sale in Minnesota. A violation is a misdemeanor. But the difficulty of proving the difference between the two types of wild rice makes it hard to enforce the state law. A University of Minnesota agronomist has suggested that it would be more meaningful to consumers to label the natural lake rice and market it as a premium product.[22]

Although the production and worldwide sale of wild rice is an economic asset to Minnesota, the state's Indians receive only minimal income from it. For some, it provides a little additional cash in the fall as they sell their excess harvest. Tribal efforts to get involved in production, processing, and marketing have not been very successful. It is considered an especially emotional and political issue on the reservations.[23] In 1983, Bois Forte Reservation did some processing on a small scale, and Leech Lake began a program. There are now 140 acres in paddy rice production at Leech Lake, but the tribe finds it hard to become enthusiastic about paddy rice.

Urban Businesses

No business development programs targeted to Indians are available for urban Indian organizations, which must compete with all other groups for funding. The Minneapolis Indian community, with great persistence over seven years, was able to put together a program and funding to create Franklin Circle Shopping Center, including a supermarket, auto supply, and other stores in two blocks on Franklin Avenue. The project is providing stimulus for additional renewal in the Indian community. The American Indian Business Development Corporation, which owned the center, expected to sell it in 1984 to a retail center management business. The proceeds were to be used to further economic development of benefit to Indians and the Indian community.

Small, community-generated enterprises that provide employment within the neighborhoods and help the unskilled are receiving corporation, foundation, and government support. The enterprises perform labor-intensive projects that are contracted from various businesses. Project for Pride in Living Industries in Minneapolis, which was begun in 1982 and emphasizes Indian employment, employed as many as 55 at one time in 1983. Phillips Bindery is located in an area of high Indian population in south Minneapolis; in 1983 it had 9 full-time and 26 part-time workers.

Small Businesses

Small business operations that are individually run are at high risk for the whole population. Indians are often very skilled craftspeople, good in their trades but lacking the other elements needed for success — among them record keeping, accounting, and marketing skills. With these problems, providing dollars alone will not prevent failure; improved technique is necessary. Although the obstacles can be overcome, they are often very frustrating to the individual involved. Minority-run small businesses frequently fail, creating problems not only for the individuals involved but also for the minority group, by reinforcing the expectation that failure will occur.[24]

Minnesota Indian-Owned Businesses

Data prepared by the Census Bureau for 1977 showed 81 Indian businesses in the state, 6% of all minority-owned ones. Of these, 9 had employees and 72 did not. They reported gross receipts of $3.3 million.[25] In 1981, 147 Indian firms were listed by the Minnesota Department of Energy and Economic Development, not including tribal businesses (49 in the Twin Cities area).[26] Indians operate businesses and retail stores across a wide spectrum of products and services, with the greatest number in construction trades.

The Minnesota Indian Contractors Association has been organized to give the individual contractor greater visibility and better opportunities to get contracts. The organization had 30 members in 1980 and identified 76 Indian contractors serving Minnesota.

Government Assistance to Small Businesses

Several government programs are designed to assist minority-run small businesses. They are used by tribal businesses as well as those run by individual Indians.

State Business Loan Fund. In 1973 the state authorized the Minnesota Indian Business Loan Fund (Mn. Stat. 362.40), a revolving fund to help in economic development. The program is funded by five cents of the tax of twenty-five cents per acre on severed mineral rights (rights owned separately from the land). In 1982, $414,000 was available in the fund, with about $70,000 added by the tax annually. Increased funding from a more reliable source was recommended in 1984 by the governor and Indian leaders.

In 1984, administration of the program was transferred to the Indian Affairs Council. Tribes must submit plans showing how the loans are to be used to serve members on and off the reservations. Bois Forte, Fond du Lac, Grand Portage, Leech Lake, and White Earth reservations had begun their programs in 1984.

This very-low-interest-rate (2%) loan program has received considerable criticism from the Indian community. Promised 10 years ago, it had yet to make a significant number of loans through 1983. The funds have been apportioned among the tribes on a population basis, which means that the share available for any one tribe is too small to be meaningful.[27]

Federal Assistance. The Office of Minority Business Development, US Department of Commerce (Ex. Order 11625, 1971), funds the major program reaching out to help Indians. The Indian Business Development Center, administered by the MCT, received $153,000 in 1983, and the MCT added $17,000 to the center's funding. A staff of five, with offices in Cass Lake and Duluth, provides help with management techniques and contract procurement. The program serves racial minorities and other disadvantaged groups. In 1982, about 75 individuals, Indian-owned firms, and reservation enterprises were helped. The center has sponsored annual conferences since 1980 to bring together Indian business owners, helping with skill development and providing a vehicle for networking and cooperation within the Indian business community.

Government Purchasing Programs. Under the Minority Business Development Procurement Assistance program, referred to as 8A (PL 95–507, sec. 8 [a]), the Small Business Administration (SBA) becomes the prime contractor for government procurement orders and subcontracts them to businesses owned and controlled by minorities. In 1980 there were 8A contracts with the MCT and Mille Lacs Reservation businesses.

Under federal and state "set-aside" programs, a percentage of a government contract is subcontracted to small businesses owned and controlled by "socially and economically disadvantaged individuals" (including Indians). The SBA enforces the federal program. Minnesota requires that 6% of all state purchases be from such individuals (Mn.

Stat. 16.083). Similar requirements for purchases from disadvantaged persons apply to the University of Minnesota (Mn. Stat. 137.31, subd. 3). Local and regional governments are also authorized to have minority set-aside programs.

The set-aside provisions for government purchases are seen as having a high potential for assisting minority-run small businesses, but they are often a source of frustration to those they are designed to help: the paper work is extensive, technicalities can be used to circumvent the law's intent, and compliance is poorly monitored. A legislative audit of the Minnesota minority set-aside program in 1981 concluded that "the broader goals of the program have not been well served by the manner in which [it] has been carried out."[28]

Other Aids for Small Business

Assistance for all small businesses, not restricted to minorities or disadvantaged, is provided by the SBA, which has programs guaranteeing loans and making financing available that otherwise might be denied. Technical assistance, workshops, and help with loan packaging are services offered by the Small Business Development Center (funded by the SBA) and the Small Business Assistance Center (Minnesota Department of Energy and Economic Development).

In the private sector, minority vendor and business trade fairs have been annual events in the Twin Cities since 1976, offering an opportunity for purchasing agents and minority vendors to get acquainted. Corporate-Minority Business Exchange puts on the fairs in cooperation with minority community organizations like the Indian Business Development Center. Minnesota Minority Purchasing Council is a group of firms that have pledged to buy supplies from minority firms.

The business community also sponsors the Metropolitan Economic Development Association, a group available to advise minority business people; and SCORE, Service Corps of Retired Executives, a Chamber of Commerce program to help individual businesses improve their financial and management skills.

Summary

Economic development means jobs, personal dignity, and tribal independence from changeable government policies. It is a long, hard struggle, but success brings more success, as some of the reservations are finding as they invest profits into expanding opportunities.

Indians lack sufficient resources, however, and they lack access to the means to obtain the needed investment. Government is still the key, and the trust/sovereign status of the tribes requires that government be involved if investment is to be made. A long-term, dependable commitment is essential if what has been achieved is not to be lost.

The Indian position was summarized by a Leech Lake RBC member during testimony to a congressional committee in 1982:

> We believe that economic self-sufficiency is an attainable goal on our reservation. We have made some beginnings. Our development efforts are at a crucial stage where the next several years will spell the difference between success or failure for many of our undertakings. We have over the past decade used federal programs in combination to strengthen tribal government, to improve our planning and management capabilities, to finance construction, to train manpower for tribal business enterprises and to provide for the educational and health needs of our people. Since we have already come part of the way toward the goal of a viable economy for the reservation, this is the worst time imaginable for us to be thrown off balance by changing policies and budget cuts on the part of the federal government.[29]

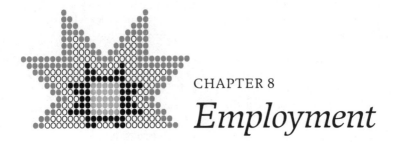

CHAPTER 8

Employment

Most people can't conceive of what our unemployment is
like. It just doesn't seem real to them. Whites look at the
numbers, and they think they must be wrong. Their
parents tell them about the Depression, and what they
don't know is that our unemployment is worse now than
the Depression ever was for whites.[1]

Lack of employment is not new to Indians. In northern Minnesota,
they suffer along with non-Indians from that area's chronic economic
depression. The economic recession in the early 1980s has added to the
problem, at the same time that government programs providing training
and employment were cut.

These conditions, combined with other factors that contribute to
perennial low Indian employment—lack of education, lack of work
record or experience, discrimination in employment—made the 1982–83
situation extremely bleak. For urban Indians or those coming to the
major cities to find something to do, the situation was the same: no jobs
and no hope of jobs, especially for Indians without skills and experience.

Assessing the Numbers

The Employed

Indians who are employed work in greater proportion in low-skilled jobs and in government than do other groups (tables 8–10). Large private firms (100 or more employees) hired the lowest percentage of Indians in 1978 – 0.5% – despite being the greatest source of jobs numerically. The prevalence of employment in lower skilled positions was shown by Indians being 0.9% of laborers and only 0.2% of professionals in private industry. Manufacturing provided the greatest employment, for 28% of all Indians, with service industries next at 16%. Construction firms employed 6.5% of Indians and had the highest percentage of Indian employees, 1.7%, of any employment group.[2] Indian union members are overwhelmingly in the building trades.

The federal government in Minnesota employed a higher percentage of Indians than did any other sector – 1.6% in 1979. Many of these

Table 8. Employment of Minnesota Indians in Industry and Government

Indian Employees	Number of Indians	Percentage of Employees
Working age Indians (16 and older), 1980	22,033	0.7%
Private industry[a] employees	3,293	0.5[b]
Referral union members[a,c]	384	1.1[d]
Building trades members	373	1.2[d]
Federal civilian employees	382	1.6[e]
State employees	217	0.7[f]
Minneapolis employees	47	1.1[g]

[a]With 100 or more employees.

[b]US Equal Employment Opportunities Commission, *Minorities and Women in Private Industry: 1978* (1980), 1:394–404.

[c]Using a hiring hall or similar method of referring persons to jobs.

[d]EEOC, *Minorities and Women in Apprenticeship Programs and Referral Unions: 1978* (1980), Minnesota.

[e]EEOC, *Federal Civilian Work Force Statistics: Minority Group Study of Full-Time Employment: November 30, 1979*, table 2–051.

[f]Pat Herndon, Equal Opportunity, Minnesota Department of Employee Relations, interview with author on 26 Jan. 1982.

[g]City of Minneapolis, *Affirmative Action Management Program*, 24 Dec. 1981.

Table 9. Employment in Minnesota Private Industry

Position	All Employees (N = 646,011)	Indian Employees (N = 3,293)
Officials, managers, professionals	21%	12%
Technicians, craft workers	16	19
Office, clerical, sales workers	26	17
Operatives, laborers, service workers	37	52

Source: EEOC, *Minorities and Women in Private Industry: 1978* (1980), 1:394–404.

federal jobs are connected with Indian programs, which give employment preference to Indians. The number of Indian employees was dramatically lower in other federal jobs. For example, they were only 0.3% of those employed in Minnesota in the postal service. Indians in federal service work at a much lower average employment grade. The state's average grade was 8.29, whereas the grade for Indians was 6.33.[3]

In Minneapolis, where Indians constitute 2.0% of the work force, they were only 1.1% of all city employees in 1981. An aggressive program to increase minority employment in the protective services (police and fire) has made a major difference in Indian employment there: more than half of the city's Indian employees were in those departments, where they were 2.9% of all employees.[4]

Table 10. Indian Employment in Government in Minnesota
(Excludes Tribal Employees)

Position	Sample of State and Local, 1975[a] (N = 281)	State, 1982[b] (N = 217)	Minneapolis, 1981[c]	
			Indians (N = 47)	All Employees (N = 4,451)
Officials, managers, professionals	21%	23%	2%	16%
Technicians, craft workers, paraprofessionals	24	11	9	23
Office, clerical	12	19	6	18
Protective services	9	NA	51	19
Operatives, laborers, service workers	34	47	32	24

[a]EEOC, *Minorities and Women in State and Local Government: 1975*, report 4.
[b]Pat Herndon, Equal Opportunity, Minnesota Department of Employee Relations, interview with author, 26 Jan. 1982.
[c]City of Minneapolis, *Affirmative Action Management Program*, 24 Dec. 1981.

The Unemployed

The 1980 census sample data provide figures on employment and unemployment. Individuals 16 and older are characterized as being in the labor force, either employed or unemployed, or not in the labor force. Unemployment for Indians was four times that for whites (table 11), and the percentage of the population over 16 that was not in the labor force was also higher.

The Federal Bureau of Labor Statistics does not compile unemployment data on Indian workers in Minnesota because the numbers in the sample are too small. The BIA, however, compiles a labor force report of those employed, the potential labor force, and the unemployed living on or adjacent to reservations in the state (table 12). The percentage unemployed of the potential labor force has always been many times higher than shown in state unemployment figures. The percentages are calculated somewhat differently, and the definition of "adjacent" is not precise; however, the BIA figures do demonstrate the great numbers of Indians without employment.

Although there is a great deal of difference among the reservations, total employment as reported by the BIA decreased from 3,118 in 1979 to 2,532 in 1983. Unemployment percentages increased between 1981 and 1983 for all reservations except two Sioux communities.

The 1983 report illustrates the effects of worsening economic conditions and the cutback in federal employment programs. White Earth Reservation, which has always suffered from extreme unemployment, had an employment drop of 40%, from 493 people employed in 1981 to 295 in 1983; the unemployment rate increased 13% to an unconscionable 82%. Leech Lake Reservation had a drop of 566 jobs between 1979 and

Table 11. Minnesota Employment Figures for Indians and Whites

Category	Minnesota Indians	Whites	Minneapolis Indians	Whites	Phillips Neighborhood (Minneapolis), Indians
Number employed	9,954		2,291		505
Number unemployed	2,563		679		215
Total	12,517		2,970		720
Percentage unemployed	20.5	5.2	22.9	4.8	30
Number not in labor force	9,516		2,537		883
Percentage not in labor force	43.2	34.7	46.1	34.5	55.1

Source: US Census, 1980 sample data.

Table 12. Indian Employment On and Near Reservations

Reservation	Dec. 1982-Jan. 1983		April-May 1981		1979
	Number Employed	Percentage Unemployed	Number Employed	Percentage Unemployed	Number Employed
Bois Forte	220	64%	163	58%	122
Fond du Lac	387	41	369	40	177
Grand Portage	76	43	86	34	68
Leech Lake	526	70	610	54	1,092
Mille Lacs	205	51	205	51	185
White Earth	295	82	493	69	440
Red Lake	686	63	947	41	891
Lower Sioux	34	35	68	47	40
Prairie Island	16	77	46	43	17
Shakopee-Mdewakanton	54	23	30	14	49
Upper Sioux	33	39	33	53	37
Total	2,532		3,050		3,118

Source: BIA, Minneapolis Area Office, *Labor Force Report*, 1979, Apr.-May 1981, and Dec. 1982-Jan. 1983.

1983, a number greater than those actually working in January 1983.

Unemployment figures for urban Indians are even more difficult to document. In reporting on the need for training assistance in 1982, Project Search of Minneapolis summarized Indian sources as putting unemployment between 46 and 89%.[5]

Another measurement of unemployment is the number of job applications made to Job Service, Minnesota Department of Economic Security. In 1981, a total of 5,183 Indians applied—1.7% of the state's total applicants. The percentage is remarkably stable, ranging between 1.75 and 1.9% in reports for 1974, 1976, and 1979.[6] In 1981, the Twin Cities counties of Hennepin and Ramsey had 2,573 applications from Indians, half of the applications from the state's Indians. In Hennepin County, Indians were 4% of all the county's applicants.

Data on Indian employment may be limited, but the Minnesota department concluded, "Unemployment is at unacceptable levels in almost any Indian community. Anyone can see that. It doesn't really matter so much if the rate is 30 percent, 40 percent or 50 percent. More important is whether those unemployed who do show up looking for work are helped."[7]

Problems

The demographics of the Indian population contribute to the problem. A high percentage of Indians are young people, and youth—especially minority youth—are the largest unemployed group in the country.

Employment opportunities are especially limited in northern Minnesota, where most of the reservations are located. In February 1982, the state unemployment rate was 7.7%; in northern counties with reservations, it varied between 9.5% in Beltrami and 23.4% in Clearwater counties. These same counties have high percentages of Indians applying for jobs to Job Service; in 1981, Indians were 35% of the applicants in Mahnomen County, 17% in Cass County, 12% in Beltrami County, and 10% in Becker and Clearwater counties.

When government had a policy of assisting the chronically unemployed in the early 1960s, the results were dramatic. White Earth Reservation had 61% unemployment in 1962, but that figure was reduced to 36% in 1966 through the antipoverty programs, worktraining, and two Job Corps centers on the reservation.[8] These programs were eventually changed or phased out as policy directions changed, and unemployment increased to 69% in 1981 and to 82% in the fall of 1982.

The change was reflected in lower levels of funding. For example, in 1978 White Earth Reservation had $2 million in federal Comprehensive Employment and Training Act (CETA) funding. By the summer of 1982, less than $400,000 was available. Leech Lake's CETA public service employment program of over $1 million in 1981 was cut by two-thirds the next year; the program went from 120 to 22 employees.

For most Indians, additional training and skills are also needed to qualify successfully for employment. The nature of work is changing from unskilled labor to jobs requiring special training, from basic production industries to service and higher technology positions. Government employment programs stress the training aspect, teaching job interview and job search skills and providing specialized training and perhaps subsidized employment for a while.

But the training is wasted if there are not enough jobs for the workers. Mille Lacs Reservation pointed out in its 1980 economic development report that people have been trained as welders, plumbers, bookkeepers, carpenters, auto mechanics, heavy equipment operators, cooks, waitresses, secretaries, auto body workers, dental technicians, child care aides, chemical dependency counselors, and nurses. "People get trained and then released to collect unemployment benefits instead of or in addition to welfare benefits."[9] Training programs have no lasting effect unless there are businesses or other opportunities to provide for the continuing development of trained employees.

Indian Culture and Work

Cultural misunderstandings about Indians and the white work

ethic go back to the beginning of contact between the two races. A report to Congress in 1888 stated:

> The Indian should be taught not only how to work but also that it is his duty to work; for the degrading communism of the tribal reservation system gives to the individual no incentive to labor, but puts a premium upon idleness and makes it fashionable. . . . The Indian must therefore . . . be taken out of the reservation. . . . He must be imbued with the exalting egotism of American civilization, so that he will say "I" instead of "We," and "This is mine," instead of "This is ours."[10]

The Indian response, as stated by Wamditanka (Big Eagle) of the Santee Sioux, was, "The whites were always trying to make the Indians give up their life and live like the white man . . . work hard and do as they did . . . and the Indian did not know how to do that, and did not want to anyway."[11]

Some facets of Indian culture are at odds with the stereotype of the work ethic. Although Indians may not value competitiveness and material possessions or strict adherence to a rigid schedule as whites do, firms that work closely with tribal Indians and their governments report that "Indians are model workers. Properly directed, Indian workers display an untiring methodical approach to their work. Properly trained, they dedicate their skills to the company. Properly motivated, their loyalty is boundless."[12]

Particular problems may arise out of cultural differences:

- Family ties are very important to Indians. An Indian employee may quit or leave a job to attend a funeral, not realizing that time off can be arranged or perhaps feeling hesitant about asking permission.
- The employee may be unfamiliar with city living. Transportation is a major problem if the employee has no car and is reluctant to use public transportation. Lack of a telephone or change of residence may make employment follow-up offers impossible.
- Excess bureaucracy and delays in filling out applications or having to come back for testing, referral, interviews, or physical examinations may be very intimidating and discouraging.

An Indian running a jobs program for low-skilled Indians in Minneapolis noted that one thing those who kept their jobs had in common was a close personal relationship with their immediate supervisors. "For

[Indians], that one-to-one relationship is important. Perhaps more important than just getting a pay check."[13]

A support system of Indian employees to ease difficulties is helpful. Business executives who have worked closely with tribal Indians around the country stress the importance of Indian role models. "Installing well-trained Indian supervisors and managers is essential. If the Indians see one of their own in charge, they know they can master the job and meet production goals."[14]

The management of Control Data's plant in Bemidji, which was located there to ease the area's unemployment, reported that 22% of their 400 employees were Indian (1982). As a result of a strong training program and the tight economic situation, the company had had very little turnover.

Programs

Indian Employment Preference

Indians have preference in hiring and promotion by the BIA, the IHS (25 USC 472), Indian education programs, the programs that have been contracted to the tribes under the Indian Self-Determination Act, or by other employers when they receive federal money for programs to benefit Indians. Preferential treatment is also allowed in the employment of Indians in businesses on or near Indian reservations where preference has been publicly announced as an employment practice (43 USC 2000 [e 1]). Off the reservation and outside of other specific situations where Indian preference is authorized, federal, state, and several city ordinances prohibit discrimination in employment on the basis of race.

Affirmative Action

Many government units also encourage businesses to take affirmative action by seeking out members of disadvantaged groups. Minnesota requires state certification by the Department of Human Rights of an affirmative action plan for the employment of minorities, women, and the disabled by any firm that does more than $50,000 in business with any state agency. The certification and contracts can be revoked if a good faith effort to comply is not made (Mn. Stat. 363.073).

Affirmative action plans and their review is required of private companies doing business with the federal government under Executive Order 11246. The program is administered by the Office of Federal Contract Compliance, US Department of Labor. Some local governments also have affirmative action officers, plans, and programs. Minneapolis requires a business to file an affirmative action plan before it can sign a contract with the city.

Some units of government have affirmative action plans that include goals for hiring and promotion of protected classes. Changes have been made in the employment systems of government to eliminate the barriers to employment that have been identified by minorities. In the hiring process, several approved names are to be sent to the hiring authority (10 in state government) to give minorities a greater opportunity to be considered. Formal education and testing requirements that do not pertain to the job have been dropped.

Many of these efforts have fallen short of expectations. During a period of funding cuts and layoffs, minority workers, frequently those most recently hired, have been laid off because they lack seniority. It is estimated that the 1982 cutback in hourly factory workers at one of the area's major manufacturing companies removed 80–85% of the company's Indian employees.

A League of Women Voters member who has observed Minneapolis government pointed out several problems Indians have in obtaining city employment, in spite of affirmative action efforts. Information about job openings is obtained primarily through word of mouth from personal friends at city hall; with so few Indians employed, this networking system does not work for them. Affirmative action plans, goals, and percentages are usually in terms of "minorities" and do not address specific groups. Programs and efforts designed to reach the Black community are not as effective in reaching the Indian community. Several Indians have expressed the opinion that the city's affirmative action is a program to help Blacks, not Indians.

Job Service

Job Service, the state's employment program, is totally funded by federal funds from the US Department of Labor. Some counseling and testing is provided, but the agency primarily receives applications from those looking for work and makes referrals to those seeking employees. People must register with Job Service in order to receive unemployment compensation and some welfare program funds (Aid to Families with Dependent Children [AFDC], General Assistance, and food stamps). In 1981, 5,183 Indians statewide submitted applications. Most Indian applicants were low skilled and economically disadvantaged, the groups least likely to be referred or placed.

In the 1960s and early 1970s, Job Service programs were directed toward seeking out the hard-core unemployed and doing what was necessary to make them ready for jobs. Serious efforts were made to reach the unemployed with neighborhood offices, personnel placed in Indian centers, minority employees, and mobile units to serve the reservations.

Federal funding then became contingent on the number of placements. Programs to help Indians were discontinued because they were viewed as nonproductive. "The number of placements does not justify the expense." As there were cuts in federal funding, "marginal services such as Job Service representatives at the reservations and urban centers were cut."[15] By 1982, all of the outreach for Indians was gone. In the reservation areas, Indians must now travel to offices far distant, and transportation is often a problem.

Besides the inaccessibility of Job Service offices, other problems for Indians using the agency were pointed out in a 1980 study published by the department. Job Service needs more Indian employees and greater sensitivity to Indian culture. Interviewers recognizing Indians are apt to assign them to the laborer category even if the person is highly educated. They rarely ask Indians about other work experiences that would help in getting jobs. The bureaucratic system is also too cumbersome for Indians. From registration to referral may take four to five weeks, with three trips required: to register, to come back for testing, to come back for referral. "Indians can't wait that long."[16]

Other Employment and Training Programs

The tribes have been successful in combining job training and education programs from various funding sources with reservation employment needs. For instance, Red Lake has placed trainees in the police department and the schools; training programs assisted in the building of the Leech Lake Firewood Company and the Ojibwa Training Center on White Earth Reservation.

Federal Employment Assistance. In October 1983, CETA became the Job Training Partnership Act (JTPA). The purpose of the law is to provide job assistance to low-income, hard-to-employ people by training and developing the job skills that lead to permanent employment.

Until 1981, a major portion of the CETA program was in public service employment. This program was especially useful to reservations, where there are few employment opportunities outside of public service; the training and service programs both benefited by the combination. When CETA stopped the program, many of the opportunities ended.

JTPA focuses on private employment and directing people into high-technology growth fields, but there are concerns that the program's priorities will make it difficult to serve minorities. Indians generally lack the educational preparation to qualify for "high tech" training. Although tribal industries can be used as private employers, these opportunities are very limited.

Performance standards (and consequent funding) of JTPA are tied to the number of people placed in jobs. This incentive to focus on people who can be employed easily leads to fears that the program will "cream"— that is, concentrate on the best prospects and avoid the hard-core, low-income minorities and handicapped.

JTPA is administered by the US Department of Labor. Most of the program funds go to the state, which distributes them through service delivery areas. The employment agencies that serve major Indian populations include the Minnesota Concentrated Employment Program (MNCEP), which is active in 19 counties that include White Earth, Red Lake, and part of Leech Lake reservations; the Arrowhead Economic Opportunity Agency, including Bois Forte, Fond du Lac, Grand Portage, Mille Lacs, and part of Leech Lake reservations; and separate programs for Minneapolis, St. Paul, Duluth, Hennepin County, and Ramsey County.

This state-directed effort, when it was operating as CETA, served more than 2,000 Indians in 1981, or 4.5% of all those assisted. MNCEP had 2 Indians on its staff of 10 in 1982, and Indians were 26% of those helped. In 1981, Indians were 3.2% of those served in the St. Paul program, 1% in suburban Ramsey County, and only 0.8% of those in Minneapolis. A summer youth employment program, providing career information and job search assistance, operates on all reservations and for urban Indians.

A separate Indian program begun under CETA and continued under JTPA comes directly from Washington. It allows funding of community service employees in an amount linked to the Indian unemployment rate (using 1980 census or BIA labor force reports). This program was very significant in the past: at its height, in 1978, $6 million was used for Minnesota Indian programs. By 1982, cutbacks had reduced the amount to $2 million.

Funding for 1984 was distributed on the basis of the 1980 census employment figures, which led to great shifts in its distribution. All reservations had major cuts, ranging from 56% at Fond du Lac to 16% at White Earth. Urban programs, on the other hand, received significant increases—25% for Minneapolis, 27% for Duluth. In November 1983, a special census taken on Fond du Lac Reservation confirmed a much larger population than the 1980 census figure; consequently, program funding should be increased there in the future.

Indian organizations are involved in program administration. The MCT provides technical assistance for the programs. The American Indian Fellowship Association of Duluth administers the services at Grand Portage Reservation in addition to those at Duluth and at Superior, Wis. The Minneapolis American Indian Center handles the program for the four Sioux Communities and for the St. Paul American Indian Center.

In Hennepin County, the American Indian Opportunities Industrialization Center, Minneapolis, is responsible for the program. This center, with the first opportunities industrialization program for American Indians, was begun in 1981. Its program is designed to serve the hard-core unemployed. Students are first helped to achieve job readiness through a program dealing with work attitudes and personal problems. The center provides classroom training and actual work programs, including on-the-job training, community service employment, work experience, and a youth program that allows students still in school to work in the private sector.

The Native American Sector Initiative Program (Title VII), an Indian set-aside of the federal program focusing on private sector employment training, is used to train people in tribal businesses. In 1984, Leech Lake, White Earth, and Red Lake reservations and MAIC on behalf of the four Sioux Communities received grants on a competitive basis. Red Lake was funded for over $0.5 million, the largest award nationwide under the program.

State Program. In 1983, Minnesota began an emergency employment program under the Minnesota Emergency Employment Development Act (MEED), providing jobs for 26 weeks to the long-term unemployed. Applicants for General Assistance welfare who had marketable skills applied to the state's Job Service for either job training or placement under the MEED program; payment similar to General Assistance was provided until employment was found.

MEED jobs were to be 40% in the private sector, 60% public employment. Private sector employers paid back to the state 70% of the employee cost. If the employee was retained longer than 26 weeks, the obligation diminished; it was forgiven if the employee was retained for a year beyond the initial six months. Funds were distributed for the MEED program through the service delivery areas, according to the number of unemployed people in each area. White Earth Reservation, for instance, was to have 27 employment slots; Leech Lake was assigned 23.

BIA Programs. The BIA funds two employment programs, which are administered through the tribes. The major one in terms of dollars spent has been the Vocational Training Program (see chap. 9). The BIA Area Office estimates that about 65% of the students completed training and 60% were placed in 1981; the program assisted about 150 students from the MCT, 40 from Red Lake, and 3 from the Sioux Communities.

The other program, Direct Employment Assistance, helps in moving reservation Indians and their families and providing the additional assistance needed to get the family established in an off-reservation location where employment opportunities are better. Help can be provided for up to two years, after which the person is no longer eligible for BIA assistance. In 1981, about 100 Indians were helped in Minnesota, most of whom moved to the Twin Cities.

Senior Community Service Employment Program. Senior Community Service Employment is a federal program under the Health and Human Service Department that provides up to 20 hours of work a week at minimum wage for people 55 and older. The MCT and its separate reservations had 18 employees in this program in 1983. The Upper Midwest American Indian Center in Minneapolis employed five seniors under the program, with the funding channeled through the Urban League.

Work Incentive Program. AFDC welfare recipients are required to register and participate in job placement programs unless they are under 16 years of age, over 16 but still in school, or caring for children under six years of age. The Work Incentive Program (WIN) provides a full range of job-training and job-seeking services to help AFDC recipients get into nonsubsidized, permanant jobs in private employment. The program has been oversubscribed, and recent funding cuts have closed it in several counties.

For 1981, 1,591 Indians in Minnesota had registered for the WIN program, 4.7% of all registrants. In the Minneapolis Area WIN (Hennepin, Scott, Carver, and Anoka counties), 8% (443) of the registrants were Indian.

Project Search. Project Search at Heart of the Earth Survival School, Minneapolis, is a program that helps individuals to evaluate their interests and skills in relation to work and to explore careers through the use of computer data about jobs and attitudes. Designed to assist those enrolled in other training, it is funded by $123,000 from the Indian Education Act, Title IV. The three-year program began in 1983.

Summary

"Minorities still face discrimination, are generally less educated and skilled and experience higher unemployment rates than whites. . . . The situation for Indians is worse, complicated by cultural difficulties."[17] The first need is jobs, but if the massive unemployment of Indians is to be corrected, the problem must be approached from several directions.

Economic development and employment sources not dependent on government are needed in reservation areas to provide jobs. Much more education and training for employment is needed. Beyond this, the help with personal needs and assistance in developing work skills that are often necessary should be recognized as training costs. Successful Indian role models in business, networking support systems, and the building of close interpersonal relationships with co-workers are all proven techniques that lead to success in employment. The staggering level of Indian unemployment demands attention.

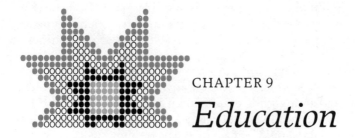

CHAPTER 9

Education

People say to me, "What's wrong with your kids that they come to our schools and drop out?" I answer, "What's wrong with your schools that they're causing our kids to drop out?"[1]

History

From the very beginning of white contact with Indians, education was seen as the mechanism for "civilizing" and Christianizing the "savages." As stated by the commissioner of Indian affairs in 1899, "This [education] policy . . . is based on the well-known inferiority of the great mass of Indians in religion, intelligence, morals, and home life."[2] The challenge for education was put very bluntly in 1818, as the House Committee on Indian Affairs debated what was to become the first federal statute on Indian education: "In the present state of our country, one of two things seems to be necessary; either that those sons of the forest should be moralized or exterminated."[3]

Education of Indians in Minnesota followed the national pattern. Missionaries came to convert Indians, and they also offered education. An Ojibway spelling book had been prepared by 1833, and teaching missionaries were active in the state.[4] Among the Dakota, two Pond brothers arrived in 1834 and devised a written language; over the next

122

several years, they prepared grammar books and the first Dakota dictionary.[5]

Most of the treaties signed in Minnesota included provisions for education and the teaching of agricultural skills. At first there were day schools, but boarding schools—which could remove children from their home atmosphere and totally regiment their lives—were seen as much more effective.

Boarding Schools

Boarding schools dominated Indian education into the 1920s, and memory of them continues to influence Indian attitudes today. They were operated on and off the reservations by the government and by religious denominations, with student tuitions paid by the federal government. Many Minnesota Indians were sent to the government schools in the Dakotas.

The children were taken at an early age, six or even younger. Absence from home could last the full six years of elementary school. They were forbidden to speak their language, their hair was cut, and native ways were not allowed. It was intended that all Indian culture be replaced with white values and Christian philosophy. Congress made the education compulsory in 1893, denying rations and subsistence to parents who did not send their children to school.[6] The education system, designed to destroy Indian ways, was paid for by federal appropriations and by the Indians themselves from the proceeds of treaty sales of their lands.

Manual training education was stressed. Schools devoted half a day to classes and the other half to domestic or industrial work. For girls, the schools provided "mental and moral training . . . to give them a christian and polite education and to teach them all that is necessary for a woman to know of housekeeping and such like female duties."[7] Student labor was used in the schools and on the farms connected with them, keeping operating costs low. It is questionable whether the manual work had much educational value, and the drudgery often led to hatred of the experience.

By the 1920s, the boarding school concept began to come under attack. The federal boarding schools had suffered from serious neglect, and funding was woefully inadequate. The Meriam survey in 1928 found them to be overcrowded; the sanitation inadequate; the children undernourished, overworked and severely disciplined; and the staff unaccredited and poorly paid.[8] In Minnesota, federal boarding schools were phased out at this time. St. Mary's Mission Boarding School at Red

Lake changed to a day school in 1940, and the White Earth mission school closed in 1945.

Minnesota Public Schools

Public schools in the state had been teaching Indian children as early as 1899, with the federal government paying tuition. By 1926, the change in Indian education responsibility had become obvious: 65% of the state's 3,527 Ojibway students were in Minnesota public schools, 825 (23%) were in government day and boarding schools, and 425 (12%) were in the two mission schools.[9] The education of Indian students became fully a state responsibility in Minnesota in 1936, under a contract between the state and the BIA as authorized by the federal Johnson-O'Malley Act.

The legacy of the federal policies and programs is "a deep-seated mistrust of education from boarding school days. There is no more emotional an issue. Indians fear that schools will brainwash the children and rob them of their heritage."[10] Even though many of the overtly coercive aspects of education have been eliminated, "American education has not lost its basic assimilative objectives."[11]

Indians within the state system are treated as are any other students, with the same standards and funding. In addition, the federal government continues to provide extra funding because of the special needs and unique Indian status. Several state and federal programs are targeted to help with special problems that may have unusually high Indian representation; for example, federal Title I funds for special educational needs associated with poverty and additional state money to schools with children from AFDC homes. The state has put additional resources into upgrading Indian education, including funds for pilot programs to bring Indian culture and language into the full school curriculum, programs to encourage Indian students to continue their education, and scholarships for postsecondary and graduate study.

The state's Indian educators have provided leadership in developing curriculum materials, working to improve the public schools, originating the alternative Indian school, and successfully operating tribal schools. These are major accomplishments.

In contrast with 1945, when there were eight Indian high school graduates in the entire state, in 1981 the state's public schools reported 503;[12] the MCT also identified 24 from alternative and tribal schools.[13] The 1980 census reported that 55% of adult Indians were high school graduates, up from 32% in 1970. Although the 1970 census found that only 2% of Indian adults were college graduates, in 1980 the percentage had more than doubled to 5%.

Measurements of Indian Educational Problems

The 1980 census sample data showed that 55% of Indians over 25 years were high school graduates, a figure 18% lower than for the state's general population. Twenty-one percent of Indians had not gone beyond eighth grade. The 730 Indians with 16 or more years of school (college graduate level) were 5% of the state's Indian population, while 17% of non-Indians had a similar education level. Table 13, based on a hypothetical sample of 1,000 Indian and 1,000 white students, shows the differences in the school experiences of the two groups.

Counting Indian Students

Counts of Indian students in Minnesota vary, depending on the source of the data. By state law, schools take a "sight count" in October of each year that is reported to the Minnesota Civil Rights Information

Table 13. Indicators of Problems in Indian Education
(Per 1,000 students)

Indicator	Indian Students	All Students	Ratio
In one year:			
Would drop out (7–12)	108	26	4.00:1
Would be suspended (7–12)	193	70	2.75:1
Would be labeled:			
Seriously emotionally disturbed (K-12)	11	5	2.20:1
Specific learning disabled, including special learning and behavior problems	61	43	1.50:1
Would be in:			
Advanced math (7–12)	79	117	0.66:1
Advanced science (7–12)	39	77	0.50:1
Gifted program (K-12)	18	37	0.50:1
On a given day, would not be in:			
Elementary school	80	60	1.33:1
Secondary school	130	80	1.63:1
Urban secondary school	180	90	2.00:1

Note: Based on 1981 data, except figures for absences (1977–78).
Sources: MINCRIS, *Summary,* 4, 6–7, 10; MDE, *Indian Needs Assessment,* 1977–78, III:18–19.

System (MINCRIS) along with a great deal of information about programs and practices. The data are used to monitor compliance with various antidiscrimination laws. Information is not received from private, tribal, or alternative schools.

The count for the federal Indian education program, available to all schools with more than 10 Indian students (Title IV), is done each spring by Indian people in the schools who are knowledgeable about the Indian community. The 1980 census sample data count has information on students in kindergarten through twelfth grades. The census total of Indian students in the state was 11,516. In 1981, the MINCRIS total from 435 school districts was 10,972, and the Title IV count was 9,786 from 53 school districts.

The League of Women Voters analyzed October 1981 MINCRIS data from 17 school districts in northern Minnesota on or near reservations and containing 33% of the state's Indian students,[14] from the three big city districts (Minneapolis, St. Paul, and Duluth) with 27% of the Indian student population, and from state totals. The analysis showed that the Indian student population is growing, which means the lower grades have greater numbers and a larger percentage of Indians.

The *Indian Needs Assessment*, a study done for the state Department of Education in 1977–78, found similar age distributions in the districts selected for study. The report also noted that the non-Indian population was just the opposite, increasing in numbers as grade levels increased.[15]

Dropouts and Suspensions

The needs assessment study reported very high dropout statistics. Of every 100 Indian students starting seventh grade, fewer than 50 rural students graduated; only 40 urban students graduated. When student files were examined, the dropout records were found to be quite inaccurate: actual numbers probably exceeded those reported by the schools.[16] School district reports to the Minnesota Department of Education for 1982–83 showed even higher Indian dropout percentages statewide.

The Minnesota Pupil Fair Dismissal Act of 1974 discourages suspensions and directs schools to find alternatives. Cass Lake School District was investigated by the State Board of Education for an excessive number of suspended Indian students in 1979–80. The board ruled that the school's actions constituted racial discrimination. "A two to one ratio of suspensions is disproportionate by a wide margin, and violates the Civil Rights Act, Title VI."[17] The school subsequently remedied the situation.

The reports to MINCRIS for October 1981 showed that 921 individual Indian students were suspended in Minnesota during 1980–81, 19% of all Indian secondary students. The 17 northern reservation school districts were the main users of suspension, having suspended 500 Indian students. These districts had 14.5% Indian students in grades 7 through 12, but over 28% of those suspended were Indian. This figure is very close to the two-to-one ratio found unacceptable by the State Board of Education in 1980.

Attendance

School attendance dropped as students got older, but the drop was greater for Indians. The *Indian Needs Assessment* found that students in grades 7 through 12 attended 92% of the time, Indian students only 87%.[18] Minneapolis Indian student attendance was lower, 74%, with tenth graders in school only 67% of the time.[19] It was also in the tenth grade that the greatest number of Indian students dropped out.

Nonattendance poses great problems for teaching, and a mobile life-style contributes to the problem. In a three-month period, Minneapolis schools recorded at least 300 children who moved on and off the school census list.[20] The needs assessment found that "Indians were significantly more mobile than were non-Indians, and that . . . mobility increases where there are larger concentrations of Indian students."[21]

Measurements of School Achievement

"Indian students score lower than non-Indian students in all tests at all grade levels," according to findings of the *Indian Needs Assessment*, which looked at 25 school districts.[22] To be more accountable for educating minorities, the Minneapolis Public Schools have made standardized test results by race available to the public.[23] The elementary level tests showed significantly lower language skills than the national norm for Indian students and an even greater discrepancy when compared with those of white students in the Minneapolis system. There was a further drop by the tenth grade.

On the other hand, in mathematics Indian students were at or close to national norms, and this was maintained through tests given in the eighth grade. By the tenth grade, however, there was a large drop. Although the 1981–82 scores were low, the report indicated that there had been improvement over similar tests taken two years previously.

Special Education Programs

"Overall, it appears that what is more clearly a cultural problem of majority dominance and minority alienation is being treated as a behavior or learning problem."[24] According to the needs assessment, one out of eight Indian students was in a special education program, while only one of 20 non-Indians was. MINCRIS reported similar figures: 1,299 Indian students were in special education, 12% of all Indian students in Minnesota in 1981.[25]

Special education programs for the mentally retarded, physically handicapped, or speech-impaired had the same proportion of Indian and non-Indan students as regular classes. A significantly higher number of Indian students were labeled "learning disabled" or "special learning and behavior problems."

Middle-ear infections are an unusually severe problem among Indian children throughout the state, and they can result in temporary and permanent hearing loss. Poor school achievement may result if the teacher is unaware of the problem. A 1977–78 study in Minneapolis documented that Wechsler IQ verbal scores were significantly lower than performance IQ scores among Indian students. The authors speculated that middle-ear infections and subsequent hearing loss may be responsible for the differences.[26]

Major Problems in Indian Education

Following is a look at possible reasons why the state's education system is doing such a poor job reaching Indian students.

Clash of Cultures

Indian traditions, values, language, and culture are all markedly different from those of the dominant culture. Many parents and students see as the goal of the schools to turn out people who will adapt to a predominantly white, middle-class society and be assimilated into it.

There are Indian parents who do not believe that the education presently available in the public schools is desirable or essential to the well-being of their children, and they do not encourage their children to participate. "We want our children to attend school with their own . . . [to] grow up together so that their Indian values are reinforced and those values will remain intact."[27]

The clash of cultures and insensitivity to Indian values has been the common experience of all Indians to a greater or lesser degree as they have gone through the education system. Competition is a school-honored value that is especially troublesome to Indians.

The instructional process itself is alien to an Indian's approach to learning. According to the director of Indian education for the Minneapolis Public Schools, time and space concepts are different for Indians. A school curriculum is organized on building-block units. Step one is taught, mastered, and tested, then step two is taught, and so forth. Mastery is needed at each step of the way. Indians learn by absorbing everything, but the components may not be put together until many years later.[28]

The distrust of education also extends at times to the Indians who have become professionals and are giving leadership to the Indian communities. "Educated, middle-class Indian people are made to feel apologetic about their education, and in some undefined way, are made to feel less Indian because of their education."[29]

But, paradoxically, Indians also know that they need education. The MCT requires its top administrators to have college degrees, and the economic development plans of the reservations give high priority to having trained Indian administrators. Communities strongly support their students in the education process: dinners and publicity recognize graduates, whether from Head Start or medical school.

According to an Indian educator, "If you want to be corrupted by white society and its values you can be. And if you don't want to be, you're not. It's a balancing problem, integrating the contradictory experiences of growing up Indian in a white world. . . . Chuck Robertson calls it 'a well-adjusted schizophrenia'. . . . If education isn't something people can undergo and still remain Indian, we're up a creek. . . . To be a doctor you have to go to med school."[30]

Poverty and Parental Support

An Indian educator lamented, "In the 70s . . . we said education will solve the 'Indian problem.' We've made a tremendous effort to bring children to school, to develop a curriculum relating to culture, to provide more peer models for them. In the meantime, people were still starving, their families were still splitting up. There was no employment. The anticipation that education alone will heal the Indian community's distress allows us to blame the Indian people when it does not work."[31]

The correlation of poverty and poorer educational results is well documented for all races. Poverty often means that parents are burdened by lack of everyday needs; they don't have the energy to spend with children and to provide a stimulating, educationally supportive environment. They may have limited education themselves. The child, seeing no jobs available, may find little purpose in getting an education.

A very high proportion of Indian students in Minnesota's schools come from low-income families. The *Indian Needs Assessment* found a correlation between low income and poorer academic achievement.[32] Enormous social problems that are not being dealt with adequately impinge on the child's performance and attendance. The school is expected to have answers and to solve all problems.

Not everyone, however, believes in "socioeconomic determinism"—the school's expectation that low socioeconomic status means low achievement. The Minneapolis Urban Coalition points out that schools try to avoid responsibility for failing to teach minority students by blaming outside factors.[33] Roger Buffalohead has stated, "They appear now ready to blame the victim for not being educated, to say that the parents are bad. There is no indication that achievement results will be tied to teacher accountability."[34]

Control of Education

School district boundaries, dividing reservations among several different districts, make it very difficult to elect Indians to school boards. The 1,250 students at White Earth Reservation are divided among seven districts; they are the racial minority in all but two elementary schools. None of the other schools has an Indian enrollment higher than 25%.[35] As decisions affecting educational programs, such as closing schools, are made by each school district, Indians feel they have no voice in what will happen to their children.

Many districts are facing the need to close schools and reduce staff. In the sparsely settled, rural areas, it is a difficult step to take. The ensuing busing takes the children far from the supporting community. Small Indian elementary schools are vulnerable. The White Earth Elementary School was closed in 1982; Naytahwaush on the White Earth Reservation and Grand Portage Elementary School may face closing in the near future.

Where there are sufficient numbers of Indians, voting power has been used to influence school board elections and make the school system more responsive to Indian needs. This occurred in the Cass Lake School District in 1980 with very positive results for the children, the school system, and the whole community.

The MCT has recommended that the State Board of Education look at the geographical location of Indian population and the percentage of school board members and "provide feasible options which may insure equitable representation of Indian people on local school boards."[36]

Because in the past federal funds targeted for Indians were not used for them, some programs now require a large degree of Indian control. Elected groups—local Indian education committees—may administer the federal Johnson-O'Malley program for Indian students in public schools independent of the school administration. In other programs, such as Title IV of the Indian Education Act, Indians have a major voice in deciding how the money is to be used (see Federal Legislation below).

Curriculum

Incorporation of Indian history and culture into the curricula of all schools, funded by local monies and not dependent on special categorical aid, has been a major Indian goal. Some state and federal funding has made possible special programs. Supplemental units have been written, bibliographies prepared, and language classes begun. Yet, very little local money has gone into programs for Indian students, and the Indian programs have not been maintained when federal funding ended. Until each school district rewrites its curriculum throughout the grades, little will happen.

A 1980–81 study of Indians in the St. Paul school system found that half of the 60 Indian parents surveyed were dissatisfied with the way the schools taught their children about their cultural background. When five Indian students who had dropped out were interviewed, four said they would have stayed in school if the curriculum had included Indian culture. The interviewer commented, "Nothing in school related to their culture whatsoever. It was sort of tragic to hear that history or social studies had nothing to offer these students."[37]

A few signs of change are encouraging. The state-funded American Indian Language and Culture Education program has brought about curriculum changes and has exposed substantial numbers of non-Indians to Indian culture in the schools where it operates. During the summer of 1983, the Minneapolis School District for the first time incorporated Indian culture units that had been prepared by the Indian Education Section into the ongoing district curriculum revision.

Textbooks

Evaluations of textbooks indicate that, with a few exceptions, they perpetuate stereotypes of the savage; the vanishing American Indian; or the lazy, shiftless, drunken Indian. "How can you teach about the United States without Indians? Now there is nothing taught about who they were, what they valued, how they lived, the speeches of Sitting Bull and Black Hawk. There is a lot of material now, but it is not in the school system."[38]

Materials that present Indians in highly offensive ways continue to be used in the schools. "An example of an offensive stereotype is author and illustrator Maurice Sendak's drawing of an alligator wearing an Indian headdress with a feather and carrying a tomahawk and sacred peace pipe. That would be like an alligator carrying a Christian cross."[39]

Lack of Indian School Personnel

In all categories except teacher aides, Indians were underrepresented among the state's public school employees in 1981 (table 14). The lowest percentage of Indian employees was classroom teachers. The 17 Indian administrators in the state were a sharp drop from the 28 employed in 1980.[40]

The percentage of teacher aides was almost double the Indian student percentage, which reflects the use of programs funded to serve Indians and having Indian community involvement. Very few Indians were employed in the less skilled or unskilled positions—only one-third to one-half of the Indian student percentage.

Many schools indicate that they try hard to recruit Indian teachers but that being few in number, the teachers can command more money elsewhere. Indian teachers may also be reluctant to accept token minority positions in districts where they feel a lack of administrative support for Indian education. Programs that have Indian preference in hiring are more successful in locating Indians. Of the 51 professionals hired to set up and run the state's Chapter 312 Indian language and culture programs in 1979–80, 46 were Indian. All of the other 35 employees, including staff, aides, and coordinators, were Indian.[41]

Certification of Indian Teachers

There is a shortage of Minnesota-certified teachers skilled in Indian languages and knowledgeable about Indian culture. Chapter 312 established a process for "eminence" certification, licensing teachers with competence in those areas (Mn. Stat. 126–49). A college degree is not mandatory.

Hamline University provides a two-week course in classroom management and other teaching skills to help with the certification. Red School House provides a practice teaching opportunity. The testing for competency in Indian language and culture is done by each tribe, which certifies a teacher as qualified to teach for that tribe. The Minnesota Board of Teaching records those certified, who then have standing equivalent to teachers with general licenses. Fewer than 50 had been certified by fall 1982.

Table 14. Indians in the Schools as Students and Personnel

Position	Minnesota Indians		17 Districts in Northern Reservation Areas, Percentage Indian
	Number	Percentage	
Students	10,972	1.5%	17.1%
Administration/principals	17	0.6	4.3
Classroom teachers	94	0.2	2.3
Other professionals	45	0.8	10.7
Teacher aides	115	2.4	31.3
Less or unskilled workers	77	0.5	8.4

Source: MINCRIS data for Oct. 1981.

Teacher and Counselor Attitudes toward Indians

Since the mid-1970s, all Minnesota teachers have had instruction in human relations. Many in-service programs have been held to increase sensitivity to special needs; schools with Indian students have had extra funding and personnel to focus attention on the great unmet needs of these students. Yet, the problem of insensitivity by school personnel persists.

A national study of teachers of Indian children found that "most had never visited an Indian's home but they were positive the home background was undesirable."[42] A needs assessment taken in the Red Lake School District produced teacher comments that the teachers did not like visitors, did not like the PTA.[43]

An Indian attorney with two children, one with Indian-looking features and the other looking more non-Indian, found that the Indian-looking child was having problems in school while the other was not. "Some teachers communicate that they don't see the need for Indians to attend school."[44]

Attempts to provide Indian culture training for mainstream teachers have been dropped. Moorhead State University and Concordia College, Moorhead, no longer place student teachers on a reservation. Bemidji State University students practice teach on a reservation by student request only. The MCT has recommended that all teachers on or near an Indian reservation be required to take special Indian culture classes.[45]

Non-Indian counselors are seen as limiting rather than challenging Indian students. "Indian students stated quite forcefully that they would not visit school counselors to discuss personal problems at home or problems with teachers or other school staff" was the finding in a St. Paul study.[46] The responses of MCT higher education scholarship recipients showed that over 80% were given no information about vocational choices, choosing a college best suited to their needs, or what to expect in college, nor were they helped in getting accepted by a college.[47] There were only six Indian counselors in the state in 1981.

Effects of Desegregation Laws

Segregation has been used as a way of denying opportunity to minorities, and the country has benefited from those laws passed to prevent it; however, forced desegregation is seen as a problem for Indian students and Indian education programs. Keeping Indian students together helps them feel more comfortable and secure with their peers; the school system can concentrate more of its resources on Indian study materials, and Indian programs can be more effectively targeted.

It is exceedingly difficult to involve parents and community people when the children must be bused out of their area. Indian parents are strongly opposed to forced desegregation. In Duluth, a parent committee was successful in convincing the school board to refrain from widely dispersing Indian students.

In the Minneapolis school desegregation court cases, the school board asked permission to increase minority student percentages, particularly to increase concentrations of Indian students. The request was rejected; however, the issue of possibly exempting Indians from school desegregation laws was not specifically addressed (see *Booker v. Special School District No. 1*, appendix C).

The state law on desegregation requires that no school building have more than 15% above the total minority population for that grade level in the district. Schools with nearly 100% Indian enrollment (Red Lake, Pine Point, Nett Lake) do not have trouble with the law because the school districts have a similarly high Indian population.

Tribally controlled schools are considered "not segregated." The Office of Civil Rights (Department of Health, Education and Welfare) held in 1975, "Tribes may exercise powers of self-government, including providing for the education of their members, and may do so without running afoul of Title VI, Civil Rights Act of 1964."[48]

Government Responsibilities for Educating Indians

Sources of School Revenue

The major portion of public school funding, 55%, came from the state in 1981.[49] Local districts, on the average, raised 40% of their expenditures, and about 5% came from federal sources.

The financing of schools in the 17 northern districts with high Indian enrollment varied considerably from the state average, in part due to the financial impact of Indian students. Because of large amounts of tax-exempt federal, state, county, and Indian trust lands, the locally raised portion was only about 25%. Federal impact aid, paid to districts in lieu of taxes, accounted for 9% of revenues to the northern school districts. The state average amount of impact aid received was less than 1%.

The northern districts also received much higher than state average state funding for having large numbers of AFDC families (distributed on the assumption that these children are more difficult to educate)—8% of their funding, compared with 2% statewide.

Specific Indian education programs, federal and state, provided an additional 3% to the funding of the northern districts. The state also funded "sparsity aid" for districts with large areas and few children. School lunches for low-income students were also subsidized.

Indian children bring a great deal of money into some school districts. Considering the state's poor educational results with Indian students, one can question whether the money is really being used to meet targeted needs of Indian students.

Tribal Administration

Increasingly, tribes are running their own tribal schools (also called "contract schools") to meet special needs unmet in the public schools. Each of the seven Chippewa reservations has an education department and director to deal with all aspects of education, from preschool through postsecondary. They work with school districts, local Indian education committees (LIECs), and parent advisory committees in providing training and technical assistance.

Federal Legislation

Johnson-O'Malley Act and Other BIA Programs. Historically, the Johnson-O'Malley Act (JOM; 25 USC 52) has been the major federal program affecting Indian education; it was under this act that the state contracted for Indian education in the 1930s. Although no longer the major source of federal funds, in 1982 JOM provided $764,000 to an estimated 5,228 eligible students.

The money is spent for supplements to basic education, including home-school coordinators; teacher aides; tutoring programs; and special student needs, such as purchase of school supplies, athletic or band and orchestra expenses, and other costs that parents are unable to bear. To qualify, a student must have at least one-fourth Indian ancestry and be a tribal member.

None of the funds go to school districts; they are all administered by tribal governments or LIECs. About 35–40% of the total funding, however–$286,000 in 1981–[50] is spent through the schools. Each reservation handles its own program, working with the school districts on that reservation, except for Bois Forte, Grand Portage, and Leech Lake. Their programs are administered by the MCT, which also handles the JOM funds for the Indian tribal and alternative schools. The LIEC conducts an annual needs assessment to decide how the funds are to be spent; no funds can be spent without LIEC approval. There is Indian preference in hiring and the purchasing of materials.

The BIA also provides direct funding for school construction on Red Lake Reservation. In 1983, an elementary school was being constructed at Ponemah; a new high school was to be built at Red Lake in 1984.

Title IV of the Indian Education Act. Title IV (PL 92–318, 1972) has made it possible for Indian students throughout the state to learn some of their language and something about their culture. "Grandmother smiled when she heard my son speaking Ojibway. It was something she had never expected to see, speaking Ojibway again. I was never taught by my parents and grandparents because they didn't want me to be beaten."[51]

Title IV, the largest program in Indian education, is operated by the US Department of Education. During 1982, $3,544,000 was allocated in Minnesota, $1,855,000 to 57 school districts serving 12,199 students, $330,000 to two Indian-controlled schools, and $1,256,000 for five pilot projects.[52] Title IV reaches most Indian students in the state. To qualify, they must be enrolled in a tribe or have at least one grandparent who is enrolled. A school must have 10 or more Indian students to have a program.

The programs are conducted through the schools, with Indian parents assessing needs and deciding how the money is to be spent. Committees that are at least half Indian and including elected parents, a secondary student, and teachers oversee the programs. Major uses of the funds are Indian language and culture programs, counseling, tutoring, and meeting special student needs. The programs must be totally supplemental and for qualifying Indians only. If they are remedial, they cannot take the place of Title I programs, which must also be used. There is Indian preference in hiring and the purchasing of materials.

Schools usually combine Title IV and JOM funds, which are used for similar supplemental purposes; the same LIEC may be used, but it is not required. The programs differ on who is an Indian (Title IV is much more inclusive), when the fiscal year begins (October 1 or July 1), and paperwork required. The Cloquet School District, for example, received $17,000 from JOM funds and $42,000 in Title IV funds in 1982. It had two LIECs, one for each program.[53]

Who is to be counted as an Indian and the proof required have been the major controversies over the Title IV program. The definition of "Indian" was intentionally made broad to provide Indian culture and identity to Indian children no longer associated with reservations and in need of help in learning about their heritage.

In recent years the program has been changed to require much more proof of qualification, resulting in substantial drops in the numbers served. The drop statewide from 1982 to 1983 was 20%. Forms must be signed by the parent or guardian stating the name of the tribal member who makes the student qualified and giving the tribe enrollment number. "The form is very legal looking. Parents don't want to sign it. There is anger and frustration that 'now we have to prove we are Indian.' "[54]

The grandparent may have been enrolled, but no one has been since and nobody knows the details. Only about 3% of St. Paul's 950–1,000 Indian students have enrollment numbers.[55] With large numbers of children adopted or in foster care, enrollment details may not be known. The Anoka School District estimates that one of five of its Indian students is either in foster care or adopted. One district with 25 or 30 Indian children had no Indian parents to serve on the parent committee because the children were all living out of Indian homes.[56]

Impact Aid. The impact aid program (PL 81–874), helps school districts that have large numbers of students whose parents live or work on federal land, including reservations. The school qualifies if it has more than 3% qualifying children, equaling 10 or more. If the school has 20% or more Indian students, an additional 25% in aid money is provided. The funding level is meant to be comparable to what the state and local effort would have been if the land were subject to taxation.

In 1981, Nett Lake Elementary District received one-third of the school's funds from impact aid; Red Lake, one-fourth.[57] During 1982, four school districts with the highest concentration of Indian students from the White Earth Reservation received nearly $500,000 from impact aid.[58]

The funding goes to the school districts and is not earmarked for special Indian programs, but Indians must be consulted on its use. The money goes with the child who qualifies, and it is available for tribal schools.

Title I. Title I of the Elementary and Secondary Education Act, administered by the Department of Education, is targeted to children who need compensatory assistance in reading and math and who live in areas where family incomes are below the average. Supplemental teachers and tutors are provided; the funds cannot be used to replace other funding. The program provides large amounts of money to districts throughout the state.

Many Indian children are eligible. In the schools studied for the *Indian Needs Assessment*, 30% of the Indian chidren qualified for Title I funds, compared with 11% of the non-Indian children.[59]

Other Federal Legislation. Title VII of the Elementary and Secondary Education Act provides funds for a bilingual and bicultural program to help school districts whose students come from an environment in which a language other than English has had a significant impact on the level of English language proficiency. In 1983, the program provided Ojibway language instruction at the Red Lake alternative school (K-6) and at St. Mary's Mission School.

The US Department of Agriculture provides commodities and funding for free school lunches for children of low-income families; the state also participates. Most Indian students qualify for the program. Minneapolis has an additional free breakfast program in areas with high concentrations of low-income children.

State Programs

The State Board of Education adopted a policy in 1982 to encourage the development of programs and services to meet the unique education needs of Indians; to involve Indians in the total educational program; to incorporate Indian language, literature, and heritage into the general curricula; and to provide viable programs that will permit Indian people to compete and excel in life areas of their choice.

The Indian Education Section of the Minnesota Department of Education administers the state Indian programs, American Indian Language and Culture Education Act (Chapter 312), Post Secondary Preparation Project, Indian Adult Basic Education (administered from Duluth), and Minnesota Indian Education Scholarship Program (administered from Bemidji). It assists with the Social Work Aide training program that has been used in combination with Title IV and JOM programs to meet special Indian needs. Indian advisory groups are a strong part of the state program. Separate task forces advise the State Board of Education on the scholarship program and Chapter 312.

Chapter 312. Under Chapter 312 (Mn. Stat. 126.45), the state funded 12 pilot projects in 1983 and an additional 2 in 1984 that were designed to make Indian language and culture an integral part of mainstream curricula. The programs extend from preschool through high school, some during the school year and others in the summers only. They are in reservation area and urban schools, both alternative and public.

A 1981 evaluation noted, "Because of Chapter 312 . . . seven high schools offer Ojibwe or Dakota for credit; curriculum development has added over 60 units in ten school districts; several hundred teachers have participated in in-service sessions on curriculum, history, culture, and . . . several thousand children have been exposed to positive cultural experiences."[60] Funding has been set at $547,000 for 1984 and $568,000 for 1985.

Other Special Indian Education Legislation. The state appropriates small amounts of money ($18,000-$40,000 in 1981) for five schools with high concentrations of Indian students: the elementary schools at Pine Point, Nett Lake, and Grand Portage; and the schools at Mahnomen and Red Lake. In 1979, when JOM basic support was eliminated, the state picked up the cost with the intent to phase it out as other funds became available. In the absence of other funds, the legislature has appropriated $163,000 for each of fiscal years 1984 and 1985. Some additional aid was provided to Pine Point in 1983 to help in debt reduction.

Pine Point has been a unique Indian school in terms of receiving state legislative attention. When the Indian elementary school was slated to become a part of the Park Rapids School District in 1970, the Indians requested that it become an experimental school—an Indian-run alternative school. Permission was granted and renewed, with some additional state funding, until 1981. With a declining enrollment at the school, costs had become excessive. Legislation in 1981 allowed the Indian community to vote on the school's future. A large majority voted to keep it a community school, a special school district with mandatory enrollment administered by the White Earth tribal government.

Specific Programs

Preschool

The 1980 census sample data showed that 694 Indians (5% of the Indian student population of the state) were enrolled in nursery schools.

Early youth programs have been well supported by the Indian community in northern Minnesota.

Early Childhood and Family Education. A state pilot program, Early Childhood and Family Education, assists young children's development by helping parents to provide learning experiences. Three of the programs operate on White Earth and Leech Lake reservations, and at Nay Ah Shing School on the Mille Lacs Reservation. The Mille Lacs program focuses on child-parent activities, providing parenting resources, educational toys, and home visits. It is a part of that reservation's comprehensive early childhood program, along with three age groups of day care and the Head Start Program.

Head Start. The major program for three to five year olds is Head Start, which is based on helping a child develop by building a positive self-image. It prepares the disadvantaged child for school academically, physically (through medical checkups and improved nutrition), and socially. It fosters parental interest and involvement through home visits by teachers, use of mothers as aides, and establishment of parent policy-making committees.

The MCT provides training, technical assistance, and supervision on its six reservations and Red Lake. Funding is from the Indian and Migrant Program Division, Department of Health and Human Services. Leech Lake RBC supplements its program of 10 Head Start centers (180 students in 1982–83) with $50,000 in tribal funds. White Earth operates four centers.

At Red Lake, where the program is coupled with Chapter 312 funding, special techniques are used to develop early reading skills. The results have been very encouraging: tests showed a gain of 18 months in mental ability and 14 months in physical skills in the 9-month school year 1981–82. These results have remained constant through several years of the program. Although designed for 125 children, the Red Lake program is so well received that there were 184 children enrolled in 1983–84.

Fond du Lac started a Head Start program in 1983, replacing its own Ojibway Preschool, a three-generation sharing program begun in 1977. The tribe provides half of the funding of Head Start from bingo revenue.

Head Start programs are not consistently reaching other Indian children. The Community Action Program is supposed to fund Head Start services. The Lower Sioux Indian Community has Head Start available at Morton, but the Shakopee-Mdewakanton Sioux Community has no program and the Goodhue-Rice-Wabasha Citizens' Action Council has not served Prairie Island Indian Community children for the past three years.

In the urban areas, Duluth concentrates on Ojibway culture with Chapter 312 funds in a preschool program. Little Earth of United Tribes housing complex in Minneapolis has a Head Start program as well as day care after school.

Programs in the Schools

A great deal of new curriculum has been written for use in the schools (K-12), and materials are available for purchase by school districts. Extensive work has been done by Minneapolis, St. Paul, Duluth, and Red Lake school districts; the other schools involved in Chapter 312 programs; and the Red School House, St. Paul, through Indian Country Press. The MCT is publishing tribally written histories of the reservations and other educational materials, including a publication on Indian women funded by the Women's Education Equity Act, US Department of Education.

To expand the Indian aide programs, some districts have linked them with special education, using 40% Indian funds and 60% from the special education programs. In 1983, 53 people were involved in the Indian Social Work Aides Program. Part of the program provides community outreach to promote understanding of programs for these students. Outreach is also mandated in the Chapter 312 programs; teacher aides are required to "visit the homes of children enrolled" (Mn. Stat. 126.50).

Programs with an Indian focus are too widespread to discuss individually. At least 55 school districts are involved, with local decision making and great variation in the extent of programs, responsiveness to Indian children, and involvement of parents and the Indian community. Generally, Indian support has been strong. Bagley has an annual Amerind spring banquet honoring Indian students and their parents. Student Indian clubs are active in several districts, including Walker, Bemidji, Red Lake, Minneapolis, and Deer River.

Duluth's 1981–82 program, which was administered by the district's Indian Education Department, shows the type of special effort being made. The program provided youth advocates who worked with Indians in special education; tutors; Indian culture resource people; a secondary school teacher of Indian language, culture, and history; a preschool program funded by Chapter 312; and a chemical dependency prevention program with JOM funds through the Fond du Lac Reservation.

A staff of 18−15 Indian−served 526 students. Funding totaled about $275,000, with 38% from Title IV, 22% from Chapter 312, 11% from JOM, and 29% from state and district funds, including special education. For 1982–83 the total budget was $225,000, a cut of 18%.

Minneapolis has by far the largest Indian school enrollment in the state−well over 2,000, or about 20% of the state's Indian student population. (Red Lake and St. Paul have the next largest numbers.) The district's Indian Education Section, with a staff of 54 (48 Indian) in 1980–81, administers several programs. It is one of only two locally funded Indian education departments in the nation. The director is paid by the school district. Special Indian focus programs using social work aides and a project for the gifted, North Wind Warriors, were incorporated into regular district programming in 1983–84.

Two programs have been especially successful. A curriculum project, Gi-Ki-No-A-Ma-Di-Win, is an introduction to Ojibway language and culture that is brought into the classrooms. In-service training for teachers is emphasized, and the units are being integrated into the regular classroom curriculum during the on-going curriculum revision.

The summer school program, Niibin, is carried out in cooperation with the Indian Health Board and Minneapolis American Indian Center. It provides Ojibway culture; math and reading classes; and nutrition, health, and family communication programs. A very successful feature has been the mandatory parental involvement: for each child, an adult in a parenting role must also attend. Parents and children learn together from the classroom teachers and from each other. Adult education classes are offered, too. The program uses regular classroom teachers, thus exposing them to the special curriculum, to Indians, and to Indian ways of learning and behavior styles.

Alternative Education in Public Schools

Two Indian-focused schools with regular school district funding operate as alternatives for students alienated from the regular school system. At Ponemah, on the Red Lake Reservation, Bakaan Gwagak School ("a different way") serves as a junior high school. It was begun with assistance from the Council on Quality Education, which awards state funds for innovative education programs. The program has increased attendance and improved retention of students through high school. In 1981–82, 48 students attended.

Nah Way Ee Neighborhood Center School (called Center School), Minneapolis, is budgeted through the Minneapolis Public Schools, with additional funds from foundations and religious groups. Episcopal

Community Services is the funding agent. It receives no special funding from Indian sources, although it serves a predominantly Indian group of students. In 1981–82, there were 88 students in grades 9 through 12, with 56 the average daily enrollment and a six-week waiting list for additional enrollments. About half the staff is Indian.

Students come with multiple problems; 98% are low income. The school provides academic education along with Indian culture, individual development, employment help, advocacy, social services, and counseling.

Indian-operated Schools

The Education Commission of the States noted, "It is congressional intent that Indian-operated schools be used as alternatives when public school districts do not satisfy Indian tribal communities."[61] The American Indian Policy Review Commission called community-controlled schools "the most significant education system for Indians today."[62]

Included are both alternative schools in the urban areas and tribal schools on the reservations. They serve students whose needs have not been met by the public schools. The *Indian Needs Assessment* pointed out that they are "students who have been failed by the public school sector and who, as a consequence, demonstrate anomie and distrust."[63]

These schools have been successful, with increasing enrollment each year. A larger percentage of the staff members (73%) were Indian than in any public school, including high proportions of the professionals.[64]

The Indian-operated schools receive no state aids beyond the same supplemental services received by other private schools. Although the BIA funds the tribal schools, the urban ones must spend major amounts of time looking for money. Tuition is not possible for the low-income families served. Because these alternative schools are successfully educating the chidren and benefiting all of society, Indians involved with their programs argue that they should receive state aid.

Reservation Tribal Schools. Tribal schools are authorized by 25 USC 2010, under the policy "to facilitate Indian control of Indian affairs in all matters relating to education." Tribal governments administer the schools on contract with the BIA. Elected school boards hire the administrators and make policy. The schools must comply with state standards in curriculum and teacher certification, are accredited, and may graduate students. The state has four tribal schools; in 1982 three of the four received $610,000 from the BIA.[65]

Chief Bug-O-Nay-Ge-Shig School (named for the Leech Lake Reservation leader, Chief Hole-in-the-Day) serves kindergarten through twelfth grade. It has operated since 1975 when Cass Lake High School rejected a proposal to provide an alternative education program for Indian children. In 1983–84 the school had 150 students. A new building to serve 200 students was constructed in 1984 at a cost of $4.3 million. Nay Ah Shing School serves grades 7 through 12 on the Mille Lacs Reservation. It began in 1979 in response to strong Indian dissatisfaction with a local public school. Circle of Life School began at White Earth in 1978. With the closing of White Earth Elementary school, Circle of Life began offering instruction for kindergarten through twelfth grade in 1983–84. Seventy students were enrolled. Ojibway School, Fond du Lac Reservation, opened in the fall of 1981. A new gymnasium was built in 1982 with matching money from the Department of Housing and Urban Development. In April 1982, 65 students were enrolled in grades 7 through 12. Twenty students are bused to the school daily from Duluth.

Urban Alternative Schools. The two urban alternative schools—Red School House, St. Paul, and Heart of the Earth, Minneapolis —are survival schools begun in 1972 by AIM. The schools adhere to a twofold concept: contemporary Indian problems come from being caught between two worlds, and survival comes through strengthening the Indian's self-image as an Indian. Emphasis is then given to learning the basic skills necessary to survive in both of the culture worlds. Funding comes through Title IV, Title I, Chapter 312, JOM funds allocated by the tribes, and contributions from foundations, corporations, and individuals.

Boarding Schools

The BIA-operated boarding schools, another alternative for educating Minnesota Indian children, fulfill the needs of many children who have not been helped by the public schools. The children benefit from living and studying together and learning more about their culture. Minnesota had 140 Indian students in boarding schools in 1981–82, primarily at Wahpeton, North Dakota, and Flandreau, South Dakota. The largest group came from Red Lake Reservation, with about 15 from MCT reservations.

Programs to Encourage Postsecondary Education

Several programs attempt to keep Indian students in high school and to encourage higher education. In 1984, the state began funding the

Post Secondary Preparation Project for students who show the potential to benefit from further education but who need some extra preparation in basic skills. Funds, set at $300,000 a year for 1984 and 1985, are distributed to school districts based on grant proposals.

Upward Bound. Upward Bound (20 USC 1070d) is a federal program designed to encourage and assist in the transition from high school to higher education. It has two programs that have been especially successful in reaching Indians in Minnesota.

In the Minneapolis Public Schools, Upward Bound focuses on younger students, grades 8 through 10. The program has a strong Indian emphasis, built on Indian culture. A summer program for 60 students is held at the University of Minnesota, St. Paul Campus. It provides tutoring, remedial help, career exploration, and communication and assertiveness classes. Stipends are paid contingent on participation, and there is a work program for students who are old enough. The staff of 15 is two-thirds Indian.

During the school year, about 85 students are assisted by the program offered in targeted senior and junior high schools. The Upward Bound students attend regular classes and come to the program for counseling and tutoring. Follow-up shows that the Upward Bound students are far more successful in graduating on time, with fewer dropouts than the average for Indian students. From 1974 to 1977, 52% of the Indian students in Minneapolis were known dropouts and only 12% graduated on time.[66] Only 25% of the Upward Bound students dropped out, and 40% graduated on time.[67]

A similar summer Upward Bound program is offered at the Bemidji State University campus, for sophomores and juniors from area high schools. During the school year, follow-up visits are made. Career education and counseling, along with help in getting into college, are important parts of the program. The program has a large Indian enrollment—47% of the students in 1981.

A "bridge" program of two weeks of intensified courses is provided during the summer for high school graduates who will enter college the following fall. An Upward Bound program also operates on the University of Minnesota, Duluth (UMD), campus.

Talent Search. The MCT administers Talent Search, a program that focuses on helping Indian students on the reservations to move toward higher education. Another program operates in the Twin Cities. Talent Search works through the schools, providing counseling for the students with funds from Title IV of the Indian Education Act.

Achievement through Communications. An afternoon program at Migizi Communications, Indian radio in Minneapolis, serves 40 senior high school students each trimester, providing communication skills and career awareness. Title IV funds this pilot project.

Programs to Foster Medical Careers. UMD has two summer programs to interest and encourage students into medical careers. In the Howard Rockefeller Program, students in tenth to twelfth grades participate in academic medical classes, and each student is teamed with a faculty member from the School of Medicine to learn about research through experience.

Native Americans into Medicine exposes students from high school through the second year of college to classwork and laboratory experience in the medical professions. The program is funded by the Health Career Opportunity Program, Department of Health and Human Services.

Higher Education

The number of Indians who go to college is low but growing. Records kept by the Minnesota Indian scholarship program show that in 1955, three Indian students received scholarship help. Forty were helped in 1960, 142 in 1970, and 894 in 1983; a high of 1,215 were helped in 1980. Between 1973 and 1982, 2,036 Indian students completed their programs—927 in vocational education, 602 in four-year colleges, and 507 in two-year colleges.[68]

The 1980 census showed 730 Indian college graduates in Minnesota, and the sample census counted 1,312 Indian college students in 1980. A comparison of the number of students given scholarship assistance and the census counts shows the great importance of the program.

The type of education being sought has changed over the years. Indians enrolling in four-year colleges were 69% of all Indian scholarship recipients in 1976. By 1981, both the percentage and the actual number of students enrolled in such schools had declined: less than half of the scholarship recipients were seeking four-year college degrees.

Community college enrollments had the largest increase. In 1981, 27% of the recipients were enrolled in these two-year programs. Vocational education was the choice of one-fourth of all recipients in 1981.[69] Limited scholarship funds and preference for less costly programs have probably been major factors in causing these changes.

Very few Indians are enrolled in professional education and graduate degree programs. The Minnesota Higher Education Coordinating

Board reported that in the fall of 1978, 28 Indian students were taking the six-year professional programs in medicine, law, and dentistry; and 22 more were in graduate school.

Comparative figures for 1976 and 1978 show major shifts of Indian career interests, with registered nursing program enrollments cut one-third while those taking the shorter licensed practical nursing program more than doubled. The number of students preparing to be teachers declined one-third, from 109 to 73.[70]

Completion Rate

As dropout statistics are used to evaluate high school programs, the percentage of students who graduate measures university programs. Relatively few Indian students finish.

The director of Indian Education Studies at Bemidji State University (BSU) estimated that fewer than 10% graduate in four years, although 10–12% graduate eventually.[71] It has been noted that there is value to college work, even without graduation. "Non-graduates . . . gain a lot from being in college. They gain confidence, are more employable, and the value will emerge with their children, who will be better prepared to go to college and to stay longer."[72]

Barriers

Three major reasons account for the poor completion rate: lack of sufficient financial aid, lack of preparation for college work, and family or personal problems. Analyzing reasons why minority students drop out, researchers noted, "Many students come from low income families, have families of their own to support, and have to study very hard due to their inferior academic preparation."[73]

Need for Financial Aid/Scholarships. Most Indian students cannot afford advanced education without outside help. A study of 125 MCT scholarship recipients over 10 years ending in 1981 found that two-thirds of those who completed their studies called "lack of money" the biggest obstacle to overcome. Of those who did not complete their courses, 87% said that the lack of adequate money was a significant reason.[74]

Financial assistance programs for low-income students are available to Indians. Major ones are the federal Pell Grants (20 USC 1070a) and Supplemental Education Opportunity Grants (20 USC 1070b); Minnesota's scholarship (based on need and achievement) and grant-in-aid programs; loans; work/study; and other programs, such as veterans' aid, Social Security, and privately funded scholarship programs.

Those who work with Indian students are generally reluctant to saddle them with loans because of the burden imposed if the students are unable to complete the course of study. Because students frequently have family responsibilities and need to do catch-up studying, outside employment is not feasible.

Two major scholarship programs assist qualified Indian students to get advanced education that would otherwise be financially impossible. The BIA federal program makes awards good for four years of study (not for graduate school). Students need not live on a reservation to qualify. The program is contracted for the most part to the tribes for administration to their members.

In 1982, $1,108,000 was spent in Minnesota to assist over 1,100 students. There were contracts with the MCT for $840,000, Red Lake Reservation for $220,300, and the Sioux Communities for $47,700.

The MCT combines the funds it has under contract for scholarships with money for vocational education also contracted for from BIA. Together, these programs provided $1.5 million in 1980–81 to help 1,240 students.

The Minnesota Indian Scholarship Program, begun in 1955, has been innovative and exceedingly helpful in assisting more than 5,000 of the state's Indian students. "Most of the Indian persons now in responsible positions in Minnesota have been assisted by the program."[75] Through the help these people have given the state and its Indian people in return, the program has paid dividends.

The program assisted 894 on $625,000 in 1981–82. The appropriation per year for 1984 and 1985 was $1.5 million. To qualify, students must be one-fourth Indian and residents of Minnesota for the previous year for reasons other than education. They are not required to live on a reservation. Most of the scholarships are for four years, although a limited number have gone for graduate studies.

About 60–65% of the funds from the Minnesota Scholarship Program have been distributed to members of the MCT, 15% to Red Lake Reservation members, 4%-5% to Sioux Communities members, and 17% to qualified Indians who are not enrolled in or identified with a Minnesota reservation.[76] Because the tribes handle their programs in different ways and the state administers its program separately, there is no total count of individuals helped by all programs.

Special programs also provide some scholarship assistance for Indian students, as in the program at UMD (see below). Title IV of the Indian Education Act, which provides a few fellowships for graduate study, assisted seven Minnesota Indians in 1981. The BIA also helps Indian students to go to BIA programs at Haskell and Santa Fe Institute; 15 attended from Minnesota in 1982.

In 1983–84, the MCT began a loan program for members at the advanced undergraduate or postgraduate level who are working for degrees in professions for which the tribe has a critical need. Loans will be forgiven after the recipients have worked for two years serving the Indian community.

Special Indian programs serve many Indian students, but other students lack the technical qualifications for any Indian assistance by having less than one-fourth Indian ancestry or being unable to verify their ancestry. St. Scholastica College, Duluth, estimates that six to eight of its 35 Indian students are not considered Indian for any program.[77]

Poor Academic Preparation. High schools are faulted for their poor preparation of Indian students. One-third of the students who completed degrees called the lack of study skills and poor academic preparation in high school their most significant obstacle to overcome; only 21% considered themselves well or very well prepared academically for college.[78]

A 1975–77 study of Indians at the University of Minnesota, Twin Cities (UMTC), found that they had entered with lower academic proficiency than "average" students and were performing generally below minimal college standards.[79] Citing these statistics, one report commented, "[This] could lead one to the conclusion that Indian students at the University had been doing poorly primarily because they did not have the background required to excel."[80]

In trying to adjust to the academic requirements of college, "a majority find themselves in a position of trying to compete while catching up."[81] For success, remedial programs, support, and tutoring are usually needed. High school deficiencies in counseling were also identified as a major problem.

Family Circumstances and Motivation. Family ties are very important to Indians, and family needs often interfere with school. Day care, family support costs, health needs, transportation costs, family crises are all possible causes of financial and personal difficulties that may place enough of a burden to cause withdrawal from college.

Personal motivation is obviously a primary factor. Students who had career goals when they entered college were likely to complete more years of school than those who did not, as were students who received parental and friend support and those whose parents had gone further in school themselves.[82]

Ingredients of Success in Higher Education

From studies and League of Women Voters interviews with people involved in postsecondary programs, several important ingredients for successful achievement in higher education have been identified. If some ingredients are missing, the student may still achieve. But identifying the factors that contribute to success can help the individual and the educational system to deal with the problems. Although the following discussion focuses on colleges, much of it also applies to vocational education.

The Institution's Commitment. Willingness to provide the services needed to attract and assist Indian students was seen as the first step. A priority at UMD's School of Social Development is to "meet the needs and interests of American Indians as a major part of an overall commitment to eliminate racism and discrimination."[83] Commitment to funding and incorporating Indian courses and services into the regular budget indicates positive support. The programs of several private colleges that were reaching out to Indian students in the early 1970s have totally disappeared because of lack of commitment and funding.

Support Services. Several useful programs to provide support have been identified. An outreach program for recruitment communicates an institution's interest in the student, in the school, and in obtaining Indian community support. Counseling help—staffed and run by Indians—is perhaps the most important service; it has been important in the expanding program at Augsburg College and in keeping a program alive at Macalester College. Programs with large Indian enrollment provide an Indian center for cultural and social activities.

Peer Group. A peer group of other students of the same racial or ethnic background is important for support and friendship. Indian student clubs are active on several campuses. A private college study concluded that a minimum enrollment of 10–15 students is crucial.[84] Although the College of St. Theresa, Winona, brought Indians to the campus and tailored programs to their needs, the community lacked an Indian population. The Indian students, who were from Montana, found it hard to live so far from home and their culture; the program was eventually dropped.[85]

Indian Faculty and Staff. Faculty and staff provide role models and are invaluable sources of support and encouragement. Minnesota had only 25 Indian faculty at institutions of higher education in 1979, 0.3% of the total. Of all the staff, Indians were 0.2%.[86] In addition, the institutions need non-Indian faculty and staff with an awareness and appreciation of Indian culture. One-third of the MCT graduates surveyed cited "individual faculty who cared" as important in helping them remain in school.[87]

Indian Studies. Several institutions offer classes about Indians, but programs leading to a major in Indian studies are available only at the University of Minnesota, Twin Cities (UMTC), and at Bemidji State University. The University of Minnesota at Duluth and Mankato State University (MSU) offer minors. Except at BSU, most of the students taking Indian studies classes are not Indian.

Indian language and culture curricula are needed to prepare teachers for the incorporation of these subjects into the public school curriculum and to meet the needs of Indian alternative schools. Four years of Ojibway are available at BSU. An average of 40 freshmen take the language classes, with 6 students at the advanced level.

Scholarship and instruction in Minnesota Indian languages pose unique problems. The written languages are not being used for personal use, record keeping, or tribal purposes, and there is very little historical material. An Ojibway dictionary is being prepared at BSU. UMTC has prepared a model curriculum.

Specific Higher Education Programs

According to a 1976 report of the US Office of Civil Rights, the largest Indian student enrollments were at UMTC, with 283; BSU, 163; UMD, 88; and MSU, 58. The percentage of Indian students in 1978 was highest at UMD, with 12.2%. Those with more than 2% were BSU; UM, Morris; St. Scholastica; Minneapolis Community College; and Minneapolis College of Art and Design.[88]

UMTC. The Department of Indian Studies, first in the nation to offer a degree program, was begun on the Twin Cities campus in 1969. It has not developed as its early supporters envisioned, and by 1983–84 a staff of only four teachers remained.

All ethnic studies programs have been challenged as not providing marketable skills, having declining student interest, and being too isolated from other academic disciplines. The Indian experience is that the programs are serving Indian needs and that graduates are being employed, frequently on the reservations.

Proposals have been made to integrate UMTC's Indian studies curriculum into the other disciplines, such as literature, history, and political science. Some think this would strengthen the scholarship: the classes would no longer be seen as supplemental, and there would be greater security for their continuation. Several people close to the Indian studies program fear that if the classes were scattered there would be no focus—no visible Indian role at the university to serve Indian students, provide leadership, and work with the Indian community.

UMD. The Duluth campus has a strong Indian program assisted by an advisory board of Indian community and university leaders. Special Indian-oriented programs are offered in science: a two-year program for upper-level Indian students to gain research experience and a similar program in marine science. The students earn their bachelor's degrees and are prepared to continue into graduate research programs.

The UMD School of Social Development has had Indian faculty since it began; three out of eight faculty members were Indian in 1982. It offers the American Indian Projects program, funded by the National Institute of Mental Health, which trains students in social work through service on reservations and in other communities. The institute, through the MCT, also funds the American Indian Mental Health Training Program. It prepares students as chemical dependency counselors or other health workers through either a two-year associate or four-year bachelor's degree program.

UM, Morris. The Morris campus began as a Catholic boarding school for Indians. It became a federal Indian school in 1896. It was transferred to the state in 1909 with the stipulation that Indians might attend tuition free (Mn. Stat. 137.16, subd. 1). It was intended that Indians and whites would attend together, but during the next 50 years, only two Indians were students.[89]

It was not until the Minority Student Program was started in 1971 that any significant number of Indians came. Since then, 136 have enrolled and 14 have graduated. In spite of being tuition free, however, the campus has had only a small Indian enrollment.[90]

State Universities. BSU has a strong Indian program with special appeal to students from the three major reservations nearby; reservation representatives serve on the advisory board. It offers a degree program in Indian studies, with classes averaging 175 students a quarter, mostly Indian.

The Education Development Center of BSU provides a two-year program of sheltered classes and remedial help for low-income, minority, academically deficient students who are not ready to enter the mainstream of college-level work. The program serves about 400 students, 50–60% Indian, and is very important in helping Indian students over-

Grand entry, Indian Health Board Pow Wow, Minneapolis. Photo by
Terry Smith © 1983.

Amos Owen, Prairie Island Indian Community, pipe ceremony. Photo by
Randy Croce © 1978.

Indian mother in Minneapolis. Photo by Randy Croce © 1978.

Harvesting wild rice on Bowstring Lake. Photo by Monte Draper.

Traditional dancer, Red Lake band.
Photo by Richards Publishing, Gon-
vick, MN 56644.

Red Lake Reservation automobile
license. Photo by author.

Leech Lake Reservation. Photo by
author.

Minneapolis American Indian Center. Photo by Terry Smith © 1983.

Rudy Perpich, governor of Minnesota, and Roger Jourdain, Red
Lake band chairman. Photo by Red Lake staff photographer.

Tribal Executive Council, Minnesota Chippewa Tribe, 1983. Photo by
Ourselves, MCT.

Che-Wa-Ka-E-Gon, Cass Lake, Leech Lake Reservation. Photo by author.

Ojibwa Building Supplies, White Earth Reservation. Photo by author.

Little Six Bingo Palace, Shakopee-Mdewakanton Sioux Community, Prior Lake. Photo by *St. Paul Dispatch*.

Construction, Shakopee-Mdewakanton Culture Center, Prior Lake. Photo by Terry Smith © 1983.

Fond du Lac Manufacturing Company, Fond du Lac Reservation. Photo
by Terry Smith © 1983.

Woodcutting, Indian Wood Incorporated, White Earth
Reservation. Photo by White Earth Reservation
Business Committee.

Dr. Kathleen Annette, Minnesota's first Indian woman doctor. Photo by
Terry Smith © 1983.

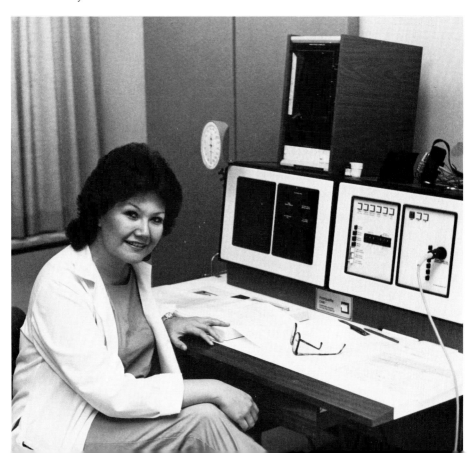

Bait research project. Photo by American Indians in
Marine Science Program, University of Minnesota,
Duluth.

Street project, instructor and student at Leech Lake Reservation. Photo by
Ourselves, Minnesota Chippewa Tribe.

Dakota school, Lower Sioux Agency ca. 1900. Photo courtesy of Science Museum of Minnesota (Bishop Whipple Collection).

Heart of the Earth Survival School, Minneapolis. Photo by Randy Croce © 1983.

The drum, singers, dancers, and spectators, St. Paul American Indian
Center Pow Wow. Photo by Randy Croce © 1977.

Trail of Broken Treaties March on Washington, DC, 1978. Teepee, Heart of the Earth Survival School, Minneapolis. Photo by Gianfranco Gorgoni. © Gianfranco Gorgoni/Contact.

come academic deficiencies. Moorhead State University has an Indian staff person located at White Earth Reservation, where there are 15 full-time and about 25 part-time students.

Community Colleges. The Minneapolis Community College program grew from 25–30 Indian students in the early 1970s to 122 in the fall of 1982–83, graduating its largest group of Indian students ever — 22 — in 1983. The college offers classes in Indian studies and provides credit courses in Indian culture and basic skills at the American Indian Opportunities Industrialization Center.

Arrowhead Community College combines the former community colleges of Itasca (Grand Rapids), Hibbing, Virginia, Ely, and Rainy River (International Falls). A strong Indian program, Service to Indian People, had been offered at Rainy River, enrolling an average of 70 Indian students (15% of the student body) by 1982. The Blandin Foundation funded a three-year, $250,000 project to expand the program to the other campuses.

Private Colleges. The experience in Minnesota's private colleges shows most clearly the importance of having a special Indian program and support services. Throughout the 1970s, many of the state's private colleges worked together through the Minnesota Indian Consortium for Higher Education. Major private funding was used to encourage and help private colleges build Indian programs, have Indian staff, encourage and financially assist Indian students to attend.

At St. Olaf College, for instance, a program was begun in 1971. By 1973–74, there were 14 Indian students. When the Indian counselor left and was not replaced, there was a drastic drop in Indian enrollment. A study in 1975 noted, "What the college has finally come to recognize is that the college is more in need of the Indian student presence and culture than the Indian students are in need of St. Olaf."[91] The college did not revive the program, however, and had only two Indian students in 1981–82.

In 1975, the eight colleges involved in the consortium had 174 Indians enrolled. The League of Women Voters surveyed nine private institutions in 1982 and found about 100 Indian students, but practically all were at the three colleges that had Indian programs: St. Scholastica, Macalester, and Augsburg.

College of St. Scholastica, Duluth, had an Indian major program and three Indian professors until the late 1970s. In 1982, only one Indian professor remained; several Indian classes were offered. Macalester College, St. Paul, also cut back on a strong minority student program that operated throughout the 1970s. By 1984, there was only one Indian staff person and 19 students. Augsburg College, Minneapolis, began the American Indian Student Support Program with an Indian staff person in 1978. Student enrollment increased (to 29 in 1983–84); since 1980, 15 have graduated. The program has an 80% retention rate.[92]

Minneapolis College of Art and Design, offering a four-year arts program, attracts a relatively large number of Indian students. It has an Indian staff person. Although it is one of the higher tuition private colleges, scholarships assist in meeting the costs.

Postsecondary Vocational Education Program

The Area Vocational Technical Institutes (AVTIs) provide education in vocational skills throughout Minnesota. For Indians, the AVTI programs have provided the "most dramatic improvement" in postsecondary education in the past 10 years, with 60% retention rates.[93]

The AVTIs reported 1,087 Indian students (2.5% of the total) as of October 1981.[94] In 1979, the state vocational program and the tribes began cooperating on satellite programs on the reservations, an effort that has greatly expanded their use. Detroit Lakes AVTI serves White Earth and Red Lake reservations, and Staples AVTI provides instruction on Fond du Lac, Bois Forte, and Leech Lake reservations. Detroit Lakes AVTI alone reported 448 Indian students, 41% of all Indian AVTI enrollees. In addition, Minneapolis had 177 Indian students; Bemidji, 49; Duluth, 41; and Red Lake Reservation, with its own AVTI, 18. Through careful planning, training programs have been linked to reservation employment needs.

Indian students at AVTIs have problems similar to those of other postsecondary students. Poor preparation in basic skills is a major handicap; consequently, early assessment tests and remedial training are very useful for successful completion of the courses. The MCT expects students to complete their high school equivalency degree along with the training if they are not high school graduates. Support and counseling services are important, particularly if staffed by Indians.

A major obstacle is lack of funds. At the same time that there is increased interest in the training, fewer dollars are available. Almost all Indian students need help; many must support families.

Scholarships similar to those available for college programs are offered. In addition, the BIA has the Vocational Training Program that provides a student with tuition, books, supplies, and a stipend while attending a technical school. Time spent in the program is limited to 24 months per student. The Sioux Communities program is handled by the

BIA, Sioux Field Office. The MCT contracts for and administers its share of the funds. The MCT pools BIA vocational and scholarship money with Minnesota scholarship funds and makes its own allotments to vocational education students. Because of funding cuts, the MCT program declined from $650,000 helping 340 students in 1980–81 to $436,000 for 232 recipients the next year.

The Federal Vocational Education Act (20 USC 2301) provides funds for the state vocational education programs and requires states to use part of the vocational money for "disadvantaged" students, those with academic or economic hardships, and minorities. Minnesota adds to the funding to provide minority vocational advisers to help recruit and provide counseling and support. The state has 26 positions; five were Indians in 1981.[95] Although Indian teachers are sought, the percentage of Indian staff is low. Of 3,816 full-time positions in 1981, 30 (0.8%) were held by Indians.

Adult Education

Special adult education programs have been provided for Indians in Minnesota since 1968. Many Indians have been assisted in obtaining general education development (GED) certificates (high school diploma equivalency). From 1970 through 1973 alone, over 528 GEDs were awarded to Indians. The program is open ended; students can come into it when they wish, and about half complete it.

The major program is Indian Adult Basic Education, primarily federally funded and channeled through the state. Leech Lake, White Earth, and Red Lake reservations administer their own programs. The state administers programs on Bois Forte, Grand Portage, Mille Lacs, and Fond du Lac reservations, at International Falls, Cook County, and in Duluth. Programs to serve the Sioux Communities have been tried in various places, but they have received no sustained interest. The state program is administered by a staff of three located in Duluth.

Other regions of the state are served by the regular adult basic education programs of the school districts. Generally, they do not have Indian-oriented programs. In St. Paul, however, the school district offers a program with Indian staff and content. The Minneapolis American Indian Center continued its program, paying for it totally out of bingo revenue, when federal funding ended in 1982.

The Federal Indian Education Act, Title IVC, pays for special adult education programs on a grant basis. These grants have been used by Heart of the Earth Survival School to offer a GED course at the American

Indian Opportunities Industrialization Center and to provide programs in the prisons (see chap. 14).

Summary

Minnesota Indians have shown their great concern over the education of their children by becoming involved in education programs and demanding changes so that programs will better meet their needs. Improving education levels is a necessary part of solutions for the many other problems facing Indians. Until the non-Indian community is much better informed about Indians and takes responsibility for remedying past injustice, and until Indians feel they have educational options that meet the needs of their children and communities, education will continue to be a major problem requiring expanded government and citizen attention.

CHAPTER 10

Welfare

Poverty diminishes the spirit. A person whose sole concern is survival on the most minimal level . . . does not
have time for culture, for making art or song, things that
are so deeply ingrained in Indian tradition. . . . We are
rightly concerned about the diminishing of our cultural
values.[1]

Indian Poverty

History

Ever since they were forced onto reservations, Indians have had to
depend in large measure on support from the government. The restrictions of the reservation and the destruction of timber and other natural
resources denied access to traditional food supplies. On some reservations starvation was imminent and the government began to supply
food rations on a regular basis. (The sight of men heaving loaves of
bread out of trucks with pitchforks is still clear in the memory of some
Minnesota Indians.)

The supplying of rations continued until criticized by the Meriam
report in 1928. "It worked untold harm to the Indians because it was
pauperizing and lacked any appreciable educational value."[2] Ironically,
rations and other services had been paid for out of the Indians' own

money. In 1901, for instance, all but $7,000 of $205,000 recorded for Ojibway relief in Minnesota had come from tribal funds.[3]

When Indian money ran out, Congress began appropriating "gratuity funds" to continue some programs. After 1924, when they became citizens, Indians had an equal right with all citizens to state welfare services. The Social Security legislation passed in the 1930s expanded assistance to all those in need.

During the many years of total federal domination, Indians were not allowed to make their own decisions; the government acted for them. These experiences robbed many Indians of the expectation that they would manage their own lives and established the pattern of dependency.

Lack of employment opportunities, joblessness, poor health, substandard housing, discrimination, alcoholism, limited education, teenage pregnancies, and large families are some of today's realities. These current multiple problems, plus the scars from past treatment, the severe pressures of the recession, and the economic decline in northern Minnesota all contribute to the Indians' need to use government assistance.

Current Economic Status

The most recent and complete picture of Indians' economic status is provided by the 1980 census (table 15). By every measure, Indians as a racial group are on the lowest economic level in the state. Demographics alone show the major problem of a young, dependent population, many children for few productive-age adults.

Women and Children. Families headed by women have incomes significantly lower than male-headed families and are more apt to experience poverty. Indians have almost four times as many families headed by females as the general state population. The Minnesota Indian figure is also significantly higher than for Indian families elsewhere in the country. Ohoyo Resource Center, analyzing 1980 census data for 19 states with the largest Indian populations, found an average of 24% Indian female-headed families, as compared with 38% in Minnesota.[4] Minneapolis has the highest percentage in the state.

The figures for children living with nonrelatives probably reflect the role of foster care and other out-of-home placements made when Indian families are disrupted. The larger numbers are in urban and suburban areas. In comparison with the general population, Indian children are more apt to be living with relatives other than their parents, as many as 15% in the state's reservation areas.

Table 15. Socioeconomic Characteristics of Minnesota Indians
(1980 Census Except Where Noted)

		Indians				
Characteristic	All Minnesotans	Minnesota	Nine Northern Counties[a]	Minneapolis[b]	Twin Cities Suburban	Minnesota, 1970
Population under 20	33%	49.6%	51%	49%	48.6%[c]	55.3%
Population 65 or over	12%	4.5%	6%	3%	2%[c]	4.8%
Median age	29.2	20.1	19.8	20.4	20.6[c]	17.2
Average number of persons per family	3.29	3.88	4.21	3.77	3.68[c]	4.61
Families with children under 6	24%	39%	36%	42%	37%[c]	46%
Families with female householder	10%	38%	31%	57%	23%[c]	28%
Families with children under 6 headed by women (no husband present)	10%	42%	32%	65%	21%[c]	—
Persons under 18 living with a married couple	84%	47%	52%	28%	63%[c]	—
Persons under 18 living with female householder (no husband present)	10%	31%	23%	50%	21%[c]	—
Persons under 18 living with other relatives	2.5%	11%	15%	11%	4%[c]	—
Persons under 18 living with nonrelatives	1%	4%	4%	5%	5.5%[c]	—
Those 25 and older:						
High school graduates	73%	55%	—	53%	72%[d]	32%
College graduates	17%	5%	—	4%	7%[d]	2%
Avg. income, 1979	$24,110	$14,667	—	$11,964	—	—
Population below poverty line, 1979	9%	30%	—	41%	12%[d]	38%
Income less than $10,000, 1979	16%	43%	—	52%	25%[d]	—
Those 16 and older in the labor force:						
Males	73%	49%	—	67%	69%[d]	62%
Females	52%	41%	—	43%	65%[d]	36%
Those in the labor force unemployed:						
Males	6.2%	24.4%	—	28%	10.4%[d]	17%
Females	4%	15.7%	—	16.2%	9%[d]	11.2%
Households with no vehicles	9%[e]	31%	—	59%	7%[d]	—

[a]Includes St. Louis County less Duluth, and Becker, Beltrami, Carlton, Cass, Clearwater, Itasca, Mahnomen, and Mille Lacs counties, for a total of 12,060, or 34% of the state's Indian population.

[b]Includes 8,933 Indians, or 26% of the state's Indian population.

[c]Includes Anoka and Dakota counties, Hennepin County less Minneapolis, and Ramsey County less St. Paul, for a total of 3,534, or 10% of the state's Indian population.

[d]Includes seven metropolitan counties, excluding Minneapolis and St. Paul, or 12% of the state's Indian population.

[e]White population only.

Income. Because income defines poverty, the census figures showing that average Indian income in Minnesota in 1980 was $9,443 less than that of the general population (61% of the state average) are a clear statement that poverty is a major, if not all-consuming, problem for Indians. Thirty percent of Indians were below the poverty level, compared with 27% of Blacks and 18% of those of Spanish origin.

The Metropolitan Council has reported that of the 25 largest metropolitan areas, the Twin Cities had the lowest proportion of people living below the poverty level (6.8%). The Indian population, however, had the second highest poverty rate in the nation, exceeded only in Phoenix, Arizona.[5]

Unemployment. According to the 1980 census, the percentage of Indians over 16 years of age in the work force was a great deal lower than that of the general population, both males and females. Unemployment rates for Indians were truly staggering, four times those of the general population. Unemployment figures by reservation were reported by the BIA in December 1982–January 1983 (see chap. 8). Unemployment was as high as 82% on White Earth; no major reservation had less than 40%. The director of a Minneapolis Indian center estimated that 50–70% of Indians were unemployed in 1982.[6]

Demographic Changes since 1970. In 10 years, the size of the average Minnesota Indian family decreased, and the median age increased by three years. The number living below the poverty level declined 21%. These are indications of an improved economic life during the decade, but discouraging trends were the increase in female heads of household and a 40% increase in the percentage of men unemployed.

Effects of Recession and Program Cuts. Cuts in welfare eligibility and level of benefits came at the same time that opportunities for employment declined. Eligibility for AFDC was changed in 1981, primarily to prohibit recipients from earning income in addition to the AFDC payment. General Assistance (GA) was cut to those considered as having marketable skills. (In the latter case, eligibility standards were reinstated in 1983.) The cuts in the GA program were especially hard on the Indian community, since those with "marketable skills" were unable to find employment either on reservations or in the urban centers.

Emergency needs of those with no other sources of help have been an increasing problem, especially in the cities. A 1982 study by Hennepin County of users of emergency shelters found that almost half were racial minorities.[7]

Records kept by the Division of Indian Work (DIW) in Minneapolis show the rapid increase in needs since 1981. Under DIW's Emergency Assistance Program, 16,000 services were provided in 1981; for 1982, the number had increased to 33,000. The figure for 1983 was 48,000, a tripling in two years of services provided.

Mobility. The mobility of the Indian population is a factor in the welfare situation. Typical is migration to the Twin Cities from the reservation, the individual looking for work and a better way of life.

> A man arrives here with his pregnant wife and the family in a car. They don't have any money. They don't have a job. They don't have a place to stay, and the car's out of gas. They think things are going to be wonderful down here. . . . So we get him a place to stay and enough money to tide him over until he starts work, and then he gets a job, works a few months, then heads back to the reservation. He'll shuttle like that, back and forth for the rest of his life.[8]

The Indian Health Board of Minneapolis noted that in 1981 new patients registered at the clinic represented 32% of the total patients for the year, a much higher figure than the average mobility factor of 20%. "This higher figure is an indication of economic factors pressing Indians to move from the reservation to the urban areas."[9]

The worsened economic conditions have also increased returns to the reservations. Red Lake has noted that its population usually increases in the summer and decreases in the winter, when people leave to find employment elsewhere. During the fall of 1982, increased numbers came back to the reservation from the Twin Cities.[10]

Minnesota Welfare System

With minor exceptions on Red Lake Reservation, Minnesota Indians qualify for all state welfare programs as do any other state residents. The programs must be available to all who meet the eligibility criteria, regardless of race. The major income maintenance programs include AFDC and Medical Assistance (MA or Medicaid), which are funded with federal, state, and county monies; and GA and General Assistance Medical Care (GAMC), from state and county funds only.

Social services are also funded by all three levels of government. The decisions about what programs to offer and the level of their funding are made primarily at the county level, and most programs are administered by county welfare departments. The services generally provided are for child welfare, chemical dependency, mental illness, mental retardation, and several other areas of concern.

Special state welfare funds are provided as "distressed county aid" (Mn. Stat. 245.74) to the poorest counties, those with the heaviest welfare recipient rates. Several of the northern reservation counties with major Indian populations receive this aid. The 10 counties that received the funds in 1982 had 38% of the state's Indian population outside of the Twin Cities and Duluth.

Specific Programs for Indians

The state has two welfare programs specifically for Indians: reimbursement to counties of their portion of Red Lake Reservation costs, and the Indigent Indian Account. Minnesota Statute 245.76 states, "The care and relief of persons of Indian blood is declared to be a matter of special state concern and responsibility." The law allows up to 75% reimbursement of the costs of direct relief, maintenance of children, medical care, and burial for Indians who are at least one-quarter blood and do not reside on Red Lake Reservation. Although mandated by the law, state rules have not been written setting standards or priorities for administering the funds.

In 1981, 24 counties submitted to the state over $3.5 million in expenses (63% from Hennepin County). With only $1,240,000 appropriated, the reimbursement was limited to that amount, 37% of the submitted expenses.[11] This funding, however, was greater than the counties would have received from the state for such programs as regular foster care or out-of-home placement for emotionally handicapped. The same amount has been appropriated for each fiscal year 1984 and 1985.

The law and its funding process raise several questions. Indians point out that it is a program intended to help Indians, yet there is no Indian participation in decisions about how the money is spent or the program administered.

Some Indians are concerned that the availability of this special money for Indian foster care may make taking children out of their homes seem a financially better alternative than working with the families. (Of the submitted Indigent Indian Account expenditures, 72% were for foster care.) Although the program appears to be intended to help counties with large numbers of Indians, one-third of the applications in 1981 came from counties with fewer than 135 Indians.[12] The Indian Affairs Council has recommended that the law be changed to allow reimbursement to tribal governments and urban Indian groups as well as the counties for Indian welfare expenditures.

Problems

Eligibility

Generally, Indians who qualify for income maintenance programs receive them as does any other applicant. Local funding, however, becomes a serious burden in those counties with heavy welfare costs and limited local resources—often those with high Indian populations. Consequently, the level of benefits may be reduced in the state-county programs; services may be denied; nonresidents may be pressured to return to their home counties for services; or the counties may seek special funding from the Indigent Indian Account, rather than use accounts for which the client would otherwise qualify.

When a person resides in one county and needs services in another, generally the county of residency is responsible for payment. For medical care, this has the potential of forcing Indians to return to reservations for Indian Health Service care, which is not a cost to the counties. For GA welfare and detoxification programs, the county where the client is located is financially responsible.

Other technical problems with the welfare system have been noted by Indians: If a mother enters a residential chemical dependency treatment program, she loses welfare assistance. When she returns, in order to get her child back she must first have a suitable home. But she cannot afford the housing without AFDC, and without her child she cannot qualify for AFDC. County welfare systems also have problems in trying to make foster home or other placements outside the county. Getting the other county to license the home is difficult, monitoring the placement can be expensive, and business is denied to homes already licensed.

County Administration of Social Services

Some social service programs must be provided to serve vulnerable populations, such as emotionally disturbed, dependent, neglected, or abused children; pregnant adolescents; parents under 18 years of age and their children; adults in need of protection; the mentally ill or retarded; the drug dependent and intoxicated. How this is done and the quality of service are left to the county. In general, it is the remedial, preventive programs that are bearing the brunt of funding shortages.

The Community Social Services Act (CSSA) is the state welfare block grant to counties. Funds are distributed based on population, number of elderly people, and welfare burden. The legislature assumed that local government is best able to define local problems, set priorities, and allocate resources. County boards must prepare plans every two years to allocate funds, using citizen testimony on needs. The assistant commissioner of the Department of Human Services (formerly the Department of Public Welfare) noted, "Indians are not one of the special target groups in the law, but there is an 'other' designation. Indians need to be planned for. Counties should work with Indians."[13]

A review of the 1981 CSSA plans of the six counties that contain parts of the White Earth or Leech Lake reservation showed that only two of the six mentioned Indian needs. In these two counties, the MCT had participated in the needs assessment process. The other four counties did not reach out to hear from Indian representatives, although presumably Indian needs for programs such as foster care, homemaker assistance, and help with chemical dependency were a major portion of their programs.[14] In 1982 no county had involved the MCT in its plan or evaluation of the effectiveness of the plan.[15]

The CSSA lacks effective safeguards to ensure that vulnerable populations will be heard and have their needs met. Legislative auditors, checking CSSA plans as they apply to chemical dependency programs, found that only 20% had been filed with the state as required. Those that were filed were considered especially weak in their assessment of needs in the communities.[16]

A 1982 survey to evaluate county-funded social services and the Community Action Program (CAP) found that, in the opinion of CAP directors, county decisions are shaped in part by "local passions and prejudices against certain groups. Women on AFDC, Indians, and unemployed single adults are often deemed to be morally culpable and therefore undeserving." The researcher concluded, "Local prejudices attached to 'deserving' and 'undeserving' groups endanger the principle of equity. Disfavored groups are especially vulnerable given the monopoly role assigned to elected county commissioners under CSSA."[17]

Critics have recommended that the Minnesota Department of Human Services monitor more closely the counties' CSSA decision making to ensure that the needs of vulnerable populations are being adequately met; further, that the department establish a grievance procedure for groups that are inadequately served. Since as much as half of the social service money being used by the counties is federal or state funds, some have suggested that tribes be recognized as governmental units eligible for a share of this money. The tribes could then operate their own programs.

Welfare Agency Attitudes

The attitude of welfare agency personnel towards Indians, their lack of understanding of Indian culture, and the Indians' perception of welfare agencies pose major barriers to the effective utilization by Indians of available services. The barriers are a significant problem in the provision of child welfare services (see Child Welfare, below). Only 7% of the Indians interviewed in a 1979 survey in St. Paul and Minneapolis mentioned seeking public services when help was needed. They were concerned about insensitive, "don't care," and "hostile, dehumanizing" attitudes on the part of those providing public services.[18]

An Indian advocate now working in a battered women's shelter commented that even though she had worked for the welfare system and knew it, when the need arose in her own life she was reluctant to walk in. "I felt that as an Indian they would treat me like a stereotype, they would give me disrespect. And they did. . . . Only when I went to the Indian advocate could I relate. . . . When Indians feel vibrations of disrespect they don't stay to explain, they just leave."[19]

In some instances and in some Indian communities, the use of Indian advocates also causes difficulties because of the wish to maintain privacy. The Indian community is small and people know each other. Sometimes anonymity is almost impossible. In other interviews, the League of Women Voters found Indian leaders, especially professional social workers, very complimentary about the county personnel they worked with.

In the early 1970s, the solution for insensitive personnel in welfare departments was the use of training sessions on Indian culture to increase understanding. Although the Indian professors in the School of Social Development at UMD do some of this, most welfare departments are no longer stressing culture awareness or sensitivity.

Indians working in the social service field are unanimous about the importance of having Indian staff if Indian problems are to be alleviated. "Indians have multiple problems and they don't know where to start. No one can understand the problems like an Indian."[20] The professionals point out that non-Indians are not aware of the extensive family systems and cultural strengths that can aid in working out strategies to meet the problems of Indian families. Efforts by non-Indians to help may become hindrances to improvement because of this lack of understanding.

Hennepin County supplies some staff and funding to provide Indian-oriented social service programs. It has three Indian welfare advocates with offices in Indian centers, and one Indian social worker. Ramsey County has two Indian social workers.

Burials

Covering the expense of burials has posed a special problem for Indians, especially in the urban areas. A reservation burial is often desired. County welfare assists in the Twin Cities, but the cost of transporting a body to another county for burial poses problems.

In 1982, Ramsey County proposed to provide only cremation for welfare burials. This would have been in conflict with Indian religious beliefs. The St. Paul Indian community was successful in having the plan changed.

Welfare Services on Reservations

Red Lake Reservation

The state welfare system does not extend to Red Lake Reservation, with the exception of the federally funded income maintenance programs (AFDC). The Minnesota Supreme Court ruled in 1963 that since Beltrami County can not enforce state law on the reservation, it does not have to provide the programs. The BIA funds the General Assistance and social service programs; in 1982, it provided $0.75 million for GA, child care services, and administrative costs. State-recommended funding standards, higher than those used by neighboring counties, are applied for GA payments.

Unless federally funded income maintenance programs (including AFDC) extend equally to all people in the state, the state is subject to the cutoff of federal funds. Beltrami and Clearwater counties are responsible for AFDC on Red Lake. Beltrami County has a staff of two caseworkers and four financial workers on the reservation. The state, however, pays the county share of the expense (Mn. Stat. 245.965).

In 1981, 8% of Clearwater County cases were reservation residents (127 of 1,611) and the county was reimbursed $22,000. Beltrami County, with 31% of its 5,123 welfare recipients on the reservation, received $280,000 from the state. For each year 1984 and 1985, $496,000 has been appropriated for reimbursements.

Other Reservations

A few social service programs are administered by the MCT and the reservations, primarily in child welfare, chemical dependency (see chap. 13), and other programs listed below. Full-time professionals, several with social work degrees, are available on each reservation to assist with meeting needs and to provide liaison with county agencies and the court system.

The Fond du Lac tribe has a close working relationship with UMD's School of Social Development. Students are placed on the reservation as part of their training to prepare for practice with American Indians. Assistance provided to Fond du Lac has included work on planning and developing a day-care system.

Commodity Distribution

The federal Commodity Distribution Program (7 USC 612c), administered by the Department of Agriculture, is designed to help increase the use of food acquired under price-support programs and to encourage consumption of agricultural products. It is an alternative to the food stamp program.

The law specifically authorizes the program for Indians when the tribal organization requests it, with the directive that the department "shall improve the variety and quantity of commodities supplied to Indians in order to provide them an opportunity to obtain a more nutritious diet" (see chap. 12).

To qualify, families must meet low-income eligibility standards. Each month they have the option of getting food stamps instead of commodities. The supplies of commodities are maintained on the reservations. As many as 41 different dried, canned, and packaged foods are provided at a time to meet total nutritional requirements; no fresh foods are provided.

The improved commodity program has been operating since 1980 or 1981, depending on the reservation. It has been well received and is widely used. The White Earth Reservation program has been federally recognized as a well-administered program. It served an average of 2,300 people (760–800 families) per month in 1982, including more than 100 who received home deliveries.

Each reservation in the state operates the program except the Shakopee-Mdewakanton Sioux Community, which is no longer eligible because of its success in raising the income level of its members.

WIC Program

Extra commodities or food stamps are provided to pregnant women, nursing mothers, and young children whose health is considered at risk through the Supplemental Food Program for Women, Infants and Children (WIC). It is funded by the Department of Agriculture and administered through health programs (see chap. 12).

Community Action Programs

Begun under the Economic Opportunity Act of 1964 with the objective of letting the poor determine their own needs and have a voice in how their problems were to be met, CAPs continue in most of Minnesota's counties (26 organizations in 1982). The agencies are paragovernmental, largely independent of established government units and providing advocacy, strategies for social change, and service delivery for the low-income populace. They are run by boards composed one-third of elected county commissioners, one-third low-income population representatives, and one-third community group representatives.

The CAPs are funded by federal community service block grants, channeled through the state, along with state funds and a small amount of local money. State law provides that Indian reservations are equally eligible along with the county CAPs (Mn. Stat. 268.52). Urban Indian centers, however, are not eligible. The reservations have the option of getting funding directly from Washington or through the state. In 1982, all 11 Minnesota reservations chose the state program. Minnesota was the only state to have complete participation.

The study of rural CAPs in Minnesota, published in January 1982, found that they were better able to represent low-income populations than were county social service administrations.[21] The League of Women Voters, however, found that the CAP programs often were not reaching low-income Indians. Indians were usually not involved in the decision-making process and were not hired as employees in numbers corresponding to the ratio of the Indian population in need. Only 7% of the Beltrami/Cass counties CAP staff was Indian. In the Sioux Communities, CAP programs were not effective in serving the reservation populations. For instance, there was no Head Start program on Prairie Island in 1982.

The former Indian Community Action Program has become the Administration for Native Americans, run by the Department of Health and Human Services (42 USC 2991) directly from Washington. It funds programs at the urban Indian centers and on reservations. Proposals are approved on a competitive basis.

Energy Programs

With the rapid increase of fuel costs in the mid-1970s, programs were begun to help cushion the shock of these expenditures on the poor and to help them make home improvements that would reduce their need for fuel. Energy Assistance is a federal block grant to the Minnesota Department of Economic Security for distribution to the poor through local CAPs.

Significant numbers of Indians use wood. They are paid directly based on the average cost of wood being cut in the area. Reservations have also used the funds to provide wood for members' homes. During the 1981–82 winter, nine of Minnesota's reservations contracted directly with the state to operate the program; the two remaining Sioux Communities were served by the CAPs in their areas. A much smaller program, the Energy Crisis Assistance Program, was used by Grand Portage Reservation in 1982 to sweep chimneys in all the homes in the community.

The state sets aside for Indian reservations 2% of the funding received through the federal weatherization assistance program for low-income persons (42 USC 6861). In calendar year 1982, $409,000 was used by the reservations to provide insulation, caulking, storm windows, and other improvements for about 300 homes.

Programs for the Elderly

Older Americans Act

The federal Older Americans Act, under the Department of Health and Human Services, funds several types of programs for the elderly. Reservations may get their grants directly from the federal government under Title VI (12 USC 3057); Fond du Lac, Mille Lacs, and Red Lake reservations do this. The Minnesota Indian Area Agency on Aging is the other major funding conduit. These funds, channeled through the state under Title III, are used by the remaining four MCT reservations. County programs provide the services to the Sioux Communities, but not all services are available. The Minnesota Board on Aging (Mn. Stat. 256.975) reviews the programs that come through the state and provides technical assistance to the local agencies.

In the urban areas, responsibilities for the programs are divided.

Some difficulties—mainly transportation problems—interfere with Indian utilization of the urban programs.

The program with greatest use is the Elderly Nutrition Program (Title III C), which provides for congregate dining and home-delivered meals. Congregate dining brings together for a hot lunch those 60 years or older and their spouses of any age. Social activities are usually associated with the program. Contributions are suggested, but each person decides what to pay and the meals are provided even if the person pays nothing. Most of the programs operate five days a week. The program's funding is federal; the Department of Agriculture provides commodities or cash and the Department of Health and Human Services administers the program.

There are strong programs on the reservations, with several dining sites on the larger ones. In the town of Cass Lake, the Leech Lake Reservation Neighborhood Facility Center provides the program for the whole community—Indians and whites—and is building bridges of understanding.

The major congregate dining program serving Indians in Minneapolis is located at the Minneapolis American Indian Center (MAIC). It serves 80–100 at two seatings daily, five days a week. The Volunteers of America provides the food service under contract.

Providing transportation to bring the elderly to the center has been very important. When transportation funding was cut in 1981, attendance dropped by 65%. The Indian elderly did not attend centers closer to their homes, as had been proposed by Metropolitan Council policy. Eventually money was found to provide two vans, but about 75 Indians no longer attend because of lack of transportation, according to the MAIC director.[22]

The home-delivered meals program in Minneapolis has not been effective in reaching Indians. In Ramsey County, less than 1% of recipients of the home-delivered meals were Indians in 1981. The congregate dining program to serve Indians in St. Paul has also had problems.

Records kept on the dining programs by the Minnesota Board on Aging indicate that in 1981 3,521 Indians received services, 1.8% of the total number served. The figures do not include Red Lake, Fond du Lac, and Mille Lacs reservations, which deal directly with Washington.

Title IIIB of the Older Americans Act provides for social services, the Homemaker Chore program, transportation, and legal services. In Minnesota in 1981, 1,706 Indians received services from this program, 3.7% of the total. Legal help in northern Minnesota is provided by Anishinabe Legal Services program, Cass Lake. In the Metropolitan Area, Indians have had minimal use of Title IIIB programs, 1% or less.

Senior Community Employment Program

The Senior Community Employment Program (42 USC 3056) provides employees on each reservation of the MCT and two at tribal headquarters, 18 in all. The MCT administers the program of part-time employment (20 hours a week) for those 55 and over to provide them with supplemental income. The program is funded through the Minnesota Department of Economic Security. Fond du Lac also has a senior companion program; the employees visit elderly, homebound people and provide services for them.

Other Urban Programs for Seniors

The Minneapolis American Indian Center offers a drop-in center, a crafts program, limited health services, transportation, and emergency help for seniors. The program serves about 220 individuals a month, almost all Indian and with very low incomes (95% have less than $7,500 a year).

Concerned about shut-in and forgotten elderly Indians, Upper Midwest Indian Center in 1982 began the Interventive Assistance Program. By February 1982, 28 shut-ins had been located and involved in the Indian community. An advocate program for senior Indians was begun by Family Health at Pilot City Center on the north side of Minneapolis in 1984.

Child Welfare

History of the Problem

For many years, large numbers of Indian children were taken from their parents and placed in boarding schools, often not to return home for several years (see chap. 9). This separation was made for the "benefit" of the child, in order to "civilize" the race: parents were viewed as unsuitable to raise their own children. The modern form of taking has been to place Indian children in white foster care or adoptive homes where for their "own good," a "better" environment can be provided.

In the mid-1970s, public attention was focused on the wholesale separation of Indian children from their families. White systems and white personnel were applying cultural values and social norms inappropriate to Indian life to remove children from their parents.

Poverty, poor housing, lack of modern plumbing, and overcrowding were used as proof of parental neglect. Child-rearing practices of another culture were misinterpreted as neglect or letting the child "run wild." Whereas abuse of alcohol by a parent was one of the most frequently advanced grounds for removing children, this standard was rarely applied to non-Indians.

Parental rights were often terminated without due process and true understanding. The child's rights to tribal membership and an Indian heritage were totally ignored. The procedure was not only an attack on the people involved, but it was threatening the destruction of Indian tribes and Indian culture.

Minnesota was cited to show the extent of the problem. One out of every 5.4 Indian children under 21 in the state was either in a foster family or adoptive home in 1972. Indian children were removed 5.2 times more often than non-Indian children in the state. In 1975, 98% of adopting mothers were white.[23]

Indian Child Welfare Act

Passage by Congress in 1978 of the Indian Child Welfare Act (25 USC 1901) was an effort to put an end to the abuses by giving tribes the opportunity to control what happened to Indian children. The act states that "no . . . resource is more vital to the continued existence and integrity of Indian tribes than their children." The United States, as trustee, has a direct interest in protecting Indian children who are tribe members.

Tribes are to be notified when a member or someone eligible for membership comes before a court to be placed outside the home, if parental rights are to be terminated, or if a child is to be transferred from one foster home to another. (Divorce or criminal case placements do not come under the act.) If the tribe is not known, the BIA is to be notified and has 15 days to provide the information.

The tribe may intervene and request transfer to its own court or may intervene at any point in the proceedings. A tribe does not have to take a case; but if the tribe requests that the case be transferred to its own court, "absent objection by either parent" or in "absence of good cause to the contrary," the state court must transfer it. Tribal court actions are to be accepted by all states.

The act stresses programs to help families in preventing the removal of children. A wide range of programs are authorized to provide family services, help tribal courts, license and work with Indian foster homes, and provide legal representation on and off the reservations.

If there is placement, the child's or parent's preference is to be considered. Beyond that, first consideration is given to the extended family (including second cousins, brothers- or sisters-in-law, stepparents). Second preference is tribal members; third, other Indians.

In court proceedings, the act puts the burden on the county to show that efforts have been made to help the family and that they were unsuccessful. It must also provide evidence, including testimony of "qualified expert witnesses" (assumed to mean someone familiar with Indian culture), that continued custody by the parent is likely to result in serious emotional or physical damage to the child.

Records must be kept showing efforts to comply with the preference order and must be available to the tribe and the BIA. Final decrees, including information about tribal membership, are to be sent to the Department of the Interior. Adopted children 18 years or older may apply for information about tribal affiliation and biological parents.

If the law has been violated, the tribe, the child, or a parent can petition the court to invalidate a placement, voluntary or involuntary. In 1983, Red Lake band was challenging on behalf of a tribal mother a placement made in Missouri without notification of the tribe as the law mandates.

Neither the MCT reservations nor the Sioux Communities had juvenile courts when the act was passed. By state-tribe agreements (1980), the state was authorized (after notifying the child's tribe) to exercise jurisdiction on and off the reservations. The agreements can be revoked upon six months' notice, at which time the tribes could reassume jurisdiction. Several MCT reservations are interested in having their own courts.

State Law. In 1983 the state legislature passed the Ethnic Heritage Protection Act (Mn. Stat. 257.071), which is similar in intent to the Indian Child Welfare Act. Race or ethnic heritage is to be given preference in making foster care or adoption placements. Special efforts are to be made to recruit minority foster families. Records are to be kept by race, including an annual report of children in residential facilities. While the law generally lacks a strong enforcement provision, the court is empowered to require county welfare departments to continue efforts to find a minority family if one is not immediately available.

Effects of the New Legislation

The experience in Minnesota is that the Indian Child Welfare Act has already made significant changes, all to the good. The law has worked in many instances to keep the child in the Indian culture. It is making county welfare personnel aware of Indian needs, and there is greatly improved cooperation and respect between counties and the tribes.

A Hennepin County juvenile court judge commented, "The counties have taken a great number of steps. There have been seminars, an Indian guardian *ad litem* program [court appointees to represent what is best from the child's viewpoint]. People are trying. There has been change, with increased sensitivity to other cultures. Foster care standards are more accommodating. They are learning about Indians."[24]

Great improvement has been noted in the declining number of Indian adoptions. From 1977 through 1981, the number of Indian children adopted each year averaged 51, less than one-third of the peak of 159 adopted in 1972 (4% of all adoptions).[25]

The law puts responsibility on the tribes to be informed and become involved, if that is their decision, all over the United States. Conversely, in a major urban Indian area like the Twin Cities, children belonging to literally dozens of tribes throughout the country may come under the act. Hennepin County's 171 Indian children placed out of their homes as of December 1982 were 87% Ojibway, 6% Dakota, 2% Winnebago, 5% other, and 15 children "unknown."[26] Even with the Ojibway and Dakota, the tribe could be outside of Minnesota.

In 1981, the MCT had 256 cases under the act. Although 59% were handled in reservation counties, the single largest load was in Hennepin County, with 28% of all cases (35% in the metropolitan counties). Fourteen cases (6%) were out of state in Colorado, California, Alaska, Texas, and Washington, as well as in other Midwest states.[27]

Between June and September 1982, Red Lake Court had 12 off-reservation cases, including a case in Los Angeles; and a Sioux community social worker was supervising from afar a case in Oregon. In off-reservation cases the tribes have the options of not participating, recommending an approach to be used, sending someone to represent the tribe, or using representation already in the community (like legal services or public defenders).

Tribal Responsibilities

Each reservation has its own foster care standards, licenses and supervises the homes, and maintains active programs to recruit and work with Indian families willing to adopt children or provide foster care. The MCT reservations had 30 licensed foster homes in 1982. With small staffs funded by the BIA, the reservations coordinate casework and court work with county social service programs to ensure that there is compliance with the law. Some federal child welfare funds, $50,000 in 1983, are channeled to the MCT through the state Department of Human Services.

Red Lake Reservation has a juvenile court. In 1982 it had 15 licensed foster homes, including a group home at Ponemah. Long before the Indian Child Welfare Act, the tribal court had stressed using the extended family; very few placements are made in foster homes. There were no placements made in 1981 or 1982, and the eight children in court-ordered foster care in September 1982 predate that time. The Red Lake Court handles adoptions of tribal members; during 1982 there were four adoptions, all voluntary.

State Programs

There is no way to determine the amount of money being spent in Minnesota on Indian child welfare cases. Twenty-four counties reported expenditures of $2.5 million for foster care in 1981 under the Indigent Indian Account, or 5.6% of the state total expenditures for foster care.[28] It was only a portion of the full cost, however.

Funding cuts and decisions about how social service monies are to be spent are resulting in cutbacks in the very programs that help keep children in the home: homemakers programs, early intervention and family support, day care, parenting classes. Funding pressures are also encouraging less placement or shorter placement in the more expensive foster care, group homes, and institutional care.

Instead, the state is encouraging counties to use family-based service whenever possible. The multiple problems that may be present can be addressed with a continuum of services offered to the whole unit rather than an individual client. Keeping the child in the family setting and helping with the family's crisis not only prevents the needless trauma added by the child's removal, but pilot projects have shown that it saves money.[29]

This type of approach is being used in Itasca County, which has a large Indian population. In 1981, the county had the lowest foster care costs and disproportionately low costs in comparison with the Indian child protection case load of the six counties serving White Earth and Leech Lake reservations.[30]

In addition to contracting with the MCT for some of the state's federal child welfare funds, the Department of Public Welfare in 1983 provided funding to the 14 counties with Indian reservations with the understanding that they enter into purchase service contracts with the reservations for child welfare services. This action was taken to resume the relationship that the MCT had established under a grant program.

When that funding ended, all counties except Cass had refused to contract with the MCT, saying they did not have money for "extra" Indian services.

The professional staff and services that the reservation programs are able to provide have contributed to good working relationships among the reservations, the state, and most counties. "The counties have come to rely on the tribe's staff."[31] Cass County, for example, had a good relationship with the MCT even before the state program began. The county notifies the tribe within 24 hours of the time an Indian child begins to receive welfare services, access is provided, and information on treatment is shared.

Problems

In spite of the intent of the Indian Child Welfare Act, Indian children in Minnesota are still being taken from their homes and from the Indian community well in excess of their percentage in the state population. Indian adoptions in 1980 (56) were 2% of the state total, while Indians under 18 years were 1.3% of the state population. In 1981, 79% of the 42 children adopted joined families with white mothers.[32]

Placements of Indian children in foster care administered by the state's departments of welfare declined between December 1972 and October 1981, from 737 to 594. But an Indian child was still eight times more apt to be placed than the state's other children. The combined out-of-home placements administered by welfare departments, calculated as of 1981, show that one out of every 10 Indian youths under age 21 was not in his or her natural home, a rate 2.7 times the state figure (table 16).

More recent data document the continued excessive removal of Indian children in the state from their homes. Minnesota has an unusually high ratio of out-of-home placements to deal with juvenile problems. In a 1982 national one-day count of children in foster care, Minnesota was ninth nationally in the rate of white children placed, 37 per 10,000 population. In the same count, Minnesota ranked first in the nation in the placement rate of Indian children, 345 per 10,000, far in excess of any other state—twice that of Wisconsin, for instance.[33]

Major family and child welfare problems in the Indian communities need assistance. For instance, the rate of reported cases of maltreated children in Minnesota in 1981 was four and one-half times greater for the Indian population than for the general population.[34] Judge Allen Oleisky, Hennepin County Juvenile Court, reported that of 900 cases he heard in 1983, 200 involved Indians, affecting more than 400 children.[35] The issue that is being raised by the Indian communities is

Table 16. Minnesota Children under 21
in Adoptive or Foster Homes in an Average Year

	1972[a]		1981	
	Minnesota Indians	Minnesota Non-Indians	Minnesota Indians	Minnesota Non-Indians
Population under 21[b]	12,672	1,572,514	18,090	1,397,363
Adoptions:[c]				
Average number	103	3,271	82[d]	3,075[d]
At any one time	1,594	50,543	1,263[e]	47,534[e]
Ratio of adoptees to population under 21	1:7.9	1:31	1:14.3	1:29
Ratio of Indian to non-Indian adoptees	3.9:1		2:1	
Foster Care:				
Number	737	5,541	594[f]	5,672[g]
Ratio of foster children to population under 21	1:17.2	1:284	1:30.5	1:246
Ratio of Indians to non-Indians	16.5:1		8.1:1	
Combined:	2,331	56,084	1,857	53,206
Ratio of both to population under 21	1:5.4	1:28	1:9.7	1:26
Ratio of Indians to non-Indians in out-of-home placement	5.2:1		2.7:1	
Percentage of population under 21 in out-of-home placement	18%	3.6%	10.3%	3.8%

[a]Data from *Report on Federal, State and Tribal Jurisdiction* (Washington, DC: American Indian Policy Review Commission, 1976), 210.

[b]Census data from 1970 and 1980.

[c]Data for 1972 adoptions: averages between 1964 and 1975; data for 1981 adoptions: averages between 1971 and 1981.

[d]DPW, *Adoptions: Annual Report*, 30 June 1981.

[e]Calculations via the same cumulative adotions-per-year method used to calculate the 1972 figures; contact the League of Women Voters of Minnesota for details.

[f]Survey by the League of Women Voters of Indian children in out-of-home placement on 1 Oct. 1981. Responses from all counties where Indian placements were probable except Anoka.

[g]DPW, *Children in Out of Home Placement*, 1 Oct. 1981.

not whether there are problems but that they be allowed to assist in helping these people.

Dealing with Indian Children in the System. Court-ordered placements because of dependency or neglect are over twice as frequent for Indian children as for the population statewide. In these cases, children are taken from the home because parents are not providing proper care or are willfully mistreating them. In 1981, 28% of Indian out-of-home placements were for dependency or neglect, in comparison with 12% of the general population placements.[36] Welfare department records for Hennepin County as of December 1982 showed that 58% of the Indian children in placement were dependency or neglect cases, 21% were voluntary, 14% were delinquents, and 8% involved termination of parental rights.[37]

Placement data show that Indians are most likely to be put in foster homes, with much fewer using group treatment facilities. This is true in absolute terms and percentages relative to all children involved. State-wide data collected by the League of Women Voters showed that 78% of the Indian children had been placed in foster care, 11% in group homes, 9% in institutional care for the emotionally handicapped, 1% in care for mentally retarded, and 1% with relatives (539 responses, October 1981).

Hennepin County data show major racial differences (table 17). Indian children were placed at a younger age in foster homes, whereas white children were older and more apt to be placed in group treatment facilities.

Table 17. Children in Out-of-Home Placement
in Hennepin County, December 1982

	Indian	White
Placed in foster homes	63%	56%
Placed in group treatment facilities	15	27
Under 3 years old at placement	35	17
Over 11 years old at placement	24	49

Sources: Hennepin County Community Services Department, *Comparison of Children in Placement: Child Welfare and Child Protection Divisions*, 1983, tables 3 and 5; *Addendum to the 1981 Comparison of Children in Placement by Racial Group*, 1983, table 2.

Blacks and Indians are less likely than others in the population to terminate parental rights to their children at birth. They give up their children at a later age than is the pattern for the white state population. In 1982, over 40% of all court terminations of parental rights were for children under one year of age. In Black and Indian cases, only 12% were.[38]

Perceived Hostility of the System. An Indian advocate in St. Paul noted, "If you work with welfare on a positive note and are willing to work on your problem, welfare will bend over backwards. But there is a real fear of welfare by Indians, though. There is the fear that welfare will grab your kids and run."[39]

Joseph Westermeyer, a University of Minnesota psychiatrist, documented in 1977 the cases of eight Indian families who had come to institutions of society seeking help.[40] Instead of offering help, in each case the institutional worker had the children removed from the home. Chemical dependency problems increased, there were two attempted suicides, and "within a few weeks of the seizure of the children, all of the six couples still living together had separated."[41] Removal of the children had the same effect in all eight cases: it effectively destroyed the family unit, and it exacerbated the problems of alcoholism, unemployment, and emotional duress of the parents.

Indians view the welfare systems as placing Indian children in substitute homes where they may remain a long time. When the case goes to court, it can be demonstrated that a permanent, loving, caring home has already been found and "bonding" has been established. Experts are brought in to testify to the traumatic effects of separation and return to the family home. The listing of parental failures is presented, with no mention of the strengths of the family or of Indian culture and community.

This is seen as "ganging up" on the mother, helping to make her look bad so that the recommendation will be adoption by the foster family. The social workers can claim that the removal of the child to the questionable home of the Indian parents or relatives would inflict severe, long-lasting, and traumatic damage to the child. And the parent's rights are terminated.[42]

"Best Interests" Placements. As the system makes decisions about a child, perhaps most controversial is the standard used to provide for the "best interests" of the child. Judgments of social workers and judges may be based on their own cultural values, which can be quite different from the values of the family.

The decision that is made also has great impact on parents. A complaint of child neglect or abuse may have a very debilitating effect. There is the bewilderment at confronting the formal legal process and the sense of worthlessness when a court takes the child. Removing the children may so undermine parents' self-confidence that their ability to function successfully is impaired; it may also remove their incentive to struggle against their difficulties.

Records kept by Hennepin County show that Indian families are less apt to visit children who have been removed from their homes. Within a typical month in 1982, a family visit was made in only 39% of

Indian placements because of dependency or neglect (58% of such white children were visited). Voluntarily placed Indian children received even fewer visits: 35%, compared with 74% of whites.[43] Only 29% of the Indian families visited when the child was in a white foster home.[44]

Identity Problems of Indian Adolescents. In adolescence, Indian children adopted by white families may be subject to discrimination; they have questions about who they are, and they may become a problem to their adoptive parents. They may leave or be dumped by the parents, who "terminate the parental relationship."

Many older adolescents are coming to Indian communities seeking their identities. It becomes the burden of the urban Indian agencies to help "teach seventeen-year-old youths trying to find out who they are, how to be Indian."[45] These young people bring with them many emotional scars, the devastating rejection by their adoptive parents, the uncertainty about themselves. The stress may be so damaging that they can never relate or fit in either the Indian or the white world.

The degree of the problem is difficult to assess. All of the Indians interviewed by the League of Women Voters who work with children were aware of specific instances. A juvenile court judge commented, "The adolescent returnee does exist. The full impact has not yet hit. It will get worse, but on balance I believe there are limited numbers of Indians in that situation."[46] In any case, when it comes to evaluating the "best interest" of the child, it appears important to add, "What about the best interest of the adolescent child and the adult?"[47]

Indian Foster Homes. If the goals of the Indian Child Welfare Act are to be achieved, more nonreservation Indian foster homes are needed. Through county and tribal program efforts, the number of Indian foster homes has generally increased in the past few years. Hennepin County had 23 in 1979 and 52 in December 1982, with an Indian shelter home and a group home for small children. The county, which provides programming for all foster families with Indian children, has a goal of 60 Indian homes. An additional short-term foster care group facility was started by the Indian Health Board in Minneapolis in 1984.

Ramsey County had only seven licensed Indian foster homes in 1982, as did St. Louis County; a group home opened in Duluth that summer. Beltrami County, with up to 60 Indian children needing foster care, had only three Indian homes in 1982.

A major reason for the lack of foster homes, according to those who work with the programs, is the unwillingness of many Indians to get involved with the welfare system. They are hesitant to come forward and be evaluated by white standards.

State rules on foster homes provide that the evaluation of applicants should consider cultural differences, and in general state requirements are not considered a barrier for Indians. However, administrative procedures do limit participation. It is very difficult for a single, working parent to be approved. From the viewpoint of the welfare department, continuity with one adult is important; and placing the child in day care is not acceptable. As a rule of thumb, most welfare departments will not allow placement when there is more than a 40-year difference in age between child and adult.

Fire departments may require the homes to make fire safety changes that potential foster families cannot afford. In 1983, eight Indian families in Ramsey County that had gained welfare department approval were refused licensing by fire departments, and the families gave up trying to provide foster homes.[48]

Indian Resources Not Used. Very few Indians are employed by the county systems that make decisions about Indian lives. The Indian Child Welfare Act funds a few individuals to observe what happens in the courts and to respond if directed by the tribe. Hennepin County has a few Indian advocates and two guardians *ad litem.*

The lack of Indian involvement makes it difficult for the counties to comply fully with the act. In Hennepin County, an Indian guardian *ad litem* noted that social workers were not checking on tribal membership and enrolling children if this had not been done. Of 29 cases in 1981–82, 13 children who should have been enrolled had not been.[49]

Social workers may not be aware when a child is Indian and may fail to make contact with the Indian workers. In May 1982, only three of a case load of 15 Indian children had had contact with an Indian advocate.[50] Unless Indians are involved, it is unlikely that the social worker will know the child's extended family and be able to use the placement preferences that the act requires.

Professional staff appear to be less interested in assisting Indians than others, according to 1982 Hennepin County statistics. The placement plan of treatment, which must be prepared within 30 days, had not been completed by the social worker in 36% of the Indian cases (23% of white cases). For voluntary situations, in 19% of Indian cases the agreements had not been prepared within 30 days, whereas in only 7% of the white cases were the workers delinquent.[51]

To remedy the deficiencies in the current system and to make Indian child placements in an Indian way, the St. Paul American Indian

Center in 1984 established the first Indian-controlled private child placement agency in the state, American Indian Family and Children Service.
The program, licensed by the state, has the capacity to assist both urban
and reservation children.

Problems with the Act. To clarify and strengthen the law, a state
version of the Indian Child Welfare Act was proposed in 1984 by tribal
and urban Indians who work with Indian children. Under the proposed
law, the tribe would be notified as soon as a child (including any placed
voluntarily) entered the welfare system so that the Indian community
could provide assistance much earlier in the process. At present, as
many as 18 months pass before the tribes are notified. The proposed
state legislation did not pass in 1984.

Other problems remain, especially the lack of funding from the
federal government to provide the needed tribal services. With a small
staff of one to two social workers each, the reservations have an overwhelming burden in just meeting the needs of the local children. Inability to assist the children living away from the reservations is a major gap
and a source of frustration. Decisions about the funding that does exist
are made by the BIA and not the tribes. As a result, tribes at times have
made only limited use of the BIA-designated urban representatives.

The power to become involved in a child's case rests solely with the
tribe. It is only the tribe that is notified under the federal law. Unless
there is good cooperation, these procedures fail to make full use of the
urban community, with its extensive knowledge and networking capa-
bility.

In the one case where the Red Lake Court requested jurisdiction,
this decision was accepted by the Minnesota county court; however,
questions have been raised about the transfer process. The issue of who
is to pay if the tribe takes jurisdiction of a case is in the courts. In 1982,
the county refused to pay and the BIA was funding the handling of the
case.

Dealing with Canadian Indian children raises questions not only of
tribe-state relations but also international dealings. In the early 1970s,
many Indian children were intentionally brought from Canada for adoption; an estimated 45% of all Indian children adopted in Minnesota during 1968–74 were Canadian.[52] Although this practice has stopped, Canadian children continue to be involved in the Minnesota system, where
they pose unique problems. They do not come under the Indian Child
Welfare Act and lack the protection that it offers.

Summary

Indians are the poorest and most dependent group of Minnesota's citizens. Poverty tears Indian families apart, and many other problems compound the situation. As misery grows, families disintegrate and children are placed in damaging situations—and the cycle goes on.

Until agencies realize that Indians must be involved meaningfully in the decision-making process and that there must be Indian outreach, sensitivity to Indian culture, willingness to modify bureaucratic procedures if necessary, and additional Indian staffing, the cost of Indian services will continue to rise but their effectiveness will not.

Indian communities are strongly objecting to the processes that have taken so many children from their Indian homes and culture. They are insisting that they be involved and have a right to control their children's future. Better funding and better understanding among the many interests involved are needed if there is to be a truly "best interest" solution for each Indian family and child who needs help.

According to an urban Indian community leader, "Indians are tired of being a welfare class, 'downtrodden.' They want to be middle class economically with the comfort and strength of their culture."[53] Before Indians can break the pattern of dependency, they must have not only jobs, decent housing, better health, and schooling, but also self-confidence and hope.

CHAPTER 11

Housing

Without question our people rank as the worst housed
segment of population in the United States. It is not un-
common that Indian people on our reservation still live in
shacks without the benefit of running water, electricity, or
adequate insulation. . . . Minnesota winters are long and
cold.[1]

Indian housing is inferior to that of other state citizens. The 1980
census pointed out several ways in which housing for Indians and
others in the state differed (table 18). Statewide, well over half of all Indians lived in rented homes, while the state average was around one-
fourth. In Minneapolis, 83% rented their housing, compared with 49%
of whites. Indian homes were also much more overcrowded and apt to
be substandard.

Reservation Housing Needs

The 1980 census recorded that more Indian housing on reservations was overcrowded and below standards than was Indian housing
statewide. In identifying housing needs in 1975, the MCT found conditions even worse than those reported in the census (table 19),[2] and the
MCT figures are probably more accurate. According to a 1981 BIA report
on reservation housing, 22% of the homes needed extensive repairs or

Table 18. Indian Housing Compared with All Minnesota Housing

Characteristic	Minnesota Indians	Total Population
Total houses occupied	8,932	1,445,222
Percentage of renters	57	27[a]
Among owners, median value of home	$33,200	$53,100
Average number of persons per family	3.88	3.29
Median number of people per unit:		
Renters	2.66	1.67
Owners	3.64	2.71
Crowded: more than 1.01 persons per room	1,329 (15%)	32,832 (2.3%)
Severely overcrowded: more than 1.5 persons per room	401 (4.5%)	6,910 (0.5%)
Without adequate plumbing[b]	605 (6.8%)	42,950 (2.8%)

Source: US Census, 1980.

[a]White population only.

[b]Adequate plumbing means hot and cold running water, flush toilets, and bathtub or shower.

replacement, and 35% additional homes were needed. Information compiled by the MCT in 1982 indicated an even greater need for housing.

The goal of government housing programs is to provide decent housing for low-income Americans. These programs have been active on the reservations, but the effort has not been enough to meet the needs. Requests for housing by tribal members who wish to return to

Table 19. Indian Housing Needs on Reservations

Housing Need	MCT Survey, 1975[a]	1980 Census	BIA Inventory, 1981
Total houses occupied	–	2,506	2,604
Crowded: more than 1.01 persons per room	33%	576 (23%)	
Severely overcrowded: more than 1.5 persons per room	16%	202 (8%)	
Without adequate plumbing	21%	288 (11.5%)	
Needing extensive repairs	–	–	102 (4%)
Needing replacement	–	–	459 (18%)
Requests to return to reservations	–	–	440
New housing needed	1,126[b]		899

Sources: MCT, *Housing Needs and Programs,* 1976, 7, 14, 22; BIA, Minneapolis Area Office, *Consolidated Housing Inventory,* 1981.

[a]Does not include Red Lake Reservation or the Sioux Communities.

[b]1982 calculation of requests for reservation housing by the MCT.

the reservations have increased substantially. A Leech Lake Reservation official testified to the Senate in 1980 that the reservation was 10 years behind its projected construction needs and that the population was increasing at a rate more than twice the projection.[3]

Financing Reservation Housing

Conventional channels for providing housing are not an alternative for Indians on reservation land. As a federal trust responsibility, the land cannot be mortgaged voluntarily or involuntarily. In case of default, the land cannot be taken in foreclosure. Where the land belongs to the tribe, individual families only have lease use of it, not ownership.

Officers of financial institutions are frequently far distant from reservations, are unfamiliar with them, and are generally reluctant to serve any group of low-income people. If a private financial institution is to invest, the federal government has to act as the guarantor. Almost no programs relying on private investment have provided housing for reservation Indians, and government programs are the only alternative.

Some reservation Indians may have the attitude that the federal government owes them adequate housing, and the idea of debt housing is difficult to accept. Because some programs that serve the reservations are grant programs with no repayment obligation, the attitude is reinforced.

Reservation Land

On some of the reservations, especially the small Sioux Communities, additional housing is not possible unless more land is obtained. The communities' comprehensive plans of 1980 point out the problem: "All land is assigned and there are considerable requests for housing sites from eligible members."[4] "Several are waiting to move in as soon as building sites are available. There can be replacements, but no room for new housing development without expanding the community."[5] Land purchased for Prairie Island and Shakopee-Mdewakanton was being processed by the BIA in 1982.

The Upper Sioux and Prairie Island Indian communities have the problem of significant amounts of land in the floodplain. Over half of Prairie Island's land is in the 100-year floodplain area. At the Upper Sioux Community, steep banks also limit housing sites.

Urban Housing for Indians

In the cities, many Indian households are headed by women. Families are large, and there is high mobility. Seeking community and preferring to live near family and friends, Indians tend to concentrate in certain areas, often doubling up with family members in crowded circumstances. Large amounts of family resources, not uncommonly 50–60% of income, must be spent for shelter. Day-to-day survival is a struggle, "a question of whether to feed the family or pay rent."[6]

Because affordable, decent housing for low-income people is severely limited, many Indians have to live in substandard and unhealthful conditions. The slum nature of the housing is associated with many of the other problems considered in this book: poor health conditions, chemical dependency, criminal activity and aggressive police supervision, and the very severe problem of providing a good environment for raising children.

Many urban Indians live in old apartment buildings with code violations and frequently changing owners. In 1980, the city of Minneapolis reported that the Phillips neighborhood, an area with a large Indian population, had almost 3,000 units of substandard housing, including 62% of all one- and two-unit homes.[7]

A survey in 1978 by the Upper Midwest Indian Center found that the median Indian home was 70 years old, whereas the citywide average was 55 years. Various problems were noted in 10–30% of the homes, and 25% of the renters stated that the owner seldom or never made repairs.[8]

The reality of "nowhere else to go" leaves Indians at the mercy of indifferent owners. Even substandard units are not affordable. If all code violations were corrected, the additional rent needed to cover the costs would put them even more out of reach.

Rental policies add to the difficulties. Owners frequently require not only the first and last months' rent as a deposit but also a damage deposit, expenses that can easily amount to $1,000. For a family living on a basic welfare grant of $600 per month, the advance payment is not possible.

"The housing prospects for low-income people are very bleak in Minneapolis," according to an Indian housing advocate at the Minneapolis American Indian Center.[9] In 1981, 1,500 Indian clients sought assistance; housing was located for less than half.

Discrimination

Discrimination in housing is a problem faced by many Indians. The survey done of Minneapolis Indians in 1978 found that 27% had experienced housing discrimination; 466 problems were cited. The major categories mentioned were discrimination based on race, 27%; because of children, 24%; and for being on welfare, 12%. Although there are state laws and city ordinances forbidding these kinds of discrimination, only 14% of those surveyed had ever made a formal complaint.[10]

Discrimination is also a factor in getting conventional housing in reservation areas. An MCT report stated, "Not obtaining adequate housing is often due to problems with the existing housing supply mechanism. . . . Discrimination on the part of realtors, sellers, and/or landlords is certainly not unique to urban minorities alone."[11]

The state Indian housing program and federal programs on the reservations have the right to maintain their Indian character, according to laws and court decisions. In 1983, a federal court in Minneapolis ruled (*St. Paul Intertribal Housing Board v. HUD*) that the federally subsidized program for low-income people can be used for urban Indian housing programs.

Need for Supportive Services

Having to rent run-down, dilapidated housing in communities where no one seems to care about the quality of homes can result in a similar attitude by tenants. Renters who are not responsible for repairs do not have a strong incentive to put their scarce resources into maintenance, and overcrowding adds to these problems.

The Indian community has pointed out the need for supportive and education services for city dwellers. Minneapolis funds an Indian housing advocate located at the Minneapolis American Indian Center whose function is to help in finding housing; however, the related service needs—education in money management, home maintenance, and tenant rights; counseling and support—have not yet begun to be met.[12]

Need for Emergency Housing

Another important unmet need is emergency housing to provide temporary shelter for families who are suddenly displaced or who have migrated to the cities. In the 1970s, the Minneapolis Housing Authority set aside several housing units for stays limited to a few weeks. That program no longer operates, leaving a void in providing emergency housing assistance.

Programs

Housing programs to help low-income people with home ownership and rent subsidies are equally available for Indians who do not live on reservation trust land. Federal and state housing programs have been adapted to meet the unique circumstances of the reservations, and the state program for Indian housing also extends into urban areas.

Adaptations for Reservations

Federal government assistance for housing began in 1937, but it was not until the early 1960s that efforts were made to extend the programs to Indian reservations, with tribes being allowed to establish housing authorities. In 1968, the US Housing Act was amended to authorize assistance to low-income families in Indian areas, and funds are set aside for that purpose (42 USC 1437). Minnesota's reservations are served by the Chicago office of the US Department of Housing and Urban Development's (HUD) Indian housing program.

Housing Authorities. All the reservations have housing authorities, although it has only been in the 1980s that the smaller reservations were allowed to enter the program. The Minnesota Dakota Indian Housing Authority administers the HUD programs for the four Sioux Communities.

Reservation housing authorities are government subdivisions established by the tribal governments, with independent boards. They are responsible for proposing housing projects and supervising the building. Under contract with HUD, they own and manage the projects. Individual projects can last 25–40 years, depending on the program. It is the housing authority's responsibility to see that rents are collected on time and that the homes are maintained.

Home Ownership. HUD home ownership programs for Indian reservations generally involve some form of mutual help, in which the individual provides the land, participates in the building, does the maintenance, and pays for utilities. These apply as "sweat equity" against the purchase price. Ownership rests with the housing authority until the house is paid for.

Under the ownership programs, the monthly payment is based on income level—set at 15% of income in 1982—with the understanding that utility payments must also be made. The excess over administration and insurance costs is used to pay off the mortgage and speed up ownership. If the owner gets into dire financial straits, a minimum of $30 a month must be paid to cover administrative costs and insurance. A person can be carried only 30 days without foreclosure.

Rental Programs. Reservation rental programs are operated by the housing authority, which makes utility payments and provides maintenance. Rent payment is based on income under federal guidelines, with HUD making up the difference. Financially strapped renters can be carried without paying rent; however, the utility equivalent must be paid. In addition to regular rental programs, there are special programs for the elderly.

Problems with HUD Programs

Income Too Low. Many Indian families, urban as well as reservation, cannot meet the minimum requirements for participation in government housing programs for low-income people. The programs frequently limit a family's monthly payment to 25% of income, but they also require as an absolute minimum payment enough to cover utilities and administrative expenses of the housing authority. The required costs alone often exceed the 25% ceiling. A 1977 survey of housing on Leech Lake Reservation found that 18% had housing payments in excess of 25% of gross family income.[13]

HUD Bureaucracy. Developing HUD projects is a time-consuming effort taking three or more years. On Mille Lacs Reservation, construction was begun on 30 HUD units in August 1982; the planning had begun six years before.

Programs are also very complex. The US Senate Select Committee on Indian Affairs noted in 1979 that the bureaucracy and regulations were a burden for Indian housing authorities, which lack funds for professional employees. The committee stated that HUD rarely funds sufficient technical assistance or administrative help and "then blames the 'incompetent' housing authorities for delays."[14]

Collecting Payments. "Many Indian housing authorities are experiencing great difficulties in collecting rental and home buyer payments."[15] The poverty of the occupants, exacerbated by the recession, makes it difficult for them to meet the required charges. Tribal leaders and courts may be reluctant to enforce collection and eviction policies because there is often no other place on the reservation for evicted people to be housed.

In 1982–83, both Red Lake and Leech Lake reservations were notified that their collection records needed to be improved. Innovative efforts have been made to improve collections, including payroll deduction for those who are employed by the tribe, improving understanding of the importance of the programs, and a drawing for a prize among families that have made monthly payments on time throughout the year.

Maintenance and repair are often problems. The housing authorities lack funding and staff to provide upkeep, and the occupants may fail to understand their obligations.

Funding. In the early 1980s, no further funds were provided for HUD housing because a substantial backlog of unused funds remained. By the spring of 1983, however, only an estimated one and one-half years' worth of money for construction remained. Because of the lag time between allocation of money and actual construction, if new money is not allocated soon the programs will come to a halt.

Community Development Block Grants

In addition to funding home construction and supervising the housing authorities, HUD also distributes the community development block grant funds. This money goes to local governments, including Indian tribes, for community priority purposes as determined by the local government. In several instances, the tribes in Minnesota have used these funds for housing, rehabilitation programs, or—in Fond du Lac and some of the Sioux Communities—purchase of land.

Bureau of Indian Affairs Programs

Under the Housing Improvement Program, the BIA provides funds to the tribes, which make grants to individual Indians. Money may be used for repairs and major rehabilitation ($20,000 maximum in 1980); for down payments on housing loans ($5,000 maximum); and, to a limited extent, for building new homes ($45,000 maximum). The programs are only for the very poor, frequently the elderly, and only if assistance is not available from other sources.

In the case of a new home, ownership passes to the individual, although there may be a period of time before the transfer. Funds may not be used for mobile home purchases or for renovation of HUD-funded homes unless those homes have been completely paid for.

The BIA also assists in reservation housing programs with site development and the building and maintenance of roads. There has been criticism of the latter program because funding has lagged and road work is many years behind needs. Road problems identified on White Earth Reservation in 1982 included dirt access roads as long as three to five miles that are difficult to travel in bad weather.

Indian Health Service Programs

The IHS constructs water and sewer facilities for the new housing on the reservations. Its priorities, within available funding, are HUD homes first; then BIA housing improvement construction; and third, "other," which includes the state-funded housing. When IHS funds are not provided, the purchaser pays for the facilities as part of the construction cost. (Problems with the maintenance of water and sewer systems are discussed in chap. 12.)

Farmers Home Administration Programs

A major federal supplier of housing assistance for low-income rural people who cannot get credit elsewhere is the Farmers Home Administration (FmHA), US Department of Agriculture, which is specifically authorized to provide loans to Indian tribes and individuals (42 USC 1471). There is no down payment, and interest was as low as 1% in 1983.

To obtain a loan, an enforceable mortgage is required. For Indian families, a leasehold from the tribe for one and one-half times the period of the mortgage meets the requirement. If there is a default, FmHA may foreclose and sell the house to anybody; but, at the end of the leasehold period (50 years on a new home), the land reverts to trust status, unencumbered.

With a few exceptions, Indians have not used the FmHA program. The 1979 Senate Select Committee report on Indian housing noted that FmHA had very little outreach to Indians and, by being closely linked to county governments, "cannot avoid being influenced by the often deep-seated tensions between county governments and tribal governments at the local level."[16]

FmHA has funded one major reservation program, a 30-unit congregate housing project for the elderly at White Earth. The $1 million facility, one of two such demonstration projects in the country, is for those aged 62 and older who can continue independent living. Many support services are available, including meals, transportation, personal care, housekeeping, public health nursing (IHS), and social and recreational services. The residents pay rent limited to 25% of income.

Weatherization: Federal and State Funding

Weatherization is a combined federal (42 USC 6861) and state (Mn. Stat. 268.37) program, administered through the state Department of Economic Security. Tribes have the option of using the state-coordinated program or getting funding directly from Washington. Minnesota reservations use the state program, getting 2% of the total funding.

Grants are provided for material and labor to weatherize homes. In calendar year 1982, $410,000 was received, varying from $5,000 for Grand Portage and $13,000 for the four Sioux Communities to $99,000 for Leech Lake.

Only a few homes can be assisted yearly. The housing director on the Bois Forte Reservation has noted that the program would benefit from an increase in the funds spent on each house. "Most dwellings require major repairs before an adequate weatherization project can be initiated."[17]

Impact on the Reservations

Commenting on the housing programs, Red Lake Reservation's health plan noted, "There has been no other single development that has done so much to improve the standard of living and general welfare of the population."[18] The BIA-compiled figures for 1981 indicate that 65% of all reservation housing in Minnesota had been built in the previous 18 years, an average of 94 new homes a year (table 20).

Economic Importance

Besides providing decent, warm housing, the programs have been of great economic importance to the reservations in bringing employ-

Table 20. New or Improved Housing on Minnesota Reservations

	Total	MCT	Red Lake	Sioux Communities
Total houses, 1981	2,604	1,672	802	130
New homes built, 1963–1981				
HUD:				
Ownership	298	68	230	–
Rental	447	382	65	–
BIA Housing Improvement				
Program	561	421	84	56
Other[a]	378	173	198	7
Total built since 1963	1,684 (65%)	1,004 (62%)	577 (72%)	63 (48%)
Repairs and improvements, 1963–81[b]	1,752	455	959	338

Sources: BIA, Minneapolis Area Office, *New Homes Constructed, FY 1963–81; Housing Improvement Repairs,* 1963–81.

[a]Includes Minnesota Housing Finance Agency program.

[b]Includes BIA Housing Improvement Program, community development block grants, weatherization, and Minnesota Housing Finance Agency Program grants and loans.

ment and employment training. Several reservations have their own construction companies and are successfully bidding for and carrying out the projects.

For instance, the Fond du Lac Equipment and Construction Company had built 100 houses and done some 165 repair projects by 1982. The homes use the wood-gas furnaces built by the Fond du Lac Manufacturing Company. The congregate housing project built in 1983 at White Earth used eight Indian subcontractors, and two-thirds of the work force was Indian. In the state Indian housing program, 75% of the new homes built through 1983 used Indian labor.

The housing construction programs have continued at about the same pace during the early 1980s, while other employment opportunities have become very scarce. "Without housing, the reservation would be in a very bad way," commented the executive director of the Fond du Lac Reservation.[19]

Minnesota Housing Finance Agency

In the early 1970s, Minnesota began home ownership and home improvement grant and loan programs, administered by the state's Housing Finance Agency, to assist in providing housing for low-income residents. After extensive lobbying by the Indian communities, a program specifically designed to provide housing for the state's Indian residents was begun in 1976 (Mn. Stat. 462.07, subd. 14).

Minnesota is the first state in the nation to recognize and assist with the housing needs of Indians through a program operated by Indians. By summer 1983, the program was operating through three tribal organizations and two urban groups: Minnesota Chippewa Tribal Housing Corporation, for the six MCT reservations and their members and as administrator of the Duluth Urban Indian Housing program; Red Lake Housing Finance Corporation, Red Lake Reservation; Minnesota Dakota Indian Housing Authority, administering the program for the four Sioux Communities and the Twin Cities suburban program; St. Paul Intertribal Housing Board, for the St. Paul Indian Housing program; and the Minneapolis Community Development Agency, for the Minneapolis Urban Indian Housing program.

These programs have extensive Indian involvement. At the state level, the Urban Advisory Council of the Indian Affairs Council assists in planning the urban programs. The Minneapolis program has a contract with Little Earth of United Tribes to provide advisory assistance.

In Duluth, the MCT administrators use the Duluth Urban Indian

Advisory Committee composed of Indian residents of the city. The St. Paul Intertribal Housing Board has brought together representatives from the city's major Indian organizations. The Minnesota Dakota Indian Housing Authority is made up of two representatives from each of the four communities' five-member housing authorities.

How the Program Works

The program provides housing loans for Indians with low and moderate incomes who are a reasonable credit risk. One spouse must be enrolled in a federally recognized tribe (not necessarily a Minnesota tribe). The law requires that the programs "take into account the housing needs of all Indians residing both on and off reservations," providing for a "reasonable balance" between the groups (Mn. Stat. 462A.07, subd. 14).

The state money is in a revolving fund that totaled $22.46 million in 1983, $3 million designated for urban Indians and $19.46 million allotted to the tribes. The 1984 legislature added $1.75 million more for tribal housing and $750,000 for the urban program.

Tribal money was distributed by a population formula, 62.5% to the MCT, 29% to the Red Lake band, and 8.5% to the Sioux Communities. When the program first began, an additional $600,000 was provided for rehabilitation grants; 139 were made to low-income Indian families.

Each administering agency makes its own contract with the state. In general, the home ownership loans require no down payment and run for 30 years; home improvement loans are for 15 years. Each tribal program sets its own limits on family income, value of the house, and interest rate (which varies from 3.5% to 5%). The record of loan repayment has remained good. With the loans going into their sixth year, delinquency rates were about 2–4%, depending on the program.

The Tribal Contracts

As of March 1984, the MCT Tribal Housing Corporation had made 520 loans, and Red Lake Housing Finance Corporation had made 144 loans. In addition, 10 single family homes were built and operated under a rental program.

The Sioux Communities had provided 41 loans for ownership and home improvement. In addition, state-provided grant money was packaged with funds from community action agencies, FmHA, BIA, and weatherization programs to provide home improvement grants to 50 people. The Minnesota Housing Finance Agency contributed from $500 to $6,000 per grant.

Urban Housing Program

A housing program with money specifically set aside for urban Indians was added to the law in 1978. One provision, however, required that funding be obtained from other sources also (Mn. Stat. 462A.07, subd. 14), which made it difficult to get several of the programs started. In 1983, legislation exempted Duluth from the requirement. By spring 1984, all the programs were operational and had committed the available funds.

The state money is used to help with down payments and to lower monthly mortgage costs. Additional funding has come from a variety of sources, depending upon the program: traditional mortgage financing obtained by the individual; state bond funds; city revenue bonds; community development block grants; HUD home ownership program; and, in the Minneapolis and St. Paul programs, the HUD-subsidized rental program, Section 8. The Minneapolis/St. Paul Family Housing Fund, with money from the McKnight Foundation, federal programs, and city bonds (used to subsidize interest rates for low-income people), has also been used.

By March 1984, eight loans had been made in Duluth and eight more in the Twin Cities suburbs, concentrated in areas with large numbers of children being served by Title IV Indian education programs. In St. Paul, the program was held up until the court decided that Section 8 funds could subsidize rents in a program for Indians only.

The Minneapolis program includes a provision for families to rent at the beginning and, as financial stability is demonstrated, move into home ownership. Families are chosen through a lottery among those who meet HUD standards of income level, job stability, credit worthiness, and marital status. Because general housing program funds are used, about one-fifth of the participants in the Minneapolis program cannot be Indian. As of June 1983, about one-half (76) of the units had been prepared, 24 of new construction and 52 rehabilitated. Of these, there were renters in 17, owners in 30 (27 Indian), and 29 were vacant.

The program has some major problems. Some of the people selected had not previously been accepted in the Section 8 program, and further Section 8 slots were not available. The renting feature was difficult for the agency to administer, and Indians who rented were having difficulty qualifying for ownership. Questions have been raised about who would replace Indian families who move out of homes. There appears to be no guarantee that Indians will be found and assisted to replace them. Efforts were being made in 1984 to resolve the issues.

Little Earth of United Tribes, Minneapolis

Little Earth of United Tribes in Minneapolis was the first HUD-financed urban Indian project in the nation, and it has continued to be the only Indian-controlled one. The complex of 212 units, housing some 900 residents (1982), was built in 1974. It was reorganized in 1975 when the American Indian Movement took over management and HUD assumed the mortgage; Section 8 housing rent subsidy was obtained. As of 1982, the renters were 98% Indian. A day-care center and child care personnel training program were operating at the facility in 1983.

HUD, citing the large mortgage payment in arrears, proposed in 1982 that the housing project be sold. This was strenuously resisted by Little Earth's board of directors, and the issue was taken to court.

A housing project like Little Earth is very difficult to operate on a financially sound basis. Extensive work needs to be done: a 1982 city evaluation of the property estimated that $2.8 million in repairs is needed. Many similar projects started in the early 1970s to serve urban areas have ended in abandonment or foreclosure.

The fate of Little Earth is not certain. A court-appointed receiver was managing the property as of fall 1983. To the Indians involved, it is very important that the project continue to serve low-income people, remain under Indian control, and stay a focal point for the Minneapolis urban Indian community.

Summary

The uniqueness of reservation housing problems requires public housing efforts. The Minnesota state program has been most helpful in providing flexibility to serve Indians. HUD is the major federal supplier of housing funds, and it will be out of money around 1985. A successor program with major funding must be put in place.

But even with these various programs, the demands on reservation housing are increasing at a faster pace than housing starts. The US Senate Select Committee on Indian Affairs has stated that a means must be found to bring private investment funds onto the reservations. The problems of reservation housing cannot be solved until both the public and private sectors become heavily involved.[20]

In urban areas, before Indians can be extricated from the bind of exorbitant rents, degrading dilapidation, negligent owners, and long waiting lists for public housing, the supply of inexpensive rentals will have to be vastly increased. The Minnesota housing program is an attempt to help, but it is not reaching the low-income group that has the greatest needs. Indians should have greater roles in designing programs that they know will meet their needs. Greater emphasis on home maintenance and housing management skills are a necessary part of improved urban living.

CHAPTER 12

Health

A young lady was seriously ill with hepatitis. She felt that she was being treated like dirt by the nurses at the hospital and she checked herself out. She refused to go back. A few days later she tried to get into another hospital; . . . she went into a coma; . . . three days later she died. . . . A young mother brought her child into the emergency room because the child had fallen and gotten badly hurt. They treated her as if she had beaten the child. She vowed never to go back there again. . . . These cases exemplify the seriousness that results from the inability to be culturally sensitive and responsive to Indian needs.[1]

Background

Indian Medicine

Traditional Indian medicine included a strong spiritual component and an extensive knowledge of herbs, drugs, and other pharmaceutical remedies. The non-Indian medical profession is only now beginning to recognize the validity of much Indian medicine.

The Indian doctor or healer dealt with the whole of life—natural, spiritual, and physical—to cure an illness. To Indian people, this concept of life was not theoretical but fundamental. "Traditions were passed

199

down within the clans. . . . Elders transmitted their knowledge to the younger family members. A great deal of care was taken passing this information along, not only because it was of a religious nature, but also because some of the medicines could be very dangerous if administered improperly."[2]

Although Indian communities vary and, to some extent, the old ways have now been forgotten, the Indian medicine man, with healing powers received as a gift from the spirits, continues to help the people. "Much secrecy surrounds the field of traditional medicine even today. If people talk about it at all, they do so reservedly, somewhat fearfully, not wanting to show disrespect."[3]

White Medicine in the Early Days

Diseases introduced to the Indians for the first time by the whites decimated Indian communities. Being forced onto reservations led to a permanent and more communal living pattern than that of traditional small bands moving with the food supply and seasons.

White medical care was often promised to Indians in treaties during the mid-nineteenth century. As with other services, health care was paid for with money due the Indians for land they had sold. Red Lake Hospital, for instance, started in 1914, was funded by tribal money until the late 1940s.

Once these funds ran out, Congress continued the programs with federal money. The Meriam report of 1928 explained the need for the federal program:

> The advent of white civilization has forced on the Indians new problems of health and sanitation. . . . The presence of their villages in close proximity to white settlements made the health and sanitary conditions in those villages public questions of concern to the entire section. . . . Both the Indians and their white neighbors are concerned in having [Indians] live according to at least a minimum standard of health and decency. Less than that means not only that they may become a menace to the whites but also that they themselves will go through a long drawn out and painful process of vanishing. They must be aided for the preservation of themselves.[4]

The Role of Federal and State Governments

The federal government has continued to be the major health provider on the reservations. In 1955, PL 83–568 transferred the Indian

Health Service (IHS) from the BIA to the US Public Health Service under the Department of Health, Education and Welfare (now Health and Human Services). The responsibility of IHS was clarified and expanded to include care of Indians living near reservations. In 1976, a major effort was begun to upgrade facilities and improve health services to Indian reservations with the Indian Health Care Improvement Act (PL 94–437), which also provided some funds for urban Indian health care.

Because of the availability of federally funded Indian health programs, the state role in providing Indian health services has been far smaller than in other program areas. Minnesota, however, was one of the first states to act in dealing with Indian health problems. As early as 1911, it was concerned about tuberculosis and trachoma (an eye disease that causes permanent injury) among the state's Indians. Minnesota assigned public health nurses to work with Indians in 1923, the first state to begin such a program.

Vital Statistics and Health Problems

Tremendous improvements have occurred in Indian health. The Meriam report quoted 1925 statistics for Minnesota. Among 13,910 Indians, there were 255 deaths, 18.3 per 1,000 population. (All the following birth and death rates are given per 1,000.) The state's general population death rate at that time was 9.7.[5] In 1980 there were 199 Indian deaths in a population of 35,016, a rate of 5.7.[6] Some major causes of death in the 1920s are no longer a problem: tuberculosis caused 60 deaths in 1925, 24% of the total.[7] This disease is now very rare.

Current vital statistics are based on reports filed with the Minnesota Department of Health and published annually in *Minnesota Health Statistics*. Studies done by Indians knowledgeable of their communities have shown a failure to accurately identify Indians on death certificates, resulting in an undercount.[8] The statistics that follow are from the state reports for the year or years indicated. Although the Indians may be undercounted, these figures are used because they are the only ones available. The 1980 census figures are used for rates based on population.

High Birthrate

The Indian birthrate in Minnesota is twice that of the general population. In 1979–81, it was 33.6; the total state rate was 16.5 for the same period. For the same three years, Minneapolis had a higher Indian birthrate than the state average, at 38.7, while that city's general population birthrate was slightly lower, 16.0.

The Indian population is increasing at a much faster rate than the general population. Indian births were six times Indian deaths in 1980 (1,223 births; 199 deaths), while the ratio for the state's total population was two births for every death.

Infant Mortality Rate

Infant deaths (mortality) are an important measurement of the health of a population group. Infant mortality rates are calculated as the number of deaths of infants under one year of age per 1,000 births. Indians have a higher rate than the general population, but there has been substantial improvement in infant mortality — especially in the reservation areas, which are served by the IHS (table 21).

Table 21. Infant Mortality Rate in Minnesota
(Deaths per 1,000 Births)

Years	Minnesota		Reservations[a]		Urban[b]	
	Indians	All Races	Indians	All Races	Indians	All Races
1970–72	20.7	17.2	16.9	19.0	21.5	17.4
1974–76	19.3	14.0	11.3	14.0	28.2	14.9
1979–81	14.2	10.3	–	–	–	–

Sources: Minnesota Department of Health, *Minnesota Indian People: Selected Health Statistics,* 1980, 74; *Minnesota Health Statistics,* 1979–81.
[a]Area served by the Indian Health Service.
[b]Hennepin and Ramsey counties and the city of Duluth.

The 1979–81 state infant mortality rate for Indians was about one and one-third the total state figure. It was also higher than the IHS figure of 13.8 for Indians nationwide.[9] In Minneapolis, however, the figures were 25.1 for Indians and 12.5 for the city as a whole, or two to one. Although the city's figures were higher for all people, they were significantly higher for Indians.

Reservation infant mortality showed a major decline between 1970–72 and 1974–76, and it remained considerably lower than the infant mortality of the general population of the area.[10] In the urban setting, however, there was a major increase in Indian infant mortality between the two periods, while the overall urban rate declined.

Postneonatal Mortality Rate

Statistically important in the infant mortality figures is the postneonatal death rate; that is, deaths that occur after 28 days and before one year. Deaths during this period may reflect poor care provided by young and inexperienced mothers, poor quality or lack of follow-up medical care and child care instructions, or parental chemical abuse problems resulting in child neglect.

Postneonatal infant deaths occur much more frequently among Indians than they do in the general population. For 1979–81, 64% of Indian infant deaths were postneonatal, compared with 34% in the general population. The postneonatal mortality rate was 9.1 for Indians, two and one-half times the rate for the state's general population (3.5).

The difference between the reservation and urban Indians is also large, again indicating the more readily available medical care on the reservations and, perhaps, a more extensive nurturing network for infants. In 1974–76, the IHS service unit rate of postneonatal deaths was 4.8; the urban Indian rate, 15.3 — more than three times greater.[11]

High-Risk Births

High-risk births are measured by several indicators, and special help — such as the nutritional supplements of the WIC program — is available in areas of high-risk concentrations. Statistical measurements show the Indian population at greater risk than the general population.

Low Birth Weight. Research has found that smaller babies, born at 5.5 pounds or less, are at higher risk of early death than those born over that weight. Low-income and minority mothers are more apt to have low-weight babies. In 1974–76, 7.3% of all Indian births were at the low birth weight, compared with 5.5% of those of all races. Again, the percentage was lower in the area served by IHS (6.4%) and higher in the urban area (8.2%).[12]

Mother's Age. The mother's age is another statistically significant factor in high-risk births. It has been going up for the Indian population as well as the state generally, but Indian mothers are two and one-half times more apt to be under 20 years of age at childbirth than are those in the state's general population. In 1974–76, 32.5% of Indian mothers were under 20 at the time of the child's birth, compared with 12.6% of all mothers; for 1978–80, the figures are 27.4 and 10.7%, respectively.[13]

The problems of early-age pregnancies and frequency of children are priorities of the community health programs throughout the state. More attention is needed to sex education at the junior high school level, including emphasis on postponement of childbearing, as well as parenting skills classes and support programs for single-parent homes.

Children Born Out of Wedlock. A majority of Indian births in the state are out of wedlock: 53.2% in 1978–80, compared with 10.8% of all births. The numbers are especially large among mothers under 20 years of age: 79.4%, compared with 46.3% of all mothers under 20.[14] The figures for 1974–76, analyzed for reservation and urban populations, show the Indian out-of-wedlock percentage at 40% in the IHS service area and 60% in the cities.[15]

Length of Prenatal Care. Professionals agree that care should begin within the first three months of pregnancy. The increased risk group is measured as those who get care only during the last three months of pregnancy or get no care at all. In 1974–76, the percentage of Indians who received the poorer care was over four times that for the state's general population: 18.2%, compared with 4.3%. Pregnant Indians on reservations, while receiving somewhat better care than those in the urban areas, were still far more likely to receive only late prenatal care than the general population in the area: 17.5%, compared with 5.5%. One-fifth of all urban pregnant Indian women did not get medical care or got it only in the third trimester: 20.7%, compared with 4.4% for the general population.[16]

Life Expectancy

Nationally, Indians have a life expectancy of 71 years, as compared with the general population average of 74 years.[17] Life expectancy for Minnesota Indians cannot be determined because it takes a death level of at least 1,600 a year to determine an accurate death rate for a population. However, Indian deaths in Minnesota have been compared by age at time of death to all deaths (table 22).

The distribution of deaths by age shows the much higher incidence of infant death among Indians than for all races, especially in urban areas, where the Indian percentage was eight times higher than that for

Table 22. Percentage of Deaths at Various Ages in Minnesota, 1975–76

	Indians			
Age at death	Statewide	IHS Service Area	Urban[a]	All Races
Under 1 year	9.9%	5.0%	19.6%	2.4%
1–24 years	15.0	15.4	13.7	3.6
25–44 years	17.3	11.1	26.2	3.7
45–64 years	23.2	24.0	20.2	19.0
65 and over	34.6	44.4	19.6	71.3

Source: Minnesota Indian People, 46.
    [a]Hennepin and Ramsey counties.

all Minnesotans. Fewer than half as many Indians as people of all races lived long enough to die at 65 or older.

A study of all death certificates in Minnesota for 1970–81 found that Indian males died at an average age of 50.2 years and white males at 59.4 years. Indian women died at a significantly earlier age, 44.5 years, compared with white women, who died at the average age of 60.1 years. Indians were the only racial group in which women died at a younger age than men.[18]

Causes of Death

Heart disease, not including strokes, is the primary cause of death of Minnesota Indians, as well as the general population. Causes of death vary considerably in rank between the two population groups after that: heart disease, cancer, and strokes—the top three causes of death among the general population in 1979–81 (72% of all deaths)—caused only 40% of deaths among Indians (table 23).

A close second cause of death for Indians was accidents, which was much less significant among the general population. Accidents, homicides, suicides, and other violent deaths, combined as a single category, were the leading cause of death among Indians. At a rate of 147.6 per 100,000 (27%), violent deaths occurred among Indians two and one-half times more often than among the general population in 1979–81.

High rates of suicide are frequently mentioned as a particularly

Table 23. Leading Causes of Death in Minnesota, 1979–81

Cause	Indians			All Races		
	Rank	Percentage of Deaths	Rate per 100,000	Rank	Percentage of Deaths	Rate per 100,000
Heart disease (not including stroke)	1	24.2	132.2	1	40.8	328.0
Accidents	2	20.0	109.4	5	5.5	44.1
Neoplasms (cancer)	3	10.3	56.3	2	21.0	169.1
Respiratory disease	4	6.4	35.1	4	6.9	55.7
Chronic liver disease	5	5.6	30.6	8	1.0	8.4
Cardiovascular disease (stroke)	6	5.0	27.7	3	9.8	79.1
Homicide	7	3.0	16.3	14	.3	2.6
Infant mortality	8	3.0	16.3	9	1.0	7.9
Suicide	9	2.8	15.1	7	1.3	10.7
Diabetes	10	1.7	9.4	6	1.5	11.8

Source: Minnesota Health Statistics, 1979–81.

important health problem for Indians. In Minnesota, the Indian rate of death from suicide in 1979–81 was almost one and one-half times greater than the rate for the general population. Even so, suicide may not be as severe a problem for Indians in Minnesota as it is for Indians nationwide. A 1972 study noted that, in contrast with some tribes, the Ojibways and other Indians in Minnesota had a relatively low suicide rate.[19]

Homicide takes even more Indian lives yearly. It was over six times more prevalent among Indians in 1979–81 than among the general population.

Chemical dependency (see chap. 13) is a pervasive, severe problem of great concern to the Indian communities. Its impact is reflected in many of the mortality and morbidity statistics.

Morbidity

Morbidity statistics for 1976–78, as reported by the three IHS ambulatory patient care programs at Red Lake, Leech Lake, and White Earth reservations, show that respiratory diseases were the major cause of patient visits.[20] At Fond du Lac's Min No Ya Win clinic ("good health to all"), 30% of the cases were from this cause in 1983. This illness was also the most prevalent one dealt with by the Indian Health Board in Minneapolis in 1979–81.[21] Respiratory and infectious diseases often correlate with conditions of poverty; overcrowded, inadequate housing; and poor sanitation.

High blood pressure (hypertension) was the second major problem that brought people to the IHS clinics. In the summer of 1983, the IHS unit director at White Earth reported an increase in high blood pressure, along with other stress-related illnesses, resulting from the worsened economic conditions.[22] Diabetes was the third major problem in 1976–78.

Acute otitis media, middle-ear infection among children, was one of the top reasons for visiting the IHS facilities. At the Fond du Lac Reservation clinic, it was the third most frequent cause for visits, 10% of all cases. In its chronic form and in situations where the infection and subsequent fluid retention are not treated, the disease contributes to hearing impairment. Related to upper respiratory tract infection associated with environmental problems, it is estimated to affect 20–60% of all Indian children, in contrast with about 5% of children in the general population.

A 1977 study of children at Anderson Elementary School, Minneapolis, found that nearly half of the Indian children had evidence of the chronic form of the disease. Among similar low-income, non-Indian students, the incidence was only 20%.[23] The prevalence of the disease and the hearing impairment it causes no doubt contribute to learning difficulties and poor educational achievement.

Physical Impairment

The relatively greater health needs of Indian children were reported in the state Indian education needs assessment, for which Indian and non-Indian children placed in special education programs in 1977–78 were evaluated. The assessment covered over 3,000 Indian students in 25 school districts. The Indian rate of physical impairment (orthopedic, hearing, or visual) was 2.7 per 1,000 students. For non-Indian students in the same buildings, it was 1.75 per 1,000 students.[24]

Poor Nutrition

Proper diet is a problem for many Indians because of low income and lack of understanding of nutritional needs. A survey conducted by the St. Paul American Indian Center Community Food and Nutrition Program found that diets were extremely high in fats, sugar, and salt, and low in protein and vitamins. Greater amounts of vegetables were needed.[25]

For many reservation Indians, the commodity food program is the sole food supply, and it is not supplemented by other purchases. Although recipients may choose on a monthly basis to take food stamps instead, this entails a good deal of paperwork that discourages people from participation. Commodity program foods include canned meat, fruits, and vegetables, and other products that can be stored without refrigeration; no fresh foods are provided.

It is possible to get a properly balanced diet from the commodities program if the recipient has a good understanding of nutrition. Unless careful choices are made, however, the diet is high in calories, starch, sugar, salt, and cholesterol. This imbalance becomes a significant problem to those with diabetes, high blood pressure, obesity, and other problems that require special diets. The commodity program has no provision for meeting these dietary needs, and no other resources are provided. Using these foods to provide a special diet is exceedingly difficult. In addition to making wise food selections, the individual must wash salt or sugar off the foods and remove the fat.[26]

Indian Health Service

The major supplier of health care to Indians living on reservations in Minnesota is the Indian Health Service. It provides preventive, cura-tive, rehabilitative, and environmental health services on reservations, and it funds services in certain urban locations.

In the 1976 law (PL 94–437), Congress stated that federal health services are required because of the federal government's historical and unique legal relationship with, and responsibility to, the American Indian people. In view of this statement and the many years the federal government has provided medical care, "the Indian Health Service program is generally viewed by the Indian community as an obligation of the federal government assumed in return for the cession of Indian land."[27]

Eligibility

Eligibility for health care services varies with the type of program. Direct facilities—hospitals or clinics—provide whatever services are available at the facility to any person considered Indian, from a federally recognized tribe, who comes in. The individual need not be formally enrolled and may be from any tribe, not just from that reservation. There is no means test, and until 1983 there was no billing of third parties for reimbursement. Beginning in 1984, efforts were made to collect from insurance if the patient qualified.

When the facility does not provide some services (for instance, no major surgery is done by the IHS in Minnesota), or when the reservation does not offer direct care, IHS contracts for services from other health care providers.

Tribal members of a reservation who live on or near the reservation qualify for contract care. ("Near" means within the same county as the reservation or in an abutting county.) Indians not of the tribe are also eligible if they live on the reservation or near it and have close social or economic ties with it. For these Indians, the tribal council approves eligibility, as in the case of a nontribal member who works for the tribe. Legislation in 1983 (PL 97–394) terminated services for non-Indian spouses and other non-Indian household members.

Funding for the contract program requires annual congressional appropriations, whereas the direct care has continuing funding. The contract program tends to be less well funded and more subject to restraints, with services limited to the funding that has been provided. Contract care funding is viewed as residual or supplemental and is only provided when qualifying Indians are ineligible for services funded by other programs.

To keep within financial limits, the contract health program assigns priorities to medical procedures. Low-priority services cannot be provided until the end of the financial period to ensure that money is available. These services include eye examinations and eyeglasses; physical therapy; and elective surgery for cataract removal, hernia repairs, hysterectomies, gall bladder removal, tubal ligations, vasectomies, and coronary artery bypass. The result is that Indians who are dependent on the IHS for medical care may be unable to have these medical needs taken care of. In 1983, the IHS contract care funding was cut by 4%.

Eligibility Issues

Eligibility for IHS assistance is a "continual source of friction among Indians and the IHS," noted the American Indian Policy Review Commission Task Force on Health in 1976.[28] With limited dollars, not everyone can be served to the extent of meeting all medical needs. Reimbursement of the IHS direct care facilities for costs of patients who qualify for public health funding would greatly increase the costs of these programs to local governments. Most state and local governments, as well as Indians, believe that primary responsibility for Indian health care rests with the federal government.

As for collecting from those with the ability to pay or from third-party sources, Everett Rhoades, IHS director, is quoted as saying, "To require an individual Indian, whether economically secure or destitute, to pay for a service already considered to have been paid for . . . a service viewed as stemming from the trust relationship—would be a fundamental change . . . in the relationship between the Federal Government and the Indian tribes."[29] It is also questionable, given the high unemployment on reservations, whether major amounts of money could be raised. The issues involved in extending programs to urban Indians are discussed in chapter 6.

Physicians

The major source of physicians to staff IHS facilities is the Commissioned Corps of the US Public Health Service. The federal government provides medical scholarships to assist students through school and then requires a payback of two to three years of service, which can be military or with the IHS. All doctors get the same "military" pay and benefits. The federal government also funds a scholarship program to encourage Indians to go into medical professions.

Maintaining the quality and quantity of doctors is a concern. Scholarship funding has been cut back, and priorities have been changed to benefit the military service, with which the IHS must compete. The pressures of the volume of patients, the overcrowded facilities, inadequate supplies and equipment, and lack of support staff put a strain on doctors and their ability to provide quality care, thus contributing to "burnout."

Indian Preference

Like the BIA, the IHS follows Indian preference in hiring and purchasing services and, at tribal request, can enter into contracts for tribal management of programs (under the Indian Self-Determination Act). Most of the reservations operate their own community health and sanitation services. Red Lake Builders was the first tribal company in the nation to manage the building of a reservation hospital and new staff housing.

Minnesota Services

The Bemidji Program Area of the IHS has responsibility for health care programs on Minnesota reservations. Although most of the professional staff is non-Indian because of the limited number of Indian physicians, nurses, and other health professionals, 54% of all employees are Indian.

The two inpatient facilities on Red Lake and Leech Lake reservations and the ambulatory care facility at White Earth are administered by the IHS. The hospitals, both accredited by the Joint Commission on Accreditation of Hospitals, take care of general medicine, low-risk obstetrics, and pediatric cases. The new $9 million Red Lake Hospital opened in March 1981. The Leech Lake facility, with 23 beds, was built in the 1930s and was being remodeled in 1983.

The three facilities are served by physicians (11 in all), nurses, and full supportive staff. Dental services, optometry, audiology, lab services, radiology, and pharmacy programs are also provided.

Ambulatory outpatient programs are offered in satellite facilities on the three reservations and at clinics on the other four MCT reservations. Fond du Lac Reservation operates on contract its Min No Ya Win facility and a satellite clinic in Duluth. Mille Lacs Reservation's facility, Ne-ia-Shing, was built in 1979.

Bois Forte and Grand Portage have small clinics; most of the medical care is provided by contract with outside health providers. The Minnesota Sioux Communities, which use contract health services, administered their own programs in 1984, except for the Lower Sioux Indian Community. Other health services, such as immunizations, were provided through the counties.

Community health services that are available on most reservations include public health nursing, nutrition, environmental health, health education, and mental health/alcoholism/social services; and clinics in maternal and child health, diabetes, hypertension, family planning, and immunization.

Community Health Representatives are a link to the community to make medical treatment more acceptable and understandable. They provide follow-up support of hospital and clinic services, assisting when help is needed in the home and providing transportation. Some have been trained to assist in special programs such as dental or eye care, blood pressure screening, or helping school nurses. The program has been one of the largest employers of local people in the health services. In 1982, it provided staff on all the reservations, including the Sioux Communities. The administration has proposed the elimination of the program, and funding was cut 20% in 1983.

Emergency medical and ambulance services are provided by Indian-run programs on the seven northern reservations. Help is available on a 24-hour basis; on the more populated reservations, equipment is placed at two or more sites. While the IHS provides some funds, the programs also rely on community fund raising, tribal funds, and third-party payment for services.

Usually a small paid staff heads a program that relies on volunteers who have been trained in emergency health procedures and are state certified. As the programs are the only emergency care in the areas served, Indians and non-Indians come together as volunteers to staff them.

Abortion and Sterilization

Federal funding may be used for abortions under IHS regulations only if a physician states in writing that carrying the fetus to term would endanger the life of the woman. Medical Assistance cannot be used for abortions. The urban centers that serve Indians do not do abortions, but information is provided about counseling and services that are available. In relation to the total number of births in Minnesota for 1980, 10% of Indian pregnancies were aborted; 20% of pregnancies in the general population were aborted.[30]

Sterilizations require the following of strict IHS guidelines. They are not done at IHS facilities in the state, only through contract care. During 1981, 38 were authorized in Minnesota.[31] There is concern that overt or implied pressure from welfare workers is forcing sterilizations on Indian women in the Twin Cities. A case in Hennepin County in 1980 involved a pregnant Indian woman with two children in foster care who was told to give up her baby and be sterilized or give up her rights to the other children. The legal case was decided in favor of the Indian mother.[32]

Meeting Sanitation Needs

In addition to medical care, the IHS is responsible for constructing sanitary facilities, providing safe drinking water, and meeting environmental health needs (PL 86–121). It works along with the housing programs to install the facilities in new construction, and it assists with maintenance and upkeep. Over a 20-year period (1962–1981), the IHS provided 1,021 wells and 1,426 septic systems to serve approximately 1,500 scattered site homes on Minnesota reservations. Community water systems were installed to serve 1,181 homes; and community sewer systems, for 776 homes.[33]

The community systems are usually directed by a commission that is responsible for maintenance and for collection of user fees. Occupants of homes that have their own individual systems are responsible for upkeep and maintenance. Keeping the systems operating and protecting against unsanitary conditions is often a major problem. In January 1982, the IHS reported that sanitary facilities at 479 Minnesota reservation homes needed upgrading, and 140 homes needed first-time service.[34]

The IHS Environmental Health Program includes food sanitation, insect and rodent control, chimney/firewood burning safety, and emergency preparedness. A major antirabies vaccination program for cats and dogs has operated on the reservations since rabid animals were identified in 1981, when 25 people had to have rabies shots. White Earth and Leech Lake reservations contract for their own environmental health programs. The Red Lake program provides services to Bois Forte and Grand Portage.

Federal Programs for the General Population

The Urban Health Initiative Program of the Community Health Centers Act (PL 94–63, Section 330) serves medically underserved urban populations: those with low incomes, high infant mortality, large numbers of high-risk pregnancies, high numbers of elderly, and low physician ratio. The Indian Health Board of Minneapolis was the first urban Indian program in the country to be funded under the law.

The WIC program provides supplemental, highly nutritious food for pregnant women, nursing mothers, and children up to five years old who are considered high health risks. Participants in the program must make monthly visits to a nurse and keep up immunizations. The program is funded by the US Department of Agriculture (42 USC 1771) and is administered through the Minnesota Department of Health and the counties (Mn. Stat. 145.893). Tribes can also contract directly for the program. All Minnesota reservations and urban Indian health programs have WIC.

State and County Programs

Community Health Services

Health services for the general population in Minnesota are administered through the counties. The Minnesota Community Health Services Act of 1976 (Mn. Stat. 145.911) provides funds for local health services and requires that counties prepare health plans to identify needs and set priorities among a broad range of community health services. An advisory committee with at least one-third consumers is required.

Health needs of minorities must be included, services are to be accessible to all persons on a basis of need, and no one is to be denied services because of race. The plans are reviewed by regional development commissions (such as the Metropolitan Council) and the state commissioner of health. Although the state reviews the plans, it has no authority to cause them to be changed if some needs are not being met.

County Programs for Indian Health

A few counties target some programs specifically to serving Indians, usually public health nursing and home health aides. For instance, four of the clinic sites on Leech Lake Reservation have county public health nurses. Cass County, in addition, provides its homemaker chore program to Indians on the reservation.

Hennepin County, in its health plan for 1982–83, identified Indian needs and programs totaling $1,200,000 for calendar year 1982. Although most of the funds came from state or federal programs and were passed through the county, $150,000 of county funds were expended on the Indian programs. Hennepin County also staffs an Indian advocate at Hennepin County Medical Center to assist Indian patients.

Counties generally provide very little funding for Indian health needs, however, and do not incorporate them into the health plans. The Bois Forte IHS service unit requested two additional persons for community health services in its 1979 health plan, noting, "The tribe has had only limited success in obtaining services from state and county agencies in recent years due to their isolation."[35]

The 1982–83 health plans of two of the northern county groups that serve Indian areas showed no indication that they had sought out or tried to meet Indian resident needs. Beltrami County, for instance, had no Indians on the advisory committee and no Indian employees working for Beltrami County Health Services.

Welfare Medical Programs

Cuts and restrictions on Medicaid (primarily federally funded) and General Assistance Medical Care (GAMC, state and county funded) have caused problems not only for the individual Indians coming under one of these programs but also for the facilities seeking reimbursement for serving welfare patients. The GAMC program has had the most drastic limits. It does not cover eyeglasses, hearing aids, psychologists, or in-home care. Several private providers of drugs, dental services, and psychiatric care will no longer accept GAMC patients.[36]

Urban Indian Programs

The importance of having Indian-oriented programs was documented in a study done by the Community-University Health Care Center in the early 1970s. When Indians were hired for the noncertified positions and an Indian supervisor was put in charge, Indian use of the facility doubled.[37] In its health plan for 1982–83, Hennepin County identified health service problems of Indians as resulting from the failure of Indians to "seek, find and use and inability to pay for health care." Its objective was to encourage the use of health services by having them accessible and acceptable to the Indian population.

The state provides some funding for urban health programs through the Special Native American Block Grant. In 1982, $150,000 was provided, giving some support to the St. Paul Urban Indian Health Center; American Indian Fellowship Association, Duluth; and, in Minneapolis, to the Family Practice Clinic associated with Fairview Deaconess Hospital, the Community-University Health Care Center, and the Indian Health Board.

Indian Health Board

The Indian Health Board in Minneapolis is a national model for urban Indian health programs, one of the largest in the country. It was the first such program developed and built by local Indians to meet local needs. The board was incorporated in 1971 and a demonstration project was begun. It was "quickly overcome by the level of need discovered."[38]

The IHB has been heavily used by the Indian community, serving over 6,300 individuals annually. Its clients are very poor (55% below the poverty income level and only 4% covered by private insurance). The program includes outpatient medical care, dental services, a mental health program, prenatal care, well child services, family planning, WIC, and transportation services. In 1982, the staff numbered more than 30 (80% Indian), including two physicians, three dentists, and a consulting psychologist. The clinic was open five days a week, with 24-hour emergency help available. Patients who needed hospitalization were referred to hospitals in the city.

Funding comes from a variety of sources. The IHS provides over half, and a little under one-fourth each comes from the federal program to help underserved urban populations (Urban Health Initiative) and from patient fees and third-party payments such as Medicaid. In 1982, small amounts came from the state's block grant ($60,000), family planning and WIC program funds, and about $30,000 from Hennepin County funds.

In May 1983, the IHB moved into new facilities across from Fairview Deaconess Hospital. The newly constructed building, which cost over $800,000, was totally funded by the IHB. In 1984, money was borrowed against the building to make major needed expansions in programming.

Other Minneapolis Programs

The Family Health Program at Fairview Deaconess is an Indian-directed psychiatric program that provides a variety of mental health services, counseling, testing, information and referral, advocacy, and consultation with schools. About 60% of the clients are Indian.

Two other health service programs designed to reach underserved Minneapolis residents are located in Indian population areas of the city and make special efforts to reach the Indian community. The Family Practice Clinic located at Fairview Deaconess is an affiliate of the Hennepin County Medical Center. It operates two facilities, including a satellite clinic in downtown Minneapolis. The program, which uses an Indian advocate, focuses on family practice, obstetrics, pediatrics, family planning, and WIC. In 1984, about 15% of its participants were Indian.

Community-University Health Care Center offers clinic services, including a mental health program. It has special programs for young mothers, with a full-service health clinic at South High School two mornings a week. About 22% of its patients were Indian in 1984.

Services in St. Paul and Duluth

Health services targeted at the Indian communities in St. Paul and Duluth are on a much more limited scale. The St. Paul Urban Indian Health Center operates a clinic at the Red School House and an office at Hosanna Lutheran Church (1983). The American Indian Fellowship Association in Duluth provides some clinic and outreach services, although there is some confusion about the services offered by the association and the Fond du Lac satellite clinic in Duluth. The latter is a direct service facility of the IHS that is available to all Indians.

Mental Health Problems

One of the greatest deficiencies in Indian health care is in mental health services. The needs are demonstrated by the high incidence of families in crisis, the number of foster home placements, problems in school, job adjustment problems, problems of alcohol misuse, depression, and violent deaths.

Nature of the Problem

A study done in 1978 by the Indian Health Board in Minneapolis showed that 10–12 clients each day had serious mental health needs. The report concluded that Indian children and families have significant and multiple mental health needs and that resources then available were inadequate.[39] The IHS estimates that only half of the reservation Indians with mental health needs are reached at all.[40] The impact of the economic situation on mental health was noted in August 1983 by the IHS unit director at White Earth Reservation, where suicide attempts "have been as high as three to four a week and are becoming one of the most frequently treated emergencies."[41]

Major differences in diagnosis between Indian patients and a sample of Euro-Americans were noted among the institutionalized mentally ill in a 1982 study. Schizophrenia was the most frequent diagnosis, although it was made for fewer Indians (23%) than for the control group (33%). Alcohol abuse was associated with 40% of the Indian patients, but it was diagnosed in only 12.5% of the Euro-Americans. The third largest Indian group, 18%, was diagnosed as having "personality disorders," an ambiguous term. The researcher commented, "One wonders if this 'catch-all' diagnosis is more likely to be made when communication fails, cultural misunderstandings occur, and/or when the principal behavioral pattern is a rebellious 'acting out' of hostilities against a discriminatory society."[42]

Indian Aspects of Mental Illness

Indians are reluctant to use the state treatment systems. Of 2,827 clients served by Hennepin County Mental Health Center in 1981, 57 (2%) were Indians. Although the percentage is around the Indian population figure, it is a good deal lower than the Indian percentage in the various measurements of mental health problems. Ramsey County Mental Health Center reported serving only 30 Indians in 1981.

The study of institutionalized patients found that Indian families are less likely to commit members or to seek professional treatment than non-Indian families. If there is a problem, the Indian family is more apt to rely on extended kin and community support systems.[43] However, once a diagnosis is made, Indians gather around, "are supportive of people with problems and do not place blame on the individual."[44] Whites are apt to back out and abandon the patient.

Indians who are institutionalized are principally those who come to the attention of judicial or social services and who have been committed by the courts.[45] For Red Lake Reservation, where state court jurisdiction does not apply, legislation approved in 1983 allows state courts to accept the Red Lake Tribal Court action in commitments (Mn. Stat. 253B.212).

Indian patients frequently suffer from the dual problems of mental illness and chemical dependency. Neither treatment system is equipped to deal with those with dual disabilities: the professionals have not been trained and facilities are not licensed to deal with the other problem, and patient histories are not taken with both problems in mind. Treating a mentally ill patient with medicine may make the individual unacceptable to Alcoholics Anonymous as drug dependent. The problems of handling patients with dual disabilities have yet to be dealt with.[46]

Indian Recommendations

At a 1979 conference on Indian mental health problems, Minnesota Indians urged that the Indian community's values be "incorporated into the goals and objectives and processes of mental health programs serving . . . Indians."[47] More Indian mental health service providers need to be trained, and non-Indian mental health workers need to be assisted in learning effective ways of interacting with Indian people. Recommendations included creation of an Indian board to plan programs and funding.

Indian studies have pointed out that the mental health resource networks and follow-up programs are disjointed, unconnected, and often at odds with each other. Getting follow-up care after returning to the reservation may be difficult because mental health programs are not well planned for by the IHS.[48]

The conference report also recommended that programs to help deinstitutionalized Indian patients stress traditional, holistic healing practices, planned and managed by esteemed members of the local Indian community. Given the background of the patients (35% urban residents and predominantly young males), urban centers as well as reservation programs are needed, with resources focused on Indian youth, especially adolescent boys and young men. However, "it is imperative that the de-institutionalization movement not be used as an excuse for neglect . . . that the economic and human resources be allocated to American Indian reservations and urban communities so as to develop effective mental health prevention and treatment programs."[49]

Services for the Mentally Ill

Services are provided for mentally ill Indians on the reservations by the IHS. Upper Mississippi Mental Health Center offers professional help to Red Lake, White Earth, and Leech Lake reservations. For instance, a physician visits Red Lake twice a month. The health center reports that about 20% of its case load is Indian, corresponding closely to the area's Indian population.

A combination of federal block grant mental health funds and assistance from the McKnight Foundation made $94,000 available in 1983 to expand Indian utilization of mental health programs. Fond du Lac is using some of the funds for native practitioner services on the reservation; on Leech Lake, the program helps with mental health needs of women clients. Part-time "positive living workers" are provided at three of the Sioux communities.

Traditional Medicine

Traditional Indian medicine is getting increasing attention. The 1982 service unit reports of several of the state's reservations mentioned community interest.

Fond du Lac Reservation stated, "Traditional medicine has always been a part, recognized or unrecognized, of the Fond du Lac health system."[50] With the resurgence of interest in traditional ways and the growing awareness of holistic medicine, counseling sessions on the proper way to proceed with traditional medicine have been made available.

The IHS encourages cooperation with native practitioners in considering the health needs of the patient. Funding is permitted through contract care if authorized by a physician and if funds are available. However, "many Native Practitioners, while permitting gifts and offerings from the client, neither accept or permit or request payment of fees from a third party."[51]

Summary

Minnesota Indians have greater health needs than the general population. They die at a younger age, with major problems including urban infant deaths, deaths from violence, diseases and deaths related to alcohol abuse, and respiratory and environmentally related diseases. Conditions of poverty, lack of education, and ignorance of how to get services in the urban setting all contribute to the problem.

Where federal health care through the IHS is available, health improves, especially in the area of infant mortality. Indian-run, Indian-oriented health clinics in the urban areas are meeting the needs of many Indians.

Problems of mental health have received little attention. Indian communities, having assessed their needs, should be listened to and assisted in developing programs that will help meet these needs.

Funding of existing health service programs and assurance of their continued availability are major concerns. Much more still needs to be done, especially in urban areas, to meet the federal goal to provide the "highest possible health status to Indians and to provide existing Indian health services with all resources necessary to effect that policy" (25 USC 1602).

CHAPTER 13

Chemical
Dependency

The problem is devastating: imagine 95% of all people
affected either by drinking themselves or with an alcoholic
problem in the family. Indians can't afford that. Nobody
could afford that, but with Indians, it might mean that we
won't survive, if something doesn't change.[1]

Dimension of the Problem

Stereotype of Indian Drinking

Indians were not familiar with alcohol until Europeans introduced
them to it, and their culture did not have built-in social controls for its
use or abuse. Whites on the frontier often took advantage of Indians by
using alcohol as a tool of economic control, an aid in getting treaties
approved and land taken.

The stereotype grew that drinking affected Indians in a specific and
unusual manner, and the federal government gave official recognition
to it by prohibiting the sale of alcohol to Indian people. The ban lasted
over 120 years, from 1832 to 1953. That "did more to nourish the stereotype of the 'drunken Indian' than to remedy the situation."[2] The imposed controls were largely futile, contributing to abusive ways of drinking rather than leading to moderation. Of the reservations in Minnesota,
Red Lake still has a tribally imposed prohibition on alcohol sales, although the law is poorly enforced.

220

Indians strongly resent the assumption that as a matter of racial heritage all of them have problems with alcohol, although it is widely acknowledged that alcohol is a major problem for Indians. There are Indians who do not drink, and, as with all other segments of the population, not all who drink are alcoholics. Different tribes, subgroups, and individuals have different use patterns and are affected in different degrees by alcohol. Although particular patterns of alcohol consumption can be correlated to different racial groups, race is not a causative factor. The cause of alcoholism is not known.

The destructiveness of the stereotype can be seen in the view that alcoholism is the cause of Indian problems, a view that may lead to the ignoring of urgent political and economic issues. A major study of Indian drinking patterns in St. Paul in 1981 concluded, "Alcoholism is a severe problem among Indians, but so [are] . . . a number of other problems that need to be resolved to insure the possibility of a decent life. The 'solution' to alcoholism has as much to do with improving the conditions of life for Indians as it does with improving treatment programs."[3]

Association with Other Problems

"The problem of excessive drinking cannot be understood apart from Indian history, social values, movements from reservation to city and the realities of social and economic discrimination which have characterized Indian life."[4] Restriction on reservations and subjugation to "white civilized society" created inducements to drink to forget, to release inhibitions, to vent anger, to dull pain, and to avoid the necessity of facing a world that was no longer theirs or under their control.

The daily reality of unemployment, poverty, boredom, and lack of good education and skills contributes to low expectations and self-esteem. Some individuals begin the cycle of seeking relief from problems in alcohol, with alcohol in turn causing problems, and the pattern is repeated into succeeding generations.

The economic and social realities have further ramifications. Motivation to seek treatment for alcoholism is often lacking because sobriety will still not bring jobs, and the discrimination will not end. Those who are successful in treatment must face the same difficult circumstances, including recurring economic crises.

Social Drinking

Socializing within the Indian community usually includes all age groups, from the very old to the very young. Most of the Indians surveyed in St. Paul mentioned social reasons for starting to drink. They began drinking with family and friends because "everybody else was doing it."[5] Drinking by leaders, parents, and peers makes this the accepted role model for young people. Given alcohol's role in social situations, abstinence often means a rejection and separation, a loss of community. This additional obstacle must be overcome for successful treatment.

The pattern of heavy weekend drinking on the reservation is similar to that of the rest of northern Minnesota. A treatment worker in Bemidji noted that alcoholism in northern Minnesota is 4% higher than the national average. "Alcohol is our drug of choice." In her experience, alcoholism is not greater among Indians than whites, just more visible. "Whites get intoxicated at home or at friends' homes or at the country club. Indians are drunk on street corners."[6]

Other Drugs

These aspects of Indian abuse of alcohol also apply to abuse of other drugs, which is a growing problem. On some reservations, the inhaling of volatile solvents—"sniffing"—is a serious abuse among young children. But because Indians have less access to drugs other than alcohol, and because they cost more, these substances are not considered as big a problem. The remaining discussion focuses on alcohol abuse, although the treatment of other drug problems would be similar except for the additional fact of their illegality.

Measurement of the Problem

Number of Alcoholics

Minnesota's Comprehensive Chemical Dependency State Plan, 1982, sets the number of Indians in Minnesota who are considered chemically dependent at 15,750. The figure is based on estimates by the National Institute on Alcoholism and Alcohol Abuse and by the IHS that 40–49% of the total US Indian population has or is seriously affected by the disease of alcoholism.[7]

The state used the figure of 45% in arriving at its total. The state plan estimated that the general state population includes 280,873 problem drinkers, or 6.9%.[8] Based on these estimates, alcoholism is a 6.5 times greater problem in the Indian communities than among the population statewide.

Families of individuals with an alcohol problem are also greatly affected. One hundred respondents in the 1981 study cited 777 close relatives as having serious drinking problems and 161 relatives as having alcohol-related deaths.[9] The Minnesota Alcohol and Drug Abuse Authority puts the combined total of family members involved at 46% for the general population and 90% for the Indian population.[10]

Number in Treatment

Statistics show that Indians are involved in chemical dependency programs at a rate that far exceeds their population percentage of 0.9%. During 1980, Indians were 18% of all admissions (duplicated numbers) to state detoxification centers, with 5,767 admissions.[11] They were a significantly higher percentage of admissions in Hennepin County, with 25%.[12] Indians living in Hennepin County were 30% of the state's Indian population and 52% of all Indian admissions to detoxification centers statewide.

State statistics also show that Indians use the other chemical dependency treatment programs well in excess of their population numbers. On 30 September 1980, they were 5.5% of those in residential treatment (8.5% of those in state hospitals), 19% of those in nonresidential treatment, and 10% of those in halfway houses. During calendar year 1980, Indians were 15% of halfway house admissions (duplicated numbers).[13]

Social Indicators of Alcohol Abuse

Several statistics on health and social problems reflect the severity of alcohol abuse within the Indian community (table 24). Violence (accident, murder, or suicide) is the leading cause of death among Minnesota Indians. These deaths, along with those caused by cirrhosis of the liver, are often associated with alcohol abuse. In 1979–81, violence and cirrhosis accounted for one-third of all Indian fatalities in the state.[14]

Postneonatal infant deaths, child abuse, and placement of children in foster care are considered related to the incidence of alcoholism. Arrests for liquor law violations also measure alcohol abuse.

A University of Minnesota psychiatrist has noted that crimes that result in imprisonment of Indians are almost always associated with the use of alcohol: "Homicide rarely occurs outside the drinking context."[15] Minnesota Indians are incarcerated at a rate much higher than their percentage of the population. A study done for the American Indian Court Judges Association estimated that over half of the federal cases (major crimes) arising from violations committed on Indian reservations involve alcoholic intoxication.[16]

A 1983 study of institutionalized, chronically mentally ill Indians in

Table 24. Social Indicators Associated with Alcohol Abuse in Minnesota

Indicator	Indians	All Races	Ratio, Indians to All Races
Cause of death, per 100,000:[a]			
Accidents	109.4	44.1	2.5:1
Homicides	16.3	2.6	6.3:1
Suicides	15.1	10.7	1.4:1
Total violent deaths	147.6	58.6	2.5:1
Cirrhosis of the liver	30.6	8.4	3.6:1
Postneonatal deaths, per 1,000 live births[a]	9.1	3.5	2.6:1
Substantiated child abuse cases, per 1,000 population[b]	20.1	4.2	4.8:1
Children removed from their homes, percentage 21 and younger[c]	10.8	3.8	2.8:1
Arrests for liquor law violation:[d]			
Per 1,000 population	10.1	2.3	4.4:1
In Minneapolis	32.2	3.7	8.7:1
Arrests for driving under the influence:[d]			
Per 1,000 population	14.6	6.6	2.2:1
In Minneapolis	20.2	4.2	4.8:1

[a]*Minnesota Health Statistics*, 1979–81.
[b]DPW, 1981.
[c]Refer to table 16.
[d]Minnesota Crime Information System, *Uniform Crime Report*, 1981.

Minnesota found that 40% had dual disabilities, with additional alcoholism or drug dependency problems. The Euro-American control sample had only 12.5% with the dual problems.[17]

Many Indians admitted to hospitals for nonalcoholic problems are alcoholics who are being treated for the symptoms rather than the disease of alcoholism. Drinking is responsible for a good deal of Indian medical costs for accidents and the physical disabilities they cause. Problems with alcohol are also linked to birth defects, pneumonia, and malnutrition; spouse and child abuse; school dropouts; unemployment; and the need for welfare. As the American Indian Policy Review Commission commented, "One could almost conclude that the use of alcohol and drugs causes 80–90% of the problems of Indian people."[18]

Statistics may show a correlation between alcohol and many other problems, but they do not prove a causal relationship. Navajo homicide statistics have remained constant since the 1880s, while alcohol use has increased.[19] Similarly, arrest rates for crimes involving alcohol may be more reflective of police practices than of problems specifically Indian. "Problems with alcohol abuse bring Indian people to the morgue, to prisons and jails, and to foster homes," but the statistics are more an indictment of the poor record of problem solving in the majority society than of Indian drinking patterns.[20]

Characteristics of Alcoholic Indians

To a large extent, Indians in detoxification centers are "street people." "About 90% are regulars, with no family, no homes. Not many of them work. They are mostly police pickups. The people have nothing and have nothing to motivate change unless they are sick enough," according to the Indian worker at Ramsey County Receiving Center.[21]

The 1981 study found that the street people had the highest level of fluency in tribal languages, the shortest length of time in the urban area, and the greatest preference for Indian-oriented treatment programs. They had a high level of independence and a tremendous capacity for survival.[22]

In a 1973 comparison of hospitalized alcoholics at Willmar State Hospital, little difference was found between the drinking behavior of Indian and non-Indian male patients, except that Indians were considerably less likely to hide their drinking behavior (12% of the Indians hid drinking; 52% of the non-Indians). Indian alcoholics tended to be substantially younger, from an urban residence (57%, compared with 29%), not steadily employed (38%, compared with 11%), and not raised by their natural parents. Of the sample, 46% of the Indians were raised away from their biological parents, compared with 20% of the non-Indian sample.[23]

Only 5–8% of the sample groups with drinking problems in the 1981 study had been raised by foster parents; however, 30–44% were not raised by their biological parents. Grandparents were the major non-parental childrearers.[24]

Chemically Dependent Indian Women

The severity and nature of chemical dependency problems among Indian women have received little attention. An analysis was made of the Minnesota death certificate records for 1979–81 of those who had died from cirrhosis of the liver, a disease highly correlated with chemical abuse; Indians are four times as apt to die from this cause as whites. Quite unexpectedly, it was found that Indian women not only had a death rate from cirrhosis seven times higher than that for white women, but that they also had significantly higher rates than Indian males. Per 100,000 in the population, 41.4 Indian women died, compared with 33.1 Indian men.[25]

As a group, chemically dependent women were found in one study to be low income, male dominated, and lacking in education.[26] Because of early motherhood and large numbers of dependents, they were locked into a dependency on systems and people. They did not feel good about themselves and lacked the power to change or control their lives. Besides needing help with the chemical dependency, they frequently had related problems of physical abuse, domestic violence, placement of their children in foster care, and dependence on public welfare. Fear of losing their children was a barrier to seeking treatment in some cases.

Indian women received substantially fewer of the "hard" services in chemical dependency treatment: primary residential care, detoxification, and aftercare. Staff and counselors of the programs were primarily male, especially in Indian programs, and had difficulty in relating to Indian women. Women used more of the "soft" services of community education and support groups, but many needs were unmet.

The researchers recommended basic general improvements in treatment: orienting treatment to families; providing comprehensive care for women and children; improving transportation; providing more services on the reservations; and making treatment more appropriate to Indian women, either with more female counselors or additional training of male counselors. With $100,000 provided by the 1984 legislature for research and training to help with the problems identified, the Minnesota Indian Women's Resource Center was opened in Minneapolis.

Minnesota Treatment System

Services that have been developed to deal with chemical dependency include prevention programs and education; intervention (referral); detoxification (holding individuals up to 72 hours); primary treatment, either residential or outpatient; aftercare, including halfway houses that provide supportive help in returning to the community; and support groups, such as Alcoholics Anonymous or Alanon (for family members).

The Community Social Services Act (Mn. Stat. 256E) requires that counties provide chemical dependency programs along with other social services (see chap. 10). Detoxification services must be provided, and treatment is not to be denied because of prior treatment.

Programs for Indians

Funding for Indian chemical dependency programs is provided under both federal and state laws. When the federal programs were combined into block grants to the states in 1981, Indian tribes were allowed to continue to get direct funding rather than sharing in the funds at the state level. Red Lake's Drug Abuse Program continues to be funded federally, whereas the remaining reservations participate in the state programs.

The Indian Health Service does not provide direct treatment of chemical dependency on the reservations; as a "residual" provider of medical care off the reservations, it considers the funding of such treatment for reservation Indians to be a county or other third-party expense. IHS has picked up programs formerly funded by the National Institute on Alcoholism and Alcohol Abuse, and it provides some assistance to Indian treatment programs in the state. In 1983, $370,000 was spent.

Minnesota is a leader among the states in providing assistance to Indians. The state program for Indians is headed by an Indian, who is special assistant to the director of the Chemical Dependency Program Division, Minnesota Department of Human Services. By law, an Indian advisory council participates in establishing policies and procedures for the programs and is involved in recommending which programs are to be funded. According to the law, "All programs shall be designed to meet the needs identified by the American Indian community and appropriate recognition shall be given to the cultural and social needs of American Indians" (Mn. Stat. 254A.035). A plan of affirmative outreach is to be developed for these services.

Employees in the programs serving the Indian communities must have "considerable practical experience in alcohol and other drug abuse problems and understanding of social and cultural problems related to [these problems] . . . in the American Indian community" (Mn. Stat. 254A.03, subd.1[j]). County programs that serve Indian communities follow the same employment guidelines.

A report analyzing the state programs noted, "American Indians receive more services than any other minority group, which seems appropriate given the state's emphasis on American Indian chemical dependency programming and the seriousness of American Indian chemical dependency problems."[27] Funding for these Indian programs is a line item in the state budget; $1.25 million was provided in 1983. This money, together with $458,000 in federal funds administered by the state, provided 29 Indian-designated programs.

Some counties fund Indian-oriented programs out of their social services money. Cass and Beltrami counties assist with programs at Leech Lake Reservation; Hennepin County funds several major Indian programs. As an indication of the importance of Indian programming, in Hennepin County 89% of all Indian clients served by halfway houses in 1980 used Indian-oriented facilities.[28]

Indian-oriented Services

Mash-Ka-Wisen

Mash-Ka-Wisen ("be strong, accept help") is the nation's first Indian-owned, Indian-operated chemical dependency treatment center. The 28-bed facility serving both men and women 16 years and older opened in August 1978 near Sawyer, on the Fond du Lac Reservation about 10 miles from Cloquet. The tribe donated the land and buildings, and the state provided $530,000 for the first stage of construction.

Mash-Ka-Wisen is run by the nonprofit Minnesota Indian Primary Residential Treatment Center; the board is composed of tribal chairmen from Minnesota's reservations. Major funding comes from the county and third-party payment for services. The state also assists, and, beginning in 1984, the IHS funds those ineligible for other services.

Treatment emphasizes the philosophical and spiritual aspects of Indian heritage, along with conventional chemical dependency treatment. The Ojibway language is used. Since opening, the center has served about 1,000 Indians, and the 24-member staff is all Indian. Funds were being raised in 1983 to add a juvenile facility.

The program has been very successful in reaching Indian clients. Independent evaluations have found that although it serves people for whom the usual motivations of jobs and social status do not work, Mash-Ka-Wisen has been as successful in patient program completion rate as private chemical dependency facilities.[29]

Reservation Programs

All reservations have some chemical dependency services, with programs focusing on youth or on prevention and intervention for adults.

A detoxification center, Mineo Detox, operates on Leech Lake Reservation; Cass County and the state Indian program provide funding. The center is used by several counties and also serves Red Lake Reservation. A White Earth Reservation facility was closed at the end of 1983 for lack of funding.

The White Earth Board and Care Center, located at the former Job Corps facility, accommodates six male chronic alcoholics, usually 60 or older, who have detached themselves from their families. In a homelike atmosphere with positive peer pressure, they can gain in self-worth and lead a more dignified life during retirement. No drugs or alcohol are allowed. The costs are paid by the individuals' Social Security and pensions, with the counties paying the balance.

Both Leech Lake and Mille Lacs reservations have halfway houses. Leech Lake's facility, Ahnji-Be-Mah-Diz Center ("change of life") has room for 17 men. The Mille Lacs Halfway House serves six males and two females. Both programs assist the individual to return to successful community living by providing counseling, group therapy, and help in education, training, and finding jobs.

Red Lake Reservation

Red Lake Reservation uses regular state programs for detoxification and primary residential care. Adults go either to Brainerd or Fergus Falls State Hospital, and juveniles to the Freeway Program at Fergus Falls State Hospital. The Red Lake Hospital has an outpatient drug abuse counseling program called Indian and Free. The Alcohol Rehabilitation Program provides group therapy, counseling, and outreach and assists with job search skills. Alcoholics Anonymous and Alanon programs function at Red Lake and Ponemah.

Red Lake also has the Drug Abuse Program, directed at youth; state funding is provided. The program at Red Lake has been followed since 1977 in a research project by Colorado State University. Its 1981 survey of elementary school children showed that for the first time there had been a 20–30% decrease in first use of alcohol, marijuana, and inhalants.[30]

Programs Off the Reservation

Duluth has two 10-bed Indian halfway houses, Thunderbird for men and Wren for women; a staff of 10 serves the two facilities. The IHS provides major funding, and counties of residence pay for client usage. The North American Indian Fellowship Center at International Falls has chemical dependency programs for youth and adults, with funding channeled through the MCT. The state provided $16,000 in 1982 for an Indian chemical dependency program at the Minnesota Correctional Facility at St. Cloud.

Hennepin County. Hennepin County funds several Indian-oriented programs in Minneapolis. New Visions Center, begun in 1981, is a 21-bed inpatient primary treatment program that draws on Indian culture and religious experience. The staff of 17, which is 85% Indian, operates a program similar in philosophy to that of Mash-Ka-Wisen. There is a strong aftercare program.

Male and female halfway houses serve Indians in the Minneapolis area. American Indian Services has facilities for up to 20 men. Winaki House accommodates 14 women, 16 years of age and older. Waniki II is a residential house for the children of the women when they are in treatment. The Eden Youth residential program for juveniles 12 to 17, a part of Eden House, serves about 75% Indian clients.

The Indian Neighborhood Club has filled the otherwise unmet need for an environment free of alcohol and drugs for street people of Minneapolis, primarily Indian. In 1984 the county ruled that the club could no longer provide sleeping accommodations. The American Indian Chemical Dependency Diversion Project in Minneapolis provides counseling, court evaluation, and legal aid to those in the criminal justice system.

Chemical dependency prevention programs for youth are run by the Minneapolis American Indian Center. The counseling program helps about 12 clients a month, and group counseling is provided for aftercare. A preventive education program run by the center works with elementary students.

Nah Way Ee Neighborhood Center School also has a youth prevention and intervention program. The Indian-oriented drug abuse program in the Minneapolis schools is a part of the school district's regular programming. The Indian Health Board began in 1984 to provide a social center for Indians in Minneapolis where whole families could congregate in a chemical-free setting.

Ramsey County. Juel Fairbanks Aftercare Residence is a 20-bed halfway house in St. Paul for men and women. The staff of 17 is about 70% Indian; control resides in an all-Indian board. In 1982, about 50% of the admissions were Indian, some 65–75% from Ramsey County. The utilization rate was over 90%, with a waiting list for admission. A primary treatment outpatient program is also offered, the only Indian program licensed for this service.

In addition to the halfway house, a three-quarters house of four beds allows for advanced independent living. In 1982 an eight-bed home was started for chronically alcoholic Indian women, those who had exhausted the treatment program and would not be eligible for further help otherwise. Juel Fairbanks programming also includes family outpatient, youth, and prevention programs. State and IHS funds help provide the services. A drug education program is also in operation at the Red School House, St. Paul.

Problems with Treatment Programs

Cultural Differences

A respondent to the State Planning Agency's survey of Indian needs reported, "Money for chemical dependency treatment is often 'wasted' because it is spent on programs which are not Indian run or Indian oriented."[31] The frequently used confrontational or "hot seat" approach of getting a chemically dependent person to understand the problem does not usually work with Indians. Direct confrontation is not a part of historic Indian culture. To many Indians, it is degrading and destructive to self-esteem.

The standard treatment motivations of regaining a job or acquiring material possessions are not likely to work with Indians: there is probably no job, and Indians do not value economic things that highly. The Indian sees no value in what is being said and may either not participate or may leave. The achievement of well-being and personal health are far better motivations.

Counselors who do not understand Indians often have serious problems working with them, becoming frustrated because the expected responses and reactions to motivation do not occur. In a survey of 30 Minnesota providers of chemical dependency and mental illness services, a majority of the respondents believed that there are cultural differences between Indian and non-Indian clients. The most common view was that the Indian client is less "likely to verbalize and address a problem through the traditional, verbal therapeutic mode."[32]

Current treatment programs focus on the individual, only later involving the family; children may be left out of the picture entirely. For Indians, what constitutes "significant" family may be far more extensive than treatment programs usually consider. For success, Indians stress that the entire family needs to be involved and make changes together.

Measuring Success

Criteria for successful treatment are difficult to establish. The studies cited below indicate that Indians receive less benefit from the programs as measured by several standards. Indian workers point out, however, that more limited goals may be highly significant to an individual who has wasted a large part of a lifetime. Keeping an individual sober, even for a time, has an effect in the Indian community.

Indians are far more apt to leave before completing a program than are whites. A 1979 study of Ramsey County halfway houses showed that 76% of the Indians left against staff approval, as compared with 38% of the white clients; only 2% of the Indians completed the program, and 17% of the whites.[33]

In addition to the high dropout rate, there is a low "cure" rate for Indians. The Ramsey County evaluation found that chemical dependency treatment programs were helpful in lowering recidivism to detoxification centers, welfare program usage, arrests, and involvement in the correctional system. For the Indian portion of the sample, however, the various measures of program effectiveness either showed no improvement or a worsened condition. The study recommended that "minority planners and minority service groups explore different methods of providing these needed services to minority populations."[34]

The statewide evaluation of halfway house program effectiveness in 1980 followed up a sample of individuals 90 days after discharge. Whereas whites and Blacks maintained or achieved an abstinence rate of 65%, the Indian rate was only 28%.[35]

There is agreement, as acknowledged in state law, that when cultural and social needs of American Indians are recognized, programs can be more successful. In treatment programs that were doing a better job assisting Indians, "there was a heavy emphasis on having Indian staff and counselors and making more use of Indian culture and spiritual values in the course of treatment."[36] Hennepin County targets its limited social service funds into programs sensitive to Indian culture where this understanding is thought to have the greatest impact, such as primary chemical dependency treatment.

County Systems and Funding Policies

By law, detoxification services are provided wherever a person needs the services; any further treatment is the financial responsibility of the county of residency. Decisions about having chemical dependency programs beyond detoxification, the funding levels, and locations of services are all made by the counties.

State law directs the Department of Human Services to "set criteria for appropriate level of chemical dependency care for each recipient of public assistance" taking into account family relationships, past treatment history, medical or physical problems, arrest record, and employment (Mn. Stat. 254A.04). Although this requirement would seem to mandate a clarification of the level of treatment for low-income people who receive public assistance, the rules had not been established by

1983. A 1981 legislative audit recommended that treatment be refocused to serve disadvantaged groups better and that financial barriers to appropriate care be eliminated for dependent people.[37]

Chemical dependency is the only illness that has a limited treatment time based on available funding. Many counties are adopting shorter treatment schedules, with primary treatment usually limited to 28 days or less. At Mash-Ka-Wisen, which bases the stay on individual needs, the average is 32 days.[38]

Ramsey County will pay for only two months at a halfway house. Juel Fairbanks has about a five-month program and does not force people to leave. Given the gap between the time for which county funding is available and the time required for the program, money becomes a major problem.

In cases involving a frequent repeater, a county may deny further treatment in the belief that nothing more will be gained. Ramsey County has set a limit of three treatment admissions.

Funding Determines Choices. If a person seeking chemical dependency treatment is employed and has private insurance, many choices are available; Indians generally are not employed, however, and they have very few choices. State reports showed that of those who entered the detoxification program at White Earth Reservation in 1981 (89% Indians), 90% had no insurance, public or private, to help with treatment costs. Statewide, 55% of those in detoxification programs were without insurance.[39]

In Ramsey County, and Indian without private insurance but qualifying for welfare Medical Assistance (AFDC recipient) is usually treated at St. Paul-Ramsey Hospital. For a patient without Medical Assistance, state hospital treatment is the only option.

Counties rely heavily on state hospitals for treatment, mainly because the state assumes 90% of the cost. The counties are assigned to specific hospitals and have a limited number of slots available for clients; however, state hospitals generally do a poor job helping Indians.

Because of government policies, funding is often not available to allow Indians use of the Indian-oriented primary treatment facility, Mash-Ka-Wisen. When more state funding was available in 1980, the facility had an 85% monthly occupancy rate. In 1982, the state met only $35 of the $83 daily cost (a rate comparable with that of similar facilities). The remaining amount had to be paid by the client, a third party, or a county (only 6% of the clients had health insurance).[40]

Four counties with large Indian populations continued to use the facility, providing 80% of the clients. Indians were not sent from the

Twin Cities area unless they were committed by the courts, thus requiring the county to pay. In 1982, because of the cutbacks, the occupancy rate was only 55%. The increased use of the facility made possible by IHS funding in 1984 raised this rate to 75%.

The relatively small percentage of Indian youth in treatment programs in 1981—3% on a specific day, 5% of the yearly total—may also reflect funding policies. Participation in these programs often requires that patients have private insurance.[41]

Insufficient Funding. Indian professionals at the state's Chemical Dependency Program Division have projected a need for 58 counselors (1982) at a cost of two times the dollars allotted to the Indian program.[42] In St. Paul, where the Juel Fairbanks Aftercare Residence serves primarily Indians as a halfway house facility, "during much of the year the waiting list . . . is equivalent to three or four times its twenty-bed capacity."[43]

The evaluation of Indians in the state correctional system found that the "most commonly cited problem was a shortage of Indian-oriented alcohol treatment programs . . . especially . . . in the rural areas of the state."[44] Other programming needs that were frequently stressed by people working in the field are greater supportive help for the Indian returning from treatment and safe holding houses in which people can wait the one to two weeks it takes to get into primary treatment or a halfway house.

In 1982, people were forced to return to the streets to await further treatment, frequently negating the progress that had already been made. "Nobody will take these people for that short a stay. With the paper work, they can't afford to for that brief a time."[45]

State funding earmarked for Indian programs declined from $1.5 million in 1981 to $1.25 million in 1983. One of the sharpest cuts was in state support for the Indian residential primary treatment program, Mash-Ka-Wisen, from $0.5 million to $250,000 in 1983, a 50% cut; Juel Fairbanks Aftercare Residence had a 30% funding cut. The 1984 legislature restored $200,000 to the Mash-Ka-Wisen program and appropriated an additional $200,000 for prevention and programming focused on women.

Summary

Minnesota has major social and human costs in the prevalence of chemical dependency problems in the Indian communities. The American Indian Policy Review Commission recommended that comprehensive alcohol and drug prevention and treatment programs be accorded the highest possible health priority. Minnesota has done well in acknowledging alcoholism as a problem and in funding programs to help. The state's Indian community has provided nationally acknowledged leadership in designing, implementing, and staffing programs.

But a great deal remains to be done. Continuing and additional funding is needed, and existing programs should be better utilized. The total scope of the problem urgently needs to be faced. "The well-being of future generations may well depend on the course of action to be followed in the next few years."[46]

CHAPTER 14

The Criminal
Justice System

Almost every young man who has come off [White Earth]
reservation has been in jail or prison. They think of any
reason to throw you in.[1]

History

Before the immigration of Europeans to America, Indian tribes had
well-established codes of conduct and ways of dealing with crime. If a
person violated another's rights, penalties were culturally sanctioned.
Crimes against another individual and not the tribe called for restitution
to the injured party. When the price was paid, the matter was settled.
Public shame and humiliation were the major punishments of the
group, to let the individual know of its disapproval and to accentuate
the guilt and shame already felt by the offender. Counseling was done
by tribal elders until behavior changed.

Other penalties included spiritual disenfranchisement, prohibition
from participation in ceremonies, isolation, and temporary banishment.
Banishment was the ultimate punishment because it represented the
loss of one's people and status, as well as almost certain death. It was
used for the most serious crimes, in the most extreme situations.

Individuals were taught by example to become personally responsible for their conduct. An individual's conscience included not only
personal values but also those of the entire culture. White men were

236

amazed, during the frontier years, when an Indian would voluntarily ride miles unescorted to appear in court to be sentenced. Indians did not have an adversary system of justice, in which one could plead innocent and leave the burden of proving guilt to the courts.

With the reservations came pressures from the federal government and program administrators to extinguish traditional Indian society and to accept the white system. Formal legal systems with police enforcement were set up under civil and criminal codes devised by the secretary of the interior. The law was used to impose an alien form of government on Indian society.

Courts of Indian Offenses, with Indian judges, were established in 1883; Indian police imposed the laws and federal agency regulations. The Indian court was limited to crimes of Indians against Indians. But in 1885, when it was realized that Crow Dog would not be hanged for killing Spotted Tail because federal courts lacked jurisdiction, legislation was passed giving federal courts responsibility for handling major crimes on the reservations (18 USC 1153).

When allotment, fee patenting, and sale of land on the reservations began, many legal jurisdictional problems arose. The secretary of the interior ruled in 1903 that even if land title had passed to the Indians, they were still under federal control.[2] The states claimed legal jurisdiction on non-Indian lands within the reservations, at least for the purpose of controlling white citizens; but the crazy-quilt pattern of trust lands made enforcement all but impossible.

The local police authorities usually gave up. Law enforcement was "left largely to the Indians themselves. . . . There has been a hiatus in law enforcement authority."[3]

The transfer of criminal jurisdiction on all the reservations (except Red Lake) to the state in 1953 under PL 280 was seen as a way of dealing with the problems arising out of the lack of law enforcement. The change of jurisdiction also included some civil authority, but regulation of hunting, fishing, and wild-rice gathering was specifically exempt.

State jurisdiction in criminal matters did not necessarily mean improved law enforcement. The counties were responsible for providing service, and they complained that the federal government did not provide the funding to hire the needed personnel. Those enforcing the laws were often considered prejudiced by the Indian communities. In 1973, the Minnesota legislature approved the request by the Bois Forte Reservation to return to federal jurisdiction in criminal matters. Both Bois Forte and Red Lake reservations have their own criminal codes, tribal courts, and BIA-funded police forces (see below).

Today's criminal justice system is complex, involving at least five separate systems of government that include the police, those making decisions about prosecution, those defending the accused, the courts, and corrections. The Minnesota Department of Corrections funds three programs for Indians: Anishinabe Longhouse, a halfway house for adult Indian males released from prison; Leech Lake Youth Lodge; and Indian spiritual programs in the correctional institutions (partial funding). In 1983, $420,000 was allocated for these programs.

Federal funds to upgrade and improve law enforcement, the judicial system, and corrections were provided throughout the 1970s by the Law Enforcement Assistance Administration. In Minnesota, Indian needs received priority; and several programs were developed that received $500,000 or more annually. The federal funding, which ended by 1983, was used for youth programs, group homes, improvements of reservation police services by employing Indians there as part of the local sheriff's staff, and rehabilitation programs for offenders. As they proved useful, the programs were expected to be continued at the county level with regular funding. With very few exceptions, however, Indian programs were not continued.

The Minnesota Community Corrections Act (Mn. Stat. 401.01) provides financial incentives for staff training and development of local prevention, treatment, and diversion programs. An advisory board must include representatives of ethnic minorities—at least two if the county's total minority population exceeds the state percentage. (As with other efforts to involve minority communities, the actual influence of the representatives is open to question.) Hennepin, Ramsey, St. Louis, Cook, and Carlton counties, with major Indian populations, operate under the act; the remaining northern counties with high Indian populations do not.

Indians and Crime

Many factors not related to race correlate with a high crime rate. Although breaking the law is a personal decision, regardless of the experiences an individual has had, a compounding of circumstances may contribute to the commission of a crime. Youths, the economically disadvantaged, alcohol and drug abusers, the unemployed, and the poorly educated are all groups with high crime rates. The Indian population is disproportionately large in all these groups.

The criminal justice system is also wholly non-Indian. "Indians just don't believe in the white court system."[4] When dealing with it, Indians often believe that those who run it will not understand them or will exhibit overt or covert racial prejudice. The Indians' response may be to withdraw. A common comment from attorneys representing Indians in court is that they are not active in their own defense, they do not communicate well, and witnesses frequently do not appear.

This lack of trust in law enforcement is an obstacle to those trying to prevent criminal activity. County sheriffs note that Indian people are reluctant to pass on information or to testify, through fear of retaliation or, perhaps, because kin or friends are involved.

Indians note that it was not until after the passage of PL 280 in the late 1950s and the large migration to the cities that Indians came into the state correctional system and began the disproportionate involvement with it that they have in the 1980s. The effect of the migration has been to isolate individuals and to break down social structures. Traditional Indian values have been weakened, and the peer pressure to maintain community standards has diminished.

The complex legal status of Indians has added to the problem. An Indian is confronted by multiple jurisdictions, different laws, and even different definitions of "Indian." Being on Indian trust land may mean one set of laws, being on privately held land within the reservation may mean another set, and being outside the reservation may mean still another. These changes in jurisdiction can occur daily to an individual.

Life may consist of constant shuttling between Indian and white worlds, with varying norms of acceptable conduct and with the contradictions of urban and rural or reservation culture. In remote reservation areas, law enforcement may be nonexistent or seen as intrusive. "Friction between the sheriff's department and those on the reservation who feel state law should not supersede tribal sovereignty is real."[5] In urban centers, Indians may feel that they are under constant, hostile police surveillance.

Indian Adults in the Justice System

Indians are represented in the law enforcement and criminal justice system far in excess of their numbers in the general population. Although Indian adults were only 0.7% of the state's population in the 1980 census, and 0.8% in Hennepin County, they were 4.4% of arrested adults (5.9% in Hennepin County) in 1981. Those arrested for index (most serious) crimes were 5.8% statewide, 9.5% in Hennepin County.[6] Indian adults were 8.0% of the inmates in state correctional facilities, and they were 5.6% of those on state parole.[7]

Over two-thirds of the Indian inmates (69%) came from the metropolitan counties, with only 25% from nine northern counties.[8] Ojibway were 74% of the group; Dakota, 18%; and Winnebago, 2%. Although the average Indian inmate had lived on the reservation five to six years, many had never been reservation residents.[9] Indian inmates were less well educated than others: only 20% were high school graduates, although a higher number had received GED certificates—23% of admissions in 1981.[10]

Comparatively, Indians enter the correctional system younger, have more frequent contacts with the courts, and spend more time in correctional facilities, based on surveys of halfway house clients (table 25).

Table 25. Criminal Histories of Men in Halfway Houses, 1975
(Median Figures)

History	Anishinabe Longhouse (Indian)	Other Halfway Houses (85% Non-Indian)
As Juveniles		
Number of apprehensions	2.8	0.9
Times found delinquent of status offenses (truancy, loitering)	1.5	0.8
Times found delinquent of other offenses	1.3	0.8
Age at first conviction	13.7	14.9
Months in correctional facilities	5.8	0.8
As Adults		
Number of arrests	7.5	1.6
Number of misdemeanor convictions	3.5	1.2
Number of gross misdemeanor and felony convictions	1.8	1.6
Months in jails or workhouses	5.5	3.5
Months in correctional facilities	16.2	16.3

Source: Minnesota Crime Control Planning Board, Anishinabe Longhouse Final Report [1977].

Potential for Bias in the System

Throughout the process, from arrest to correctional institution, a great deal of discretion is allowed. Whether formally defined or not, decisions determine what neighborhoods receive more concentrated police enforcement efforts and therefore have higher arrest rates. Poorly defined criteria may determine who is detained in jail rather than released before trial; who is allowed bail and how high it is set; what charges are brought and whether they are reduced, dropped, or plea bargained.

Where there are standards, they usually contain such factors as residential stability; employment record; problems with alcohol or drugs; perceived eagerness, sincerity, and willingness to change; and previous criminal record. These standards allow for a good deal of subjective opinion by the evaluators and can be detrimental when used by those not familiar with Indian people.

Indians are highly mobile, suffer from excessive unemployment, are perceived as having excessive alcohol problems, may not communicate well with non-Indian officials, and often have earlier and more extensive criminal records. Even within the structured framework of determinate sentencing, judges can choose among several courses of action or inaction. As discretion is used throughout the administration of justice, questions have been raised about possible discrimination against Indians.

Two major studies of Indians in the correctional system reached similar conclusions: racial bias may be one of the causes of the unusually high representation of Indians throughout the process. A 1979 study that tracked Indian and non-Indian cases through the entire system commented, "Although the conclusions of this study must be carefully interpreted, they suggest the possibility of systemic bias in the criminal justice system of Minnesota."[11] A 1981 study of Minnesota's sentencing guidelines concluded, "It is also likely that there is some racial bias in sentencing."[12] This research, updated through 1983, found that there had been improvement in the racial neutrality of sentencing; however, "there is still room for improvement, especially regarding sentencing of American Indians."[13]

Arrest and Treatment in the Courts

In 1981, Indians were arrested in far greater numbers than whites in relation to their total population—in many categories, as much as 10 times or more (table 26). Indians are more apt to be arrested if they are in the Twin Cities: in 1981, 65% of adult Indian arrests in the state were in Minneapolis and St. Paul alone.

During 1973-75, a larger percentage of Indians than whites were involved with Minnesota courts and they were dealt with more severely: a higher arrest ratio, greater numbers held in jail prior to court arraignment (43%, Indians; 22%, whites), fewer cases dropped before arraignment (88%, compared with 95%), fewer released on bail (29%, compared with 36%), and far fewer getting outright release (7%, compared with 19%). About 85% of both races who came before the court pleaded guilty. At final court disposition, Indians were somewhat more apt to have acquittal or dismissal (24%, compared with 20%). A substantial number of Indians thus spent time in jail only to have their cases ultimately dismissed.[14]

Table 26. Arrest Rates of Minnesota Indian Adults, 1981
(Per 1,000 Population)

Offense	Minnesota Indians		Minnesota Whites		Minneapolis Indians	
	Rank	Rate	Rank	Rate	Rank	Rate
Larceny[a]	1	32.6	2	3.6	1	80.9
Driving under influence of alcohol	2	26.1	1	9.0	4	35.4
Disorderly conduct	3	20.6	3	1.8	3	36.5
Assault[a,b]	4	18.4	4	1.6	5	33.8
Liquor law violation	5	16.1	5	1.6	2	56.7
Burglary[a]	6	8.3	7	0.8	6	13.4
Vandalism	7	5.0	8	0.7	8	9.8
Robbery[a,b]	8	4.0			7	12.4
Auto theft[a]	9	3.5			10	6.0
Narcotics violation	10	3.3	6	1.3		
Prostitution and other sex offenses			9	0.5	9	7.8

Sources: Minnesota Crime Information System, *Uniform Crime Report*, 1981; US Census for 1980, adult populations, for rate per 1,000.
[a]Felonies.
[b]Crimes against persons.

In 1981, the state adopted a determinate sentencing system in felony cases. When the sentencing guidelines were imposed, it was expected that minority prison populations might increase, but only slightly. Significant increases did take place, however. By 1981, the state's prison population was 33% minority. From 1978 to 1981, there was a 50% increase in Indian inmates but only a 17% increase in whites.

Analysis showed that Indians received more severe sentencing in variance from the guidelines than did whites, both in terms of being sent to prison and receiving longer sentences. Although minorities were found to have committed somewhat more severe crimes within the same general categories than whites did and had more extensive criminal histories, factors contributing to severity of sentences, this did not account for the much more severe treatment they received.[15]

The courts in Hennepin and Ramsey counties imposed longer sentences than courts in other parts of the state on people who committed the same crimes and had similar criminal histories. This was true for all races. However, both the Sixth and Ninth Judicial Districts (northeastern and northwestern Minnesota) dealt more severely with Indians than with whites. In 1983, those districts sent 33 Indians to prison. If the pattern of sentencing used for whites had been followed, only 21 Indians would have been committed.[16]

Although the guidelines prohibit the use of employment status, more severe sentences were given to those unemployed. Of the offenders studied, 90% of the Indians were unemployed and 60% of the whites. Of the unemployed Indians, 34% were imprisoned; but only 19% of the unemployed whites were imprisoned. Of those working, very few whites were imprisoned (5%), whereas 23% of the Indians were.[17]

Statistics also show a disproportionate severity of sentences given Indians when records include misdemeanor as well as felony cases. The accompanying tabulation shows the Hennepin County Court Services sentencing dispositions for both types of cases in 1981.

	Indians	Whites
	(N=119, 7% of total)	(N=1,014, 61% of total)
Probation	20%	36%
Workhouse	52	47
Prison	28	15
Other	0	2

Whites were far more apt to receive probation and were less apt to be sentenced to the workhouse. Indians received almost twice as many prison sentences as whites.[18]

Judges determine grand jury selection procedures, which may be highly personal and subjective. Petit juries, by law, are drawn randomly from such sources as voter and driver's license rolls, on which Indians are apt to be underrepresented. People working with the courts in Bemidji report that there are very few Indians drawn for jury duty: 2 to 4 in a panel of 30, or less than their proportion of the population. Those Indians drawn are disproportionately nonreservation.[19]

White community attitudes toward Indians in northern Minnesota may be a factor in jury decisions. Although attorneys representing Indian clients are sensitive to local prejudices, most felony and gross misdemeanor cases are tried before juries. In the opinion of a public defender with the Ninth District Court in Bemidji, juries tend to consider Indian poverty and lack of opportunities and to show reverse prejudice in minor cases; but in major cases, "there is a definite bias against Indians."[20]

Correctional Institutions

The types of crimes for which people are incarcerated in state correctional institutions differ by race. Indians are more apt to have been sentenced for burglary (property crime), somewhat more apt to have been sentenced for robbery or aggravated assault (crimes against persons), and less frequently sentenced for rape or homicide (table 27).

Table 27. Crimes Leading to Incarceration

Crime	Indian Adults, 1981		General Population, 1 July 1980	
	Rank	Percentage	Rank	Percentage
Burglary	1	29	2	17
Robbery	2	23	1	21
Aggravated assault	3	10	6	7
Larceny	4	9	5	10
Unauthorized vehicle	5	6	8	3
Rape/Sex crimes	6	4	3	15
Homicide	6	4	4	14

Source: DOC, *Characteristics of Adult Institutional Populations, American Indians,* 1981, 59; *Biennial Report,* 1979–80, 20.

Correctional institutions are not very successful in changing the behavior of any inmate, and less so with Indians. Of adults released from state correctional institutions in 1980, 43% of the Indians—in comparison with 33% of all races—were back in prison within two years.[21]

Heart of the Earth Education Program. The first and only Indian adult education program within a correctional institution in the United States has operated at Stillwater since 1978. Heart of the Earth Education Program is offered as a full-time work assignment, five days a week and six hours a day. Indian instructors (eight teachers and one counselor in 1982) are brought in to provide classes in basic math and English, GED preparation, life coping skills, and Indian culture and language.

The voluntary program, which is funded under the Indian Education Act, Title IV, served 104 Indian inmates in 1982; it is administered by Heart of the Earth Survival School, Minneapolis. In addition to serving the Stillwater facility, the school provides cultural programming at the Lino Lakes and Shakopee institutions.

The Minnesota attorney general's opinion of November 1980 stated that the program did not appear to be in violation of antidiscrimination laws. "Failure to make meaningful provision for the safety, well being and possible rehabilitation of the inmates of correctional facilities has been established as constitutionally intolerable."[22]

A 1981 evaluation of the program noted that the Indian-oriented education and cultural experience had improved attitudes and self-concept. More Indian inmates were involved in education programs than previously, and they were doing as well as or better on tests than those involved in the institution's regular education program. The report recommended that the institution support the program with the same level of enthusiasm as it did other programs.[23]

Anishinabe Longhouse. Anishinabe Longhouse, Minneapolis, was developed by Indians in 1973 during the early days of funding from the Law Enforcement Assistance Administration. It is now funded by the Department of Corrections as its only adult, community-based Indian program. The halfway house serves up to 15 men released on parole from state institutions or felons whose sentences are stayed pending good behavior at the longhouse.

The program was set up in consultation with elders in the Indian community. It uses Indian spiritual values, traditional strengths, and stresses the importance of community. Indians are offered a way to break free of the criminal justice system. The program provides treatment, counseling, and help in securing jobs to ease clients into community life. The average stay is 78 days. An evaluation by the Minnesota Crime Control Planning Board around 1977 found that "no clients who satisfactorily completed residence were convicted of felonies or [had parole revoked] during the twelve months following residence."[24]

Legal Services

There are several unique dimensions to serving Indians; unless attorneys are sensitive to the differences, "the attorney-client relationship will be superficial, and unsatisfying to everyone involved."[25] According to a public defender in Bemidji, "It is hard to gain the confidence of the defendant. It is hard to get facts from witnesses. Families may report a crime but then will not testify. . . . Indians are noncommunicative."[26]

Attorneys who represent Indians in Minneapolis have found that their clients often have no hope for justice in a white court and little faith in the helpfulness of agencies. The attorneys need to work with their Indian clients to create some confidence in the legal process. While developing in the client an understanding of the process involved, attorneys need to respect the client's decision making and to vigorously present the case.

Public Defenders. The public defender program is used by many Indians in the Ninth Judicial District, which is headquartered in Bemidji. An estimated 95% of the Indian defendants used the program, making up 35–40% of its clients.[27] Bemidji has two Indian attorneys in private practice available to serve as court-appointed public defenders.

State-assisted Programs. As an alternative to public defenders, state-assisted legal services targeted to Indians are available in Minneapolis, St. Paul, and Duluth. Help is provided to low-income people in criminal and juvenile cases. The state also makes funds available ($53,000 each in 1983) to the White Earth and Leech Lake reservations with which they can contract on their own for attorneys.

The state-assisted, Indian-oriented programs include the Legal Rights Center, Minneapolis, which was begun in 1969 with AIM help to provide legal services in criminal cases to low-income people. It is directed by a community-based board. Minority paralegal employees who know the community are very important to the program. Two of the staff and 40% of the clients were Indian in 1981. Funding sources include United Way, foundations, corporations, law firms, and individuals. Minnesota provided $55,000 in 1983.

Neighborhood Justice Center in St. Paul, a similar program, uses community workers. One of the 10-person staff is Indian. It also has legal education programs in the community, including a project of training legal advocates at the Red School House, St. Paul. Funding was about 40% private and 60% public in 1982; state funds provided $95,000 in 1983.

Indian Legal Services in Duluth provides legal assistance for Grand Portage, Bois Forte, Fond du Lac, and Mille Lacs reservations as well as for Indians in Duluth. In addition to criminal cases, the office handles civil cases involving divorce, domestic abuse, and landlord-tenant problems. County social service funds are used for juvenile cases in St. Louis County alone. The program is heavily dependent on state funds, $85,000 in 1983. Programs have been cut, and state funding has not increased in four years. As a result, the staff of 14 was reduced to 3 attorneys and 1 office worker by 1982.

Federally Funded Legal Services. Legal Services programs are available statewide to provide assistance for low-income people in civil matters such as wills; estates; domestic relations; cases involving children; landlord-tenant disputes; and problems with taxes, Social Security, welfare, and public benefit programs. Criminal or fee-generating cases cannot be taken. The program, which is federally funded by the Legal Services Corporation, suffered a cut of 25–30% during 1981 and 1982 that caused major staff reductions. Individual offices may have funding from other sources.

Anishinabe Legal Services, Cass Lake, provides a legal services program primarily targeted to Indians. It serves the Leech Lake, White Earth, and Red Lake reservations area, operating from six offices.

Legal Aid Society of Minneapolis serves Hennepin County and provides legal services in a 20-county area. It has three offices, including one on Minneapolis's south side and one on the north side. In 1981, 3% of the clients were Indian. Southern Minnesota Regional Legal Services, St. Paul, serves 33 counties. It provides services at the St. Paul American Indian Center. Legal Aid Service Northeastern Minnesota, Duluth, serves 11 counties, and 2% of its clients were Indian in calendar year 1982. Once a month it provides legal assistance to senior citizens at Fond du Lac Reservation.

Indians in the Juvenile Justice System

The numbers of Indian youth arrested, sentenced by the courts, and removed from home and community are well in excess of Indian juvenile percentages in the state's population. According to the MCT, "The facet of the problem hardest to bear is the waste of so many young Indian lives."[28]

Arrest

Overall, Indian juveniles were arrested three times as frequently as their percentage in the population (1.3% statewide, 5.3% in Minneapolis) in 1981 (table 28). Arrests of Indian juveniles are much more frequent in the Twin Cities than in the rest of the state; 72% of all juvenile Indian arrests were in Minneapolis and St. Paul alone in 1981. The arrest rate for Indian youth is consistently higher than for the white population.

One of the major differences in arrest patterns between the races is that white juveniles are much more apt to be arrested for status offenses. Statewide, 10% of all Indian juveniles were arrested on this charge, compared with 22% of white juveniles. The difference is much

Table 28. Arrests of Indian Juveniles, 1981

Offense	Minnesota		Minneapolis	
	Number	Percentage of Arrests	Number	Percentage of Arrests
Index crimes[a]	635	4.1	355	16.9
Status offenses	144	2.1	55	13.9
Other crimes	604	4.9	358	16.2
Total	1,383	4.0	768	16.3

Source: Minnesota Crime Information System, *Uniform Crime Report*, 1981.

[a]The eight most serious crimes: homicide, rape, robbery, assault, burglary, theft, auto theft, arson.

smaller in Minneapolis, where status offense arrests were fewer for both races, although relatively higher for whites (7 and 10%, respectively).

Court System

Detention. Hennepin County data show that as the county processed juveniles in 1981, Indians were involved at a consistently higher rate than their population percentage of 2.0% (table 29).

Table 29. Detention of Indian Juveniles in Hennepin County, 1981

| | Hennepin County Juvenile Center | | |
	Arrests	Intake Referrals	Detentions
All races	10,482	6,406	2,342
Indians	830	389	288
Percentage Indian	8	7	12

Sources: Minnesota Crime Information System, *Uniform Crime Report*, 1981; Hennepin County Court Services, 1981.

The Hennepin County Juvenile Center is used for intake and, after court action, as a detention facility. Although severity of crime and fear that the youth will fail to appear in court may be factors in the disproportionate detention of Indians, cultural differences also play a role. Extended family members may not fit the court system's criteria for people who may assume responsibility for the juveniles, even when they serve the juveniles in a parental capacity.[29]

A statewide study using 1981 data showed that white juveniles were more apt to be charged with the less severe status offenses (25% of white youth, 18% Indian), whereas Indians were two to three times more apt to be charged with the most serious crime, offenses against persons (17% of Indian cases, 6% whites).[30]

Placement choice varied with the severity of the offense. For the most and least serious offenses, no significant association was found between race and sentencing. But "the greatest amount of true decision-making lies with those cases in the middle. . . . Native Americans . . . are more likely to be placed out of home than whites for these mid-range offenses. . . . Blacks and native Americans have a significantly higher probability of being placed in correctional facilities than whites who have committed the same offense."[31] The report also showed that Metropolitan Area courts placed significantly more children out of home; the less serious the offense category, the greater the disparity between Indians and whites.

Correctional Facilities

In 1981, 12% of the 1,629 residents at seven of Minnesota's juvenile correctional facilities were Indian.[32] At Red Wing and Sauk Rapids, state institutions for the most serious juvenile offenders, Indians were 13% of the population (29 of 222)—10 times the state's Indian juvenile population, according to the 1980 census. Of those under parole from state institutions, Indians were 8% (43 of 521).

Programs for Indian Youth

A few youth programs serve the reservations, funded by the tribes and, in some cases, small amounts from the state's Youth Intervention Program. Leech Lake Reservation's Youth Development Project and the White Earth Youth Advocacy Program provide prevention, counseling, and referral services.

Midway Home on the White Earth Reservation is a residential facility for up to 10 youths at a time, serving a five-county area. It assists young people in need of a home in a crisis and receives court-assigned status offenders; it cannot by law take delinquents. The clients are mostly Indian, and ages can vary from 10 to 18 years old, with most in the older age group. The home, a restored farmhouse, provides food, shelter, recreation, counseling, and referral services. Through December 1983, it received federal juvenile justice funds. Additional funding comes from the counties that use the services.

A home for Indian delinquent boys, Leech Lake Youth Lodge, is operated by the Leech Lake tribe. Funding is provided by the Minnesota Department of Corrections ($68,000 in 1982) and by the counties, which pay the cost for their residents. The home had a total budget of about $150,000 in 1982.

The Youth Lodge, begun in 1973, is a residence for youth from all over the state who are court-assigned dischargees from Red Wing, Sauk Center, and chemical dependency and other programs. The current facility is a former resort on Portage Lake within the reservation. It consists of a lodge and three cabins that can accommodate up to 16 people. The remote location of the lodge has been a major improvement in the program. The youth are provided counseling and program help at the lodge while attending school in Cass Lake.

Other northern Minnesota facilities do not have programs geared specifically to Indians. For instance, the Northwest Minnesota Regional Training Center at Bemidji State University is a residential program with strong educational and vocational emphasis. One-third of the clients are

Indian, but no Indians serve on the staff or on the board directing the program.

A major Indian youth counseling program, American Indian Youth Alternatives, operates at the Minneapolis American Indian Center. It serves court-assigned juveniles by working with them and their families as an alternative to incarceration. Services include chemical dependency counseling, recreational programs, education, and employment assistance. The program has received federal juvenile justice money. Funding is also provided by Hennepin County.

A few other programs serving juveniles in Hennepin County are seen as Indian-sensitive and are used for court placement: chemical dependency treatment programs at Eden Youth and Winaki; the Group Home of the City; and the Hennepin County Home School, a juvenile correctional facility. In Ramsey County, a juvenile intervention project has assisted youth at the Red School House.

Conflicts between Indians and the State Systems

Police

"The feeling that black and brown people are just more likely to be picked up and arrested in the first place has been a source of police and community tension for years."[33] Crime rates are higher in low-income areas, with large numbers of young people and renters—areas where many Indians live. Social problems of alienation, family disintegration, and drugs are higher in these neighborhoods. The police concentrate their attention on areas where they see greater need, but the people who live there may view this attention as harassment.

Besides feeling unfairly harassed by police, Indian communities testify that the police respond slowly to calls for help and that they avoid areas of high Indian population (such as Little Earth Housing Project in Minneapolis), especially on domestic calls. Reservations that receive police protection from the counties are almost unanimous in their criticism of law enforcement services. According to Grand Portage Reservation, "Law enforcement is a problem. The Cook County Sheriff's Department serves this area and has to travel 80 miles round trip to respond to each call. It often takes hours to get them out here."[34]

Perceptions about Police. Both on the reservations and in the Twin Cities, Indians view law enforcement officials as prejudiced against Indians. A Minnesota Indian testified to the American Indian Policy

Review Commission that a deputy sheriff in Itasca County told him, "If all those Indians would kill each other, then we wouldn't have to go up there."[35]

White Earth Reservation has had episodes of alleged police harassment that provoked widespread protests from the Indian community. On the other hand, a deputy sheriff keeping peace on the reservation can feel very threatened. During three and a half years, a Becker County deputy sheriff was "shot at on three different occasions, though never hit. Once, a person was shot out of his arms. He's been assaulted a number of times and wound up in the hospital. In one incident he suffered cracked ribs and cuts and spent a month off the job recuperating."[36]

Hostility toward the police in minority neighborhoods of the Twin Cities was reported to the Minnesota Advisory Committee to the US Commission on Civil Rights. Police are considered adversaries by residents, and a Minneapolis police captain in a minority precinct acknowledged that "many residents are afraid of the police."[37]

A study of Minneapolis and St. Paul minority community perceptions of local police documented that, of all the groups surveyed, Indians frequently had the most negative response toward police. Whereas only 2% of whites thought the police did a very poor job of protecting lives and property, 18% of the Indians surveyed did. Seventy-six percent of the Indians responded negatively to the question, "Do you feel police in Minneapolis are fair in dealing with Indians?"[38]

Efforts to Improve Relations. Suggestions for improving relations between Indians and the police include establishing better communication between police and neighborhoods; increasing police sensitivity, understanding, and acceptance of group differences; providing channels for resolving citizen complaints; and increasing minority representation in the police departments. Although some efforts have been made, they are generally seen as having fallen short of making significant improvements. Community advisory councils have been established in Minneapolis at the police precinct level; however, the Indian community has found them ineffective as a channel for real understanding.[39]

An external review board that truly incorporates minorities has been sought as part of the system for dealing with citizen complaints of improper police conduct. Police officers are very opposed, fearing that it could be used to harass and cripple effective police work. Minorities see opposition to external civilian review as further reason for mistrust of the police.

Indian Employment in Criminal Justice

Very few Indians are employed in the criminal justice system. John Poupart, the director of the Indian halfway house Anishinabe Longhouse, summarized the problem:

> Indians are treated unfairly in the criminal justice system.
> It is no secret. Look at the numbers in the system. But
> look at the lack of Indian employees in the whole process.
> There are hardly any Indians who are police, parole/proba-
> tion officers, attorneys, judges, public defenders. Indians
> are not in the system. They have no voice.[40]

It is generally agreed that the employment of more Indians in police forces would bring greater acceptance of the police in Indian communities and would probably improve the perceived fairness of law enforcement. After the violent confrontations that took place between Indian inmates and institutional staff at both Stillwater and St. Cloud institutions in 1980 and 1981, the ombudsman recommended that staff training in human and race relations be integrated into the training plans of all correctional institutions and that vigorous efforts be made to recruit and hire Indian correctional officers as vacancies became available.[41] John Poupart has called for aggressive affirmative action plans, based on inmate racial composition, to recruit, train, employ, and advance Indians in the criminal justice system.[42]

The number of Indians employed is generally below their population percentage and far below the percentage of Indians involved in the corrections system. In 1975, in state and local government throughout Minnesota (48 units reporting), Indians were 0.5% of police protection employees and 1.8% of new hires. In corrections, they were 0.9%, and 1.8% of new hires.[43]

Strong minority hiring programs have made a difference where they have been implemented. In the Minneapolis Police Department in 1983, 10 of 686 officers were Indian, or 1.5%; in St. Paul in 1981, the police department had 1.4% Indians as officers and staff. In 1982, the Cass County Sheriff's Department had two Indian employees, or 15% of the staff. Duluth, however, employed no Indians as police.

There are no Indian judges in the state system and very few Indians employed as legal representatives. The first Ojibway woman to become a lawyer in Minnesota, Margaret Treuer, was appointed magistrate of the US District Court, Minnesota, in 1982.

In 1982, Hennepin County court services staff was 0.3% Indian; Ramsey County's, 1.2%. The Minnesota Department of Corrections

253 • CRIMINAL JUSTICE SYSTEM

employed 25 Indians on the classified staff (1.5%). At the institutions, Stillwater had six Indian guards, and St. Cloud had none; Red Wing's staff was 1.6% Indian. The state ombudsman, who deals with inmate problems, was an Indian, appointed in 1983.

Barriers. There are many barriers to increased Indian employment. Indians tend to shy away from jobs that make them their "brother's keeper," or "the enforcer," telling other people what to do. They would have to enforce laws that are not made by Indians and to impose non-Indian standards. A county deputy sheriff—part Ojibway—who serves on the White Earth Reservation explained: "They hate you more when you arrest them because you are an Indian and they think you shouldn't arrest them."[44]

The state has established education and training standards for beginning local police officers that include two years of college or a three-year vocational school program. Although officers may be hired with only a high school education, the courses must then be taken. Some see these formal education requirements as an impediment to keep minorities from qualifying.[45]

Indian Cultural and Religious Freedom in Prison

The expression of Indian culture and religion within state correctional institutions has been a major source of misunderstanding, friction, and occasional violence between inmates and those in authority. The administrative view is that all inmates are to be treated alike.

Cultural Activities. Because cultural activities are seen as having the potential of causing factionalism and creating power groups, they are feared as threats to security and discipline. The prison staff's evaluation of an Indian-run education and culture project at Stillwater included such negative comments as, "It is promoting a negative subculture" and "puts the Indians in a separate group instead of being part of the population."[46] Treatment that is "alike," however, really means treating Indians as if they were culturally identical to the majority population. This treatment "may ignore their rehabilitative needs and in fact be counterproductive to the goals of corrections. . . . [It is] like 'treating cancer patients in a tuberculosis ward; all persons are treated equally, but the cancer patient will surely die.' "[47]

Religious Freedom. The right to practice religion is poorly understood by prison officials where Indians are concerned. Denials and seemingly unnecessary affronts cause hostility among Indian inmates.

Minnesota law requires the commissioner of corrections to set aside time and space for religious worship, and clergy are allowed to visit inmates (Mn. Stat. 241.05 and 243.48). Opportunity for religious observance for Indian inmates is mandated by the federal American Indian Religious Freedom Act. In addition, the US Constitution, which forbids the establishment of religion by the government, also prohibits the denial to individuals of the right to practice religion. The courts have upheld that Indian inmates cannot be denied a freedom of religion equal to that of adherents of other faiths.

Despite these assurances, Minnesota Indian inmates complain that they are not allowed to practice their religion and are not being treated equally. Indians are denied free access to religious objects: they cannot have pipes in their cells, whereas there is no restriction on Bibles. Sage, sweet grass, and cedar for pipe ceremonies are restricted because the guards fear the scent may mask marijuana.[48] Guards have removed and mutilated eagle feathers, which have great spiritual significance. This sacrilegious act is offensive to Indians.

"Non-Indians don't readily grasp and therefore can't cope with a traditionalist religion that is based on custom rather than doctrine in a book. To authorities, Indian religion seems to be whatever those who adhere to it say it is. However, the status of the medicine man . . . and the tradition are not as vague as non-Indians think."[49] Consultation with Indian spiritual leaders can establish the important religious objects that should be allowed and respected by prison officials.

Ministers of other faiths have free access to inmates and immunity from package searches. State-funded Christian chaplains are available full time, but Indian worship is limited to once a week or once every two weeks.

The Minnesota Department of Corrections provides money ($34,000 in 1983) for transportation and other costs to provide a spiritual leader to conduct sweat lodge ceremonies and other spiritual activities at Stillwater and St. Cloud every other weekend. Hennepin County funds visits to the Minneapolis Workhouse by a spiritual leader as a part of the chaplains' program. Services are provided to Indians at the federal prison at Sandstone about once a month. Sweat lodges are especially valued, and Minnesota now has these facilities at Stillwater, St. Cloud, Lino Lakes, and the Minneapolis Workhouse.

An Indian culture group, Ogi-Chi-Dog, meets weekly at St. Cloud, using outside speakers and Indian community resources. Oak Park Heights has a drum group meeting once a week.

Besides being a basic right, participating in religious experiences is seen as being beneficial to the individual and the institution. The benefits of learning and spiritual growth that come with increased contact with elders can enhance the institution's other programs, lessen disciplinary problems, and improve the inmate's motivation to change life patterns.

Battered Women

Family violence, abuse, and the battering of women are acts that are strongly disapproved of by all cultures, including Indians. They are not minority nor low-income problems: rather, they occur throughout the population. Family violence is primarily a problem of male aggression that is linked to stressful personal circumstances and inappropriate ways of dealing with anger. In many instances, abuse is associated with excessive use of alcohol.

The extent of abuse of women is not really known because many cases do not get reported. For the two fiscal years 1979 and 1980, 6.7% of cases reported in Minnesota by medical, law enforcement, and human services departments were Indian. Indian women were 11% of all battered women housed in state-supported shelters during the year October 1979-October 1980.[50]

Indian women, as those of other cultures, often accept abuse rather than seek help. Generally, Indian community attitudes have not strongly condemned abuse, and this seeming "acceptance" may make it difficult for women to alleviate bad situations. Obtaining relief may mean getting another Indian into trouble with white authority. If the only alternative is to leave, this may bring reprimands from other family members. The woman sees leaving as banishment—being cut off from the Indian community, traditionally the worst punishment that can be imposed—while the abuser remains part of the community.[51]

Having to deal with white authorities can be a barrier. People who are supposedly there to help may humiliate the women, causing them to feel more victimized by society than by their problems. At shelters that provide temporary housing for women and their children, the women are apprehensive of finding racism, insensitivity, and misunderstanding. Bureaucracies and authorities are suspect because women fear that their children might be taken away.

Programs. Shelter facilities for women suffering abuse, counseling programs, police action, and the courts are available to deal with the problem of battering. Women seeking help can qualify for AFDC or General Assistance welfare. The state Task Force on Battered Women, composed of 18 women (including three Indians in January 1981), advises on the program. In 1983, $58,000 was set aside for programs to serve Indians.

Educational sessions on family violence, counseling, and support groups for men and women are operated by Upper Midwest Indian Center, the Division of Indian Work, Family Health Program and Indian Health Board, all in Minneapolis; and by the St. Paul American Indian Center. In northern Minnesota, Leech Lake Reservation has programs dealing with family abuse. Fond du Lac Reservation funds two advocates who serve all of Carlton County.

The shelter program in the Twin Cities has Indian advocates at some of the facilities. At Bemidji, the Northwoods Coalition for Battered Women is used extensively by Indian women and children. In 1981, 70% of the families served were Indian. There are women's support groups on Fond du Lac, Leech Lake, White Earth, and Red Lake reservations.

On Red Lake Reservation, battering charges are brought to tribal court as a misdemeanor crime. Many Indian women are unwilling to sign complaints, perhaps fearing that action will not be taken or that it may only add to the problem. Most complaints end up being dropped, and the women return to their homes. Some women use the shelter in Bemidji; volunteers provide transportation.

Tribal and Federal Criminal Justice Systems

The criminal justice systems on Red Lake and Bois Forte reservations are totally outside of state jurisdiction. Legal codes established by the tribal councils deal with lesser crimes, those with a maximum sentence of $500 fine and six months in jail. The tribal court on each reservation, the Court of Indian Offenses, deals with those charged with violating the code.

Serious offenses are under federal jurisdiction and are tried in federal court. The Major Crimes Act makes it a federal crime within Indian country to commit 14 serious crimes, including murder, manslaughter, kidnapping, rape, incest, assault with a dangerous weapon, arson, burglary, robbery, and larceny. Indian country is defined as land within reservation boundaries, even if it has passed into private ownership; rights-of-way such as state highways through the reservations; "dependent Indian communities"; and trust allotments off reservations.

Another law—the Assimilative Crimes Act (18 USC 13)—provides that in areas of federal jurisdiction (including Indian reservations), if an action would be a crime under state law the violator is subject to a punishment similar to that set by the state even if there is no specific federal law.

The disposition of a case involving a criminal act depends upon who the accused is, against whom the act was committed, how serious it is, and where it occurred. Anything that occurs off the reservation is a state matter, even if a reservation Indian is involved. If it is a case of a non-Indian against a non-Indian on the reservation, that, too, is a state matter.

For a crime by an Indian against an Indian, the severity of the crime determines whether it is a matter for tribal or federal court. A crime by an Indian against a non-Indian on the reservation is a matter for tribal or federal court. If the tribal code is violated by a non-Indian, it is usually a federal court matter, either under the Major Crimes Act, if that applies, or the Assimilative Crimes Act for lesser offenses.

Civil Jurisdiction

The Red Lake Court handles civil suits for reservation Indians and enforces the tribal civil code. Although that code also covers non-Indians on the reservation, enforcement is a problem. In civil matters, there is no reciprocity between tribal and state courts. The right of non-Indians to use the Red Lake Court to bring civil action was withdrawn by the Red Lake Tribal Council, but the BIA—which has jurisdiction over the court—has not approved the council's action.

At Bois Forte, civil jurisdiction was not retroceded to the tribe. The state court system is used, although the tribe can exercise concurrent jurisdiction over members if it wishes.

Jurisdictional Problems

When Red Lake Reservation Indians are arrested in Bemidji, they are not released on their own recognizance as are other offenders. Rather, they are treated like out-of-state people and are held in jail pending preliminary hearings. The court's premise is that arrest warrants will not be honored by the reservation police, the individual will not appear in court, and extradition will not be possible. This lack of cooperation and understanding between the two systems means inequitable treatment for the individual Indians arrested.

On the other hand, when the state probation system deals with a Red Lake resident, the state officer lacks jurisdiction to deal with the client on the reservation. Although there is "fairly adequate recognition by Indian police of probation officers' rights and responsibilities to see clients on the reservation,"[52] better access would improve the system.

Police and Jails

The police forces on Red Lake and Bois Forte reservations are funded and administered by the BIA. These staffs are professional police officers trained at the Indian Police Academy at Brigham City, Utah.

Red Lake has 30 police and jail employees: officers, including one woman; dispatchers; and jail personnel. The comprehensive police, jail, and juvenile facility that had been built at Red Lake in the early 1970s was destroyed in the violence of May 1979. Another building has been modified to serve as a jail, with two temporary holding cells for juveniles. The Youth Intervention Center, a 10-bed unit at Ponemah, serves as a detention facility. The program is funded by the Indian Child Welfare Act.

Bois Forte Reservation has four police officers, a criminal investigator, three radio operators, and two clerks. This staff provides 24-hour coverage. The reservation has a holding and detention facility.

Tribal Courts

The tribal code of criminal offenses at Bois Forte includes minor felonies as well as misdemeanors; Red Lake's code deals with misdemeanors only. The Courts of Indian Offenses on the two reservations are funded by the BIA and are under its jurisdiction.

Judges are selected in cooperation with the tribal council, with a two-thirds vote of the council needed for approval. They serve four-year terms and may be reappointed. Red Lake Court has three judges, reservation residents who are not legally trained. Bois Forte Court judges are attorneys who live off the reservation and provide part-time service.

All persons charged with crimes have the right to hire someone to defend them, but there is no right to free counsel for those who cannot pay. Attorneys are not considered necessary to bring cases before tribal courts, and their participation may even be discouraged. Defendants are allowed to be represented by outside attorneys before the Bois Forte Court. The Red Lake Court maintains a list of residents licensed by the tribe who are available to help defendants. An attorney can represent a client only if the attorney lives on the reservation.

The Indian Civil Rights Act provides that an accused person in a tribal court has the right to a trial by jury of not less than six persons if the offense is punishable by imprisonment. There is no right to a jury trial in civil cases. The process of appeal varies among tribes; it may involve asking the judge, acting with two associates, to rule on that judge's original decision.

Mille Lacs Reservation has established an elected Court of Central

Jurisdiction to provide for redress of grievances within the context of the tribal constitution, tribal codes, and federal law. All reservations have conservation courts to enforce their conservation codes.

Problems with Tribal/Federal Systems

The tribal justice system and the relationship between tribal and federal jurisdiction have raised various issues. The BIA and the tribes are sometimes in conflict over the operation of the police and the courts. Although the Indian Self-Determination and Education Assistance Act allows tribes to contract for and operate their own justice systems, neither tribe in Minnesota has.

The nature of reservation life makes it difficult for police or the courts to provide service that is seen as fair and impartial. Factionalism, extended family kinship systems, the closed community where everyone is known, or resentment of outside interference may lead to charges of harassment or excessive leniency.

Attention has been focused on efforts to make the Indian court system a greater part of Indian culture, and one that is used and respected by those it is intended to serve. The National American Indian Court Judges Association has been active in providing training programs and other attempts to upgrade the effectiveness of the courts.[53]

One concern is that many major crime cases are not prosecuted. "It appears that in excess of 80% of major crime cases, on the average, presented to US Attorneys are declined for prosecution."[54] They are dropped for a variety of reasons. The federal officials generally prosecute cases that they have a good chance to win. Indian cases are atypical of those usually brought into federal court, and they are frequently considered difficult to prosecute and win because of the cultural differences and remoteness of the reservation. Witnesses may be reluctant to come forward. Many of the offenses are alcohol related, which may mean that those involved have unreliable perceptions and poor memories.

If the federal government does not act, the common result is that no action is taken in any court system. When a tribal court is used, sentences are limited and serious felonies go virtually unpunished. This has led to the prevalent feeling among reservation Indians that the federal government does not consider Indian cases important, and there is widespread lack of confidence in the reservation law enforcement system. A study noted, however, that there is a "significant difference in the mobilization of criminal justice resources when the victim of the reservation crime is non-Indian."[55]

Because of isolation, jurisdictional problems, and insufficient funding, reservation court systems often have only limited options when dealing with offenders. Red Lake Reservation has a probation officer. In 1983, state legislation allowed the Red Lake Court to make commitments to state chemical dependency and mental illness facilities.

Summary

The present criminal justice system does not appear to be solving society's problems with Indian crime and, in fact, may be contributing to them. Indians believe that many aspects of the process, which is based on an alien culture, are destroying Indians rather than helping them. The numbers and treatment of Indians throughout the arresting, charging, court, and sentencing processes raise questions of possible racial bias that deserve the attention of all those who run these systems.

Indians have shown that rehabilitation designed and run by Indians within the context of the culture can be more successful with Indians than programs that ignore cultural differences. They are asking that the culture be respected and that there be greater use of Indian employees and programs. Truly significant results, however, will come only when the causes of crime are addressed. Improvements in Indian education, employment, income level, housing, chemical dependency treatment, and feelings of individual worth are all larger needs with direct bearing on the problem.

Conclusion

To Indians, maintenance of their culture, their tribes, their reservations, and their sovereignty has the highest priority. Their relationship to government is unique and complex, and they are continually threatened by unilateral government actions. But Indians also need to rely on government protection and assistance. The very existence of the tribe depends on the federal government's continued honoring of past treaty and other legal commitments.

Government actions have in many ways shaped today's problems for Indians, thereby establishing an obligation on the part of government to help with solutions. For many of the very pressing and debilitating human problems in the Indian community, government assistance is the only way to get sufficient help. This help, if it is truly to be beneficial, must incorporate Indians into the planning, directing, and staffing of the programs—programs that are shaped to Indian culture and unique Indian needs. A consistent, long-term commitment with continuing adequate funding is ncessary.

Indians are very few in number. Highly vocal and seemingly strong opponents can create political pressure against Indian efforts, especially as Indians exert long-dormant rights that challenge the interests of these groups. If Indians are to have a voice in controlling their own programs, strong bureaucracies and entrenched government systems will have to relinquish power. At all levels of government, concern and support from the general public are necessary so that Indian voices may be heard. More than any other minority, racial or cultural, they need the understanding and support of the general public to achieve their goals.

The need for all Minnesotans to care about Indian problems is as great today as it was in 1863, when Secretary of War Stanton, in response to Bishop Whipple's efforts on behalf of the Dakotas in Minnesota, told a friend of Whipple's: "What does Bishop Whipple want? If he came to tell us of the iniquity of our Indian system, tell him we know it. But this government never reforms an evil until the people demand it. When the Bishop has reached the hearts of the people of the United States, the Indians will be saved."[1]

Appendixes

Federal Treaties and Significant Legislation

Treaties and Agreements

1825   Treaty with the Chippewa, Sioux, and other tribes signed at Prairie du Chien (7 Stat. 272; II Kappler 250). Established a boundary line between the Chippewa and Sioux.

Sioux

1837   Treaty with the Sioux signed at Washington, DC (7 Stat. 538; II Kappler 493). Ceded lands east of the Mississippi River.

1851   Treaty with the Sisseton and Wahpeton bands signed at Traverse des Sioux (10 Stat. 949, II Kappler 588); treaty with Mdewakanton and Wahpekute bands signed at Mendota (10 Stat. 954; II Kappler 591). Ceded all Sioux lands in Minnesota and created two reservations 150 miles long and 10 miles wide, on either side of the Minnesota River.

1858   Treaty with the Yankton Sioux signed at Washington, DC (11 Stat. 743; II Kappler 776). Ceded the pipestone quarry in Minnesota, with the provision that it be kept open to Indians to visit and procure stone for as long as they desired.

1858   Treaty with the Mdewakanton and Wahpekute bands and treaty with Sisseton and Wahpeton Sioux signed at Washington, DC (12 Stat. 1031 and 1037; II Kappler 781, 785). Reservation land south of the Minnesota River allotted, and land north of the river to be sold.

1863   Treaties made with the four Minnesota Sioux bands abrogated and their lands and right of occupancy forfeited (12 Stat. 652). Sale authorized of Sioux lands in Minnesota (12 Stat. 819).

1886   Purchase of land in Minnesota for Mdewakanton Sioux who were in the state before 20 May 1886 (24 Stat. 39). Money provided in *1888* (25 Stat. 228), *1889* (25 Stat. 992), and *1890* (26 Stat. 349). Additional land purchased under the Indian Reorganization Act (IRA; 1934) for Lower Sioux and Prairie Island communities. PL 96–557 in *1981* removed the restriction limiting settlement to those who qualified under the 1886 provision. Upper Sioux Indian Community land purchased under the IRA.

Chippewa

1826   Treaty with the Chippewa Nation signed at Fond du Lac (7 Stat. 291). Ceded "the right to search for and carry away any metals or minerals."

1837   Treaty with the Chippewa signed at the mouth of the St. Peter River (7 Stat. 536; II Kappler 491). Ceded land from north of the 1825 boundary to the Crow Wing River.

1847   Treaty with the Chippewa of the Mississippi and Lake Superior bands signed at Fond du Lac (9 Stat. 878, 904; II Kappler 567). Ceded land intended for a Winnebago reservation that was never established.

1847   Treaty with the Pillager band signed at Leech Lake (9 Stat. 908; II Kappler 569). Ceded land intended for a Menominee reservation that was never established.

1854   Treaty with Chippewa of the Lake Superior and Mississippi bands signed at La Pointe, Wis. (10 Stat. 1109; II Kappler 648). Ceded most of the Arrowhead country; created Grand Portage, Fond du Lac, and Lake Vermilion reservations.

1855   Treaty with the Chippewa of the Mississippi (including Pillager and Winnibigoshish bands) signed at Washington, DC (10 Stat. 1165; II Kappler 685). Ceded north central Minnesota. Reservations created at Leech and Cass lakes for the Pillagers; at Lake Winnibigoshish for that band; and at Mille Lacs, Sandy, Rice, Gull, Rabbit, and Pokegama lakes for the Mississippi band.

1863   Treaty with the Red Lake and Pembina bands signed at Old Crossing of Red Lake River (13 Stat. 667; II Kappler 835). Amended in the supplementary treaty of *1864* (13 Stat. 689; II Kappler 861). Ceded land but retained a large tract around Red Lake.

1863   Treaty with the Mississippi, Pillager, and Lake Winnibigoshish bands signed at Washington, DC (12 Stat. 1249), the "concentration treaty." Renegotiated in *1864* at Washington, DC (13 Stat. 693; II Kappler 862). Consolidated and expanded the Cass Lake, Lake Winnibigoshish, and Leech Lake reservations into Leech Lake. Indians at Mille Lacs and the other 1855 reservations were to move to Leech Lake. The Mille Lacs and Sandy Lake bands, because of support they gave to the whites during the 1862 uprising, could stay as long as they remained friendly.

1866   Treaty with the Bois Forte band signed at Washington, DC (14 Stat. 765; II Kappler 916). Ceded Lake Vermilion Reservation and established the reservation at Nett Lake. Executive orders in *1881* and *1882* purchased land at Lake Vermilion and Deer Creek.

1867 Treaty with the Mississippi band signed at Washington, DC (16 Stat. 719; II Kappler 974). A further effort at concentration, with a portion of the 1864 Leech Lake Reservation ceded. Executive orders in *1873* and *1874* added land to Leech Lake Reservation. White Earth Reservation established.

1889 Nelson Act (25 Stat. 642; I Kappler 301), the allotment act for Minnesota. Rice Commission was to negotiate complete relinquishment of all reservations except Red Lake and White Earth, which were to be allotted. (Red Lake band resisted allotment.) Land not needed for allotment was to be sold. Residents on other reservations were to move to White Earth; however, if the Indians wished to take allotments on the existing reservations, they were not to be disturbed. Red Lake band sold the north part of its reservation. On *29 July 1889*, White Earth Reservation ceded four northeastern townships.

1902 Payment authorized for improvements Mille Lacs Indians had made to the land, provided they would move to White Earth or any other reservation (32 Stat. 268).

1904 Red Lake band sold 11 western townships and was allowed to remain independent of other Chippewa reservations (31 Stat. 1077).

1906 Clapp Rider removed restrictions on sales of allotments on White Earth by mixed bloods and allowed full bloods to sell when the secretary of the interior was satisfied that they could handle their own affairs.

1914 Land purchased for allotments, Mille Lacs Reservation; additional land purchased under the IRA.

1975 Over 28,000 acres of the White Earth Reservation held by the US Department of Agriculture transferred to the Minnesota Chippewa Tribe (MCT; 25 USC 459a).

Significant Legislation

1787 Northwest Ordinance passed by Congress of the Confederation. Recognized Indian sovereignty over the Northwest Territory; attempted to protect rights of Indians in the land they occupied.

1789 Constitution of the United States, Art. I, Sec. 8 (the commerce clause) gave Congress power "to regulate commerce with . . . Indian tribes."

1789 Department of War established with responsibility to handle matters related to Indian affairs. In *1824*, the Bureau of Indian Affairs (BIA) was established by order of the secretary of war. In *1849*, the BIA was transferred to the Department of the Interior.

1871 Abolishment of treaty-making method of dealing with Indians (16 Stat. 566). Instead, agreements were to require approval by both houses of Congress. No treaties previously made were invalidated.

1885 Major Crimes Act (23 Stat. 385; 18 USC 1153). Federal courts given jurisdiction over major crimes committed by Indians on reservations.

1887 General Allotment Act (Dawes Act; 24 Stat. 388) authorized allotment of tribal lands to individual Indians. Surplus lands remaining after allotment were to be sold, with proceeds used for Indian programs. Citizenship to be conferred upon allottees found competent and Indians who adopted "the habits of civilized life." (The Nelson Act, 1889, was the allotment act for Minnesota.)

1910 Probate Act (25 USC 372) gave the federal government power to probate Indian estates, determine heirship, sell, and partition allotted lands.

1921 Snyder Act (42 Stat. 208; 25 USC 13), the primary authorization for BIA programs for the benefit, care, and assistance of Indians throughout the United States. Authorization is open-ended and permanent, limited by congressional appropriations.

1924 Citizenship Act (43 Stat. 253). Indians made citizens of the United States.

1934 Indian Reorganization Act (IRA; Wheeler-Howard Act) (48 Stat. 984; 25 USC 470). Recognized inherent right of tribes to operate through governments of their own creation. Tribes given the right to engage in business; a revolving loan fund established. Indians given preference in BIA employment. Vocational education and student loan programs begun. Allotment process ended; land up for sale but not sold reverted to the tribes.

1934 Johnson-O'Malley Act (JOM) (48 Stat. 596; 25 USC 52) authorized the secretary of the interior to enter into contracts with states to provide education, medical attention, agricultural assistance, and social welfare.

1946 Indian Claims Commission (60 Stat. 1049; 25 USC 70) established to consolidate and speed up Indian claims. Ended on *31 Dec. 1983* (PL 96–217), with unresolved claims transferred to the US Court of Claims.

1953 House Concurrent Resolution (HCR) 108, Senate concurring. Established the policy of termination. Several tribes were terminated, with land removed from trust status and federal services stopped. Indians disagree strongly with the policy, which proposed to "end [Indians'] status as wards of the United States, and to grant them all of the rights and prerogatives pertaining to American citizenship . . . [by freeing them] from Federal supervision and control and from all disabilities and limitations specially applicable to Indians."

1953 Civil and Criminal Jurisdiction on Reservation, PL 83–280 (18 USC 1162; 28 USC 1360), known as PL 280. Transferred to five states, including Minnesota, civil and criminal jurisdiction on reservations, without tribal or state approval. Red Lake Reservation was excluded. States were not authorized to tax real or personal property. Indian rights to hunt, fish, trap, and harvest wild rice were exempted from state jurisdiction.

1954 Indian Health Service (IHS) transferred from BIA to Department of Health, Education and Welfare, now Health and Human Services (68 Stat. 674; 42 USC 2001). Snyder Act authorization procedures continued. Funding of environmental programs and construction and maintenance of water and sanitation systems authorized by Indian Sanitation Facilities Act (73 Stat. 267; 42 USC 2004a) in *1959.*

1956 Indian Adult Vocational Training Act, PL 84–959 (70 Stat. 986). This "relocation" act provided transportation, settlement costs, vocational training, and counseling assistance for up to 24 months.

1968 Indian Civil Rights Act, PL 90–284 (82 Stat. 73; 25 USC 1301). Extended to individual Indians some protections of the US Bill of Rights in their relations with their tribal governments (25 USC 1302). Tribes may, however, have an established religion; and free counsel is not required in court cases. Writs of habeas corpus may be sought in federal court. PL 280 amended so that states cannot assume legal jurisdiction over tribes without their consent (25 USC 1321), and responsibility can be retroceded from state to federal government if requested by the state (25 USC 1323).

1970 Presidential Message (House Document 91–363). A major change in policy, urging that Indians be allowed to become independent of federal control without being cut off from federal concern and support. Proposed were repeal of HCR 108, allowing Indians to control their own programs, helping urban Indians, expanding programs in economic development and health, and elevation of Indian affairs within the Department of the Interior.

1972 Indian Education Act, Title IV (86 Stat. 334). A greatly expanded program to meet special and culturally related education needs of reservation and nonreservation students with as little as one-eighth Indian ancestry. Indian parents given a major voice in program decisions (20 USC 241aa). Also funds innovative projects, adult education, and professional school fellowships for qualifying Indians (20 USC, 887c, 1211a).

1975 American Indian Policy Review Commission established by Joint Resolution of Congress (PL 93–580). The commission, composed of six members of Congress and five Indians, established task forces on 11 major governmental issues. The reports, completed in 1976 after extensive hearings, documented Indian needs and recommended policy changes (see report titles in selected reading list).

1976 Indian Self-Determination and Education Assistance Act, PL 93–638 (25 USC 450). Declared commitment to maintain the unique and continuing federal relationship, with responsibility to the Indian people and orderly transition from federal domination to Indian control of programs. Tribes allowed to contract to administer many BIA and IHS programs (Title I). Federal funding to continue, with additional money provided for administration. If requested by tribes, the agencies must resume administration. Indians to be given preference in contracts and hiring. Title II (funding for education) requires that BIA funds that go to public schools must be used for supplementary Indian education programs, for Indian students only, under control of Indian parents (25 USC 456).

1976 Indian Health Care Improvement Act, PL 94–437 (25 USC 1601), expanded health services by increased funding of health programs, facility construction, and education programs for health professionals. Urban Indian health programs authorized, Title V (25 USC 1651).

1978 Indian Child Welfare Act, PL 95–608 (25 USC 1901). Required that tribes be notified and given a say when tribal children are brought to court for placement decisions. Established priority preference for placement, first with extended family, then with tribal members, thirdly with other Indians. Funding to be provided to assist tribes in exerting their authority under the act.

1978 Indian Religious Freedom Act, PL 95–341 (42 USC 1966), guaranteed to Indians the right to believe, express, and practice native traditional religions.

1983 Indian Tribal Governmental Tax Status Act extended to tribes equal standing with other government bodies in exemption from federal excise tax on purchases and the right to sell tax-exempt bonds.

APPENDIX B

Significant State Legislation

Indian Affairs Council. Begun in 1963 (Mn. Stat. 3.922), the council is composed of one tribal representative from each of the state's 11 reservations and two elected by Minnesotans who are members of federally recognized tribes located in other states. Serving ex officio are state legislators and representatives of the governor and major state departments. The council makes legislative recommendations and acts as liaison between the state's Indian population and various levels of government.

Indian Burial Law. Destroying or damaging human burials is a gross misdemeanor. The Indian Affairs Council and the state archaeologist are to be consulted when remains are accidentally disturbed. If bodies can be dated to before 1700, the state archaeologist deals with them; for remains dated after 1700, if the tribe can be determined, the body is turned over to the contemporary tribe for burial. Indian burial grounds are to be identified and marked. Purchase of the sites is authorized (Mn. Stat. 307.08).

Planning. Reservations are eligible for local land-use planning grants (Mn. Stat. 4.26, subd. 1). Their governments may be reimbursed by the state for disposing of abandoned motor vehicles on the same basis as local governments (Mn. Stat. 168B.10, subd. 5). Counties making up the Mississippi River Headwaters Board were directed to negotiate with the Leech Lake Reservation in preparing zoning plans for the Upper Mississippi River (Mn. Stat. 114B.03, subd. 3).

Fish and Game. The Leech Lake band and the Department of Natural Resources confirmed the band's treaty rights to hunt, fish, trap, and gather wild rice (Mn. Stat. 97.433). In return for the Indians' agreement not to take game and fish (except rough fish) for commercial purposes, 5% of the proceeds from the sale of all licenses sold in the state for hunting, fishing, trapping, or taking min-

271

nows or other bait is paid to the Leech Lake band (Mn. Stat. 97.433, subd. 2). A similar law (97.433, subd. 1) authorized negotiations with the White Earth band to pay 2.5% of fees from licenses sold. The DNR was to evaluate the Mille Lacs band's claimed rights to hunt, trap, fish, and gather wild rice and to report on the feasibility of making an agreement with the band similar to the Leech Lake one (Session Laws 1982, chap. 462, sec. 12). No agreement had been reached with either the White Earth or Mille Lacs band as of 1984.

Retrocession of Criminal Jurisdiction. Minnesota asked the BIA to resume criminal jurisdiction over the Bois Forte Reservation (Session Laws 1973, chap. 625). Jurisdiction was accepted by the federal government.

White Earth Reservation Land Claims. To assist in resolving the White Earth Reservation land claims, the legislature in 1984 authorized transfer of 10,000 acres of state-held land to the federal government to be placed in trust for the tribe. If there is no federal agreement with the tribe by 31 December 1985, the land transfer offer is void.

Red Lake Tribal Court Commitments. State institutions may recognize commitments made by this court (Mn. Stat. 253B.212).

Taxes. The state can enter into agreements with tribal governments to refund state sales or excise taxes collected from Indian residents of the reservations (Mn. Stat. 270.60). Cigarettes can be seized or Minnesota cigarette wholesalers can have their licenses revoked if cigarettes are sold on reservations to persons who are not tribe members without payment of state sales taxes (Mn. Stat. 297.041).

Wild Rice Harvesting and Sale. In 1938, the state declared: "From the time immemorial the wild rice crop of the waters of the state of Minnesota has been a vital factor to the sustenance and the continued existence of the Indian race in Minnesota." Indians and non-Indian reservation residents have the exclusive right to harvest rice upon the public waters within the original reservation boundaries of the six MCT reservations (Mn. Stat. 84.09–10). Harvesting rice must be done in the Indian way (Mn. Stat. 84.11). Paddy-grown wild rice must be plainly and conspicuously labeled as such. Offering it for sale wholesale or retail without the required labeling is a misdemeanor (Mn. Stat. 30.49).

Business Loan Fund. A revolving loan fund for Indian businesses is established from 20% of the taxes collected on severed mineral rights. There is to be a "reasonable balance between Indians residing on and off reservations." Qualified Indians are one-fourth Indian blood and members of Minnesota tribes (Mn. Stat. 362.40). The Indian Affairs Council administers the program (Mn. Stat. 116J.64).

Imitation Indian-Made Goods. Indian goods made by someone of less than one-fourth Indian blood must be labeled "not Indian made." Indians can bring civil action and recover damages for violations. A knowing violation is a misdemeanor (Mn. Stat. 325F.43). Federal law provides for a penalty if goods are represented as Indian by a person who knows they are not (18 USC 1159).

Contracts. The State Board of Education may contract with the United

States to receive grants and disburse them for the education of Indians (Mn. Stat. 124.64).

School Census. In making their annual census, school districts are to use agencies or community groups in seeking information about Indian children residing in the district (Mn. Stat. 120.095, subd. 7).

Independent Indian Schools. Two small elementary schools in Indian areas are allowed to remain independent: Nett Lake, established as Independent District 710; and Pine Point. Pine Point School, first established as an experimental school within Independent District 309 (Session Laws 1973, chap. 683, sec. 26), was made an independent school district in 1981 and management was transferred to the White Earth RBC (Session Laws, chap. 358, art. 6, sec. 39). The legislation went into effect upon the vote of the people in the district.

American Indian Language and Culture Education Act of 1977. Known as Chapter 312 (Mn. Stat. 126.45), this law provides grants to a limited number of public, tribal, and alternative Indian schools to make curriculum more relevant to Indian children and to develop intercultural awareness among pupils, parents, and staff. Indians are given preference in staffing. Parents of Indian children are active in planning the programs, and an Indian advisory task force assists the state in administration.

Eminence Licensing. Teachers knowledgeable in Indian language or with unique understanding of Indian history and culture may be granted "eminence licenses"—full teaching licenses—provided they have the relevant education or experience and tribal approval (Mn. Stat. 126.49).

Indian Scholarship Program. The state provides an Indian scholarship program to assist high school graduates with one-fourth or more Indian ancestry to obtain higher education (Mn. Stat. 124.48). The 15-member Minnesota Indian Scholarship Committee appointed by the State Board of Education awards the scholarships.

University of Minnesota, Morris. Indians are admitted to attend the Morris campus tuition free, as stipulated when the federal government transferred this former Indian school to the state (Mn. Stat. 137.16, subd. 1).

Welfare. Reimbursement is authorized to counties from the Indigent Indian Account for up to 75% of their General Assistance expenditures for medical or hospital care, burial, child welfare, and home relief for Indians. Indians must be one-fourth Indian blood and not Red Lake Reservation residents. The state may also accept grants from the US government (Mn. Stat. 245.76). The state pays the counties' share of costs for federal welfare programs (AFDC, Medical Assistance, and administration) supplied to Red Lake members on their reservation (Mn. Stat. 256.965). To the extent that state and federal money is available, the state reimburses the counties' share of costs for other welfare programs for Red Lake Indians (Mn. Stat. 245.765).

Housing. Part of the state's housing finance program for low- and moderate-income housing is specifically extended to Indians for administration by the tribes (Mn. Stat. 462A.07). In 1979, a program was added for urban Indians (Mn.

Stat. 462A.07, subd. 15). Funds are available for long-term, low-cost mortgages for construction, purchase, or rehabilitation of residential housing.

Chemical Dependency. The special chemical dependency treatment needs of Indians are recognized. An Indian advisory council (Mn. Stat. 254A.035), state Indian staff (Mn. Stat. 254A.03, subd. 2), and Indian employees (Mn. Stat. 254A.03, subd. a [i]) are authorized. Counties are to employ Indians (Mn. Stat. 254A.06). A range of programs is authorized (Mn. Stat. 254A.031), including an Indian primary residential treatment center.

Corrections. The state may grant 100% of the costs of community corrections programs operated by Indian RBCs (Mn. Stat. 245.66, subd. 7).

APPENDIX C
Significant Court Decisions

Several principles of legal construction are important in Indian court decisions:

1. Laws are to be liberally construed and doubtful expressions are to be resolved in favor of the Indians (cited in *Bryan v. Itasca*, 426 US 392 [1973]).
2. Treaties and agreements are to be interpreted as the Indians understood them (cited in *State v. Clark*, 282 NW 2d 909 [MSC, 1979]).
3. Implicit Indian treaty rights and jurisdiction are not lost by inference. They cannot be taken unless specifically stated by Congress (cited in *US v. White*, 508 F.2d 453 [8th Cir., 1974]).
4. Treaty and statutory provisions that are not clear on their face may be clear from the surrounding circumstances and legislative history (cited in *Oliphant v. Suquamish*, 435 US 191 [1978]).

Federal Cases

Fletcher v. Peck (6 Cranch 87 [1810]). This first Indian case before the US Supreme Court stated that tribes had lost the right to govern every person within their limits except themselves. Cited in *Oliphant v. Suquamish*, 1978.

Cherokee Nation v. Georgia (30 US [5 Pet.] 1 [1831]). The decision written by Chief Justice Marshall stated, "The Constitution by declaring treaties . . . to be the supreme law of the land, has adopted and sanctioned the previous treaties with the Indian nations, and consequently admits their rank among those powers who are capable of making treaties" (30 US 17). Tribes were called "domestic dependent nations." "Their relation to the United States resembles that of a ward to his guardian. They look to our government for protection; rely upon its kindness and its power; appeal to it for relief of their wants" (30 US 17). This special relationship has been the basis of the trust relationship.

Worcester v. Georgia (31 US [6 Pet.] 515 [1832]). Georgia had illegally and unconstitutionally extended control over Indians within the state. Tribes were declared to have inherent sovereign powers. They were distinct, independent, political communities with territorial boundaries within which their authority was exclusive. This is considered the single most important decision pertaining to Indians.

US v. McBratney (104 US 621 [1881]) and *Draper v. US* (164 US 240 [1896]). States have criminal jurisdiction over crimes committed by non-Indians against non-Indians on the reservations.

Ex parte Crow Dog (109 US 556 [1883]). When an Indian was murdered on a reservation, it was realized that federal courts had no jurisdiction. The passage of the Major Crimes Act of 1885 gave jurisdiction over certain crimes to the federal government, marking the first overt congressional intrusion into Indian sovereignty.

US v. Kagama (118 US 375 [1886]). In response to a challenge of the Major Crimes Act, the court, while recognizing tribes as "separate people, with the power of regulating their internal and social relations," declared that sovereignty exists at the sufferance of Congress. Congress has "plenary" (complete, full) power over the "dependent" Indian tribes. The case has been used to limit tribal authority and to urge fiduciary obligations on the United States.

US v. Winans (198 US 371 [1905]). Treaties are not a grant of rights to Indians but are rather a grant of rights from them and a reservation of those rights not granted.

Morton v. Ruiz (415 US 199 [1974]). Indians living near reservations who maintain close economic and social ties and have not been assimilated into the general society are to receive federal Indian services.

Morton v. Mancari (415 US 535 [1974]). Indians are not a racial group but members of quasi-sovereign tribal entities whose lives and activities are governed by the BIA in a unique fashion. Indian preference in employment by the agency as stated in the law is not invidious racial discrimination but is reasonable and rationally designed to further Indian self-government.

US v. Mazaurie (419 US 544 [1975]). Tribes can regulate some non-Indian liquor sales on reservations. However, in *Rice v. Rehner* (103 SC 3291 [1983]), the US Supreme Court ruled that state liquor licensing can also be imposed on a reservation because sales can have impact beyond reservation boundaries.

Bryan v. Itasca (426 US 373 [1976]), reversing Minnesota Supreme Court (228 NW 2d 249). PL 280 granted to the states only civil jurisdiction in court proceedings, not civil regulation such as taxing and zoning powers.

Santa Clara Pueblo v. Martinez (436 US 49 [1978]). Even if a tribal government discriminates in a manner that would be in violation of federal law, the Indian Civil Rights Act does not give the federal courts jurisdiction to deal with the issues. (Federal jurisdiction is specifically granted only in criminal cases involving petitions for writs of habeas corpus.)

Oliphant v. Suquamish (435 US 191 [1978]). By submitting to the overriding sovereignty of the United States, Indian tribes gave up the power to try non-Indians in criminal cases. The decision greatly limited tribal jurisdiction.

Washington v. Confederated Tribes of the Colville Indian Reservation (447 US 134 [1980]). Indians doing business with non-Indians on a reservation can be required to collect and remit state taxes on sales to non-Indians. Tribes cannot invalidate state taxes but can impose their own.

Montana v. US (450 US 544 [1981]). The tribe did not have the authority to regulate hunting or fishing by non-Indians on non-Indian land within the reservation because there was no clear relationship to tribal self- government. However, tribes may retain inherent sovereign power to exercise some forms of civil jurisdiction over non-Indians, even on non-Indian land within a reservation: where there have been contracts and leases; and when conduct threatens the political integrity, economic security, health, or welfare of the tribe. In a later case, *New Mexico v. Mescalero Apache* (51 USLW 4741, 14 June 1983), the tribe was ruled to have jurisdiction over non-Indian hunting and fishing within the reservation. State jurisdiction did not apply.

Minnesota Cases

Hunting and Fishing Cases

Leech Lake Band v. Herbst (334 F. Supp. 1001 [D. Mn., 1971]). Aboriginal hunting and fishing rights were not abrogated by the Nelson Act of 1889. It is the termination of federal responsibility and not the passing of legal land title that determines whether a reservation exists in the eyes of the law. Judge Devitt was not persuaded, however, that the Leech Lake band had exclusive authority to regulate non-Indian hunting and fishing.

State v. Forge (262 NW 2d 341 [MSC, 1971]). Cert. denied (435 US 919). The special state tax imposed for hunting and fishing on Leech Lake Reservation is a rational compromise between unextinguished treaty rights held by the tribe and the legitimate interests of the state in regulating fishing for the benefit of all citizens.

Leech Lake Citizens Committee v. Leech Lake Band (355 F. Supp. 697 [D. Mn., 1973]). The court ruled that the agreement with the Leech Lake band on hunting and fishing was not a treaty but a settlement to bring litigation to an end. The legislature could not be enjoined.

State v. Clark (282 NW 2d 902 [MSC, 1979]). Cert. denied (445 US 904 [1980]). Indian hunting and fishing rights on White Earth Reservation were re-established through the 1864 and 1867 treaties and not removed by the Nelson Act of 1889. Four townships on the northeast corner were ceded, however, and are not a part of the reservation. In the 32 remaining townships, the state does not have jurisdiction over enrolled White Earth Indians on Indian and non-Indian land.

White Earth Band v. Alexander (518 F. Supp. 527 [D. Mn., 1981]) affirmed (683 F.2d 1129 [8th Cir., 1982]). Cert. denied (51 USLW 3442, 7 Dec. 1982). In the 32 reservation townships the band can regulate or prohibit the entry of non-

Indians on Indian-held land and can require compliance with Indian ordinances. Indians can hunt and fish throughout the reservation without state interference. The state can enforce its laws against persons who are not White Earth Reservation members anywhere within the reservation, including Indian-held land; but if the band's rules are more stringent, they can be imposed. Although the band cannot assert criminal jurisdiction over nonmembers through the tribal court, it can assert jurisdiction by eviction or by revoking tribal licenses; it may refer cases to federal authorities.

Lac Courte Oreilles Band v. Voight (700 F.2d 341 [7th Cir., 1983]). Wisconsin Indians who were a part of the 1837 Chippewa treaty (ceding land that included east central Minnesota) did not relinquish hunting and fishing rights. The Indians are free of state jurisdiction on public waters within the ceded area. In spring 1984, the case was still in federal district court. Mille Lacs Reservation is within the treaty area. The impact of the decision on Minnesota had not been resolved.

Other State Cases

Namekagon Development Co. v. Bois Forte Reservation Housing Authority (395 F. Supp. 23 [D. Mn.]) appealed (517 F2d 508 [8th Cir., 1975]). The tribe's housing authority could be sued because it relinquished immunity in receiving funds from the Department of Housing and Urban Development. *Duluth Lumber and Plywood Co. v. Delta Development, Inc.* (218 NW 2d 377 [MSC 1974]). The MCT waived sovereign immunity against suits for the Indian housing authority when it passed a "sue and be sued" ordinance.

State v. Zay Zah (259 NW 2d 580 [MSC, 1977]). The Clapp Amendment, which allowed Indians on White Earth to take title to their land and dispose of it, only applied when the Indian consented; otherwise, the trust status continued. Without Indian consent, the land could not be subject to property taxes and could not be forfeited for nonpayment of taxes. The Indian Reorganization Act of 1934 indefinitely extended the trust.

Booker v. Special School District No. 1 (Minneapolis) (451 F. Supp. 659 [D. Mn., 1978]) affirmed (585 F.2d 347 [8th Cir., 1978]). Cert. denied (443 US 915). The Minneapolis School Board asked that the desegregation order (351 F. Supp. 799 [D. Mn., 1972]) allow for a substantial increase in minority students by school, especially in schools having concentrations of Indian students, to allow Indians to get full benefit from federal Indian programs. Judge Larson, in denying the request, noted that allowing a large component of Indians would "condemn whites and Negroes and members of other minority groups to attend public schools . . . devoted primarily to the education of minority students."

State v. Keezer (292 NW 2d 714 [MSC, 1980]). The treaties of Greenville and Prairie du Chien do not exempt Ojibway Indians from state regulation of wild rice gathering in Anoka County.

Thompson v. City of Minneapolis (300 NW 2d 763 [MSC, 1980]). A Minneapolis building inspector's suspension for making racist remarks was upheld.

The First Amendment guarantee of freedom of speech does not give a public employee an absolute right to say anything he or she wants during the course of the job.

Lamb v. Village of Bagley (310 NW 2d 508 [MSC, 1981]). Racially derogatory remarks establish a prima facie case of unequal, discriminatory treatment. Because the accused is also Indian and has abused others does not make overt racist behavior acceptable. "Indian racial descent . . . is not enough to prove 'Indianness' "; cultural ties are also important.

St. Paul Intertribal Housing Board v. Reynolds (Civil Case 4–82–872 [D. Mn., 31 May 1983]). Using low-income housing subsidies (Section 8) from the Department of Housing and Urban Development for an urban Indian housing program is not a violation of antidiscrimination laws. The trust relationship extends to individual Indians as well as tribes. The program for urban Indians increases Indian self-determination "by increasing the available alternatives open to Indians in American society." An appeal by the department was withdrawn.

Red Lake Reservation Cases

County of Beltrami v. County of Hennepin (119 NW 2d 25 [MSC, 1963]). Beltrami County did not have to provide General Assistance welfare to Indians living on Red Lake Reservation because the county could not enforce state law on the reservation.

State v. Lussier (130 NW 2d 484 [MSC, 1964]). The state cannot prosecute for a burglary committed by a Red Lake Indian against non-Indian property on Red Lake Reservation.

Commissioner of Taxation v. Brun (174 NW 2d [MSC 120, 1970]). The state lacks the power to tax income from wages earned on the reservation by an enrolled member living on the reservation.

Topash v. Commissioner of Revenue (291 NW 2d 679 [MSC, 1980]). Exemption from state income taxes also applies to income earned on the reservation by members of all federally recognized tribes living on the reservation.

White v. Tribal Council, Red Lake Band (383 F. Supp. 810 [D. Mn., 1974]). Charges of improper election procedures were dismissed because it was not shown that the tribal courts could not fairly and justly rule.

US v. White (508 F.2d 453 [8th Cir., 1974]). The Federal Bald Eagle Protection Act does not apply to Red Lake Reservation because the act did not expressly abrogate the hunting rights implicitly granted in the treaties.

Red Lake Band v. State (248 NW 2d 722 [MSC, 1976]). Issuing motor vehicle license plates is an appropriate exercise of the Red Lake band's unique power of self-government. It is entitled to exemption from the Minnesota auto registration statutes and to reciprocity in recognition, as with a state or territory of the United States.

State v. Rossbach (288 NW 2d 714 [MSC, 1980]). An individual standing on Red Lake Reservation land who fired a gun at a deputy standing on Minnesota land could be tried by the state under the common law that the crime occurred where the shots took effect.

Jourdain v. Commissioner of Internal Revenue (617 F.2d 507 [8th Cir., 1980]). The income received from the band by the chairman is subject to federal income taxes.

State v. Red Lake DFL Committee (303 NW 2d 54 [MSC, 1981]). The political committee is subject to state reporting requirements when political advertisements endorsing state candidates are disseminated outside the reservation.

US v. Minnesota (466 F. Supp. 1382 [D. Mn., 1979]) affirmed on appeal as *Red Lake Band v. State of Minnesota* (614 F.2d 1161 [8th Cir., 1980]) Cert. denied (449 US 905 [1980]). In ceding land under the Nelson Act of 1889 and the Act of 1904, the band relinquished all rights to the ceded area, including hunting and fishing. Where the land reverted to the Red Lake band under the Indian Reorganization Act of 1934, the band now has jurisdiction. Otherwise, hunting and fishing is under state regulation in the ceded area.

APPENDIX D

Indian Media
and Events in
Minnesota

Newspapers

Speaking of Ourselves, Minnesota Chippewa Tribe, Box 217, Cass Lake, Minn.,
56633; Betty Blue, editor.
De-Bah-Ji-Mon . . . "telling news," Leech Lake Reservation, Cass Lake, Minn.,
56633; Erv Sargent, editor.
Anishinabe, Dee-Bah-Gee-Mo-Win, White Earth Reservation, Box 418, White
Earth, Minn., 56591; Norma Felty, editor.
The *Circle,* Minneapolis American Indian Center, 1530 E. Franklin Avenue, Min-
neapolis, Minn., 55404.

Radio and Television

"First Person Radio," Migizi Communications. A 30-minute weekly American
Indian news and information program. Produced in Minneapolis and
distributed nationwide over the National Public Radio Satellite System.
Carried by eight Minnesota stations: Duluth, KUMD-FM; Grand Rapids,
KAXE-FM; Twin Cities, KBEM-FM, KFAI-FM, KMOJ-FM, KQRS-FM, and
KUOM-AM.
"Madagimo," television program, WCTN, Channel 11, Minneapolis.
"Indian Viewpoint," television program, WDIO, Channel 10, Duluth.

Events

Ojibwe Art Expo. This juried art show of Great Lakes tribal artists is held annually in April and May at Bemidji State University and Augsburg
College.

281

Indian Week. The observance is held the first week in May each year.

Traditional Pow Wows. These annual Indian gatherings are important celebrations:

Minneapolis American Indian Center	Early May
Sah-Gi-Bah-Gah Days, Bois Forte Reservation, Nett Lake	Early June
1867 Treaty of a New Nation Pow Wow, White Earth Reservation	Mid-June
Veterans' Memorial Pow Wow, Leech Lake Reservation, Cass Lake	Early July
Red Lake Reservation Pow Wow	Fourth of July
Me-Gwitch Mahnomen Days, Ball Club, Leech Lake Reservation	Mid-July
Mash-Ka-Wisen Pow Wow, Sawyer	Early August
Ojibwe Nation Ni-Mi-Win, Spirit Mountain, Duluth	Mid-August
Rendezvous Days, Grand Portage Reservation	Mid-August
Mille Lacs Reservation Pow Wow, Vineland	Mid-August
Inger Pow Wow, Leech Lake Reservation	Late August
Prairie Island Indian Community Pow Wow	Mid-September
Dakota Wohiksage Makoce, Sibley Park, Mankato	Mid-September

Notes

Acronyms Used in Notes

Federal Agencies

BIA	Bureau of Indian Affairs
CCR	Commission on Civil Rights
EEOC	Equal Employment Opportunity Commission
HEW	Department of Health, Education and Welfare
HHS	Department of Health and Human Services
IHS	Indian Health Service

Minnesota Agencies

DES	Department of Economic Security
DNR	Department of Natural Resources
DOC	Department of Corrections
DPW	Department of Public Welfare
MDE	Department of Education
MDH	Department of Health
MSGC	Minnesota Sentencing Guidelines Commission
OLA	Office of Legislative Auditor
SPA	State Planning Agency

Others

BSU	Bemidji State University
CURA	Center for Urban and Regional Affairs
LWV	League of Women Voters
MCT	Minnesota Chippewa Tribe
RBC	Reservation Business Council
UMD	University of Minnesota, Duluth

Notes

Introduction

1. *US Pharmacopoeia* and *National Formulary*. IHS, Bemidji Program Office, *Bois Forte Service Unit Health Plan* (1979), 13.

2. John Red Horse, professor of social work, Arizona State Univ., speaking at the Child Welfare League of America Conference, Minneapolis, Minn., 27 Apr. 1981.

3. Alvin M. Josephy, Jr., *The Indian Heritage of America* (New York: Alfred A. Knopf, 1968).

4. Warren Upham, *Minnesota Geographic Names* (St. Paul: Minnesota Historical Society, 1920; reissue 1969); William Burnson, "How Did Your County Get Its Name?" *Minnesota Volunteer* (Jan.–Feb. 1982), 56-63.

5. *Reservations* are lands held in trust by the US government for specific groups of Indians. In Minnesota, there are seven reservations occupied by Ojibway Indians, four communities occupied by Dakota Indians, and a small tract of land held for Winnebago Indians that is not populated and does not enter into this discussion. In legal usage, the term also includes land originally set aside – even though no longer in federal trust – unless Congress took it away.

6. Helen Wolner, LWV, Cloquet, Minn., letter to author, 5 May 1982.

7. Sam Deloria, address on 12 Nov. 1979; reported in Janet Swenson and Gail Rosenthal, eds., *Warm Springs: A Case Study Approach to Recognizing the Strengths of American Indian and Alaska Native Families* (Washington, DC: American Academy of Child Psychology, 1980), iv.

8. Janice Command, *Minnesota Daily*, 1 Feb. 1982.

9. Ellen Olson; quoted in *Duluth Herald/News-Tribune* and reprinted in *Ourselves*, MCT, Cass Lake, Minn., Feb. 1983.

Chapter 1. Shifting Governmental Policies

1. Chief Joseph, Nez Perce tribe; quoted in American Indian Movement, *Non-Aligned Summit Meeting*, Jan. 1982.

2. President Andrew Jackson; quoted in Alexis de Tocqueville, *Democracy in America*, Henry Reve Text (New York: Alfred Knopf, 1945), 1:353.

3. *Democracy in America*, 1:355.

4. *The Minnesota Legislative Manual, 1983–84* (St. Paul: State of Minnesota, Secretary of State, 1983), 19.

5. Lee Antell, director, *Indian Education: Involvement of Federal, State and Tribal Governments*, report 135 of the Education Commission of the States (Denver, 1980), 37 (hereafter cited as L. Antell, *Indian Education*).

6. William Folwell, *History of Minnesota* (St. Paul: Minnesota Historical Society, 1930), 4:201.

7. Harold Fey and D'Arcy McNickle, *Indians and Other Americans* (New York: Harper and Row, 1959).

8. Folwell, *History of Minnesota*, 4:323.

9. Lewis Meriam, director, *The Problem of Indian Administration*, report by the Institute for Government Research (Baltimore: Johns Hopkins Press, 1928) (hereafter cited as Meriam, *Report*).

10. George S. Grossman, *The Sovereignty of American Indian Tribes: A Matter of Legal History* (Minneapolis: Minnesota Civil Liberties Union Foundation, 1979), 11.

11. Robert Treuer, *Minneapolis Star*, 11 June 1981.

12. Betty Blue, "Economic Progress One Step at a Time," *Human Development News*, HHS, Aug. 1981.

13. Albert White, chairman, Prairie Island Indian Community; quoted in *Republican Eagle*, Red Wing, Minn., 28 June 1982.

14. Presidential statement, "Recommendations for Indian Policy," 91st Cong., 2d sess., 8 July 1980, H.Doc. 91-363.

15. *Wassaja*, newspaper of the American Indian Historical Society, San Francisco, Calif., May/June 1983.

16. *Wassaja*, Sept. 1977.

17. *Wassaja*, Jan./Feb. 1983.

18. Nadine Chase, Leech Lake RBC, testimony before the House Appropriations Committee, Washington, DC, Apr. 1982.

19. Miles Lord, judge of US District Court, Minnesota; cited in *A Report to the Churches*, Indian Concerns Committee, Minnesota Conference, United Church of Christ, May 1981, 3.

Chapter 2. The Tribes and the Land

1. "Southwestern Chippewa," *Handbook of North American Indians* (Washington, DC: Smithsonian Institution, 1978), vol. 15.

2. Grand Portage Local Curriculum Committee, *A History of Kitchi Onagaming: Grand Portage and Its People* (Cass Lake, Minn.: MCT, 1983), 46.

3. Folwell, *History of Minnesota*, 2:256–65.

4. Alban Fruth, *A Century of Missionary Work among the Red Lake Chippewa Indians: 1858–1958* (Red Lake, Minn.: St. Mary's Mission, 1958), 35–36.

5. Paul McEnroe, *Minneapolis Star*, 24 Feb. 1981, 17A.

6. S. M. Brosius, *The Urgent Case of the Mille Lacs Indians* (Philadelphia: Indian Rights Association, 1901).

7. Folwell, *History of Minnesota*, 4:283.

8. Ibid., 4:261–96.

9. Josephine Robinson, White Earth Reservation; quoted in the *Minneapolis Star*, 23 Dec. 1978, 10.

10. Virginia Rogers, genealogist, White Earth Reservation; quoted in *Dee-Bah-Gee-Mo-Win*, White Earth, Minn., Sept. 1983.

Chapter 3. Indian People

1. *Wassaja*, June 1980, 15.

2. Meriam, *Report*, 727.

3. Paul Gunderson, Center for Health Statistics, MDH, interview with author, 13 Aug. 1982.

4. Office of State Demographer, SPA, "Demographic Overview of Minnesota's American Indian Population: 1980," *Population Notes* (Nov. 1983).

5. Interviews with author: JoAnne Barr, assistant director, Indian Health Board, Minneapolis, 4 Aug. 1982; Elsie Fairbanks, acting director, St. Paul American Indian Center, 2 July 1982; Vi Foldesi, director, American Indian Fellowship Association, Duluth, 13 Sept. 1982.

6. Elizabeth Hallmark, director, Minneapolis American Indian Center; quoted in *St. Paul Pioneer Press*, 11 Nov. 1979.

7. Ken Peterson, *Minneapolis Star*, 22 Aug. 1981.

8. Ibid., quoting an elderly Indian.

9. Red Horse, *American Indian Families: We Can Help* (Evanston, Ill.: American Academy of Pediatrics, 1979).

10. Hallmark; quoted in *St. Paul Pioneer Press*.

11. F. Earle Barcus, Boston University, *Representations of Life on Children's Television*, July 1982.

12. Jean Beaulieu; quoted in *Ourselves*, June 1981.

13. Arthur Gahbow, tribal chairman, Mille Lacs Reservation; quoted in *State Watch*, Minnesota Public Interest Research Group, St. Paul, Minn., Oct. 1980.

14. Hallmark; quoted in *St. Paul Pioneer Press*.

15. Kathleen Westcott, White Earth Reservation, at a showing of Indian artists, Minneapolis Institute of Art, June 1982.

16. Irving Hallowell, "Ojibway Personality and Acculturation," in *Beyond the Frontier*, ed. Bohanna and Plog (New York: Natural History Press, 1967).

17. Rosemary Christensen, "The Case of the Urban Indian" (Paper presented to hearing on rights' violations, International Tribunal, Rotterdam, Netherlands, 24–30 Nov. 1980), 5.

18. *Wig-I-Wam*, Division of Indian Work, Minneapolis, Sept. 1980.

19. Ibid., quoting Gary Green.

20. Ibid.

21. Frances Densmore, *Chippewa Customs* (Washington, DC: Smithsonian Institution, 1929; reprint, St. Paul: Minnesota Historical Society Press, 1979), 86–87, quoting Gagewin, a member of Midewiwin from White Earth Reservation.

22. Howard Anderson, executive director, Indian Ministry, Minnesota Diocese of the Protestant Episcopal Church, interview with author, 28 July 1983.

Chapter 4. Tribal Governments and Federal Relations

1. Folwell, *History of Minnesota*, 4:326.

2. Leo Krulitz, solicitor, Department of the Interior, "Criminal Jurisdiction on the Seminole Reservations in Florida," 85 ID No. 12, 14 Nov. 1978, 437.

3. Felix S. Cohen, *Handbook of Federal Indian Law* (1942; reprinted Albuquerque: Univ. of New Mexico Press, n.d.), 33.

4. Larry Leventhal; quoted in *Wig-I-Wam*, Nov. 1979.

5. CCR, *Indian Tribes: A Continuing Quest for Survival* (Washington, DC, 1981), v.

6. Ibid., iv.

7. Alvin Ziontz, attorney representing tribal interests, Seattle, Wash., address to the American Bar Association Convention, Las Vegas, Nev., 1984.

8. CCR, *Indian Tribes*, v.

9. Cohen, *Handbook*, 123.

10. Ibid., 122.

11. CCR, *American Indian Civil Rights Handbook*, 2d ed. (Washington, DC, 1980), 1.

12. Mark Anderson, solicitor's office, Department of the Interior, Minneapolis, interview with author, 8 Nov. 1982.

13. Ibid.

14. Roger Jourdain, chairman, Red Lake band, interview with author, 14 Sept. 1982.

15. Kate Stanley, *Minneapolis Star*, 31 Aug. 1981, quoting Ronald Libertus.

16. Stanley, *Minneapolis Star*.

17. American Indian Policy Review Commission, *Report on Tribal Government* (Washington, DC, 1976), 7.

18. Presidential statement on Indian policy, 24 Jan. 1983; quoted in *Wassaja*, Jan./Feb. 1983.

19. American Indian Policy Review Commission, *Tribal Government*, 63.

20. Jeff Spartz, Hennepin County commissioner, quoted in *Circle*, Minneapolis American Indian Center, Nov. 1980.

21. Stuart Thorson, chief of family practice, Hennepin County Medical Center; quoted in *Minneapolis Star and Tribune*, 12 Mar. 1984.

Chapter 5. State and Local Relations; Hunting and Fishing Rights

1. Meriam, *Report*, 93.

2. State/Indians Relations Team, *State/Indian Government Relations* (SPA, Aug. 1984).

3. Commission on State-Tribal Relations, *Handbook on State-Tribal Relations* (Albuquerque: American Indian Law Center), 32.

4. State/Indians Relations Team, *State/Indian Government Relations*.

5. Jim Schoessler, special assistant attorney general, DNR, interview with author, 11 Feb. 1983.

6. Commission on State-Tribal Relations, *State-Tribal Agreements: A Comprehensive Study* (Albuquerque: American Indian Law Center, 1981), 2.

7. Jay Kanassatega, solicitor general, Mille Lacs Reservation, interview with author, 19 Mar. 1984.

8. State-Tribal Relations, *Handbook*, 41.

9. Gahbow, "State of the Band" (speech delivered 20 Dec. 1983).

10. State-Tribal Relations, *Handbook*, 21.

11. Minnesota Indian Affairs Intertribal Board, *Annual Report, 1981* (St. Paul, 1981), 8.

12. Darrell Wadena, president, MCT; quoted in *Ourselves*, May 1981.

13. *Walker Pilot*, Walker, Minn., 22 Apr. 1982.

14. Grand Portage Reservation, *Overall Economic Development Plan* (1980).

15. Joseph Alexander, commissioner, DNR; quoted in *Forum*, Fargo-Moorhead, 22 Feb. 1981.

16. John Persell, North Star Environmental Research, Bemidji, interview with author, 20 Sept. 1982.

17. Both quoted in *Pioneer*, Bemidji, Minn., 1 Apr. 1982.

18. Upper Sioux Indian Community, *A Comprehensive Plan* (1980), 49.

19. Amendment to the Low-Income Weatherization program, *Legislative History*, PL 97-35 (1981), 1202.

20. Nadine Chase, Leech Lake RBC, interview with author, 15 Sept. 1982.

21. Mike McGuire, city manager, Prior Lake; quoted in *Minneapolis Star and Tribune*, 10 Aug. 1983.

22. Minnesota Indian Affairs Intertribal Board, *Annual Report, FY 1982* (St. Paul, 1982), 20.

23. CCR, *Indian Tribes*, 32.

24. Ibid., 32, 39-40.

25. Grace Haukoos, Election Department, Office of Secretary of State, interview with author, 29 Mar. 1982.

Chapter 6. Urban Indians

1. Meriam, *Report*, 728.

2. Upper Midwest American Indian Center and Minnesota Center for Social Research, Univ. of Minnesota, *Minneapolis Native American Housing Survey: Technical Report*, 1978 (hereafter cited as Upper Midwest, *Technical Report*).

3. Indian Health Board of Minneapolis, "Application for Federal Assistance for 1982-83," 1981, 65.

4. Stephen J. Tordella and Edward B. Nelson, "Circular Migration among Native Americans: A Preliminary Investigation" (Paper presented at the Population Association of America meeting, 29 Apr. 1982).

5. Christensen, "Case of Urban Indian," 5.

6. Ibid., 4.

7. Ronald Libertus, interview with author, 25 Feb. 1982.

8. American Indian Policy Review Commission, *Report on Urban and Rural Non-Reservation Indians* (Washington, DC, 1976).

9. Vi Foldesi, interview with author, 13 Sept. 1982.

Chapter 7. Economic Development

1. James M. Murray and James J. Harris, *A Regional Economic Analysis of the Turtle Mountain Indian Reservation: Determining Potential for Commercial Development*, Federal Reserve Bank, Minneapolis, 1978, authors' note.

2. Calvin Kent and Jerry W. Johnson, *Flows of Funds on the Yankton Sioux Indian Reservation*, Federal Reserve Bank, Minneapolis, 1976, 3; Murray and Harris, *Regional Economic Analysis*, 2.

3. Larry Oakes, First National Bank of Cass Lake; quoted in Blue, "Economic Progress."

4. *Wig-I-Wam*, Division of Indian Work, Minneapolis, Nov. 1978.

5. Murray and Harris, *Regional Economic Analysis*, authors' note.

6. Suzanne Garment, "The Indians Come to Washington One More Time," *Wall Street Journal*, 26 Feb. 1982.

7. Mille Lacs Reservation, *Overall Economic Development Plan*, 1980, 22-28.

8. *Wall Street Journal*, 26 Feb. 1982.

9. Priscilla Anne Schwab, "The Industrial Reservation," *Nation's Business*, Aug. 1981, 57.

10. Ibid., 56.

11. Mariana Shulstad, Solicitor's Office, Department of the Interior, Minneapolis, interview with author, 15 Mar. 1984.

12. Leech Lake Reservation, *Community Development Plan, A Five Year Approach* (1982), 3.

13. Murray and Harris, *Regional Economic Development*, authors' note.

14. Minnesota Agency and Red Lake Agency, BIA, Sept. 1982.

15. DNR, Division of Minerals, *Minnesota Peat Program, Final Report* (1981).

16. Study by the Walter Butler Company, 1978, reported in ibid., 72.

17. White, interview with LWV, Apr. 1982; Bob Doder, Sioux Communities liaison, Indian Affairs Council, interview with author, 4 May 1982.

18. Ernie Landgren, Bois Forte; quoted in "Harvesting the Wild Rice," *Minneapolis Tribune Picture Magazine*, 14 Oct. 1973, 11.

19. Ervin Oelke, agronomist, Univ. of Minnesota, interview with author, 2 July 1982.

20. Ibid.; and Agricultural Extension Service, *Wild Rice Production in Minnesota*, Bulletin 464 (St. Paul: Univ. of Minnesota, 1982), 5.

21. Michael Behr, *Indian Potential in the Wild Rice Industry*, Federal Reserve Bank, Minneapolis, 1977.

22. Oelke, interview with author, 20 Mar. 1984.

23. Behr, *Indian Potential in Wild Rice*.

24. Tim Donahue, Small Business Development Center, interview with author, 16 Apr. 1982.

25. Bureau of the Census, Dept. of Commerce, *Minority Owned Businesses, 1977* (Washington, DC, 1980).

26. Charlotte White, Dept. of Economic Development, *Indian Businesses in Minnesota* (1981).

27. Minnesota Indian Affairs Intertribal Board, *Annual Report*, 1980 (St. Paul, 1980), 22.

28. OLA, *Evaluation of Small Business Procurement Act Set-Aside Program* (St. Paul, 1982), ix.

29. Nadine Chase, testimony to the US House Committee on Appropriations, Feb. 1982.

Chapter 8. Employment

1. Vernon Bellecourt, former secretary-treasurer, White Earth Reservation; quoted in *St. Paul Pioneer Press*, 11 Nov. 1979.

2. EEOC, *Minorities and Women in Private Industry: 1978* (1980), I:394–404; II:182–191.

3. EEOC, *Federal Civilian Work Force Statistics: Minority Group Study of Full-Time Employment: November 30, 1979*, table 2–051.

4. City of Minneapolis, *Affirmative Action Management Program*, 24 Dec. 1981.

5. Heart of the Earth Survival School, "Project Search: Proposal" (Minneapolis, 1982).

6. Minnesota Advisory Committee to the CCR, *Bridging the Gap: A Reassessment* (1978), 21; DES, 14 Apr.1982.

7. DES, *Of Indians and Jobs* (1980), 19.

8. Comptroller General of the United States, *Effectiveness and Administration of Community Action Program Administered by the White Earth Reservation Business Committee under Title II of the Economic Opportunity Act of 1964* (1969).

9. Mille Lacs Reservation, *Overall Economic Development Report* (1980).

10. John Oberly, Commissioner of Indian Affairs, *Report to Congress*, 1888.

11. Wamditanka (Big Eagle), Santee Sioux, quoted in DES, *Indians and Jobs*, ii.

12. Schwab, "Industrial Reservation."

13. Gerald Vizenor, *Minneapolis Tribune*, 18 Nov. 1979.

14. Schwab, "Industrial Reservation."

15. DES, *Of Indians and Jobs*, 14.

16. Ibid., 12–13.

17. DES, Labor Market Information Summary (1980).

Chapter 9. Education

1. Julie Bolten, principal, Pine Point Elementary School, White Earth Reservation; quoted in *Minneapolis Star and Tribune*, 30 May 1983.

2. *Report of the Commissioner of Indian Affairs for 1899* (Washington, DC: US Dept. of the Interior, 1900), 3–4.

3. *Hearings of the House Committee on Indian Affairs* (22 Jan. 1818), 1.

4. Folwell, *History of Minnesota*, 1:173–76.

5. Ibid., 1:183–98.

6. L. Antell, *Indian Education*, 37.

7. *Schools for the Chippewa Indians Conducted by the Fathers and Sisters of the Order of St. Benedict at Collegeville, Minnesota* (1887).

8. Meriam, *Report*, 11–14.

9. Folwell, *History of Minnesota*, 4:324.

10. Dulcie Hagedorn, senior planner, Hennepin County, interview with author, 21 Sept. 1982.

11. L. Antell, *Indian Education*, 26.

12. MDE, *Minnesota Civil Rights Information System (MINCRIS): School District Reports October 1, 1981* (hereafter referrred to as MINCRIS).

13. *Ourselves*, Cass Lake, Minn., Oct. 1981.

14. The 17 school districts are Bagley, Bemidji, Black Duck, Cass Lake, Cloquet, Cook County, Deer River, Detroit Lakes, Mahnomen, Nett Lake, Onamia, Pine Point, Red Lake, Remer, St. Louis County, Walker-Hackensack, and Waubun.

15. Educational Management Services, *Final Report on the Statewide Indian and Bilingual Needs Assessment*, 1977–78 (1979), III-2 (hereafter referred to as INA).

16. Ibid., III-45.

17. Howard Casmey, Minnesota commissioner of education; quoted in *Minneapolis Tribune*, 6 June 1980.

18. INA, III-18.

19. Educational Management Services, *Final Evaluation Report Title IV-Part A Indian Education Program 1980–81: Submitted to Minneapolis Public Schools* (n.d.), 11 (hereafter referred to as EMS, Evaluation).

20. Rosemary Christensen, interview with author, 30 Apr. 1982.

21. INA, III-37.

22. Ibid., III-46.

23. "Results of Citywide Tests by Racial Group, Indians . . . Whites," *Minneapolis Star and Tribune*, 25 Jan. 1983, 11A.

24. INA, III-24.

25. Equal Educational Opportunities Section, MDE, *A Summary of the 1981–82 Minnesota Civil Rights Survey: Elementary and Secondary Schools* (1982), 10.

26. Damian McShane and James Nordin, "Middle Ear Disease: Tympanometry Screening, and Language and Educational Delay in High Risk Groups Such as Native American Children" (Unpublished manuscript, 1978).

27. Roger A. Jourdain, chairman, Red Lake band of Chippewa Indians, "Statement Regarding the Proposed Closure of Flandreau and Wahpeton Boarding Schools by the BIA" (1982).

28. Rosemary Christensen, interview with author, 30 Apr. 1982.

29. Christensen, "Case of Urban Indian."

30. Kate Stanley, *Minneapolis Star*, 26 Aug. 1981, quoting Roger Buffalohead.

31. Ibid., quoting Will Antell, MDE.

32. INA, III-58.

33. Urban Coalition of Minneapolis, *Quality Education for All* (Minneapolis: 1979).

34. Buffalohead, interview with author, 23 Sept. 1982.

35. Sharon Schmickle, *Minneapolis Star and Tribune*, 30 May 1983, 3B.

36. MCT recommendations to the Subcommittee on Indian Education, MDE, *Minnesota Indian Education Hearings Report* (1976), 110.

37. Anderson and Berdie Associates, *The Saint Paul Foundation Minority Student Education Program* (St. Paul, 1982), 63 (hereafter cited as Anderson and Berdie).

38. Flo Wiger, American Indian Learning Resource Center, Univ. of Minnesota, interview with author, 14 Apr. 1982.

39. Children in the North Wind Warriors Project, Minneapolis Public Schools; quoted in *Minneapolis Star and Tribune*, 29 Jan. 1982.

40. MDE, *Summary of Survey*, 13–14.

41. MDE, Indian Section, *Organizational Characteristics of Minnesota American Indian Language and Culture Education Projects* (1981), 9.

42. Gunn, "Indian American Children," in *Minority Students: A Research Appraisal* (National Institute of Education, 1977), 318.

43. Verna Wood, education director, Red Lake Reservation, interview with author, 14 Sept. 1982.

44. An Indian attorney, Bemidji, interview with the LWV, spring 1982.

45. MCT recommendations, *Indian Education Hearings*, 109.

46. Anderson and Berdie.

47. Larry P. Aitken and Dennis R. Falk, "A Higher Education Study of Minnesota Chippewa Tribal Students" (Unpublished manuscript [1982]), 3 (hereafter referred to as MCT Study).

48. Office of Civil Rights, HEW, memo to the MCT, 1975.

49. MDE, *General Fund Revenue, FY 1981* (1982).

50. MDE, *Federal Aid: Indian Program Expenditures, FY 1981* (1982).

51. Eileen Hudon, Indian advocate, Sojourner Shelter, Minneapolis, speaking at Conference on Battered Women, St. Paul, 28 June 1982.

52. National Advisory Council on Indian Education, *Indian Education: America's Unpaid Debt, Eighth Annual Report to the Congress of the United States* (Washington, DC).

53. Mary Bassett, coordinator for Indian education, Cloquet Public Schools, interview with LWV, Apr. 1982.

54. Judy Lunsman, White Bear Lake School District, interview with author, spring 1982.

55. John Wells, St. Paul School District, interview with author, 28 June 1982.

56. Mildred Mueller, director, Indian Section, MDE, interview with author, 3 May 1982.

57. MDE, *General Fund Revenue*.

58. Schmickle, *Minneapolis Star and Tribune.*

59. INA, III-31.

60. MDE, *Indian Language Projects,* 17.

61. L. Antell, *Indian Education,* 40.

62. American Indian Policy Review Commission, *Report on Indian Education* (Washington, DC, 1976), 265.

63. INA, III-72.

64. INA, III-75.

65. Helen Miller, education programs administrator, BIA Area Office, Minneapolis, letter to author, 16 June 1982.

66. Minnesota Council on Foundations, *Progress Report on Minneapolis School Dropout Study,* Education Committee Report, Minneapolis, 10 Aug. 1982.

67. Rick Dunn, Minneapolis Upward Bound, interview with author, spring 1982.

68. MDE, Indian Education Section, *Scholarships 1955–1980;* updated information, 1 Apr. 1981.

69. Ibid.

70. Minnesota Higher Education Coordinating Board, *Minority Enrollment in Professional Programs: Fall 1978* (1980) and *Fall 1976* (1980).

71. Kent Smith, director, Indian Studies, BSU, interview with LWV, Mar. 1982.

72. Donald F. Bibeau, Indian educator, interview with author, 24 Sept. 1982.

73. Anderson and Berdie, 82.

74. MCT Study, 3, 5–6.

75. MDE, *Scholarships,* 18.

76. Ibid., 9.

77. Clyde Atwood, Indian Studies, College of St. Scholastica, Duluth, interview with author, 13 Sept. 1982.

78. MCT Study, 4–5.

79. W. Hall and R. Armstrong, *Group Profile of American Indians Admitted to Liberal Arts and General College from Fall 1975 through Spring 1977;* quoted in Anderson and Berdie, 74–75.

80. Anderson and Berdie, 75.

81. Mueller, interview with author.

82. MCT Study, 6–7.

83. UMD, School of Social Development, "Five Year Plan," 1978.

84. Emanuel Panitz, *American Indians and Minnesota's Private Colleges,* Evaluation of Minnesota Private College Research Foundation's Indian Education Project 1971–2, 1974–5 (1976), 66.

85. Sister Lonan Reilly, College of St. Theresa, Winona, Minn., interview with LWV, spring 1982.

86. EEOC, *Minorities and Women in Institutions of Higher Education: 1979* (Washington, DC, 1980), 74.

87. MCT Study, 5.

88. US Dept. of Education, Office for Civil Rights, *Chronicle of Higher Education: Undergraduate Enrollments by Race in United States Colleges and Universities, 1978* (Washington, DC, 1981), 8; HEW, Office of Civil Rights, *Racial, Ethnic and Sex Enrollment Data from Institutions of Higher Education, Fall 1976* (Washington, DC, 1978), 96–99.

89. Wilbert Ahern, "Indian Education and Bureaucracy: The School at Morris," *Minnesota History,* Minnesota Historical Society (Fall 1984).

90. Task Force on Indian Education/Vocational Education, "Indian School in Morris," *1983 Task Force Report.*

91. Panitz, *American Indians*, 54.

92. Bonnie Wallace, American Indian Student Support Program, Augsburg College, Minneapolis, interview with author, 27 Mar. 1984.

93. Richard Tanner, director of Indian education, MCT, interview with author, 16 Sept. 1982.

94. MINCRIS.

95. Ibid.

Chapter 10. Welfare

1. Christensen, "Case of Urban Indians."

2. Meriam, *Report*, 88–89.

3. N. H. Winchell, *The Aborigines of Minnesota* (St. Paul: Minnesota Historical Society, 1911).

4. *Wassaja*, May/June 1983.

5. *St. Paul Dispatch*, 27 Oct. 1983.

6. Gene Buckanaga, director, Upper Midwest American Indian Center; quoted in *City Pages*, Minneapolis, Sept. 1982.

7. Hennepin County Office of Planning and Development, *A Preliminary Assessment of the Impact of State and Federal Budget and Program Changes on Human Services in Hennepin County* (1982), 8–10.

8. Hallmark, quoted in *St. Paul Pioneer Press*.

9. Indian Health Board, "Application for Federal Assistance."

10. Wood, interview with author.

11. Carol Schmitt, DPW, *Account 5166, Indigent Indians, Final Settlement, FY 1981*.

12. Ibid.

13. Francis Moriarity, interview with author, 22 Apr. 1982.

14. Mary Duroche, *Aid to Indian Children: New Patterns and New Funding Options in the Relations between Indian Reservations and Minnesota Counties* (Minneapolis: CURA, Univ. of Minnesota, 1982), 12–13.

15. Bob Aitken, director, Human Services, MCT, interview with author, 15 Sept. 1982.

16. OLA, *State-Sponsored Chemical Dependency Programs: Follow-up Study* (1981), 20.

17. Esther Wattenberg, "Competitive Tension in Delivering Social Services and Programs: The Role of CAPs in Rural Minnesota," *CURA Reporter*, (Univ. of Minnesota) 13 (Jan. 1983): 5, 7.

18. Anthony Genia, "Survey of Twin Cities American Indians" (Prepared for American Indian Ministries, United Church of Christ, Minn., 1980).

19. Hudon, Conference on Battered Women.

20. Norby Blake, director, Family Health Program, Fairview Deaconess Hospital, Minneapolis, at Joint Religious Legislative Conference, St. Paul, 25 Jan. 1981.

21. Wattenberg, "Competitive Tension," 7.

22. Elizabeth Hallmark Stately, director, Minneapolis American Indian Center, interview with LWV, Mar. 1982.

23. American Indian Policy Review Commission, *Report on Federal, State and Tribal Jurisdiction* (Washington, DC, 1976), 210.

24. Allen Oleisky, judge, Hennepin County Juvenile Court, interview with author, 4 May 1982.

25. DPW, *Adoptions: Annual Report* (30 June 1981); and *Annual Report of Adoptions, 1974–5*, 23.

26. Hennepin County Community Services, *Comparison of Children in Placement on July 31, 1981 and December 15, 1982 in the Child Welfare and Child Protection Divisions* (Apr. 1983), table 8.

27. MCT, *Indian Child Welfare Cases, 1981.*

28. DPW, *Foster Care Costs Annual Report: Year Ending June 30, 1981,* 6, 55.

29. DPW, *Title IV-B, Child Welfare Services* (1983), 9–11.

30. Mary Duroche, "Services for Indian Children: How Local Government Responds," *CURA Reporter* 12:3 (Sept. 1982).

31. Dwaine Lindberg, Children's Services, DPW, interview with author, 6 May 1982.

32. DPW, *Adoptions: 1981,* table 19, p. 18.

33. HHS, *Child Welfare Research Note Number 7,* May 1984.

34. DPW, *Reported Cases of Maltreated Children, 1981.*

35. Allen Oleisky, interview with LWV, Feb. 1984.

36. Supreme Court of Minnesota, Judicial Planning Committee, *Minnesota Transaction Report, Juveniles: Calendar Year 1981,* data requested by LWV. Based on 273 identified Indian juveniles and 14,000 general population statewide.

37. Hennepin County Community Services, *Addendum to the 1981 Comparison of Children in Placement by Racial Group* (May 1983), 2 (hereafter referred to as Hennepin Co. Addendum).

38. Kerry Fine, *Out of Home Placement of Children in Minnesota: A Research Report* (St. Paul: Minn. House of Representatives, 1983), 43.

39. Geena Van Avery, Ramsey County Receiving Center, interview with author, 29 June 1982.

40. Westermeyer, "The Ravage of Indian Families in Crisis," in *The Destruction of American Indian Families,* ed. Steven Unger (New York: Association on American Indian Affairs, 1977), 54.

41. Ibid., 54.

42. Evelyn Blanchard, "Question of Best Interest," in *Destruction of Families,* 57–60.

43. Hennepin Co. Addendum, 4.

44. Hennepin County, *Results of December 15, 1982 Survey of Children in Out-of-Home Care* (1983), table 1.

45. Margaret Silberberg, psychologist, Family Health Program, Fairview Deaconess Hospital, interview with author, 26 Mar. 1982.

46. Oleisky, interview with author, 4 May 1982.

47. Silberberg, interview with author.

48. Diane Roach, child welfare advocate, St. Paul, interview with author, 29 Sept. 1983.

49. Interview with author, 26 Mar. 1982.

50. Ibid.

51. Hennepin Co. Addendum, 3.

52. Steven Unger, Association of American Indian Affairs, Statement to US Select Commission on Immigration and Refugee Policy, 5 May 1980, manuscript.

53. Dulcie Hagedorn, senior planner, Hennepin County, interview with author, 21 Sept. 1982.

Chapter 11. Housing

1. Nadine Chase, Leech Lake Housing Authority, statement to US Senate Select Committee on Indian Affairs, *Federal Indian Housing Programs,* 96 Cong., 2d sess., 19 Aug. 1980, 53.

2. MCT, *Housing Needs and Programs* (Sept. 1976).

3. Chase, statement to Senate Select Committee.

4. Shakopee-Mdewakanton Sioux Community, *A Comprehensive Plan* (1980), 63–64.

5. Upper Sioux Indian Community, *A Comprehensive Plan* (1980), 54–55.

6. Housing Committee Report to the Minnesota Council on Foundations, Minneapolis, 10 Aug. 1982.

7. City of Minneapolis, *State of the City 1980* (Jan. 1981), 48–50.

8. Upper Midwest, *Technical Report*.

9. Diane Percy, Indian housing advocate, Minneapolis American Indian Center, interview with LWV, spring 1982.

10. Upper Midwest, *Technical Report*, 72, 73, 106.

11. MCT, *Housing Needs*.

12. Housing Committee Report.

13. IHS, Bemidji Program Office, *Greater Leech Lake Service Unit Health Plan* (1979), 44.

14. US Senate Select Committee on Indian Affairs, *Report on Federal Indian Housing* (1979), 24.

15. Ibid., 39.

16. Ibid., 20.

17. Fred Isham, Jr., housing director, Bois Forte Reservation; quoted in *Ourselves*, Cass Lake, Minn., Jan. 1981.

18. IHS, Bemidji Program Office, *Red Lake Service Unit Health Plan* (1979), 18.

19. Robert Peacock, executive director, Fond du Lac Reservation, interview with author, 22 Oct. 1982.

20. Senate Select Committee, *Report on Indian Housing*, 22.

Chapter 12. Health

1. Indian Health Board, Minneapolis, "Federal Funding Application," Dec. 1982, 7.

2. IHS, Bemidji Program Office, *Greater Leech Lake Service Unit* (1982).

3. IHS, *Greater Leech Lake Service Unit Health Plan* (1979), 70.

4. Meriam, *Report*, 88.

5. Ibid., 200.

6. MDH, *Minnesota Health Statistics 1980* (1983), 107 (hereafter this and other annual health statistics reports cited as MHS 1978, etc.; the 1981 report is provisional [May 1983]).

7. Meriam, *Report*, 200.

8. Indian Health Board, Minneapolis, "Progress Report," 1973.

9. "Indian Life Expectancy Increases Six Years," *De-Bah-Ji-Mon*, Leech Lake Reservation, July 1984.

10. MDH, *Minnesota Indian People: Selected Health Statistics* (1980) (hereafter cited as *Minn. Indian People*).

11. Ibid., 74.

12. Ibid., 29.

13. Ibid.; MHS 1978–80.

14. MHS 1978–80.

15. *Minn. Indian People*, 29.

16. Ibid.

17. *De-Bah-Ji-Mon*, July 1984.

18. Bruce Hutchinson, research coordinator, Chemical Dependency Program Divi-

sion, DPW, interview with author, 14 Mar. 1984.

19. Joseph Westermeyer and John Brantner, "Violent Death and Alcohol Use among Chippewas in Minnesota," *Minnesota Medicine* 55 (1972): 751–52.

20. IHS, *Leech Lake Health Plan* (1979), 66.

21. Indian Health Board, Minneapolis, *Annual Report, 1981,* 11.

22. Franklin Heisler, IHS unit director, White Earth; reported in *Dee-Bah-Gee-Mo-Win,* White Earth Reservation, Aug. 1983.

23. McShane and Nordin, "Middle Ear Disease."

24. INA, III-25.

25. St. Paul American Indian Center, *Report: Community Food and Nutrition Program* (30 June 1982).

26. Carolyn Ross, nutritionist, IHS, Bemidji Program Office, interview with author, 18 May 1983.

27. Everett Rhoades, director, IHS; quoted in *Wassaja,* Mar./Apr. 1983, 11.

28. American Indian Policy Review Commission, *Report on Indian Health* (Washington, DC, 1976), 138.

29. *Wassaja,* Mar./Apr. 1983, 11.

30. MHS 1980, 43, 80; MDH, *Abortions 1980.*

31. IHS, Bemidji Program Office, letter to author, 12 Feb. 1982.

32. Pat Bellanger, Anishinabe Legal Services, Cass Lake, Minn., interview with author, 25 Sept. 1983.

33. Tommie Flora, director, Office of Environmental Health, IHS, Bemidji Program Office, letter to author, 21 Jan. 1982.

34. Ibid.

35. IHS, Bemidji Program Office, *Nett Lake Service Unit Health Plan* (1979), 55.

36. Hennepin County, *Preliminary Assessment of Impact,* 37–38.

37. Joseph Westermeyer, Richard Tanner, and Jean Smelker, "Changes in Health Care Services for Indian Americans," *Minnesota Medicine* 57 (1974): 732–34.

38. Rosenberg Associates, *Urban Indian Health Care, an Evaluation of Three Programs Funded under Title V, PL 94–437* (Boulder: Native American Rights Fund, 1980), 22–37.

39. Damien McShane, *Overview of Mental Health Needs and Resources* (Minneapolis: Indian Health Board, 1978).

40. American Indian Policy Review Commission, *Report on Health.*

41. Heisler, *Dee-Bah-Gee-Mo-Win.*

42. J. Black, J. Kramer, R. Myers, and J. Wetmore, "Developing Community Support Systems for Chronically Mentally Ill American Indians: An Assessment of Needs," UMD, 1982.

43. Ibid.

44. Ruth Myers and Jacqueline Royce, "Dual Disabilities—An Unmet Need for American Indians," Miller Dwan Medical Center Foundation, UMD, 1983, 6.

45. Black et al, "Developing Community Support Systems."

46. Jacqueline Royce, UMD, interview with author, 17 Jan. 1984.

47. "Mental Health Service Delivery to American Indians in the State of Minnesota Conference, Final Recommendations," 20 Mar. 1979.

48. McShane, *Overview of Mental Health Needs.*

49. Black et al, "Developing Community Support Systems."

50. IHS, Bemidji Program Office, *Fond du Lac Service Unit* (1982).

51. John Buckanaga, director, IHS, Bemidji Program Office, letter to author, 12 Feb. 1982.

Chapter 13. Chemical Dependency

1. Ronald Head, American Indian Programs, Chemical Dependency Program Division, DPW; quoted in *St. Paul Pioneer Press*, 11 Nov. 1979.

2. Lawrence French and Jim Hornbuckle, "Alcoholism among Native Americans: An Analysis," *Social Work* 25 (July 1980): 277.

3. Michael Miller and Laura Waterman Wittstock, *American Indian Alcoholism in St. Paul: A Needs Assessment Conducted Jointly by the Community Planning Organization and the Juel Fairbanks Aftercare Residence* (Minneapolis: CURA, Univ. of Minn., 1981), 2 (hereafter cited as Miller and Wittstock).

4. Ibid., 2.

5. Ibid., 15.

6. Jeanne Cockrell, Upper Mississippi Mental Health Center, Bemidji, interview with LWV, spring 1982.

7. DPW, *Minnesota's Response to Alcohol and Other Drug Problems: Comprehensive Chemical Dependency State Plan* (1981), 133.

8. Ibid., 34.

9. Miller and Wittstock, 13.

10. DPW, *Minnesota's Response*.

11. DPW, *Minnesota's C.D. Programs* (Mar. 1981), 14.

12. Hennepin County, "1980 CD Client Demographic Summary" (data sheet), 468.

13. DPW, *Minnesota's C.D. Programs*, 20, 22, 25.

14. MHS 1979, 1980, and 1981.

15. Joseph Westermeyer, "Use of Social Indicator System to Assess Alcoholism among Indian People in Minnesota," *American Journal of Drug and Alcohol Abuse* 3 (1976): 449.

16. American Indian Court Judges Association, "Federal Prosecution of Crimes Committed on Indian Reservations," in *Justice and the American Indian* (1974), 5.

17. Myers and Royce, "Dual Disabiities," 3.

18. American Indian Policy Review Commission, *Report on Alcohol and Drug Abuse* (Washington, DC, 1976), 5–6.

19. Joseph Westermeyer, "The 'Drunken Indian': Myths and Realities," *Psychiatric Annals* 4 (Nov. 1974): 35. Reprinted in *Destruction of Families*, 26.

20. Westermeyer, "Use of Social Indicator System," 453.

21. Van Avery, interview with author.

22. Miller and Wittstock, 13.

23. Helmut Hoffman, "Hospitalized Alcoholic Ojibway Indians: Methodological Problems of a Cross-Culture Comparison, Willmar, Minnesota State Hospital," Aug.–Sept. 1973.

24. Miller and Wittstock, 16, 21.

25. Hutchinson, interview with author.

26. Margaret Peake Raymond and Elgie V. Raymond, "Chemical Dependency Needs of American Indian Women in Minnesota," DPW, 1982.

27. Walker and Associates, *An Analysis of Outcomes Achieved by a Sample of Halfway House Programs in Minnesota*, report to the Chemical Dependency Program Division, DPW, 1981, 30.

28. Hennepin County, "1980 CD Client Demographic Summary," data sheet.

29. E. Raymond, evaluator of the Mash-Ka-Wisen program, interview with author, 13 May 1983.

30. Don Lussier, youth drug abuse program, Red Lake Reservation, interview with author, 17 Sept. 1982.

31. A comment reported in Minnesota State Planning Agency, *Indian Needs Report* (1981), 48.

32. Myers and Royce, "Dual Disabilities," 6.

33. Carol Van Ryswyk, director, *Ramsey County Chemical Dependency Halfway House Study*, prepared for the Ramsey County Board (1979), 27.

34. Ibid., 3.

35. Walker and Associates, *Analysis of Outcomes*, 33.

36. Miller and Wittstock, 16.

37. OLA, *State-Sponsored Chemical Dependency Programs: Follow-up Study* (1981).

38. Elwin J. Benton, director, Mash-Ka-Wisen, Sawyer, Minn., interview with author, 23 Sept. 1982.

39. DPW, *Detox Report, Calendar Year 1981*, duplicated numbers.

40. Benton, interview with author.

41. Fine, *Out of Home Placement*, 78.

42. Harlan Downwind, program specialist, DPW, interview with author, 2 Aug. 1982.

43. Miller and Wittstock, 16.

44. Walter Echo-Hawk, director, Indian Corrections Project, *Indian Offender Project: An Indian Offender Needs Assessment* (Boulder: Native American Rights Fund, 1982), 33.

45. Van Avery, interview with author, 29 June 1982.

46. Raymond and Raymond, "Chemical Dependency Needs of Indian Women," 37.

Chapter 14. Criminal Justice

1. Fenton Van West, White Earth Reservation; quoted in *Minneapolis Tribune*, 3 Oct. 1982.

2. William T. Hagan, *Indian Police and Judges* (New Haven: Yale Univ. Press, 1966).

3. "Minnesota Chippewa: Treaties and Trends," *Minnesota Law Review* (June 1955).

4. Rick McArthur, community worker, Legal Rights Center, Minneapolis, interview with author, 10 Aug. 1982.

5. David Nunnelee, "Looking at the Law on White Earth Reservation," *Becker County Record*, Detroit Lakes, Minn., 22 Feb. 1982.

6. *Uniform Crime Report*, Minn. (1981), 11.

7. Bureau of Criminal Apprehension, *Individuals Remanded to the Custody of the Commissioner of Corrections, January 1, 1981.*

8. DOC, *Characteristics of Adult Institutional Populations, American Indians, Fiscal Year 1981.*

9. John Poupart, director, Anishinabe Longhouse, interview with author, 22 Sept. 1982.

10. DOC, *Characteristics*.

11. Roger Benjamin and Choong Nam Kim, *American Indians and the Criminal Justice System in Minnesota* (Minneapolis: CURA, Univ. of Minn., 1979), 45 (hereafter cited as Benjamin and Kim).

12. MSGC, *Preliminary Report on Development and Impact of the Minnesota Sentencing Guidelines* (1982), 40.

13. MSGC, *Impact of the Minnesota Sentencing Guidelines* (1984), 67.

14. Benjamin and Kim.

15. MSGC, *Impact*, 98–99.

16. Ibid., 65–66.

17. MSGC, *Preliminary Report*, 60.

18. Elizabeth Gunn, Hennepin County Court Services, *1981 Annual Report* (1982), 11.

19. Margaret Treuer, Indian attorney, Bemidji, interview with LWV, spring 1982.

20. Paul Kief, public defender, Minnesota Ninth Judicial District, Bemidji, interview with LWV, spring 1982.

21. DOC, 1 Apr. 1983.

22. James N. Bradford, Minn. assistant attorney general, letter to Robert Aufderhar, Special Services, Minnesota Correctional Facility-Stillwater, 24 Nov. 1980.

23. "Evaluation and Review of the Heart of the Earth Education Program at the Minnesota Correctional Facility-Stillwater," 1 May 1981, 13–14, 40.

24. Minn. Crime Control Planning Board, *Anishinabe Longhouse Final Report* [1977], 36.

25. Legal Services Committee, "Legal Service for Indian People," report to Minn. Council on Foundations, Minneapolis, 10 Aug. 1982).

26. Kief, interview with LWV.

27. Ibid.

28. MCT, "Indian Youth Service Project" (grant application, 1973).

29. John Brody, senior program analyzer, Hennepin County Court Services, interview with author, summer 1982.

30. Fine, *Out of Home Placement*, 52.

31. Ibid., 57–58.

32. Ibid., 85.

33. Janice Command, *Circle*, Minneapolis American Indian Center, Nov. 1980.

34. Grand Portage Reservation, *Overall Economic Development Report* (1980).

35. American Indian Policy Review Commission, *Report on Federal, State, and Tribal Jurisdiction* (Washington, DC, 1976), 16.

36. David Nunnelee, "Looking at the Law."

37. Minn. Advisory Committee to the CCR, *Police Practices in the Twin Cities* (1981), 8.

38. Roger Benjamin, *Perceptions of Local Police Performance by Ethnic Minorities in the Twin Cities: A Preliminary Report* (Minneapolis: CURA, Univ. of Minn. [1979]), 14–15, 17.

39. Donna Folstad, former Indian advocate, Office of the Mayor, Minneapolis, interview with author, 6 Mar. 1983.

40. Poupart, interview with author.

41. Theartrice Williams, ombudsman, *Investigation Report of February 19, 1981 Incident at Minnesota Correctional Facility-St. Cloud* (1 June 1981), 4.

42. Poupart, interview with author.

43. EEOC, *Minorities and Women in State and Local Government: 1975.*

44. Gene Clark; quoted in David Nunnelee, "Looking at the Law."

45. Ruth Myers, chairperson, Minn. Advisory Committee to the EEOC, interview with author, 22 Sept. 1982.

46. "Evaluation and Review of HEEP," 26–27.

47. Robert Sarver; quoted in Echo-Hawk, *Indian Offender Project*, 14.

48. Austin Wehrwein, *Minneapolis Star*, 28 Aug. 1981.

49. Ibid., 26 Aug. 1981.

50. DOC, *Minnesota Programs for Battered Women, 1981 Update* (1981), 36.

51. Hudon, Conference on Battered Women.

52. William Hajos, corrections specialist, Bemidji, DOC, interview with LWV, spring 1982.

53. Orville Olney, project director, *Indian Courts and the Future, Report of the NAICJA Long Range Planning Project*, National American Indian Court Judges Association, 1978.

54. CCR, *Indian Tribes*, 154-5.

55. US Dept. of Justice, *Task Force Report on Indian Matters* (Washington, DC, Oct. 1975), 43.

Conclusion

1. Bishop Henry Whipple, "Civilization and Christianization of the Ojibways in Minnesota," address delivered 2 May 1898; in *Minnesota Historical Collections* (St. Paul: Minnesota Historical Society, 1901), 9:141.

Selected Reading List

Selected
Reading List

Works of General Interest

Brandon, William. *The American Heritage Book of Indians*. New York: Simon and Schuster, 1961; paperback, New York: Dell, 1964. History of many of the major American Indian tribes from prehistory to 1961. Richly illustrated.

Brill, Charles. *Indian and Free: A Contemporary Portrait of Life on a Chippewa Reservation*. Minneapolis: Univ. of Minnesota Press, 1974. Photo essay of Red Lake Reservation, Minnesota. 160 photos with text by author.

*Broker, Ignatia. *Night Flying Woman: An Ojibwe Narrative*. St. Paul: Minnesota Historical Society Press, 1983. Illustrations by Steve Premo. An Ojibwe woman's journey through the cycle of life. Deals with the overwhelming chaos and change brought by the white man's encroachment and the ending of ancestral life-style.

Carley, Kenneth. *The Sioux Uprising of 1862*. St. Paul: Minnesota Historical Society, 1976. Pictorial history of Minnesota's Indian war. Includes 130 illustrations and map of major sites.

Deloria, Vine, Jr. *Custer Died for Your Sins: An Indian Manifesto*. New York: Macmillan, 1969. A strongly worded discussion of Indian problems from the Indian point of view.

Densmore, Frances. *Chippewa Customs*. Washington, DC: Bureau of American Ethnology, Smithsonian Institution, 1929; paperback reprint, St. Paul: Minnesota Historical Society, 1979. Detailed descriptions of tribal history, customs, legends, traditions, art, music, economy, and leisure activities of the Ojibway Indians. Based on ethnologic studies done primarily among Minnesota's Ojibways.

*Minnesota Chippewa Tribe. *A History of Kitchi Onagaming, Grand Portage and Its People*. Reservation History Series. Cass Lake, Minn.: Minnesota Chippewa Press, 1983. History of Grand Portage Reservation written by the MCT. First of a series of Minnesota reservation histories, to include Mille Lacs, Leech Lake, and White Earth.

*Indian authors who live in Minnesota.

Mittelholtz, Erwin F. *Historical Review of the Red Lake Indian Reservation.* Bemidji, Minn.: Red Lake Band and Beltrami County Historical Society, 1957.

Momaday, N. Scott. *House Made of Dawn.* New York: New American Library, 1966. Fiction. The heartbreaking life of an Indian man from the Southwest, torn between his world and the white man's.

*Rogers, John. *Red World and White, Memories of a Chippewa Boyhood.* Norman: Univ. of Oklahoma Press, 1974. Memories of growing up on the White Earth Reservation, 1896 through the early 1900s.

Roufs, Timothy G. *The Anishinabe of the Minnesota Chippewa Tribe.* Phoenix: Indian Tribal Series and the MCT, 1975. History of the Ojibway in Minnesota.

*Vizenor, Gerald. *The Everlasting Sky.* New York: Macmillan, 1972.

——. *Tribal Scenes and Ceremonies.* Minneapolis: Nodine Press, 1976.

——. *Wordarrows: Indians and Whites in the New Fur Trade.* Minneapolis: Univ. of Minnesota Press, 1978.

——. *The Earth Divers: Tribal Narratives on Mixed Descent.* Minneapolis: Univ. of Minnesota Press, 1981.

——. *The People Named the Chippewa: Narrative Stories.* Minneapolis: Univ. of Minnesota Press, 1984.

Collections of stories and poetic images of contemporary Indian life.

*Warren, William W. *History of the Ojibway People.* 1885. Reprint, St. Paul: Minnesota Historical Society, 1984. Introduction by Roger Buffalohead. Anecdotal history by an Ojibway, gathered from elders and chiefs of the tribe before 1853.

Selected Sources for Topics Covered in This Book

History

Folwell, William. *History of Minnesota.* 4 vols. St. Paul: Minnesota Historical Society, 1921–30.

Meriam, Lewis. Director, Institute for Government Research. *The Problem of Indian Administration.* Baltimore: Johns Hopkins Press, 1928.

Sovereignty and National Issues

American Indian Policy Review Commission. *Final Report.* Washington, DC, 1977.

——. Task Force 2. *Report on Tribal Government.* Washington, DC, 1976.

——. Task Force 4. *Report on Federal, State and Tribal Jurisdiction.* Washington, DC, 1976.

——. Task Force 5. *Report on Indian Education.* Washington, DC, 1976.

——. Task Force 6. *Report on Indian Health.* Washington, DC, 1976.

——. Task Force 8. *Report on Urban and Rural Non-Reservation Indians.* Washington, DC, 1976.

——. Task Force 9. *Report on Law Consolidation, Revision and Codification.* 2 vols. Washington, DC, 1976.

——. Task Force 11. *Report on Alcohol and Drug Abuse.* Washington, DC, 1976.

Cohen, Felix S. *Handbook of Federal Indian Law.* 1942. Reprint, Albuquerque: Univ. of New Mexico Press, n.d.

Commission on State-Tribal Relations. *Handbook on State-Tribal Relations.* Albuquerque: American Indian Law Center, n.d.

Grossman, George S. *The Sovereignty of American Indian Tribes: A Matter of Legal History.* Minneapolis: Minnesota Civil Liberties Union Foundation, 1979.

US Commission on Civil Rights. *American Indian Civil Rights Handbook.* 2d ed. Washington, DC, 1980.

——. *Indian Tribes: A Continuing Quest for Survival.* Washington, DC, 1981.

Urban Indians
Minnesota Advisory Committee to the US Commission on Civil Rights. *Bridging the Gap: A Reassessment.* 1978.

Economic Development
Kent, Calvin, and Jerry W. Johnson. *Flows of Funds on the Yankton Sioux Indian Reservation.* Minneapolis: Ninth District Federal Reserve Bank Information Series, 1976.
Minnesota Department of Natural Resources. Division of Minerals. *Minnesota Peat Program, Final Report.* St. Paul, 1981.
Murray, James M., and James J. Harris. *A Regional Economic Analysis of the Turtle Mountain Indian Reservation: Determining Potential for Commercial Development.* Minneapolis: Ninth District Federal Reserve Bank Information Series, 1978.

Employment
Minnesota Department of Economic Security. Research and Statistical Services Office. *Of Indians and Jobs.* St. Paul, 1980.

Education
Anderson and Berdie Associates. *The Saint Paul Foundation Minority Student Education Program.* St. Paul, 1982.
Education Management Services. *Final Report on the Statewide Indian and Bilingual Needs Assessment, 1977–78.* St. Paul, 1979.
Minnesota Department of Education. *Minnesota Civil Rights Information System (MINCRIS): School District Reports October 1, 1981.* St. Paul, 1982. (Reports are filed annually.)

Welfare
Duroche, Mary. "Services for Indian Children: How Local Government Responds." *CURA Reporter* 12:3 (Sept. 1982).
Fine, Kerry. *Out of Home Placement of Children in Minnesota: A Research Report.* St. Paul: Minnesota House of Representatives, 1983.
Hennepin County. Office of Planning and Development. *A Preliminary Assessment of the Impact of State and Federal Budget and Program Changes on Human Services in Hennepin County.* Minneapolis, 1982.
Ramsey County. *Out-of-Home Placement Study of Ramsey County Children.* St. Paul, 1981.
Unger, Steven, ed. *The Destruction of American Indian Families.* New York: Association on American Indian Affairs, 1977.
Westermeyer, Joseph. "Cross-Racial Foster Home Placement among Native American Psychiatric Patients." *Journal of the National Medical Association* 69 (1977): 231–36.

Health
Minnesota Department of Health. Center for Health Statistics. *Minnesota Health Statistics 1980.* Minneapolis, 1983. (Reports are compiled annually.)
——. *Minnesota Indian People: Selected Health Statistics.* Minneapolis, 1980.

Chemical Dependency
Miller, Michael, and Laura Waterman Wittstock. *American Indian Alcoholism in St. Paul: A Needs Assessment Conducted Jointly by the Community Planning Organization and the Juel Fairbanks Aftercare Residence.* Minneapolis: CURA, Univ. of Minnesota, 1981.

Westermeyer, Joseph. "The Apple Syndrome in Minnesota: A Complication of Race-Ethnic Discontinuity." *Journal of Operational Psychiatry* 10(2):134–40 (1980).
——. "Use of Social Indicator System to Assess Alcoholism among Indian People in Minnesota." *American Journal of Drug and Alcohol Abuse* 3 (1976):447–56.

Criminal Justice System

Benjamin, Roger. *Perceptions of Local Police Performance by Ethnic Minorities in the Twin Cities: A Preliminary Report*. Minneapolis: CURA, Univ. of Minnesota, 1979.
Benjamin, Roger, and Choong Nam Kim. *American Indians and the Criminal Justice System in Minnesota*. Minneapolis: CURA, Univ. of Minnesota, 1979.
Minnesota Advisory Committee to the US Commission on Civil Rights. *Police Practices in the Twin Cities*. 1981.
Minnesota Sentencing Guidelines Commission. *The Impact of the Minnesota Sentencing Guidelines*. St. Paul, 1984.
Olney, Orville. Project director. *Indian Courts and the Future, Report of the NAICJA Long Range Planning Project*. National American Indian Court Judges Association, 1978.
Supreme Court of Minnesota. Judicial Planning Committee. *Minnesota Transactional Report: Juveniles, June 1980–July 1981*. (Statewide juvenile court data; compiled annually.)
Wolk, Lauren Elizabeth. *Minnesota American Indian Battered Women: The Cycle of Oppression*. Battered Women's Project, St. Paul American Indian Center, 1982.

Educational Materials

*Aitken, Larry P. *Wanda Kee-Wan-Din*. Cass Lake, Minn.: Minnesota Chippewa Tribe, Head Start Project, 1970. Film and cassette recording. Some of the experiences of a Head Start student living on a northern Ojibway reservation. For young Indian children to see themselves in a story.
*Antell, Lee. Director, Indian Education Project. *Indian Education, Guides for Evaluating Textbooks from an American Indian Perspective*. Report 143. Denver: Education Commission of the States, 1981.
*Benton-Banai, Edward. *The Mishomis Book: The Voice of the Ojibway*. St. Paul: Indian Country Press, 1979. A richly illustrated retelling of Ojibway teachings by the Mishomis (grandfather). Indian culture-based curriculum for high school.
*Indian Country Press, 292 Walnut, Irvine Park Office, St. Paul, Minn. 55102. Indian curricular material developed through the Red School House, St. Paul.
*Minneapolis Department of Indian Education, Federal Programs, 807 NE Broadway, Minneapolis, Minn. 55413. Indian curricular material for students and teachers, all ages. Annotated bibliography of Indian educational materials.
*Minnesota Chippewa Tribe. Patricia Bellanger, program coordinator. *Contemporary American Indian Women: Careers and Contributions*. Cass Lake, Minn.: Minnesota Chippewa Press, 1983. Biographies of Indian women in diverse career fields. Students in middle school years.
*Minnesota Historical Society. *The Ojibwe: A History Resource Unit*. St. Paul: Minnesota Historical Society, 1973. A multimedia curriculum unit, elementary and secondary; filmstrip, booklets, charts, teachers' guide.
Tanner, Helen Hornbeck. *The Ojibwas, A Critical Bibliography*. Newberry Library Center for the History of the American Indian. Bibliographical Series. Bloomington: Indiana Univ. Press, 1976.

Index

Index

The page numbers of maps are followed by "m"; those referring to tables only are followed by "t."

Abortion, 211
Accidents, as cause of death, 205, 223, 224t
Achievement through Communications, 49–50, 146
Adoption of Indian children: from Canada, 182; and census, 44; court procedure in, 179; under Ethnic Heritage Protection Act, 173; number of, 174–77 *passim*, 182; and qualifications for Title IV school programs, 137; termination of, in adolescence, 180; and tribal membership information, 173. *See also* Child welfare
Adult education, 138, 142, 155–56, 244–45, 253
AFDC. *See* Aid to Families with Dependent Children
Ahnji-Be-Mah-Diz Center, Leech Lake Reservation, 229
Aid to Families with Dependent Children (AFDC), 160, 161, 163, 256; and employment services, 116, 120; on Red

Lake Reservation, 166; school aids increased for, 124, 135
AIM. *See* American Indian Movement
Air quality, 75, 101
Alcohol Rehabilitation Program, Red Lake Reservation, 229
Alcoholism. *See* Chemical dependency
Algonquian linguistic family, Ojibway language in, 19
Allotment: and citizenship, 11; claims of improper handling, 11, 34–38 *passim*; ended by Indian Reorganization Act, 10, 12, 23–24; and fee patents, 10, 11, 23; laws pertaining to, 10–11, 23, 33, 267, 268; resisted by Red Lake Reservation, 23; White Earth Reservation's special problems with, 34–35, 37
American Indian Business Development Corporation, Minneapolis, 103
American Indian Chemical Dependency Diversion Project, Minneapolis, 230
American Indian Court Judges Association, 223, 259
American Indian Family and Children Service, St. Paul, 86, 181–82
American Indian Fellowship Association of Duluth, 87, 119, 214

311

American Indian Freedom of Religion Act, 50, 254, 270
American Indian Language and Culture Education program (Chapter 312), 67, 131, 132, 138–39, 141, 144, 273
American Indian Law Center, 57
American Indian Mental Health Training Program, UMD, 152
American Indian Movement, (AIM), 14–15, 56–57, 246; St. Paul program of, 86; survival schools, 144
American Indian Opportunities Industrialization Center, Minneapolis programs, 119, 153, 155–56
American Indian Policy Review Commission, 15–16, 269; on alternative schools, 143; on BIA authority, 62; on chemical dependency, 224, 234–35; on federal program participation, 63; final recommendation of, 15–16; on health care, 209; on police relations with Indians, 251, on urban Indians, 83
American Indian Political Caucus, 84
American Indian Services, Minneapolis, 230
American Indian Youth Alternatives, Minneapolis, 250
Anishinabe, 19
Anishinabe Legal Services, Cass Lake, 170, 246
Anishinabe Longhouse, 238, 240t, 245
Area Vocational Technical Institutes (AVTIs), and Indians, 154–55
Arrests, 250–51; of adults, 5, 239–42 passim; and alcohol abuse, 223–25; of juveniles, 5, 247–48. See also Criminal justice system
Arrowhead Community College System, Indian programs, 88, 153
Arrowhead Economic Opportunity Agency, 118
Assimilation, pressures for, 9–11, 13, 17; through education, 11, 122–24; and effects on Indians, 47, 221; by police and courts, 11, 237, 253; by removing Indian children from their homes, 171; and work ethic, 113–14
Assimilative Crimes Act, 256–57
Augsburg College, Indian programs, 150, 153

AVTIs. See Area Vocational Technical Institutes

Bakaan Gwagak, alternative school, 138, 142
Bands, family groups, 19
Becker County: Indian population, 41t; Indian unemployment, 113; law enforcement, 251; White Earth Reservation in, 30
Bellecourt, Clyde, and AIM, 57
Beltrami County: chemical dependency programs, 228; and Federal Voting Rights Act, 79; foster homes in, 180; health care services in, 214; Indian population in, 41t; Indian unemployment in, 113; reservations in, 29, 31; and Red Lake Reservation welfare programs, 166–67
Bemidji, city of: and arrests of Red Lake Reservation Indians, 257; battered women's shelter, 256; economic benefit from reservations, 90; legal aid, 245; reservations near, 29, 30, 31
Bemidji Area Vocational Technical Institute, Indian students, 154
Bemidji Program Area Office, IHS, 210
Bemidji State University (BSU): practice teaching on reservations, 133; programs for Indians, 145, 151, 152
BIA. See Bureau of Indian Affairs
Bingo, 94–95
Birthrate of Indians, 201–2
Blood Roll of 1920, White Earth Reservation, 34–35
Bois Forte Reservation, 21m, 25t, 27; bingo, 95; criminal justice system, 14, 237, 256–58, 272; economic development of, 27, 95, 99–105 passim; education programs, 27, 154, 155; elderly programs, 169; employment on, 112t, 118; government, 54–55; history, 27, 266; at Lake Vermilion, 22, 266; land claims, 37t; legal services, 246; medical services, 27, 210, 214; population, 42t, weatherization program, 193
Bois Forte Tribal Court, 237, 257–58
BSU. See Bemidji State University
Buffalohead, Roger, on Indian education problems, 130

Bureau of Indian Affairs (BIA), 9, 267, 268, 269; allotments, role in, 10–11; in claims cases, 32, 35–38; and conservation, 71, 74; economic development programs, 95–96; education programs, 124, 135–36, 143, 144, 148–49, 154; eligibility for programs, 62, 83, 268, 276; employment programs, 111–12, 115, 120, 154; housing programs, 185, 191, 193; and Indian Child Welfare Act, 85, 86, 87, 172–73, 174, 182; and law enforcement, 237, 257–59; offices in Minnesota, 29, 62–63; population data for reservations, 41, 42t; power and functions, 9–10, 59–63, 83; probate powers, 268; and Red Lake Reservation welfare program, 166; relocation program of, 13, 268–69; timber resource management, 99–100; tribal sovereignty limited by, 10, 12, 54, 59–61; and trust land establishment, 95; and urban Indians, programs for, 83; as viewed by Indians, 61

CAP. See Community Action Program
Carlton County: family abuse program, 256; Fond du Lac Reservation in, 27; Indian population, 41t
Cass County: chemical dependency programs, 228; child welfare programs, 176; and Federal Voting Rights Act, 79; health care services, 213; Indian population, 41t; Indian unemployment, 113; law enforcement, 252; Leech Lake Reservation in, 29
Cass Lake, city of: BIA office in, 29; congregate dining program, 170; economic benefit from reservations, 90; Leech Lake Reservation headquarters, 29; MCT headquarters, 29, 55
Cass Lake School District, 126, 130
Catholic Charities Branch drop-in centers, Minneapolis, 85
Center School (Nah Way Ee): alternative school, 86, 142–43; chemical dependency program, 230
CETA. See Comprehensive Employment and Training Act
Chapter 312. See American Indian Language and Culture Education program
Charities, programs for Indians, 87–88
Chemical dependency: characteristics of Indians with, 221–22, 225–26; and crime, 223, 224t, 259; and economic and social problems, 221, 224t, 225, 226; and medical problems, 202, 206, 223–26; and mental illness, 216–18, 224; prevalence of, 5, 220–21, 223–25; among women, 225–26
—treatment: 141, 223, 226–34, 250; in correctional facilities, 230; counselor training for, UMD, 152; detoxification facilities, 163, 223, 225, 226, 228, 232, 233; funding of, 164–65, 232–34; provided by the state for Indians, 67, 226–35 passim, 274; regulatory problems, 163, 232–33; results, 231–32
Chemical Dependency Program Division, Department of Human Services, 227, 234
Chief Bug-O-Nay-Ge-Shig School, 144
Child abuse, 176–77, 223, 224
Child welfare: expert witnesses in cases, 173, 179; Minnesota programs, 162–63, 175–76, 177–78, 178–80, 273; termination of parental rights, 172, 178–79. See also Ethnic Heritage Protection Act; Foster care; Indian Child Welfare Act; Indigent Indian Account
—out-of-home placement: 5, 158, 159t, 174, 177–83; chemical dependency, relationship with, 223–26 passim; Indian preference in, 172–73; Indian-white disparity in, 172, 176, 177t, 225, 248; white standards used in, 171–72, 179. See also Adoption of Indian children; Foster care
Chippewa, 19–20; governments formed in Minnesota, 54–55. See also Minnesota Chippewa Tribe; Ojibway; and names of individual reservations
Cigarette excise tax, agreements on, 93, 271–72, 277
Circle, 85, 88
Circle of Life School, 144
Citizenship of Indians, 11, 158, 268
Civil cases, Red Lake Reservation, 257
Civil Rights, Office of (Title VI), tribal schools not segregated, 134

Civil Rights Act, 77
Claims: land sales, heirship problems with, 33, 36–37; and treaties, 32; of trespass, 35–38; over trust land sold improperly, 34–38 *passim*, 47t; and White Earth Reservation issues, 34–37 *passim*, 272. *See also* Indian Claims Commission; US Court of Claims
Clans, family groups, 19
Clapp Rider of 1906, 34–35, 267
Clearwater County: Indian population, 41t; Indian unemployment, 113; reservations in, 30, 31; and Red Lake Reservation welfare program, 166
Cloquet, city of, Fond du Lac Reservation headquarters, 27
Cohen, Felix: on importance of treaties, 57; on tribal sovereignty, 58–59
Commission on Civil Rights, 78; advisory committee in Minnesota, 78, 251; on goals of Indians, 78; on survival of tribes, 58; on treaties, 57
Commodity Distribution Program, 167, 207
Community Action Program, 168–69
Community Development Block Grants, 84, 93, 191
Community Health Services Act, 213
Community Service Block Grants, 76–77, 168
Community Social Services Act (CSSA): 164–65; requirements for counties under, 76–77, 164–65, 226
Community-University Health Center, Minneapolis, 214, 215–16
Comprehensive Employment and Training Act (CETA), 113, 117–19
Cook, Lee, and National Congress of American Indians, 56
Cook County: adult education program, 155; Grand Portage Reservation in, 28; law enforcement, 250
Corporate-Minority Business Exchange, 106
Corporations, programs for Indians, 87–88
Correctional facilities: culture and religion in, 253–55; Indian employees in, 251–52; for juveniles, 5, 249–50; programs for adults in, 230, 238,

244–45; statistics on inmates, 239, 240t, 242–44
Counties: distressed county aid, 162; health programs, 212–14; welfare programs, 163–65, 175–76
Court system: federal jurisdiction on reservations, 256–57; treatment of Indians in, 241–43. *See also* Criminal justice system; Tribal courts
Courts of Indian Offenses. *See* Tribal courts
Crime: and chemical dependency, 224, 238, 240, 242t, 259; correlated factors, 238–39; by juveniles, 238, 240t, 247–50
Criminal cases, jurisdictional responsibilities, 237–38, 239, 256–58, 268, 276, 277. *See also* Public Law 280
Criminal justice system: employment of Indians in, 251–53, Indian difficulties with, 238–40, 245–60 *passim*; Indians and whites treated differently in, 239–41, 242–43, 244t, 247–48; juries and Indians, 243; number of adult Indians involved in, 239–44; number of juvenile Indians involved in, 247–49; programs for Indians, state funded, 238, 246, 249; public defenders, 245–46
Crow Wing County, Leech Lake Reservation in, 29
CSSA. *See* Community Social Services Act
Culture of Indians, 44–50, adaptation to dominant culture, 47–48; and Anishinabe Longhouse, 245; art, 49; burials, 166; and chemical dependency, 228, 229–32; and child welfare decisions, 171–72, 173–74, 180; and clan membership, 19; in communications media, 49; contributions to dominant culture, 3–6; in correctional institutions, 253–55; and drinking patterns, 220-22, 223–26; economic development, impact on, 91-92; holistic view in, 64, 200, 218–19; insensitivity to, by agencies, 63–64, 164–65; missionary efforts to destroy, 51; pow wows, 48-49, 282; and program administration, 46; punishment for crimes, 236; spiritual beliefs, 50; sweat

lodge ceremonies, 50, 254; traditional medicine, 3, 200; tribal court conflicts with, 11, 259; US policy to destroy, 46–47; and urban Indians, 82, 239; values in, 44–45; vitality of, 47–48; wild rice, importance to, 102

Dakota Indians, 18, 19–22, 122. *See also* Sioux Communities; *names of individual communities and bands*
Dawes Act. *See* General Allotment Act
De Tocqueville, Alexis, 8
Deer Creek Reservation. *See* Bois Forte Reservation
Deloria, Sam, on adapting institutions to meet Indian needs, 6
Demographics, 158–60, 159t
Department of Human Rights (Minnesota), 77–78; and affirmative action plans for employment, 115
Department of Indian Work, St. Paul, 86
Dependency: on government programs, 9, 47, 61, 186; reservations fostered, 157–58
Desegregation: Indian attitude toward, 78, 134, 278; laws on, 77–78, 134
Detoxification programs. *See* Chemical dependency: treatment
Detroit Lakes Area Vocational Technical Institute, Indian programs, 154
Direct Employment Assistance, BIA, 120
Discrimination: court cases on, 46, 278–79; criminal justice system, potential for, 239–43 *passim*, 247; effect of, on Indians, 47; exemptions to laws prohibiting, 77, 78–79, 187–88, 196, 279; in housing, 187–88; prohibited in all programs, 63, 77, 115, 187–88; in school suspensions, 126–27
Division of Indian Work (DIW), Minneapolis, 85, 161, 256
DIW. *See* Division of Indian Work
Drift Inn, Mille Lacs Reservation, 98
Drug abuse, 222. *See also* Chemical dependency
Drug Abuse Program, Red Lake Reservation, 229
Duluth, city of, 87; bingo proposed with Fond du Lac Reservation, 95; chemical dependency programs, 229; education

programs, 141–42, 155; employment programs, 118–19; Fond du Lac Reservation near, 27; group home for Indian children, 180; housing for Indians, 194–95, 196; Indian health programs, 87, 214, 216; Indian population of, 43t; legal services for Indians, 246; MCT office in, 55, 84, 87
Duluth Urban Indian Housing Program, 194–95

Early Childhood and Family Education program, 140
Economic development on reservations, 92; benefits to surrounding areas, 90; construction companies, 97; difficulties in, 90–92, 98, 100, 106–7; fishing operations, 99; housing programs, importance to, 193–94; manufacturing companies, 96–97; resorts, 97–98; service operations, 98–99; timber, 99–100. *See also each reservation*
Economic development in urban areas, 103–4
Economic Development Administration, 95
Eden Youth residential program, Minneapolis, 230, 250
Education (preschool-twelfth grade), 122–46; academic achievement in school, 125t, 127–28, 149; assimilation pressures through, 11, 122–24; attendance, 125t, 127; curriculum, 131, 141, 142, 273; funding sources, 124, 134–39; manual training, 123; Minnesota programs for Indians, 124, 138–39, 148, 273; number of students and graduates, 4, 124–26, 159t, 273; problems in, 125-34; special, 125t, 128; suspensions, 125t, 126–27; teachers, 132–34, 150, 155, 273; textbooks, 132; tribally administered programs, 135–36, 143–44. *See also* Adult education; Higher education; Schools; Vocational education
Education Commission of the States, on alternative schools, 143
Elementary and Secondary Education Act: Title I, 138, 144; Title VII, 138
Employment, 108–121; affirmative action

in, 115-16; in criminal justice system, 253; housing program importance to, 193–94; Indian preference in, 16, 62, 78–79, 109–10, 115, 132, 136, 210, 227, 276; labor force, nature of, 91, 109–10, 112, 159t; Senior Community Service Employment Program, 120, 171; statistics on, 109–113, 133, 252–53; training programs, 113, 117–20; and vocational education on reservations, 154

Environmental Protection Agency, air quality programs, 75

Ethnic Heritage Protection Act, 173. *See also* Adoption of Indian children

Family Health Program, Minneapolis, 171, 256

Family Practice Clinic, Minneapolis, 214, 215

Farmers Home Administration, Indian programs, 96, 192

Federal Contract Compliance, Office of, 115

Federal revenue sharing, 92

Federal Voting Rights Act, 79

Fee patents. *See* Allotment

Fishing rights, 70–75 *passim*; commercial operations, 73, 99; court cases involving, 70–71, 72, 73, 277–78, 280; and treaties, 13, 16, 22, 73-74, 268; and tribal-state agreements, 71, 73–74, 99

Flandreau Boarding School, South Dakota, 144

Folwell, William (Minnesota historian), on Indian survival, 11

Fond du Lac Equipment and Construction Company, 97, 194

Fond du Lac Manufacturing, 96–97, 194

Fond du Lac Reservation, 21m, 25t, 27; bingo, 95; census undercount, 43, 118–19; economic development, 5, 95–97 *passim*, 105; education, 27, 140, 144, 154, 155; elderly programs, 169, 171; employment, 112t, 118; family abuse program, 256; government, 54–55; history, 22, 27, 266; housing, 194; hunting and fishing regulation, 72; land claims, 37t, legal services, 246, 247; medical services, 27, 83, 87,

206, 210, 216, 218–19; population, 42t; welfare programs, 167

Fort Snelling, 20

Foster care: administration, 163, 176–77, 180–81; in Indian homes, 175, 180–81; Indigent Indian Account funding for, 162–63, 175; placements, extent of, 5, 174–78 *passim*. *See also* Child welfare

Foundations, programs for Indians, 87–88

Franklin Circle Shopping Center, 88, 103

GA. *See* General Assistance

GAMC. *See* General Assistance Medical Care

GED. *See* General education development certificates

General Allotment Act (Dawes Act), 10, 268. *See also* Allotment; Assimilation, pressures for

General Assistance (GA), 160, 161, 163, 256; and employment services, 116, 119

General Assistance Medical Care (GAMC), 161, 214

General Council of the Chippewa Indians of Minnesota, 53

General Council of the Red Lake Band, 53

General education development certificates (GED), 155–56, 244

Government programs, 63–64; barriers to Indian participation, 186; Indian perception of hostility, 179, 180–81, 199, 255; insensitivity to Indian culture, 63, 181, 231–32, 238–39, 245, 251-60 *passim*; local, excluding Indians, 75-77, 238–39. *See also specific programs*

Government of tribes. *See* Tribal governments

Grand Portage Forest Products Enterprises, 100

Grand Portage Local Development Corporation, 96

Grand Portage Lodge and Conference Center, 28, 97-98

Grand Portage National Monument, 28

Grand Portage Reservation, 21m, 25t, 28; economic development, 28, 96–100 *passim*, 105; education, 28, 130, 139,

155; elderly programs, 169; employment, 112t, 118, 119; fishing rights problems, 73, 99; government, 54; history, 22, 28, 266; land claims, 37t; law enforcement problems, 250; legal services, 246; medical services, 210; population, 42t; weatherization program, 193

Great Lakes Indian Fisheries Commission, 73

Greater Leech Lake Reservation Advisory Alliance, 75

Greater Minneapolis Council of Churches, Division of Indian Work, 51, 85

Group Home of the City, Minneapolis, 250

Halfway houses: for chemically dependent, 229–30; for corrections, 240t, 245

Hamline University, Indian teacher training, 132

HCR 108. See House Concurrent Resolution 108

Head Start, 140–41, 168

Health care, 200–201, 268; community services, 76, 210–11, 213–14; county programs for Indians, 213–14; prenatal, 204; state programs, 201, 213–15 passim; for urban Indians, 201, 212–16 passim

Health problems: cirrhosis of the liver, 205t, 223, 224t, 225; diabetes, 205t, 206, 207; ear infection (otitis media), 128, 206; heart disease, 205; high-risk births, 203–4

Heart of the Earth Survival School, Minneapolis, 144; Indian adult education programs, 155–56, 244, 253

Hennepin County: chemical dependency programs, 223, 228, 229–30; employment programs, 118; health care services, 213–15; Indians in the criminal justice system, 238, 239, 242, 243, 248, 250, 254; placements of Indian children, 174, 177–81 passim; population of Indians, 41t; unemployment, 112; welfare programs, 162

Hennepin County Court Services, 243

Hennepin County Home School, 250

Hennepin County Juvenile Center, 248

Hennepin County Mental Health Center, 217

Higher education, 146–55; college graduates, 4, 125, 159t; community colleges, 146, 153; financial assistance programs, 146, 147–49, 209, 273; number of students in, 146–47, 150–54 passim, 159t, 273; problems for Indians in, 147–48, 149, 154; success, ingredients of, 150–51

Hinton Roll of 1910, White Earth Reservation, 34-35

Homemaker Chore program, 170

Homicide, 205, 223–25, 244t

Hoshungra (Winnebago), 18, 21m, 22, 25t, 266

House Concurrent Resolution 108, termination policy, 12–13, 268

Housing: financing of, 186, 189, 195–96; on reservations, 184, 185t, 186, 189–95; substandard, 4, 184–88 passim; in urban areas, 186–89, 194–97; weatherization, 169, 192–93

Housing and Urban Development, Department of: community development block grant funds, 191; and Little Earth of United Tribes, Minneapolis, 197; reservation programs, 189–91, 193t; Section 8 program, 196–97

Housing authorities, Indian, 189–91, 195

Housing Improvement Program (HIP), 191

Howard Rockefeller Program, UMD, 146

Hrdlicka, Ales, and White Earth Reservation Blood Roll, 35

Hubbard County, Leech Lake Reservation in, 29

HUD. See Housing and Urban Development, Department of

Hunting rights, to migratory birds, 74. See also Fishing rights

IAC. See Indian Affairs Council

ICAP. See Indian Community Action Program

IHS. See Indian Health Service

Income of Indians, median, 4

Indian Adult Basic Education program, 138, 155

Indian Affairs Council (IAC), Minnesota, 66, 271; Urban Advisory Council, 66, 84, 194; welfare recommendation, 162–63

Indian Business Development Center, 105, 106

Indian Child Welfare Act, 172–74, 181–82, 258, 270

Indian Civil Rights Act, 13, 59, 269

Indian Claims Commission, 13, 32, 268. *See also* Claims

Indian Community Action Program (ICAP), 14, 168–69

Indian Education Act: and adult education, 155–56, 244–45, 253; and count of Indian students, 126; and fellowships, 148; Title IV administration, 136–37, 269; Title IV programs, 120, 144, 145, 148

Indian Education Section, Minnesota Department of Education, 138

Indian Enterprise, White Earth Reservation, 88, 96

Indian Fellowship Center, South International Falls, 87

Indian Financing Act, BIA, 96

Indian Health Board, Minneapolis, 206, 212, 214–15, 216, 230, 256; group home for Indian children, 180

Indian Health Care Improvement Act, 201, 208, 269

Indian Health Service: abortion regulations, 211; chemical dependency treatment assistance, 227, 229, 230, 234; contract care, 208–9; direct care, 206–11 *passim*, 216; eligibility for programs, 163, 208–9; Environmental Health Program, 212; Indian preference in employment, 115, 210; on mental health needs, 216; outside the BIA, 63, 268; physicians, 209, 210; responsibilities, 201, 208–12, 227; sanitation programs, 192, 212; sterilization regulations, 211

Indian Needs Assessment, education study, 125–28, 130, 143, 207

Indian Neighborhood Club, Minneapolis, 85, 230

Indian police, 11, 237, 257–58

Indian Police Academy, 258

Indian Religious Freedom Act, 254, 270

Indian Reorganization Act (IRA), 12, 268; ended allotment, 11; influenced by Meriam report, 12; and tribal constitutions, 53, 56

Indian Self-Determination and Education Assistance Act, 15, 115, 259, 269; and BIA, 59; and contracting for IHS programs, 210–12 *passim*

Indian Social Work Aides program, 138, 141

Indian studies programs, 151–53 *passim*

Indian Wood, Incorporated, White Earth Reservation, 97

Indigent Indian Account, 162–63, 175, 273

Integration. *See* Desegregation

International Falls, city of, Indian programs, 87, 155, 229–30

International Indian Treaty Council, 57

IRA. *See* Indian Reorganization Act

Jackson, Andrew, promise to Indians, 7–8

Job Service, Department of Economic Security, and Indian applicants, 112, 116–17, 119

Job Training Partnership Act (JTPA), 117–19

Johnson-O'Malley Act (JOM): education transferred to state responsibility, 66, 124, 268; programs, 135–37, 144

JOM. *See* Johnson-O'Malley Act

Joseph, Chief (Nez Percé tribe), view of land, 7

Jourdain, Roger (Red Lake tribal chairman), 56, 61

Juel Fairbanks Aftercare Residence, St. Paul, 86, 230–31, 234

Koochiching County, Bois Forte Reservation in, 27

Lake Vermilion Reservation. *See* Bois Forte Reservation

Land claims. *See* Claims

Law Enforcement Assistance Administration, 238, 245

Leech Lake Construction Company, 97

Leech Lake Firewood Company, 97, 117

Leech Lake Hospital, 206, 210
Leech Lake Logging Enterprises, 101
Leech Lake Reservation, 21m, 24, 25t, 26m, 28–29; bingo, 95; chemical dependency programs, 228–29; corrections programs, 249; economic development, 28–29, 89–90, 95–100 *passim*, 103, 105; education, 29, 140, 144, 154, 155; elderly programs, 169–79; employment, 111–12, 113, 118, 119; family abuse program, 256; government, 54–55; health services, 28–29, 206, 212, 218; history, 23, 28, 266–67; housing on, 186, 190–91; hunting and fishing, 71–73, 75, 99, 271–72, 277; land claims, 37t; legal services, 246, 247; population, 42t; tribe-local relations, 75, 77; zoning power, 68
Leech Lake Youth Lodge, 88, 238, 249
Legal Aid Service Northeastern Minnesota, Duluth, 247
Legal Aid Society of Minneapolis, 247
Legal Rights Center, Minneapolis, 246
Legal services for Indians, 239, 245–47, 258
LIECs. *See* Local Indian education committees
Lino Lakes correctional facility, 244, 254
Liquor licenses, tribal power to issue, 94, 276
Little Earth of United Tribes, housing program, 194, 197
Little Six Bingo Palace, 94–95
Loaves and Fishes program, Minneapolis, 85–86
Local Indian education committees (LIECs), 131, 135–37
"Longest Walk to Washington," AIM protest, 14
Lord, Miles, Judge, on US Indian policy, 17
Lower Sioux Indian Community, 21m, 25t, 31; bingo, 95; economic development, 31, 95; employment, 112t; government, 56; history, 22, 31; Head Start, 140; population, 42t
Lower Sioux Indians, Mdewakanton and Wahpekute bands, 18–19, 265–66; expelled from state, 22
Lower Sioux Pottery, 31

MA. *See* Medical Assistance
Macalester College, Indian programs, 150, 153
Mahnomen County: Indian population, 41t; Indian unemployment, 113; White Earth Reservation in, 30
MAIC. *See* Minneapolis American Indian Center
Major Crimes Act, 256–57, 268
Mankato State University (MSU), 151
Marina and Tourism Complex, Mille Lacs Reservation, 98
Mash-Ka-Wisen, chemical dependency treatment center, 27, 228, 233–34
May-dway-gwa-no-nind, Chief, on protecting Red Lake reservation, 23
MCT. *See* Minnesota Chippewa Tribe
Mdewakanton: Dakota band, 18, 22, 265–66; Sioux Community membership, 22, 40
Medicaid. *See* Medical Assistance
Medical Assistance (MA), 161, 163, 211, 214
Medicine, traditional, 3, 199–200, 218–19
MEED. *See* Minnesota Emergency Employment Development Act
Menominee tribe: move to Minnesota, 20, 266; termination of, 13
Mental illness: and chemical dependency, 216, 217, 224–25; Indians diagnosed differently from whites, 216–17; services for, 216–18
Meriam report: education findings, 124; on food distribution system, 157; on health care, 200–201; legislation influenced by, 12; on state attitudes, 65; on Twin Cities Indians, 80; on urban Indian population, 41, 42t
Metropolitan Economic Development Association, 106
Midewiwin (Grand Medicine Society), 50
Midway Home, White Earth Reservation, 249
Migizi Communications, 49–50, 146
Migration of Indians, 81–83; increase in urban population, 41–44; and involvement in criminal justice system, 239, 241; and poverty, 161; relocation encouraged, 13, 83
Mille Lacs County, Indian population, 41t

Mille Lacs Halfway House, 229

Mille Lacs Lake, study of, 74

Mille Lacs Reservation, 21m, 25t, 29–30, 33; census undercount, 43; chemical dependency programs, 229; criminal justice system, 259; economic development, 29–30, 91, 97, 98, 105; education, 29, 140, 144, 155; elderly programs, 169; employment, 112t, 113, 118; government, 54; history, 22, 29, 33, 266, 267; housing, 190; hunting and fishing, 72, 73, 271–72, 278; land claims, 33–34, 37t; legal services, 246; medical services, 29; population, 42t

Mille Lacs Reservation Business Enterprise, 97

Min No Ya Win Clinic, Fond du Lac Reservation, 206, 210

MINCRIS. *See* Minnesota Civil Rights Information System

Mineo Detox, Leech Lake Reservation, 228

Minneapolis, city of: arrests of Indians, 242t, 247t; discrimination prohibited by ordinance, 77; employment of Indians, 110, 111t, 112, 115–19 *passim*; families headed by women, 158; Indian businesses, 103–4; Indian community liaison, 84; Indian housing, 184, 186–89, 194–97 *passim*; Indian infant vital statistics, 4, 202; Indian programs, 84–86; legal services for Indians, 246–47; MCT office, 55, 84; police, 251; population of Indians, 41–44

Minneapolis American Indian Center (MAIC), 84–85; American Indian Youth Alternatives, 250; adult education program, 155; chemical dependency program, 230; elderly programs, 170–71; employment program, 119; housing advocate, 188

Minneapolis Area Vocational Technical Institute, Indian students, 154

Minneapolis Center for Citizen Participation, 84

Minneapolis College of Art and Design, Indian program, 151, 153

Minneapolis Community College, Indian program, 151, 153

Minneapolis Public Schools: chemical dependency program, 230; and ear infection, 206–7; Indian education, 127, 128, 131, 142–43, 145

Minneapolis/St. Paul Family Housing Fund, 87–88, 196

Minneapolis Urban Coalition, on minority education, 130

Minneapolis Urban Indian Housing Program, 194, 196

Minneapolis Workhouse, 254

Minnesota, state of: definitions of Indian, 50; and education of Indians, responsibility for, 65-66, 124; jurisdiction under PL 280, 13, 66, 237; legislation on Indians, 67–68, 83, 271–74; seal redesigned, 67; sentencing guidelines, 241–43. *See also individual laws and programs*

Minnesota Alcohol and Drug Abuse Authority, 223

Minnesota Board on Aging, 169, 170

Minnesota Board of Teaching, 132

Minnesota Chippewa Tribal Housing Corporation, 194, 195

Minnesota Chippewa Tribe (MCT): administration, 129; conservation programs, 74; constitution, 54-55, 60; employment programs, 118; Head Start administration, 140–41; higher education financial assistance, 148, 155; and housing, 185, 194–95; Indian Business Development Center, 105, 106; Indian Child Welfare Act cases, 174, 182; liquor licenses issued, 94; membership, 39, 42t, 54; offices, 29, 55, 84; welfare programs, 167, 174, 175–76; zoning ordinances, 68

Minnesota Chippewa Tribe Construction Company, 97

Minnesota Civil Rights Information System (MINCRIS), 126, 127, 128

Minnesota Community Corrections Act, 238

Minnesota Concentrated Employment Program (MNCEP), 118

Minnesota Council of Churches, Duluth program, 51

Minnesota Dakota Indian Housing Authority, 56, 189, 194-95

Minnesota Emergency Employment
Development Act (MEED), 119
Minnesota Historical Society Indian
museum, Mille Lacs Reservation, 29
Minnesota Housing Finance Agency,
Indian program, 194–96, 273–74
Minnesota Indian Affairs Commission.
See Indian Affairs Council
Minnesota Indian Affairs Intertribal
Board. *See* Indian Affairs Council
Minnesota Indian Area Agency on Aging,
169
Minnesota Indian Business Loan Fund,
67, 105, 272
Minnesota Indian Consortium for Higher
Education, 153
Minnesota Indian Contractors Associa-
tion, 104
Minnesota Indian Scholarship Program,
67, 138, 148, 273
Minnesota Indian Women's Resource
Center, 226
Minnesota Minority Purchasing Council,
88, 106
Minnesota Pupil Fair Dismissal Act, 126
Minority Business Development, Office
of, 105
Minority Business Development Procure-
ment Assistance Program (8A), 97, 105
Missionaries, relationship to Indians, 10,
51, 122–24. *See also* Religion
Mississippi River Headwaters Board, 68,
271
Moorhead State University, White Earth
Reservation program, 153
Morbidity, causes of, 206–7, 224–25
Mortality: age at death, 204–5; causes of,
201, 202–6, 223, 224–25; infant rate, 4,
202–4; general rates, 4, 201, 205–6;
postneonatal rate, 203, 223, 224t
MSU. *See* Mankato State University

National Congress of American Indians,
56
National Indian Education Association, 57
National Tribal Chairmen's Association,
56
Native American Church, traditional
beliefs, 50
Native American Rights Fund, 57

Native American Sector Initiative Pro-
gram, for employment, 119
Native American Theological Association,
seminary program, 51
Native Americans into Medicine, UMD,
146
Na-way-ee, Center School, 86
Nay Ah Shing, tribal school, Mille Lacs
Reservation, 140, 144
Ne-ia-Shing, health clinic, Mille Lacs
Reservation, 210
Neighborhood Justice Center, St. Paul,
246
Nelson Act, allotment law for Minnesota,
10, 23, 33, 267
Nett Lake Reservation. *See* Bois Forte
Reservation
Nett Lake School, 134, 137, 139, 273
New Visions Center, Minneapolis, 229–
30
Ninth District Federal Reserve Bank,
economic studies, 90
Nonremovable Mille Lacs band, 54. *See
also* Mille Lacs Reservation
North American Indian Fellowship Cen-
ter, International Falls, 229–30
Northwest Minnesota Regional Training
Center, Bemidji, 249–50
Northwest Ordinance, Indian rights
recognized, 8, 267
Northwoods Coalition for Battered
Women, Bemidji, 256
Nuclear power plant, and Prairie Island
Indian Community, 31, 101
Nutrition: congregate dining, under
Elderly Nutrition Program, 170; home-
delivered meals, 170; problems of
poor Indians, 207; Ramsey County
program, 80

Oak Park Heights correctional institution,
254
Ogi-Chi-Dog, at St. Cloud correctional
institution, 254
Ojibwa Construction Company, White
Earth Reservation, 97
Ojibwa Forest Products, White Earth
Reservation, 100
Ojibway Bait Company, White Earth
Reservation, 97

Ojibway Indians, 18–19; language of, 122, 136, 138–39, 142, 151, 228
Ojibway School, Fond du Lac Reservation, 27, 144
Ojibwe Art Expo, 88, 281
Old Age Assistance liens, 36, 37
Older Americans Act, 169–70
Olson, Ellen, on modern-day Indians, 6

Peat development, rejected by reservation, 101
Phillips Bindery, Minneapolis, 88, 104
Pike, Zebulon, treaty with Dakota, 20
Pilot City Center, Minneapolis, 171
Pine Point School, White Earth Reservation, 134, 139, 273
Pipe ceremony, in traditional culture, 50, 254
PL 280. See Public Law 280
Police: and employment of Indians, 252–53; and Indians, 250–51. See also Indian police
Political organization: BIA model, 12; model for US government, 3–4; Ojibway, 53. See also Tribal governments
Political pressure: in bingo regulation, 95; and fear of treaty abrogation, 17; over hunting and fishing rights, 69, 72–74; in land claims, 38; needed to help Indians, 58, 262
Population, Minnesota Indian, 40–44; on reservations, 41, 42t; of suburban Twin Cities, 80–81, 158, 159t; urban, 41–44. See also US Census
Post Secondary Preparation Project, 138, 144–45
Poupart, John, on state criminal justice system, 252
Poverty of Indians: and education, 129–30; effect on Indians, 47; and housing, 190; measurements of, 158–60; from reservation conditions, 157–58. See also Dependency
Poverty level, living below, 4, 160, 159t, 215
Pow wows, 48–50, 282
Prairie Island Indian Community, 21m, 25t, 31, 186; bingo, 95; economic development, 31, 95; employment, 112t; government, 56; Head Start not

available, 141; history, 22, 31, 266; and nuclear power plant, 31, 101; population, 42t
Prior Lake, city of, 77, 94
Prisons. See Correctional facilities
Project for Pride in Living Industries, Minneapolis, 104
Project Search, 120
Public Law 280: jurisdiction transferred to states, 13, 68, 237, 268; retrocession allowed, 13–14, 269; sovereign powers retained under, 55

Ramsey County: chemical dependency programs, 230-33 passim; criminal justice system, 238, 243, 253; employment programs, 118; Indian foster homes, 180, 181; Indian population, 41t
Ramsey County Mental Health Center, 217
RBC. See Reservation Business Committee
Reagan, Ronald (US president): on dependency created by bureaucracy, 62; Indian policy, 16–17
Red Lake band. See Red Lake Reservation
Red Lake Builders, 97, 210
Red Lake Fisheries Association, 99
Red Lake Hospital, 200, 206, 210, 229
Red Lake Housing Finance Corporation, 194, 195
Red Lake Mills, 100
Red Lake Reservation, 21m, 25t, 30–31; adult education programs, 148, 155; alcohol sales prohibited, 220; chemical dependency programs, 227, 229; commitments by tribal court, 69, 217, 272; criminal jurisdiction, 259; criminal justice system, 256–58; economic development, 30–31, 97-101 passim; elderly programs, 169; employment, 112t, 118, 119; family abuse program, 256; federal regulation not applicable to, 279; fish hatchery, 74, 99; government of, 30–31; Head Start, 140; health services, 200, 206, 210, 212, 218; history, 11, 23, 30, 266–67; housing, 190–95 passim; land claims, 37t; legal services, 246, 258; membership, 39, 42t; peat development study, 101; population,

42t; reluctance to assume BIA programs, 60, 100; schools, 31, 123–24, 133–39 *passim*, 142; state jurisdiction not applicable to, 13, 69, 93, 279; and taxation, 93, 279; violence on, 61, 258; welfare programs, 162, 166, 273, 279
Red Lake School District, 133, 134, 137, 139
Red Lake Tribal Court, 11, 237, 257–60 *passim*; and child placement, 172, 174, 175, 182
Red School House, St. Paul, 86, 133, 144, 230–31, 250; and legal training, 246
Red Star program, Na-way-ee, Minneapolis, 86
Red Wing correctional facility, 249, 253
Religion: Christian denominational activities, 51-52; Midewiwin, 50; rights of expression, 50, 254-55, 269–70; traditional, 50–51, 254–55. *See also* Missionaries
Relocation, policy of, 13, 268–69
Reservation Business Committee, governing body, 54
Reservations: acreage, 25t; assimilation pressures through, 237; bands scattered with establishment, 19; definition of, 23, 256; effect on Indians, 9–10, 157–58, 200; hunting and fishing, control on, 71–72, 74; importance to urban Indians, 81–83; health services on, *see* Indian Health Service; in Minnesota, described, 24–32; for Ojibway, 22–23; rationale for, 9; rights of individuals on, 59, 258, 269, 276–77; tribal control limited on, 257, 268, 276–77; trust land remaining, 24, 25t; vital statistics for, 201–6 *passim*
Retrocession, legal jurisdiction returned to federal government, 13–14, 237, 257, 269, 272
Rhoades, Everett (IHS director), on medical care, 209
Rice Commission, 23, 267

St. Cloud correctional institution, 252, 254
St. Louis County: criminal justice system, 246; Indian foster homes, 180; Indian population, 41t; reservations in, 27

St. Mary's Mission Boarding School, Red Lake, 124, 138
St. Olaf College, Indian program dropped, 153
St. Paul, city of: discrimination prohibited, 77; employment programs, 118; housing for Indians, 194, 195, 196; Indian programs, 86; legal services for Indians, 246; population of Indians, 41–42, 43t
St. Paul American Indian Center, 86; employment programs, 119; family abuse program, 256; legal services, 247; nutrition survey, 207
St. Paul Council of Churches, Indian program, 51, 80
St. Paul Indian Health Board, 86
St. Paul Intertribal Housing Board, 194, 195, 279
St. Paul Public Schools, adult education, 155
St. Paul Urban Indian Health Center, 214, 216
St. Scholastica, College of, Indian program, 151, 153
St. Theresa, College of, Indian program dropped, 150
Sandstone federal prison, 254
Santee Sioux, Dakota band, 18
Sauk Rapids correctional facility, 249
Sawmills, 100
SBA. *See* Small Business Administration
School of Social Development, UMD, 150, 152, 165, 167
School personnel. *See* Teachers
Schools: alternative, 142–44; attendance, 125t, 127; boarding, 11, 123–24, 144, 171; dropouts from, 4, 125t, 126, 144–46, 147, 224; high school, Indian graduates of, 4, 125, 159t; impact aid to, 135, 137; lunch programs in, 135, 138; physically impaired students, 207; survival, 80, 144; tribal, 27, 134, 143–44. *See also* Education
Section 8, subsidized housing, 196–97
Senior Community Service Employment Program, 120, 171
Service Corps of Retired Executives (SCORE), 106
Service to Indian People program,

Arrowhead Community College, 88
Set-aside programs, government pur-
    chases, 105–6
Shakopee correctional institution, 244
Shakopee-Mdewakanton Sioux Commun-
    ity, 21m, 25t, 31–32, 186; annexed by
    Prior Lake, 31, 77; bingo, 93–94; and
    cigarette tax, 93; economic develop-
    ment, 31–32, 93–94, 95, 98, 112t; gov-
    ernment, 55; history, 22, 31–32, 56;
    population, 42t
Sioux, 18. *See also* Dakota
Sioux Communities: employment pro-
    grams, 119; housing, 56, 186, 189,
    193–95; Indian Child Welfare Act
    cases, 174; medical services, 210, 218;
    membership, 39–40; scholarship pro-
    gram, 148
Sisseton, Dakota band, 18, 22, 265
Small Business Administration, 105
Small Business Assistance Center, 106
Small Business Development Center, 106
Small businesses, Indian development of,
    103–6
Snyder Act, 62, 83, 268
Southern Minnesota Regional Legal Ser-
    vices, St. Paul, 247
Special Native American Block Grant,
    214, 215
Stanton, Edwin (US secretary of war), on
    saving the Indians, 262
Staples Area Vocational Technical Insti-
    tute, Indian programs, 159
State Board of Education: Indian policy,
    138; suspension ruling, 126
State/Indian Relations Team, recommen-
    dations, 67, 69
Stereotypes: barrier to service, 164–65,
    199, 255; and full-blooded Indians on
    White Earth Reservation, 34–35; of
    Indian drinking, 220–21; in the media,
    46; in textbooks, 132
Sterilization, 211
Stillwater correctional facility, 244, 252,
    253, 254
Suicide, 205–6, 223, 224t
Sweat lodges, 50, 254

Tado Teepee restaurant, 98
Talent Search, 145

Task Force on Battered Women, 255–56
Taxation: allotted land exempt from, 10;
    claims because of improper imposi-
    tion, 34, 36; court cases over, 13, 34,
    76, 276–77, 278, 279; by federal gov-
    ernment, 68, 279; on Red Lake Reser-
    vation, 69, 93, 279; by state govern-
    ment, 13, 68, 277, 278, 279; tribe-state
    agreements on, 93-94, 272
Teachers, 177–78; Indians employed as,
    132, 133t, 150, 155
TEC. *See* Tribal Executive Committee
Thunderbird House, Duluth, 229
Timber, 27–31 *passim*, 99–101; BIA man-
    agement of, 59–60, 99–100
Title I. *See* Elementary and Secondary
    Education Act
Title III. *See* Older Americans Act
Title IV. *See* Indian Education Act
Tocqueville, Alexis de, on treatment of
    Indians, 8
"Trail of Broken Treaties," AIM protest,
    14
Treaties, 7–9, 265–67; abrogation of, 7–8,
    17; agreements replaced, 9, 267; basis
    of Indian law, 57; Chippewa, 21m,
    22–23, 266–67; education provided for
    in, 123; enforcement problems, 57;
    health care provided for in, 200; hunt-
    ing and fishing rights under, 70–71,
    72–74, 277–78, 279, 280; land acquired
    through, 8, 20, 22; for Menominee to
    move to Minnesota, 20, 21m; for
    peace between Ojibway and Dakota,
    22; and pipestone quarry, 265; with
    Sioux, 20–22, 265–66; Winnebago
    move to Minnesota, 20, 21m
Trespass claims. *See* Claims
Treuer, Margaret (Ojibway lawyer), 252
Treuer, Robert, on tribal sovereignty, 14
Tribal courts, 71–72, 237, 256–60; Indian
    Child Welfare Act powers of, 172–73;
    on Mille Lacs Reservation, 55. *See also*
    Bois Forte Tribal Court; Red Lake
    Tribal Court
Tribal Executive Committee (TEC), 54
Tribal governments, 5–6, 53–56, 58–59;
    constitutions define individual rights,
    59; traditional, 53; voting qualifica-
    tions of, 54. *See also each reservation*

Tribal-local relations, 75–76, 170, 173, 175–76

Tribal membership, 39–40; and children placed out-of-home, 172; program participation requirement, 40, 83, 136–38, 172, 181, 208–9; protected by Indian Child Welfare Act, 172

Tribal-state agreements, 69–74 *passim*, 93, 99, 173, 272

Tribes: as domestic dependent nations, 275; education programs of, 135–36; financial powers of, 92–96 *passim*, 270; government of, 5–6, 53–56; Indian Child Welfare Act powers of, 172–73, 174–75, 181–82; laws affecting termination of, 13, 268–69; regulatory powers of, 68–69; survival of, 58, 262; urban programs of, 83–84, 105, 148, 194, 210
— sovereignty of: and Bill of Rights, 59, 269; court cases over, 16–17, 58, 275–77; and economic development, 92, 278; and governmental powers, 39–40, 50, 54, 55; and legal principles, 17, 58–59, 275; limited by US government, 57, 62; on Mille Lacs Reservation, 33, 54; and powers of state government, 68, 70–71; recognition or affirmation of, 5–6, 8, 12, 59; on Red Lake Reservation, 61; reservations as basis of, 23; and self-determination policy, 15–16, 269; strengthening of, 14, 15–16

Trust land: allotments of, 10–11, 23–24, 26m; BIA approval needed to establish, 95; heirship problems with, 33; mortgaging not allowed for, 92, 186, 192; "2415" trespass claims legislation, 35–38

Twin Cities Naval Air Station, AIM occupation of, 14

UMD. *See* University of Minnesota, Duluth

UMTC. *See* University of Minnesota, Twin Cities

Unemployment, 111–13, 159t, 160; and Job Service applications, 112–13

US Census: education levels measured, 124, 125t, 126, 146; Fond du Lac Reservation special, 43, 118–19; housing data from, 184–85; and Indian definition, 39; and Mille Lacs Reservation count, 43; poverty measurements from, 158–60, program cuts resulting from, 44, 118; undercount, 42–44; unemployment data, 111. *See also* Population

US Congress: plenary power over Indians, 58. *See also* US government

US Constitution: commerce with tribes regulated in, 9, 58, 267; protections and Indians, 58, 59; and treaties, 9, 57

US Court of Claims, 32

US government: definitions of Indians, 40; unilateral power over tribes, 17, 276; urban Indian programs of, 83, 136–37, 168–69, 172, 208, 215, 269
— policy: allotment, 10–11, 268; Indian Reorganization Act, 12, 268; nondiscriminatory, 76; Northwest Ordinance, 8, 267; self-determination, 15, 269; termination, 12–13, 268–69

US Senate Select Committee on Indian Affairs, 190, 192, 197

United Way, 85, 86, 88

University of Minnesota, Duluth (UMD), 81, 145, 150–52 *passim*

University of Minnesota, Morris, 151, 152, 273

University of Minnesota, Twin Cities (UMTC), 151-52

Upper Midwest American Indian Center, Minneapolis, 85; housing survey, 187; programs, 120, 171, 256

Upper Mississippi Mental Health Center, 218

Upper Sioux Community, 21m, 25t, 32, 186; employment, 112t; government, 56; history, 20, 22, 32, 266; land claims case, 37; membership, 40; population, 42t

Upper Sioux Indians, Sisseton and Wahpeton bands, 18–19, 22, 266

Uprising, 1862, by Dakota, 20, 22

Upward Bound, 145

Urban Health Initiative Program, 212, 215

Urban Indians, 80–88; programs for, 83–88; and reservation ties, 81–83; vital statistics of, 202-4 *passim*

Vocational education, postsecondary, 146, 154–55
Vocational Training Program, BIA, 120, 154–55
Voting rights, 77–79, 279–80

Wahpekute, Dakota band, 18, 265–66
Wahpeton, Dakota band, 18–19, 265
Wahpeton Boarding School, North Dakota, 144
Wamditanka, on white work ethic, 114
Welfare programs: administrative problems for Indians, 163, 165, 226, 255; for burials, 166; emergency assistance, 85–86, 160–61, 188; harmful effects of, 178–79; Indian staff important, 165-66, 181; recession increased need for, 160, 161; and Red Lake Reservation, 162, 166, 273, 279; state system, 161–65. See also Dependency; General Assistance; specific programs
Whipple, Henry, Bishop, 10, 262
White Earth Board and Care Center, 229
White Earth Community Development Corporation, 96
White Earth Garment Manufacturing Company, 97
White Earth Hospital, 206, 210, 216
White Earth Reservation, 21m, 25t, 30, 267; adult education programs, 154–55; chemical dependency programs, 228-29; Commodity Distribution Program, 167; conservation programs, 74, 75, 102; criminal justice, 249, 251; economic development, 30, 88, 96–100 passim, 105; elderly programs, 169, 192; employment, 111, 112t, 113, 118, 119; family abuse program, 256; government, 54; health services, 206, 210, 212, 218; history, 23, 30, 34-35, 37, 267, 277–78; housing, 191, 192, 194; hunting and fishing, 70, 73, 272, 277–

78; land issues, 34–35, 37–38, 272; population, 42t; the Ranch, 100; schools, 30, 130, 134, 137, 139, 144, 153, 154–55
White Earth Youth Advocacy Program, 249
WIC. See Women, Infants and Children program
Wild rice, 3, 101–3; state legislation on, 102, 103, 272; treaties and, 22, 278. See also Fishing rights
WIN. See Work Incentive Program
Winaki House, Minneapolis, 230, 250
Winaki II, Minneapolis, 230
Winnebago Indians, 18, 21m, 22, 25t, 266
Women, Indian: age at death, 4, 205; and chemical dependency, 163, 225–26, 234; families headed by, 4, 158, 159t, 160; mental health program for, 218; physical abuse of, 165, 224, 255–56; publication about, 141; unemployment of, 159t
Women, Infants and Children (WIC) program, 168, 203, 213, 215
Women's Education Equity Act, 141
Woodland Indian Craft Shop, Minneapolis American Indian Center, 111
Work Incentive Program (WIN), 120
Wounded Knee, S. Dak., AIM protest, 14
Wren House, Duluth, 229

Yellow Thunder Camp, S. Dak., AIM protest, 14
Yetka, Lawrence, Justice, on Indian exemption from taxes, 76
Youth Development Project, Leech Lake Reservation, 249
Youth Intervention Center, Red Lake Reservation, 258
Youth Intervention Program, Minnesota, 249